FRA. ♡ W9-CFZ-975

J. RIEGER

GROWING OLD IN DIFFERENT SOCIETIES

Cross-Cultural Perspectives

JAY SOKOLOVSKY

University of Maryland,
Baltimore County

WADSWORTH PUBLISHING COMPANY
Belmont, California
A Division of Wadsworth, Inc.

Sociology Editor   Bill Oliver
Production Editor   Toni Haskell
Managing Designer   Adriane Bosworth
Designer   Lois Stanfield
Copy Editor   Anne Draus

© 1983 by Wadsworth, Inc. All rights reserved. No part of this book may be reproduced, stored in a retrieval system, or transcribed, in any form or by any means, electronic, mechanical, photocopying, recording, or otherwise, without the prior written permission of the publisher, Wadsworth Publishing Company, Belmont, California 94002, a division of Wadsworth, Inc.

Printed in the United States of America

1 2 3 4 5 6 7 8 9 10——87 86 84 83

ISBN 0-534-01251-5

Library of Congress Cataloging in Publication Data

Sokolovsky, Jay.
  Growing old in different societies.

  Bibliography: p.
  Includes index.
  1. Aging—Cross cultural studies—Addresses, essays, lectures. I. Title.
HQ1061.S6538   1983   305.2'6   82-13598
ISBN 0-534-01251-5

DEDICATION

To Grandpa Max, Harry, Shirley, Joan, Rebecca, Isidore, Nancy, and the cherished memory of my grandparents Fanny, Jean, and Lou

TABLE OF CONTENTS

FOREWORD

A novel kind of revolution is under way around the world—a revolution of aging. Three centuries ago there was no place in the world where people sixty-five years of age and older constituted as many as one out of twenty-five in the total population. Now in certain parts of Europe one in every six people is elderly. The revolution is also well advanced in the United States, Canada, Australia, New Zealand, and Japan and is already perceptible in Israel, China, Korea, Argentina, and Chile. There are strong reasons to believe that this revolution will begin in all the developing nations within the next half-century.

The world is going to have to learn how to live with populations containing a much higher proportion of old people than has ever been known. This is a new phenomenon, and the societies that have first encountered it have not been notably successful in dealing with it. We have been groping and fumbling to adapt our cultures to this new demographic reality. Since the situation was never confronted before, there is no historic model.

In our reaction to the revolution of aging we can all learn from each other. This is the value of a volume such as the present one. The developed societies, which are already bearing the brunt of their aging populations, still have much to learn from each other and from developing societies, some of whom have had greater success with their elderly, albeit with admittedly smaller proportions of them. We can also learn from the minorities within our several societies; some of those minorities have a better track record than the general society in relating to and servicing the needs of their elderly members.

Growing Old in Different Societies: Cross-Cultural Perspectives is replete with illustrations of how older people have adapted to their various settings and of how organizations and communities have adapted to them. Some of these may provide suggestions in the form of individual coping mechanisms, and others have broad policy implications. The book will be useful to anyone with an interest in aging and aging populations and will be especially valuable to serious students of gerontology.

Growing Old in Different Societies: Cross-Cultural Perspectives is not just an anthology of previously published articles; more than half of the chapters were especially written for this volume. The editor has been exacting and parsimonious in his selections. The previously published items were carefully selected for their significance, timeliness, and contribution to the volume as a whole.

The collection also provides great variety. It includes a wide range of human cultures and subcultures and illustrates a variety of themes and methodologies. Several different theoretical perspectives in gerontology, including exchange theory and the modernization thesis, are explored. A number of different ethnic groups within the United States are examined. Moreover, the array of specific local settings in which older people are portrayed is impressive: a decadent farm community in Ireland; two Indian reservations in Oklahoma; a Jewish center in Venice, California; SROs in New York; some British New Towns; and a nursing home in Massachusetts.

The book will stretch the perspective of any reader. It clarifies theories and contradicts theories. By confronting stereotypes, it provides unusual answers to some current issues, for example, the Inuit answer to the "right to die" issue. The prevalent masculine bias in gerontological literature is balanced by an article on the aging woman. The idea that rural Ireland is a patriarchal gerontocracy is effectively debunked. So is the notion that habitués of SROs are isolated bums.

Most of the authors are anthropologists, and the virtues of a holistic outlook and participant observer method are amply demonstrated. As a sociologist, I welcome and applaud this further addition to literature on the anthropology of aging. I profited by reading the book. I commend it to my colleagues in all of the social sciences.

Donald O. Cowgill

PREFACE

In 1976 I was asked to put together a course on cross-cultural aging that could complement other gerontology courses in the sociology department where I teach. I originally taught the course by focusing separately on aging in structurally different societies—bands, tribes, chiefdoms, agrarian states, industrial nation-states. However, I found that while students were deeply interested in "exotic" examples of growing old, they complained at the same time of the difficulty in relating such materials to the situation of the aged in their own society. As many of my students—mostly sociology, social work, psychology, and nursing students—have career plans of working with the elderly, this was an important concern. Thus, subsequent development of the course shifted the emphasis to how specific issues relevant to the aging process could be illuminated by cross-cultural study. The organization of this book reflects this course structure.

Although I initially found many articles and book excerpts dealing with the issues of the course, these materials were widely scattered in numerous sources, with the exception of the now out-of-print *Aging and Modernization,* edited by Cowgill and Holmes (New York: Appleton-Century-Crofts, 1972). Moreover, detailed cultural analysis of such important topics as elderly women or ethnicity and aging was almost nonexistent. Fortunately, the past five years have witnessed a flourishing of research examining the impact of culture on aging. Although centered primarily in anthropology, such work has also been done by sociologists, psychologists, and geographers.

Yet it was impossible to find a single source that could provide a worldwide perspective on a broad range of gerontological subjects. The idea for this book arose with my hope of filling this gap. This text brings together both reprinted "classic" articles and "soon to be classic" original manuscripts written expressly for this volume. I have sought to include articles that have been most stimulating to my classes and that can be readily understood even by students lacking a background in anthropology.

Two of the articles have the additional advantage of being directly linked to exciting audiovisual materials produced by the authors themselves. These materials are the slide/cassette program "Aging in Samoa" by Lowell Holmes and the award-winning film *Number Our Days* by Barbara Myerhoff. The use of other films as well as a detailed discussion of how this book can be used in a cross-cultural aging course can be found in

Teaching the Anthropology of Aging and the Aged: A Curriculum Guide and Topical Bibliography by Sokolovsky (Chicago: Association for Anthropology and Gerontology, 1982).

In examining the situation of the elderly in diverse societies I have become more optimistic about growing old in the United States than I was when I began research in 1975 on the inner-city elderly living in New York City. Many creative paths to "successful" aging are currently being explored even in the face of sometimes severe poverty and isolation from lifelong social ties. Despite the frequent lamentation about the greater respect for the aged in the "good old days," I am especially encouraged by a poem my daughter wrote several years ago (at age 8) expressing how she felt about grandparents:

> *Grandparents are loving and caring;*
> *giving and sharing;*
> *or any nice thing in the book.*
> *Grandparents are helping and kind;*
> *always in mind;*
> *when you're thinking of nice.*
> *At Christmas time;*
> *on birthdays too;*
> *grandparents are ones to come through.*
> *Grandparents are nice in so many ways—even these days.*

ACKNOWLEDGMENTS

I would like to express my deep appreciation to the many people who have helped make this book a reality. Most important has been my wife Joan who not only has encouraged me to pursue research in aging but has also been a constant source of emotional support, intellectual stimulation, and editorial advice. Thanks must also go to Professors Jim Trela and Leslie Morgan for their helpful comments on earlier versions of this manuscript. Mary Pat Tucker and Judy Lotterman worked many long hours typing the manuscript pages and to them I am most grateful. Special thanks should also go to Professor David Lewis, who has never wavered in his support. Various editors at Wadsworth, Inc. have been particularly helpful in carrying this book to fruition. They are Toni Haskell, Bill Oliver, Curt Peoples, Lauren Foodim, Jean-François Vilain, and Jeremiah Lyons. Finally, I would like to express my appreciation to my students Joseph Sobus, Joan D'Adamo, and Georganne Derick who helped put together the bibliography and freely expressed their opinions about the book's contents.

Jay Sokolovsky

BACKGROUND TO COMPARATIVE SOCIOCULTURAL GERONTOLOGY

Socrates: "I consider that the old have gone before us along a road which we must travel in our own time and it is good we should ask them the nature of that road, whether it be rough and difficult, or easy and smooth."

—*Plato*, The Republic

Anthropologists have almost always been good listeners. In quest of knowledge about diverse societies, they have commonly relied on the accumulated wisdom of the aged as a potent source of information. Yet, only recently have they taken Socrates' words to heart and explored with the world's elders themselves the multitude of paths aging can take. As national attention is increasingly drawn to the needs of our own elderly population, the emergence of what I call "comparative sociocultural gerontology" or an "anthropology of aging" can make a significant contribution to the study of the aging process and old age itself.

The focus of this approach is exemplified by the issues posed by Leo Simmons more than 35 years ago:

What in old age are the possible adjustments to different environments both physical and social and what uniformities or general trends may be observed in such a broad cross-cultural analysis? More specifically, what securities for long life may be provided by the various social milieus and what may the aged do as individuals to safeguard their interests? (1945:v)

In pursuing answers to such questions, this volume of case studies and broader analytical research has as its central theme *examination of the multitude of cultural solutions available to societies for dealing with issues affecting the aged.* Exploring how the meaning of growing old has evolved in a wide context of divergent life styles, these articles take the reader to most of the world's major regions and cover the spectrum of societal complexity. The experience of aging is detailed among Arctic hunters and gatherers; herding peoples of Abkhasia (U.S.S.R.), Corsica, and East Africa; horticultural groups in New Guinea, Uganda, and Samoa; agrarian peasants of western Ireland, India, and Lebanon; as well as a variety of urban industrial contexts in Japan, Europe, and the United States.

Rather than presenting a series of tableaus about growing old on a South Seas island or in New York's inner city, I have organized this collection of articles into five sections so that the diverse research presented can be focused on specific gerontological topics:

I. Culture, Society, and Aging
II. Age Boundaries and Intergenerational Links
III. Aging, Modernization, and Societal Transformation
IV. The Ethnic Factor in Aging
V. Networks, Community Creation, and Institutionalization: Environments for Aging

These sections do not by any means exhaust the entire range of important aging studies. Instead, they represent issues that can greatly benefit from multicultural analysis. Wherever possible the discussions of the lives of "exotic" peoples are presented not as isolated case studies but as a basis for comparison with the aging processes in our own country. The intent is to provide materials pertinent to the wide range of disciplines that have embraced gerontology as a field of inquiry.

It must be noted that cross-cultural studies of aging are not the exclusive domain of anthropology. This volume of works also includes contributions from social scientists from other disciplines—Dowd, van den Berghe, Nahemow, Bengtson, Morgan, and Cohen. Indeed, the major theoretical propositions and empirical body of knowledge that anthropologists must address stem from the work of sociologists and psychologists. Important examples of such contributions are the works of psychiatrist David Gutmann (1968, 1974, 1980), who has examined personality processes over the life cycle in various cultures, and sociologist Donald Cowgill (1972a, 1972b, 1974a, 1974b), who has developed a theoretical framework to explain the impact of certain types of societal change on the status of the elderly (see Section III).

Despite the long-standing interdisciplinary nature of gerontology, the serious integration of a truly multicultural perspective within the mainstream of aging studies has just begun. The establishment of a comparative cross-cultural paradigm as an integral component of social gerontology requires not just presenting "quaint" vignettes of aging in Samoa or among the Eskimo. Rather it is crucial to show how the particular *relation* between culture and the nature of being old illuminates and confronts gerontological theory and eventually sheds light on the process of aging in our society.

THE ANTHROPOLOGICAL PARADIGM AND THE STUDY OF AGING

In trying to define the framework of a sociocultural gerontology, Watson and Maxwell (1977) see aging and dying as being defined in three complementary ways: (1) time-related changes in an individual's anatomy and physiology, (2) a sequence of developmental psychosocial processes, and (3) behaviors related to sequential passage through statuses and roles in a larger sociocultural system from which their meanings are ultimately derived (pp. 4–5). The anthropological paradigm can contribute to our understanding of these phenomena by combining two interrelated strategies for studying human behavior. The first is an *evolutionary* approach, which attempts to detail the impact of large-scale structural transformation (biological and social) upon the aging process. In taking evolution seriously we must consider the effect of change on the human species over *all* time frames and among *all* types of societies.

With the use of nonhuman-primate research, demographic data on the earliest human populations, and studies of contemporary variation in the physiological response to aging, physical anthropologists and biologists are just beginning to understand the evolutionary factors involved in the biological imperatives of the human life cycle (see especially Moore, 1981; Weiss, 1981; Beall, 1982). This area of inquiry is the least developed in the anthropology of aging, but in Section I articles by Teski and by Cool and McCabe address some of the key questions: Why is old age significant in an evolutionary sense to our species? How is longevity related to culture? How does culture mediate the reactions of women to some physiological imperatives of aging?

Another aspect of evolution with implications for aging is the alteration of societies themselves. The broad consequences of these transformations as reflected in varieties of subsistence patterns (Simmons, 1945) and low versus high energy systems (F. Cottrell, 1960) are discussed by Teski in Section I. Of major interest to gerontologists is a type of massive change process called *modernization*. This entails the spread of urban life styles and Western concepts of bureaucratic organization and efficient industrial production to so-called "traditional" societies, as well as the intensification of this process in more "modern" nations. Assessing the impact of modernization on the status and treatment of the elderly has developed into one of the liveliest controversies in gerontology, and aspects of the debate are encountered throughout this book. A more detailed discussion of this issue can be found in Section III.

The second anthropological strategy, which is the primary focus of this book, involves a *holistic* and *comparative sociocultural systems* approach. Through intensive firsthand field work and worldwide comparison this approach examines how the interplay of technology, social roles, and symbolic meaning determines the context in which people perceive and react to old age. Here a given sociocultural system establishes the collective representations and values (arbitrary conceptions of what is desirable in human experience) that shape and in turn are molded by distinct patterns of economic and leadership ,roles, kinship and marital relationships, social and political group formation, and ritual behavior. These factors, interacting with the physical environment and mediated by the means of subsistence (hunting and gathering, herding, horticultural, intensive agricultural, or industrial patterns), encompass what Teski, in Section I, calls the "total ecology" of a group. The total ecology is the broadest environment in which social units (societies), bounded by shared expectations, construct a version of reality about aging that interweaves notions of time, life cycle, intergenerational relations, dependency, and death.

Taking into account all components of the total ecology is what anthropologists mean by the term *holistic*. In applying the holistic strategy, anthropologists employ a dual view of sociocultural systems: an *emic* (or folk) perspective—seeking to understand the world from the eyes of the group under study; and an *etic* (analytic or comparative) perspective—attempting to translate the insider's "folk" view into comparable categories that can be used for constructing theories and testing hypotheses. A comparative sociocultural gerontology requires *both* perspectives.

AN INSIDER'S VIEW OF AGING

The *emic* approach to studying human behavior is grounded in the methods of modern cultural anthropology. Most basic is the emphasis on *ethnography*—gathering data by actually living for a prolonged period with the people you are trying to comprehend. The researcher learns through direct observations, participating in daily life, and recording in the native language the meanings of things, people, and actions. However, the nature of this process of participant observation goes beyond mere "hanging out" in an alien social milieu. The carrying out of an ethnography of age further involves such things as: learning the cognitive categories of age and how they relate to appropriate behavior (age norms) and roles throughout the life cycle; determining through genealogies, questionnaires, and "network analysis" (see the Sokolovsky and Cohen article in Section V) the matrix of social and economic exchange; recording myths and life histories as well as the systematic observation of group activities and ritual behavior.*

Carrying out this extension of participant observation is the basis of an emic understanding and a way of learning appropriate questions to ask. This applies as much to studying aging among the Inuit Eskimo as it does to investigating the aging process in a Florida nursing home, a California seniors center, or a Manhattan single room occupancy (SRO) hotel. Thus Maria Vesperi (Section V), in studying institutionalization of the aged, became a nurse's aid to capture the often brutal realities of nursing home placement. While researching aged members of her own ethnic group, Barbara Myerhoff (Section IV) felt compelled to try performing ordinary tasks with stiff gloves, plugs in her ears, and heavy shoes. In this way she began to know how a very old "Jewish lady" experiences life in Venice, California. During my own work (Section V) in Manhattan residential hotels, I found that asking even simple questions, in the researcher's native language, without a clear understanding of the life style of these aged can lead to worthless (albeit quantifiable) data. Initial questions such as "how many friends do you have?" or "how often do you see relatives?" led to active denial of any important relationships and to claims of being a "loner." However, through observation and a

---

*For the only available book detailing how anthropological methods can be applied to studying aging and the aged, see Fry and Keith (1980).

questionnaire developed in the field, the most vociferous self-proclaimed loners were often found to have more than the average number of social ties, some crucial to their very survival. My understanding of likely types and sites of interaction and the appropriate ways of asking about them was accomplished only after four months of field work inside the SRO hotels.

Historical Background to an Ethnographic Approach to Aging

The last several years have witnessed a literal explosion of anthropological concern, research, and publication on gerontological subjects. It would be incorrect to assert that this interest in comparative gerontology is totally new. The most thorough anthropological overview of aging and dying, *The Role of the Aged in Primitive Society* by Leo Simmons (1945), was written over 35 years ago. Yet a discipline-wide concern for this subject has arrived rather late considering that it was preceded by over 20 years of serious attention by sociologists and psychologists.

Writing in 1967, Margaret Clark, a true pioneer in the anthropology of aging, partially explained this lag as a form of "gerontophobia" (fear of the aged) by association.

To contemplate later life is often seen as a morbid preoccupation—an unhealthy concern, somewhat akin to necrophilia. Since anthropologists are indeed creatures of their own culture, it may be that prevailing American attitudes toward aging are manifesting themselves in unconscious decisions by ethnographers to ignore this aspect of the life cycle. (p. 56)

In this work and in another article, "Contributions of Cultural Anthropology to the Study of the Aged" (1973), Clark suggests more specific causes, such as the lack of great numbers of elderly in preindustrial societies, and the continuation of earlier adulthood roles by the surviving aged (Clark, 1973:79). While there is reason to question the generality of these assumptions, more salient is Clark's assertion that "culture and personality" studies—the specialty most likely to have contributed to an anthropology of aging due to its emphasis on the life cycle, rites of passage, and socialization—instead diverted attention away from old age. This research focus was dominated

by Freudian and neo-Freudian theories that predicted little personality development after childhood. Until the late 1960s, despite numerous anthropological replicas of Margaret Mead's classic, *Coming of Age in Samoa* (1928b), the delineation of important psychosocial processes seldom extended beyond adolescence or marriage. In fact, some anthropological works of the time on life cycles in primitive societies (see especially Mead and Calas, 1953) went straight from the stage of marriage to death. This lack of interest in the elders themselves is especially ironic. As Keith notes, while senior members of society have always been "in anthropology" serving as guides into traditional cultures, "the territory of their own lives as old people was seldom included in these tours" (1980b:339).

While prior to the late 1960s individual ethnographies with a focus on late adulthood were almost nonexistent, many works did contain valuable information about the life of the aged tucked away in discussions of kinship, politics, and ritual or in the writings of anthropological elders themselves (Bateson, 1950; Mead, 1951, 1967). This was especially the case for studies of East African "age-set" societies where age was the major basis of social organization (Dyson-Hudson, 1963; P. Spencer, 1965) or for research in Australia (Warner, 1937; Kaberry, 1939; Hart and Pilling, 1961), western Ireland (Arensberg, 1937), and Japan (Norbeck, 1953), where elders retained various forms of "gerontocratic" control. Another notable exception is Colin Turnbull's classic study of the African pygmy, *Wayward Servants* (1965), which provides a detailed picture of a highly balanced interdependent relationship between generations.

The "Ethnographic Veto" and Beyond

In the past one and one-half decades as anthropologists have become more aware of gerontological issues they have proceeded actively to delineate emic perspectives on growing old throughout the world (Amoss and Harrell, 1981). As if to challenge Clark's earlier claim of anthropological gerontophobia, a wide spectrum of America's aged population has also come under the ethnographic gaze, resulting in studies of rural and urban communities, ethnic groups, and newly emerging age-segregated environments (besides this volume, see Simić and Myerhoff, 1978; Keith, 1979; Fry, 1980, 1981).

This new generation of ethnographic studies offers more than glimpses of "exotic" ways of growing old beyond and within one's own nation. A direct benefit of these studies has been to provide varied cultural evidence to counter by "ethnographic veto" some recurrent myths generated by gerontology's early narrow focus on Western industrial nations. Take for example the much debated proposition of "intrinsic disengagement" postulated by Cumming and Henry (1961). This theory suggested that aging is a process entailing a universal and beneficial separation of the aged from the roles and norms of society. An examination of case studies among the preindustrial Samoans (Holmes and Rhoads, in this volume), Abkhasians (Benet, 1974), and the Middle Eastern Druze (Guttman, 1974), as well as of the industrialized settings of an American mobile home park (Hochschild, 1973) or an apartment house for retired French workers (Ross, 1977), demonstrates that "disengagement" is not a "natural" panhuman attribute linked to the end of the life cycle.

Another typical assumption is the irrevocable association of preindustrial, small-scale societies with high status and beneficial treatment of old people. The converse, inevitable degradation of elders in modernizing and industrialized nations, is also commonly asserted. This "world we lost" myth is shattered in studies of the Siriono (Holmberg, 1969), Kapauku Papuans (Pospisil, 1971; also see Teski, in this volume), and the Jivaro (Harner, 1972), which clearly demonstrate the perils of aging even in small, face-to-face tribal societies. Thus Holmberg reports that among the Siriono, semi-nomadic foragers and horticulturalists of eastern Bolivia, "the aged experience an unpleasant time . . . . Since status is determined largely by immediate utility to the group, the inability of the aged to compete with the younger members of society places them in the category of excess baggage" (1969:224–25). The other side of the myth is brought into question by the examples of industrializing China (Treas, 1979) and urban industrial Japan (Palmore, 1975a; Plath, in this volume). It is tempting to lament in our own society the passing of an idealized, small-town, agrarian, extended-family past (see Clark and Anderson, 1967:13–18

for a refutation of this). However, clinging to this "world we lost" notion has insidious policy implications if, as Keith (1980b:342) notes, it includes an assumption "that good treatment for the aged is part of a vanishing lifeway and impossible in the modern world."

This emphasis on qualitative case studies is not to deny the importance of quantitative survey methods such as those employed by Nahemow in her study of Baganda grandparenthood (Section II) or Bengtson and Morgan in their study of ethnicity and aging (Section IV). However, with the increasing stress in social science on "powerful" statistical manipulation of numbers, it is crucial to keep in mind what the data mean and how they are derived. Jennie Keith goes so far as to argue that so little is known about "the insider's view of old people that many research methods cannot be used before preliminary participant observation discovers reasonable questions and measures" (1980c:8). A potential solution is to guide quantitative survey approaches by *emic* maps of aging. Examples of such work in this volume include Johnson's study of family support systems (Section II) and my own study of social networks (Section V).

The need for ethnographic input into gerontological studies even in our own society is mandated not only by the existence of diverse groups of ethnic elderly but by the fact that young and old alike have a limited understanding of how the aged subjectively experience their lives. This is indicated by a recent national survey conducted by Harris and Associates (1975). As seen in Table 1, both the general public and the elderly themselves attributed to those over 65 much more concern over certain problems—such as fear of crime, poor health, lack of money, loneliness, not feeling needed, and not having enough friends—than the sample of older people claimed actually to experience. Interestingly, people over 65 seemed to accept the public's view that aged persons lead an unsatisfactory existence, although as individuals many did not identify themselves with that life. In this case we see that "objective" circumstances of the elderly—for example, income and rate of contact with friends—must be considered in relation to the perception of such statistical "facts." This will become especially apparent in Section IV where Bengtson and Morgan show that the "objective"

5

TABLE 1
Beliefs about Older People's Problems versus Their Actual Experiences

Problem	Percentage of Those over 65 Experiencing the Problem	Percentage of General Public Attributing the Problem to "Most People over 65"	
		By Public 18–64	By Public over 65
Fear of crime	23	50	51
Poor health	21	50	53
Not having enough money	15	63	59
Loneliness	12	61	56
Not feeling needed	7	56	40
Not enough friends	5	28	26

Source: From *The Myth and Reality of Aging in America*, a study prepared by Louis Harris and Associates, Inc., for The National Council on the Aging, Inc., Washington, D.C., © 1975. Reprinted by permission.

comparative poverty of minority aged does not always translate into a low qualitative assessment of their lives.

The pervasive negative image of old age as shown in the Harris poll also provides the backdrop for a kind of stereotyping and discrimination called "ageism." Ageism involves the perception that the elderly have a very limited set of negative characteristics, with old people "categorized as senile, rigid in thought and manner, old-fashioned in morality and skill" (Butler, 1975:12). Such beliefs persist despite overwhelming evidence based on numerous social, psychological, and biological measures that *there is greater variation among older individuals than among the younger segment of the population* (Maddox and Douglas, 1974). Yet the stereotype persists, perhaps, as Barbara Myerhoff suggests, because the elderly:

. . . *are not among us, and no doubt they are not among us because we don't want to recognize the inevitability of our own future decline and dependence. An insidious circularity has developed— ignorance, based in part on denial of our future, leading to fear and rejection of the elderly, engendering guilt that is often expressed as neglect or*

mistreatment, then more guilt, avoidance, and ignorance; ageism is characterized by the same self-fulfilling processes that operate on racism. (1978:19)

AGING FROM THE OUTSIDE, IN

The sociocultural approach to aging also requires an *etic* view, which is manifested by various levels of comparative analysis. Multicultural studies can involve either small-scale cross-cultural studies (sometimes called *controlled comparison*) or global, *holocultural* research. The former entails comparisons of two or more societies without using a scientifically selected sample. It may be possible to have highly controlled comparisions where societies are similar except for one or two features. A classic example is Nadel's (1952) study of two African societies, the Korongo and the Mesakin. While similar in environment, economics, political and kinship organization, each society differed in the degree of intergenerational conflict and the attitude of males toward aging. The key difference seemed to be the greater number of age distinctions among the Korongo, which led to a smoother passage into old age and a greater congruence between social and physical aging.

The more typical use of such comparisons has been to maximize the difference between the societies contrasted. In certain instances researchers have searched the available literature to see what could be learned about a specific aspect of aging such as: intergenerational relations (Levine, 1965; Simić, this volume); age as a basis of social organization (Eisenstadt, 1956; Stewart, 1977; Foner and Kertzer, 1978); widowhood (Lopata, 1972); and other aspects of female aging (Bart, 1969; Datan et al., 1970; Dougherty, 1978; Cool and McCabe, in this volume). Another related approach has been to bring together a group of researchers to review their notes (Smith, 1961a; Cowgill and Holmes, 1972) or actually to sponsor ethnographies (Simić and Myerhoff, 1978) based upon some central theme or hypothesis linking culture and aging.

Controlled-comparison cross-cultural research is important in at least two ways. First, it may suggest general hypotheses about the aging experience that can be tested by larger samples. In using a relatively small number of cases it is possible to retain a picture of the qualitative nature of sociocultural variables and thereby hopefully avoid overly simple theoretical models. A good example of this is found in Section I where Cool and McCabe examine various hypotheses concerning sex roles and aging based on qualitative analysis of a limited number of societies. Second, controlled comparisons can help us understand in a detailed fashion how aging in the United States differs from that experienced in other places. In doing this, such analysis can suggest alternative strategies for developing a better environment in which to grow old. A particularly good example of this is found in Section V where Barbara Hornum uses the case of British New Towns to discuss how planned environments can facilitate accommodations to growing old in our nation's urban areas.

The broadest comparative approach, *holocultural* analysis, involves "statistically measuring the relationship between two or more theoretically defined and operationalized variables in a world sample of human societies" (Rohner et al., 1978:128). Such a research design typically makes use of the major anthropological data bank, the Human Relations Area Files (HRAF), which houses ethnographic data representing over 1,000 societies. The intent of this approach is to apply the whole range of worldwide variations to the test of theoretical propositions. In this way it is hoped eventually to comprehend what aspects of aging are universal, as opposed to those factors that are largely shaped by the sociocultural system.

Leo Simmons was the first to apply the holocultural method to the subject of aging. His 1945 study examined the relation of 109 sociocultural traits grouped under habitat and economy, political and social organization, and religious beliefs and ritual. Despite some serious methodological flaws (see Section I), Simmons's book and subsequent summary articles (1946, 1952, 1959, 1960) remained the main font of anthropological knowledge on the elderly for over 25 years. One reason for this has been Simmons's attempt to go beyond numbers and treat his data as an elaborate cross-cultural analysis from which hypotheses could be extracted. Thus he maintains that in all societies five recurrent interests appear among old people (1959:4):

1. To preserve life as long as possible
2. To seek release from wearisome exertion and get protection from physical hazards
3. To maintain active participation in group affairs
4. To safeguard prerogatives—possessions, rights, prestige, and authority
5. To meet death honorably and comfortably

As with many other such generalizations from Simmons's works these are to be taken as propositions yet to be fully tested as universal verities. Indeed, the modern application of holocultural methods to aging has only recently begun to statistically examine the vast collection of anthropological knowledge in the light of gerontological or anthropological theory (Maxwell and Silverman, 1970; T. Sheehan, 1976; Silverman and Maxwell, 1978, 1982, in this volume; Maxwell and Maxwell, 1980; Glascock and Feinman, 1980, 1981; McArdle and Yeracaris, 1979).

SOME KEY QUESTIONS

Finally, the application of a cross-cultural perspective can provoke a series of important questions about the nature of growing old.

—To what extent are aspects of aging, such as longevity or senility, reflections of cultural variation rather than mandated by biological constraints?
—Are there significantly different paths to old age taken by males and females?
—Are there specific aspects of sociocultural systems that are universally linked to beneficial treatment and status of the aged?
—Under what conditions does age serve as an important basis for social group formation?
—How do value systems affect the type of support and roles aged family members can expect?
—Does modernization and industrialization of societies lead invariably to a decline in the social status of the aged?

—Is such a decline really not the case in preindustrial or noncapitalistic industrial societies?

—Are there specific cultural solutions to the problems of aging that can be transferred from other cultures to our own?

—Are there elements of our own varied social structure and ethnic mix that can be harnessed to enrich the process of growing old and approaching death?

—How are social networks and community organization related to the well-being of the aged?

These 10 questions will provide a broad framework for the issues focused on throughout this book. They are questions that are often alluded to in works dealing with social gerontology but which have seldom been confronted head-on.

CULTURE, SOCIETY, AND AGING

*"However, for a happy and long life . . .
choose your society and your sex very
carefully!"*
　　　　　　　　　—*Anonymous*

For the last 100,000 years the human species has had to deal with the implications of an unusually long potential life. With the potential to live 100 to 110 years we are outlived by only a handful of animals—tortoises, turtles, European freshwater clams, and the so-called immortal one-celled sea anemones and sponges. Although even today typically fewer than five in 100,000 persons ever reach that life span—that is, live to the age of 100—since Neanderthal times (120,000 to 40,000 years ago), at least some small proportion of persons have survived past the age of 50. Fossil evidence of the Neanderthal era indicates that early human groups came to recognize the value of maintaining such older persons even if their physical abilities declined dramatically. The Neanderthal fossil finds of "the old man" in La Chapelle-aux-Saints, France, reveal a human who lived into his fifties despite severe crippling arthritis and the loss of all his back teeth. It has been suggested that "for this man to survive, his fellows would not only have to provide food for him but also take special pains preparing it" (Jolly and Plog, 1979:260). In contrast to chimps and other nonhuman primates who provide no food to those adults too weak to forage, Neanderthal hunters and gatherers expanded the notion of usefulness to cover the latter part of the life cycle. With the growth of cultural complexity and the adaptation to very large and varied environments, recalling practical information gained by long experience or mastering control of supernatural forces came to be as crucial to long-term survival as the physical strength and endurance needed for hunting.

Despite the ancient recognition of the value of the aged, only in recent times and in certain societies have people had to deal with the implications of large numbers of people reaching even two-thirds of our species-specific span of life. Consequently, the average life expectancy has increased from a little over 30 years during the Upper Paleolithic Period (30,000 years ago) to over 70 years in America today (70.2 years for white males and 77.8 years for white females). With the concurrent drop in birth rates over the last century, populations in industrial societies have become demographically aged (Cowgill, 1974a) in a relatively short period of time. In 1900 only about 4.5 percent of the U.S. population were over 65, yet in 1981 about 11 percent were. The population segment statistically defined as elderly (over 65 years) numbered about 25 million in 1981 and is expected to increase to 32 million by the end of the century and to 45 million by the year 2020.* A great

---

*The demographic data concerning the United States can be found in a Congressional report on aging (U.S. Senate, 1981) that contains a wide range of current statistics concerning America's elderly population.

dilemma and challenge posed by these dramatic demographic changes is that increased numbers of postretirement, physically vigorous adults are entering a stage of the life cycle as yet ill defined by our cultural traditions or existing social institutions (Clark and Anderson, 1967). In consequence it is especially imperative that we at least consider the spectrum of cultural solutions that other societies have applied to the dilemma of long life.

ACCOMMODATIONS TO AGING: CONSTRAINTS AND RESOURCES

Despite repeated claims of geriatric utopias (Benet, 1974, 1976; Leaf, 1975; Davies, 1975; Beaubier, 1976; Halsell, 1976; Pitskhelauari, 1981) where the aged exist but *aging* does not, all populations must accommodate to the inevitable realities of some level of: physical decline; increased dependence; the generational transfer of power, knowledge, and the means of production; as well as unpredictable social disjunctures caused by the death of age peers.* The articles in this section explore how the sociocultural variations between and the sexual dichotomy within societies shape the possible accommodation to these realities. In the first selection, Teski combines both the evolutionary and the comparative paradigms of anthropology to examine growing old in the broadest possible light—the "total ecology of aging." Comparing a wide range of societies, Teski sees components of the physical, economic, social, and ideological environments as creating the specific resources (food, knowledge, authority) and statuses (in-law, grandparent, ritual leader) that determine the extent to which esteem can be attained during the latter part of the life cycle.

Different aging environments impose rather distinct constraints and strategies for perceiving and reacting to old age. This is apparent in the contrast between the two societies described in the first two readings: the Abkhasians of Caucasus, Russia, and the Inuit Eskimo. The Abkhasians live in large permanent villages in a benign mountain climate. Persons are integrated into large kinship groups that form residential clusters of 40 to 50 people. Elders not only have leadership roles in the named lineage groups but also participate into very late life in a formal community council of elders. The collectivized agricultural-pastoral economy, combined with exceptional levels of health, allows both sexes even in their eighties and nineties to make significant contributions to primary production. Old age appears as the pinnacle of life with no general terms for the Abkhasian elderly except that those over 100 are called "long living."

In contrast, the selection by Guemple describes the nomadic Inuit who live in small fluid communities that fragment and recombine during the annual cycle of hunting and gathering. Especially for males, Arctic hunting and the cold damp climate lead to early physical aging and being labeled "old" by age 50. The household organization is based on small, mobile, nuclear families, and political power is based on ephemeral, charismatic leadership. So there are no formal institutions with stable personnel from which esteem and support can be derived in old age. The young adult Inuit in physical prime are held in the highest esteem, and those Inuit culturally defined as old must resort to a variety of "renewal" activities to prevent their regard in the community from dropping substantially.

THEORETICAL PERSPECTIVES ON CULTURE, SOCIETY, AND AGING

Theory in social gerontology has been dominated by attempts to understand variation among the

---

*There are four populations for which hyperlongevity has been claimed: the Abkhasians of the U.S.S.R., Caucasus region; the peasants of Vilacabamba, Equador; the Hunzakut of the Karakoram mountains in Pakistan; and the inhabitants of Paros Island, Greece. In each of these localities there have been claims of many people living past the age of 100 and some beyond 130! For none of these cases has there been produced convincing evidence backing up these claims. In the case of Vilacabamba, recent work by Mazess and Forman (1979) has largely discredited the notion that an extraordinary percentage of centenarians exist in that population.

aged in life satisfaction, morale, or other measures of well-being.* A debate has raged during the last three decades over the particular types of activities and social interactions leading to "good" personal adjustment in later life. On one side of the controversy is the activity theory, which views aging as a problem involving the resolution of strains brought on by the relinquishment of key roles during the aging process. Proponents of this theory argue that the meaning of life is found through social interaction and activity. Thus, a positive self-image and high life satisfaction in old age is predicated on participation in active roles. This view of aging stems from the assumption made by gerontologist Ernest Burgess (1950) that because traditional American institutions—the work place, kinship and community networks, bureaucratic organizations—have not been arranged to facilitate participation of the older person, such individuals have been thrust into an alienated position described as a "roleless role."

A countervailing view was developed in the work of Cumming and Henry, who in their book *Growing Old* stated that "aging is an inevitable mutual withdrawal or disengagement, resulting in decreased interaction between the aging persons and others" (1961:14). In proposing this disengagement theory, Cumming and Henry contended that as people become old it is inevitable and mutually desirable to society and to the individual that they disengage from the normative constraints of society and seek more passive roles and reduced activity levels. While this theory was developed from studying 270 healthy and economically secure white adults (ages 50 to 90)—certainly not representative of the world's aged—the authors asserted that the theory applied to the "aging process in all societies" (p. 14).

During the 1960s and 1970s frequent attempts to validate these divergent views with research in Western industrial nations have proved inconclusive. Such studies have consistently refuted many of the premises of disengagement theory while having limited success in validating activity theory (Palmore, 1968; Lemon et al., 1972; Hochschild, 1975; Decker, 1978). The results of cross-cultural studies have been similar. However, such

research has typically not dealt with psychological measures such as life satisfaction but has focused on various indicators of status, security, or general treatment. For example, in his survey of preindustrial society Simmons notes:

The activities of the aged themselves have exercised an important influence upon their security. Their roles have hardly ever been passive. Their security has been more often an achievement than an endowment—an achievement in which favorable opportunities have been matched with active personal accomplishments. (1945:83)

A more recent holocultural study by McArdle and Yeracaris (1979), however, suggests that the relation between respect for the aged and the value of their activities is not as simple as Simmons has stated. This recent analysis involving 135 societies indicates that while respect for the aged is significantly associated with valued activities, this relation is strongly conditioned by other cultural variables, especially family organization. Thus, while failure of elders to continue valued activities is correlated with decreased respect in societies with independent nuclear family households, the same correlation does not appear where extended family organization prevails. In other words, apparently "factors other than activity, such as a high level of emotional interaction over time, were working toward the increased respect the elderly received in the extended family" (McArdle and Yeracaris, 1979:19).

In retrospect it seems that both the activity and the disengagement models of aging are too simplistic to explain the complexities of growing old. Perhaps the most important thing to be learned from this debate is that with regard to the question of social engagement, *age* itself is not the key variable. Rather, the nature of environmental constraints and more general cultural phenomena such as ideology, sex roles, family organization, or modes of controlling resources are what best explain variations in the integration of the aged into society. This is clearly seen in the selection by Dowd, which uses exchange theory to analyze how class and power relations are linked to the

*See Kertzer and Keith (forthcoming) for an attempt to apply the full range of anthropological theory to the question of aging.

resources the elderly can draw upon. Unlike activity or disengagement theories that assume either a need for lifelong involvement or an intrinsic beneficial withdrawal in late adulthood, exchange theory predicts that the degree of engagement varies with the nature of the flow of *power resources* among individuals, groups, and society.

UNIVERSAL COMPONENTS OF AGING, STATUS, AND PRESTIGE

One of the exciting possibilities of cross-culturally comparing the aging process is to develop models explaining how broad features of sociocultural systems determine the reaction of society to the elderly. Quite useful in this respect has been the work of Cowgill (1972b, 1974a) and Press and McKool (1972), which employs qualitative analysis of a limited number of ethnographies to elucidate universal factors linked to the well-being of the elderly. These authors have all suggested a similar set of sociocultural phenomena that would universally be associated with high status for the elderly:

1. Where knowledge they possess is important
2. When the control of key family/community resources is in the hands of the old
3. When useful and valued functions are continued as long as possible
4. When there are fewer role shifts and a greater role continuity through the life cycle
5. Where these roles sequentially involve higher responsibility, authority, or advisory capacity
6. Where the extended family is a viable residential or economic unit into which the elderly are integrated
7. Where there is less emphasis upon individual ego development

Importantly, Press and McKool also distinguish prestige from status of the aged, viewing the former as the behavioral components of status, such as deference, food privileges, obedience, and special terms of address. They further hypothesize that the factors controlling status can be economically reduced to four "prestige-generating" factors

(Press and McKool, 1972:304–5): (1) advisory, reflected in the degree to which the advice or opinion of the aged individual is actually heeded; (2) contributory, reflected in the extent to which older society members still participate actively in various activities; (3) control, reflecting the degree of direct control that the aged have over behavior or welfare of others; (4) residual, reflecting residual prestige from previous statuses. In essence what Press and McKool are saying is that the behavioral meaning of an idealized high status may be more myth than reality if the prestige components are not available in a society.

The testing of such propositions that claim to be valid in all societies requires the broadest comparative methodology—holocultural research. Unless such work is guided by clear theoretical propositions, well-defined variables, and valid sampling procedures, it is difficult to gain much insight from the quantitative data produced. The previously mentioned landmark work by Simmons (1945) is a case in point. In coding 109 cultural variables from 71 societies, this research took a literal "shotgun" approach and produced a bewildering outpouring of data and statistical correlations. Thus one reads about the negative association of polygyny (a man with more than one wife at the same time) and respect for aged women, or the positive correlation between constancy of the food supply and prestige for aged men. Yet there are many problems in accepting the validity of these results, including a poorly drawn sample (too many closely related societies), inadequate statistical procedures (no measure of significance), and imprecise definition of variables (how is respect measured?). We see in the article by Silverman and Maxwell how these methodological issues are clarified and used to test the proposition that deference toward the elderly is significantly related to their control of information resources.

THE GENDER FACTOR IN AGING

No analysis of aging is really complete without dealing with the differential impact of this process on men and women. The sexual dichotomy in aging seems universal and in certain societies such as the Chagga of Tanzania, where behavior is rigidly structured by gender, "one can, in fact, speak of separate male and female subcultures" (Simić and Myerhoff, 1978:23). Yet despite the fact that in the vast majority of societies, persons over 60 are more likely to be women than men, until recently many anthropological studies have tended to describe only one response to aging in a given sociocultural context or to portray males as the exclusive holders of significant roles in old age. A quite different picture emerges in the selection by Cool and McCabe, which takes a look at aging women throughout the world. Not only are significant gender differences noted in life cycle processes, but the authors also point out how a tendency to focus on the overt public roles of aged men can obscure more informal loci of authority where women over time can accumulate real power and gain ascendence over their aged opposite-sex counterparts.

Marea Teski

THE EVOLUTION OF AGING, ECOLOGY, AND THE ELDERLY IN THE MODERN WORLD

In this selection Marea Teski invokes the anthropological concept of *holism* to discuss the evolution of aging within the context of what she calls the "total ecology of aging." This ecology is comprised of five major elements: (1) physical ecology, (2) technosocial development, (3) stratification of society, (4) power and decision making available to the elderly, and (5) ideology and value system. Such a framework links together the effects of physical environment and sociocultural system and can help us understand how such factors shape the varying contexts in which old age is lived. A crucial point that Teski makes is that although elements of the total ecology of aging are interrelated, there can develop strong internal contradictions, especially during periods of rapid change. Using Bateson's concept of "double bind," Teski argues that our culture not only creates a negative perception of being old but also prevents easy escape from this unfavorable stereotype.

BIOLOGICAL, TECHNOLOGICAL, AND DEMOGRAPHIC FEATURES

Biology and Aging

BIOLOGICAL AND CULTURAL EVOLUTION are a unity in the human species. Certain biological features of humans have profoundly affected the ways that culture has developed. The human body and human cultural capabilities have developed together and have influenced one another as they developed. For example, increased brain size, upright posture, bipedal stance, and the use of the hand for complex manipulations probably occurred at the same time that humans were developing complex cultural systems and devising effective technology. Tax (1960) has stated that culture is part of the biology and evolution of man. If this is true, we need to constantly examine the areas of interface between biological and cultural phenomena. The question of aging and the place of the aged in human culture requires this double approach in order that we may understand the meaning and paradox of the demographic situation we face in the modern world.

The idea of the evolution of aging is an exciting one because in order to understand what happens to the old in modern society, we must look at other cultures and look back to the earliest human societies. We must consider humans in comparison with other species and see that we are rather unique in having a very long postreproductive period of life (especially females). This has crucial social and cultural implications. If we wish to understand aging, we must understand physical and cultural evolution and the importance of the relationship between man and ecological setting. There are cultural and biological reasons for longevity in the human species. There are also cultural and biological stresses which arise as large proportions of the population become elderly. We have seen this happening in the modern industrial nations today.

The longevity of the human species is striking (see Table 1). If we understand that *life span* is the species-specific number of years possible for humans to live, it is instructive to compare our life span with that of other species. Among

---

This essay was specially prepared for this book by the author. Permission to reprint must be obtained from the author and publisher.

TABLE 1
Maximum Longevity for Humans and Selected Other Species

Species	Life Span in Years
Human	120
Chimpanzee	45
Cat	21
Dog	34
Whale	80+
Indian elephant	57
Horse	62
Grizzly bear	31

Adapted from data in Encyclopedia Brittanica, *Life Span* 10:913 1975, Chicago, Helen Hemingway Benton, and *Biology Data Book* 1:229–232 1972. Reprinted by permission.

mammals, humans have the longest maximum life span, and the only other mammal species which approach our life span in length are the horse, the whale, and the Indian elephant. Among nonhuman primates, the chimpanzee has the longest life span—although it is shorter than that of the horse, whale, or Indian elephant. Few wild chimpanzees live beyond age 35, although in captivity they may live as long as 45 years. Humans can live twice as long as chimpanzees. In the 1975 Report from the Special Committee on Aging of the U.S. Senate, it is stated that in 1974 over 1.7 million Americans were age 85 or older. Over 7,000 persons are reported as being able to prove that they were 100 years of age or older.

It would seem that humans have two factors to deal with which are not significant for other species. They are: (1) the process of postreproductive aging and (2) the social significance of old age. A chimpanzee in the wild is probably dead before he can begin to exhibit many signs of physical aging. His social life also remains much the same from maturity to death. As humans we have to deal with both the physiological and sociological consequences of an extended life span.

If we accept the idea that biological features which persist in a species are *adaptive*—that is they affect positively the survival potential of that species—we must conclude that there is some

survival value in the long human life span. *Life expectancy* is an actuarial number expressing the number of years an individual is likely to live at a given age—and it is situational depending upon the country, part of the world, conditions, etc., which affect the individual. This is a constantly *changing* figure.

Typically, as countries become more modern, life expectancy increases, although in the transitional stage it may initially decrease because of poor conditions in cities and the many stresses of change. Life span, our species' potential for longevity, is a *constant*. It is the fact that we have a long life span which suggests that longevity must have positive adaptive value for the human species. That is, there must have been something about having older individuals in the group which made it more likely that the group as a whole would survive.

Katz (1978) suggests that the long human life span evolved early in the history of our species and that some elderly were probably present in most early human groups. The elongation of the human life span has a characteristic form in which both *childhood* and *postreproductive* life are prolonged. Both of these prolonged periods are significant in relation to learning and then utilizing complex cultural, social, and ecological facts. The selective pressure for long life (Rockstein et al., 1977) must be linked to some beneficial effect which the older person confers upon the reproducing members of the population.

There is an advantage in having people who have mastered the intricacies of life in a given ecological setting live long enough to get the most use of their skills and to teach these skills to younger members of the group. Obviously, biological selection must occur during the reproductive years, but since selection operates on populations, not individuals, we can see that populations with some older members may have had some selective advantage over populations without older members. Therefore, the populations with older members persisted—passing on the tendency for long life span which we still have today.

Katz (1978:5–6) speculates intriguingly on the evolutionary significance of *grandmothers*. Since the main evolutionary significance of longevity must be related to the social contributions which the aged individuals make to their offspring, we must think about possible reasons for sex differences in the evolution of longevity. The old person insures the continuity of certain forms of sociocultural adaption. Thus Katz suggests that:

Certain types of kinship systems significantly enhance the selective advantage of sex-associated inheritance of longevity by providing a social means for grandmothers to care for their sons' daughters. In other words a postreproductive (postmenopausal) female can increase her genetic representation among her grandchildren's generation by taking preferential care of her sons' daughters. (1978:5)

According to genetic principles, a grandmother has twice as good a chance of contributing her X chromosomes to her son's daughter as to her daughter's daughter. Therefore a patrilineal, patrilocal (reckoning kinship through the father's line and having sons live in the locale of the father) system would increase the chances for the survival of any X chromosome contributing to postreproductive longevity. In such a system, sons would bring their wives to the father's locale where the paternal grandmother would be a caregiver. This might begin to explain the differences between males and females in their postreproductive longevity. Males pass on only a Y chromosome which is of less far-reaching genetic significance. Katz's ideas are highly speculative, but they point out the importance of the interrelation between cultural forms and genetic inheritance in producing longevity.

Demography, Technology, and Aging

The long life span which we have as a species has not, until recent times, been lived out by most members of populations. Better conditions and medical technology have allowed more and more people to approach the upper limits of the human life span. The presence of more and more elderly people in our populations has caused us to turn our attention to this group and to explore the meaning of aging cross-culturally.

Technology and the form of society are significant in what happens to the aged. Cottrell (1960) divides all human societies into *high energy* or *low energy* societies. In low energy societies, less than five horsepower of energy per person per day is produced. In the high energy societies more than five horsepower of energy per person

per day is produced. This limit for the high energy society allows cultures with wind-driven ships to be counted as high energy societies. The original human societies and the early agricultural societies were all low energy societies. The advent of the high energy society brought about conditions where the breakup of the small community, urbanization, and rapid social change were likely. Low energy does not mean that the society in question is simple and lacking social complexity, for the difference between the hunting and gathering society and the early agricultural (low energy) states such as Egypt or China, is vast. The high energy society has more characteristics which seem more unfavorable to the old in society. This is particularly true of the societies of the West in which industrial capitalism has developed.

Simmons's (1945) survey of 71 randomly chosen societies ties participation of the elderly in daily life to climate, permanency of residence, subsistence activities, and family organization. Within low energy societies he finds a positive correlation between social and economic complexity and a favorable position for elders. Although his approach leaves out certain important questions, it does make clear that as resources come more and more under the control of the society, more people will reach old age and there will probably be enough food for the elders as well as for the younger members of the group.

However, as societies become high energy, using Cottrell's division, some of the features which favor the elderly disappear. For example, efficient transportation ties the small community effectively to the outside world, and the integrity of the small community is destroyed along with its insularity. In Europe and America consumption and production patterns became divorced from the land. With the growth of urban life and the development of market economies, the concept of "productivity" began to be applied to people. Cottrell sees the market system as imposing penalties on those who live by values which are not those of the marketplace. Because he feels that the old have used nonmarket values such as tradition and respect for age to buttress their position, when these values disappear the old are at a distinct disadvantage. In the West, the development of industrial capitalism has changed the environment of human culture. For the old, the environment has become one in which a satisfactory life style is difficult to find.

It may be more important to look at the stratification of society than to look at the low energy versus high energy, traditional versus modern dichotomy. To a point, the stratified, traditional, agricultural society may have favorable conditions for the old. In stratified societies where *kin groups* are important resource-controlling units, the position of an old person will depend upon his situation in the kin group. Age can give status, and the old person may control important resources. If, however, social stratification has developed to the point that the *strata* into which a person is born is more important than kin affiliation, then *class* rather than age will be the most significant factor in deciding one's role in society. In highly stratified societies, especially industrial ones, there are few functions available to people simply on the basis of age. Instead, the position of any elderly person will depend upon a complex convergence of factors centering around his social class and the resources which he is able to command. The development of the state, not just the emergence of industrialization and capitalism, has seemed to pose a number of threats to the well-being of the elderly at the same time as it has historically allowed their numbers to increase. In general, the development of the state has presented many new criteria which govern the access to power and status. Age alone does not give either power or a function. As the capitalist industrial state emerged, more factors which have negatively influenced the status of the elderly are added—urbanization and rapid change and, in the last 60 years, mobility of population.

Hauser (1976) calls the situation of vastly increasing numbers of older people in the population a "social morphological revolution." Although life span has not increased, life expectancy has greatly increased, altering the proportion of older people present in the population. Death rates decline in modern countries and birth rates also decline. Thus, the average age of the population is higher and the percentage of people age 65 and older increases. The dependency ratio, or number of dependent people in the population (those under age 15 or

over age 65), will change, in that a larger number of the dependents will be age 65 or older. The impact of this kind of change has already been felt in the more developed countries as we approach the year 2000 (see Table 2). For example, the more developed countries of Europe and North America are already facing the fact that they have large numbers of elderly citizens. There is little employment in these countries for the worker over 65 and the "scarcity value" of the aged has long been gone.[1] These facts are critical even though mass society does have certain advantages for the elderly such as pensions, social security, Medicare, Medicaid and other social programs. However, living longer means that more people suffer from chronic illnesses and mild or great physical impairment. Also, in mass society elderly members of minority groups may face enormous difficulties. Hauser states that in 1970, 41.6 percent of black elderly heads of household age 65 and older were living in poverty. If we look at the figure for *all* elderly for the same year we see that only 16.4 percent of elderly heads of household are listed as living in poverty (Hauser, 1976:83). The problems that the aged in general face in our society may be multiplied for the minority aged, and this group may be said to be in a position of "multiple jeopardy" which is discussed in a later chapter.

Poverty in general is the problem of the less developed countries of the world. These countries have not yet been confronted with large numbers of elderly in their populations. In the future, however, numbers of elderly and life expectancy are projected to increase in the less developed areas—particularly South Asia and East Asia. As modernization proceeds in these and other less developed areas, urbanization will increase and the traditional village and family life will have to change to adjust to the needs of changing economies. As has happened in the West, these changes may jeopardize the position of the elderly. In some ways the experience of the West may serve as a kind of rough model for developing countries, as we too have made the changes from a local to a mass, rural to urban, agricultural to industrial society. Our populations have grown older and life expectancy has increased. This experience will be approximated

TABLE 2
Population and Older Persons of World by Eight United Nations Regions,
1970 and Projected to 2000 (Medium Variant)

	Total Population				Persons 65 and over			
	Number (in millions)		Percentage Distribution		Number (in millions)		Percentage Distribution	
World and Region	1970	2000	1970	2000	1970	2000	1970	2000
World	3,632	6,515	100.0	100.0	190	396	100.0	100.0
East Asia	930	1,424	25.6	21.9	40	99	21.0	24.9
South Asia	1,126	2,354	31.0	36.1	36	99	18.8	24.9
Europe	462	568	12.7	8.7	52	71	27.1	17.8
U.S.S.R.	243	330	6.7	5.1	19	39	9.9	9.8
Africa	344	818	9.5	12.6	10	27	5.5	6.8
Northern America	228	333	6.3	5.1	22	31	11.6	7.8
Latin America	283	652	7.8	10.0	10	29	5.5	7.3
Oceania	19	35	0.5	0.5	1	3	0.6	0.8

Source: Total Population, from United Nations, *World and Regional Population Prospects: Addendum, World Population Prospects Beyond the Year 2000,* p. 13; Persons 65 and over, from same for year 2000; for year 1970, estimated from United Nations, *The World Population Situation in 1970,* pp. 46–50. Reprinted by permission of the United Nations, New York, N.Y.

in other areas of the world as we approach the year 2000.

A TOTAL ECOLOGY OF AGING

Simmons (1960) and others have pointed out the close connection between type of subsistence and the position of the elderly in society. The general picture is one in which the stable horticultural or agricultural society is favorable for the elderly. Hunting and gathering societies in recent times live too close to the edge of subsistence and are too mobile to be consistently advantageous to the less than fully productive adult. At the opposite end of the scale, the mass industrial society also has many features which militate against a favorable position for the aged. While accepting these broad generalizations, we should bear in mind that in any situation the balance of factors is so complex that a careful study of cultures individually is the best way to gain a clearer understanding of the cross-cultural meaning of aging.

A cross-cultural, cross-time perspective on the situation of the aged person and the aged as a group in society requires an expanded view of the ecology of aging. This includes adjustment to the total environment in all its aspects, not simply the physical and technological aspects. The social and political situation of a society is part of the environment in which the aged must act and, therefore, it is part of the expanded view of the ecological situation of the elderly. Analysis of the adjustment of the elderly to a total situation must take the following elements into account.

1. The ecology of the group, including:
   a. Climate
   b. Subsistence
   c. Difficulty of survival
   d. Contributions which older members made to subsistence
2. The technosocial development of the society, including:
   a. The social relations of subsistence
   b. Modernization
   c. The rate of social change
   d. Degree of incorporation within larger political groups

3. The stratification of society, in terms of:
   a. Class
   b. Sex
   c. Age
4. Power and decision making which elderly have in society, especially:
   a. Control of important resources
   b. Respect and deference
5. The ideology and values of the group which have evolved through their history

It is the totality of these elements which constitutes the environment in which the elderly as a group find themselves. It is the total ecology of their collective and individual situations. The physical, economic, social, and emotional well-being of the elderly are determined by this total ecology and how they function in it.

For example, Benet's (1974) study of the Abkhasians of Soviet Georgia attempts to examine the physical and social reasons for the long life and notable vigor of the people of this region. Biological selection for sturdiness and health was found to be buttressed by a life characterized by fairly hard physical labor throughout most of the life span and a diet that is moderate but rich in foods which promote good health. All persons participate regularly in all of the community's work unless they are ill.

Collectivization assured all people the means of subsistence until they die, and although no one is really prosperous, no one fears starvation. The process of collectivization under the Soviets was not a traumatic social change in this area of the Soviet Union. The traditional *kiaraz* or "self-help" work group was always organized in a way similar to the organization of a collective. Thus, modernization and change came very gradually and resembled old forms of organization so much as to seem almost natural. The traditional Abkhasian Council of Elders still exists alongside the Village Soviet and the Village Collective. The elders still retain power and make important decisions.

Respect and deference are given the elders because Abkhasians believe that the fact that they have maintained old customs and kin solidarity explains the survival of their ethnic group in a difficult land which has gone through a turbulent history. The elderly contribute knowledge of how to use the land, knowledge of local *flora*, and

knowledge of the unwritten traditions. This knowledge, in addition to their continued participation in the work force into advanced age, makes them the most valued members of the community.

In "Aging in Preindustrial Society" Simmons (1960) cites "influence" and "security" as being universal primary interests of the aged. He sees that rapid social change weakens the social participation of the elderly, and as they participate less, their influence becomes less. In Abkhasia as described by Benet, the rate of social change was rather slow. The basic subsistence patterns and the participation patterns of the elderly had not changed much in hundreds of years. The elderly make a large contribution to the subsistence of the local group. The slow rate of social change has allowed for traditional ways to retain their significance and for the elderly to profit from their knowledge of these old ways. The traditional kin groups and stratification by age remain unreplaced by different systems of social structure. The elderly have control over some of the communal resources and their advice is sought and taken. There are respect and deference for age and the older years are considered to be a good time of life by these people.

Therefore, it is possible to say that the total ecology of life in Abkhasia favors the aged. The longevity of the people is exceptional, and the experience of living to be very old is generally a positive one. Subsistence, technology, stratification, and the power and decision making potential of the elderly are all connected here and age is valued. Positive features in all of these areas contribute to a situation in which people not only live to be old, but seem to enjoy old age.

In highly stratified societies, there are generally few social functions reserved for people on the basis of age, yet we cannot assume that the traditional society values the elderly any more than does our own society. Although modern industrial societies tend to have features which discriminate against the elderly, it is important to remember that the position of any elderly person in any society depends on the complex convergence of factors which we have called the total ecology of aging.

For example, we can see that the traditional society does not automatically accord good positions to the elderly. Harlan (1968) looked at the position of the elderly in three Indian villages and found that caste, socioeconomic position, and sex were important indicators of whether a given old person felt valued in the village. In Burail in the Punjab (1968:465–72) caste status was the main index of occupation, economic condition, and social relationships. Fifty old men in Burail who represented various castes were surveyed. Despite the stated Hindu ideal of the coresident joint family with the *oldest* male as head, only 21 of the old men surveyed said that they were the head of a family. The other 29 said that someone else was the head of the household, usually a married son. Harlan noted that the shift from dominant to subordinate status seemed to occur before age 65, and was also related to whether or not the man had a living spouse. (A wife helps a man maintain his position.) Organization membership and being consulted about village matters were found to be related to caste status, landholding, and annual income rather than age. Lower caste, lower income old men were rarely consulted or respected.

The status of older women was examined in Rattan Garh, 18 miles away. In the case of the women, being a wife rather than a widow was most significant in regard to status. The death of a spouse was the most important reason for an older woman's losing status. The arrival of a woman's daughter-in-law was considered the first challenge to an older woman, but when she is widowed her position becomes more precarious, and she may have to resort to extreme measures to retain a little control. Harlan describes some of these measures.

These included the keeping of property under lock and key, burying family jewelry and gold in secret places, and letting it be known that the family member who was most attentive to her needs would receive these possessions at her death. (1968:474)

The only way an older woman could maintain status was to have a living husband, to be physically able to perform beneficial functions for the family, to behave well, and to have valuable possessions. Age was certainly no reason to expect respect.

Dowd's (1978, 1980) approach to the significance of social class in analyzing aging cross-culturally is obviously important in aspects 3 and 4 of the total ecological analysis of aging (see Dowd's article in this section). Class, power, and decision making all relate to the structures of inequality in society. They also determine the ways in which people try to maximize benefits to themselves and determine the valuations which are placed on different categories of people who engage in social relationships. The achievement structures of modern industrial society, where respected activities take place, such as labor markets or schools, are often unavailable to the elderly. This makes it less possible for them to engage in equal exchanges with people who *are* part of these achievement structures.

Other cross-cultural material shows that social exchange theory is helpful in understanding the kinds of power which the old have in various situations. Biesele and Howell (1981) see the !Kung Bushmen elders as having a valuable and desirable contribution to make to the community. The !Kung are hunters and gatherers. Storytelling is a function which seems to be reserved for people age 45 or older—especially if the stories are about the past or about old people. The stories are considered by the community to contain the accumulated knowledge of the people and they are valued for this reason. In this way the old retain power in social exchange to a certain extent because they possess a desired commodity. Information and stories are their resource which can be exchanged for food and security. Marshall (1976) notes that among the !Kung, a hunter is supposed to distribute some of his share of any kill to his parents and to his wife's parents.

The situation is somewhat different among the Kapauku Papuans as described by Pospisil (1964). These people are mountain horticulturalists who set great store by the accumulation of wealth. Wealth is gained through hard work in the fields, having land, and becoming an important person in social transactions. Status is determined mainly by wealth, and it is wealth which gives power in social exchange. Old age *per se* is not despised, but old age is the period when a man begins to use up, rather than add to his wealth. This has serious implications for his status.

The appearance of grey hair is the beginning of old age in this society. Men change their activities. They stop working in the fields, make nets and arrows, and educate their grandchildren in folklore and in history. The ideal personality of an older man is thought to be different from that of a younger man. He should be generous, nonaggressive, kind, and quiet. However, all these changes cause a man to use up his accumulated wealth at this stage of life. His influence declines as his wealth and physical strength decline. Pospisil states that old age and lack of health exclude a man from economic success and from important positions such as that of headman. Headmen are usually healthy and middle-aged. Old men are sometimes consultants and advisors—especially in field boundary disputes. They are also supposed to be immune to being killed during a war. Yet even with these advantages, and the feeling that it is immoral to use harsh words or violence against someone with grey hair, old men among the Kapauku Papuans lose their influence and power in social exchanges.

In contrast, a woman's situation here becomes a bit better as she becomes older. As death approaches, the danger that she will become an angry "female ghoul" increases. At about age 60, the status of the female is about equal to that of a 60-year-old male. The woman gains power because people fear her spirit, while the man loses power because he is spending all his wealth. The old man with adult or adolescent sons must obtain their permission if he wishes to sell *his own* land. This certainly indicates the old man's increased dependency. He cannot make decisions alone, or control his own resources. The old woman is more feared as she ages while the old man is considered less and less important. Thus in social exchange the man becomes more dependent while the woman gains some power which she did not have before.

Contrastingly, in modern American society, the social exchange potential of the elderly is menaced by the fact that they are, perhaps, the group most dependent upon modern bureaucracy.

Because they are often dependent on bureaucracies for their subsistence, the aged and the poor are the groups most clearly affected by the rationalization of the modern world. (Dowd, 1980:85)

In our society, people with technocratic skills and knowledge are the ones most likely to have power and privilege and to be active in decision making.

Elderly people, at this time, are not typically trained in the valued technocratic skills and knowledge. As a result, they are excluded from decision making even when they may be the group most affected by decisions. Among the elderly, those who are least able to deal with bureaucracy are those most likely to be categorized as sick, senile, and incompetent. Administrative control can only be countered by group action, but many elderly people instead tend to withdraw from social interactions because the costs for them are too great.

CULTURAL CONTRADICTIONS AND THE TOTAL ECOLOGY OF AGING

A total ecology of aging must also consider that all elements of culture are integrated into a system of communication and the ideology and values which it expresses (Hall, 1977). This system may at times be irrational or even destructive (Henry, 1963). Culture change often causes things to be "out of joint." Anachronistic relationships and dissonance in attitudes, values, and behavior may be seen (Hauser, 1976:80). Communication may be confusing. Contradictions in the culture will be expressed by mixed "messages" which emerge as conflicting social truths. In regard to mixed messages, the "double bind" theory of schizophrenia (Bateson, 1956, 1958, 1972) presents a useful model of confused and confusing communication. To restate the "double bind" hypothesis simply, it proposes that schizophrenic symptoms can arise in a subject when one or more people with whom he is in constant close communication give out injunctions which conflict with each other, making the subject "in the wrong" whatever he does. The pattern of the injunctions is as follows. A primary negative injunction is given out. This is followed at a more abstract level by another injunction which also includes a threat of negative sanctions. This second injunction is followed by a third which prevents the subject from "escaping the field" (Bateson, 1956).

Applying this hypothesis at the level of cultural communication, it becomes very clear that the elderly, as a group in our society, are caught in a "double bind" communication. The messages are as follows. (1) Primary injunction: "You must step aside for younger people," i.e., abandon a functional role after age 65 or 70. (2) Secondary injunction: "You must not be unhappy with the idea of retiring because young people have the new knowledge and skills which are needed for progress and our culture is based upon progress. . . ." The third injunction which prohibits escape from the field is (3) "You will have an increasingly long and healthy life because medical science has the means to keep you alive and well." Dying is really unacceptable because it denies the effectiveness of modern medicine and committing suicide is a sin and illegal. The old are thus placed in an impossible situation. They are told to have social life and engage in sometimes meaningless leisure activities after being brought up to believe that an adult must have a functional role in society. The retired have perhaps 30 years to be active doing nothing that matters to the society.

The comparatively recent development of geriatric medicine in the United States shows that in the past concern with the elderly has not been a priority of physicians. The elderly patient has been traditionally undesirable because of the high incidence of chronic complaints, the low incidence of complete "cures," and the fact that the patient may die sooner than a younger patient. However, the elderly patient has often been the unwilling recipient of the heroic measures of medicine which can keep a person alive in a vegetative state almost indefinitely. Recent changes in the medical field stress preventative medicine—the maintenance of good health through proper nutrition and exercise. The elderly are encouraged to use this new knowledge to keep themselves in good condition so that any decline is only the final decline preceding death. There is a general sense that if one is going to live a long time, it is better to be in good shape. Older people are responding to the message of the medical community which is now: "Live a long time and stay as healthy as possible." This is, of course, the third injunction in the "double bind" sequence which keeps the elderly from "escaping the field." They must live long and be healthy, but they must not keep young people

from having "their turn" to run things and they must not "stand in the way of progress."

The result of the "double bind" communication is confusion and guilt for everyone. The old have an undesirable place in the society, and yet they are made to feel that they should not complain or impede progress. They are called upon to prove the marvels of medical science by living longer and healthier lives, but they are denied access to the roles which society deems most important. Younger people feel guilty because they see that there is injustice in the situation, and yet they fear having to share jobs and resources with the increasingly large number of people over age 65. Political tensions have already begun to emerge in communities where there are large groups of elderly voters who vote against construction of new schools because they have no use for them.

What is the answer to resolving or removing the "double bind" situation in which our elderly find themselves? This nonproductive communication is part of our culture at this time, and culture change is a painful process at best. One way to begin to resolve the difficulty is to ask questions about the assumptions which underlie the communication. For example: "Are young people and older people really competing for the same jobs?" and "Are there jobs which can be done more effectively by older people?" We should be aware that in addition to the trend for extending the age of compulsory retirement, there is a trend for early retirement which in many ways balances it. We should also be aware that there are indications that taking second place is no longer acceptable to some groups of elderly citizens. The growing political strength of the elderly may be their answer to the second injunction of the "double bind" communication: "Do not feel unhappy about retiring and giving up functional roles." Although in some localities old and younger groups may become polarized, the ultimate resolution of the problem is in the interest of all.

Recognition of the nature of our society's message to the old is essential to the beginning of an effort to change the conditions which perpetuate this kind of communication. Biological evolution has provided the species with longevity. Cultural evolution has provided the species with the means to attain almost the maximum life span, but has failed to evolve really functional roles for those who live a long time. Looking at the roles of the elderly in cultures of the past is interesting, but it shows situations of a different order. Only in recent times are the elderly such a numerically significant proportion of the total population.

The contradictions expressed by the "double bind" communication are indicative of the impact of social change and technological development upon attitudes and behavior. The emergence of the elderly as a group with self-conscious decision-making power may be the only event which can change their present status. This would also create a new reality in which administrative bureaucracy would have to deal with the elderly at the time of planning, not just as subjects in the implementation of policy. If this were to happen, the stratification of society and power and decision making (elements 3 and 4) in the total ecology of aging would change. The elderly would then have more effect upon elements 1, ecology, and 2, technological development. This would drastically alter the meaning of old age in this society (5, ideology and values). The only question is whether the very real contradictions in society's message to the elderly will activate them sufficiently to bring about change. What would be involved would be a change in the totality of society's relations with this age segment. Demography is on the side of the elderly.

NOTE

1. In societies where few people live to old age, the elderly may be seen as especially favored. Fischer (1978) in *Growing Old in America* mentions that in early 18th century America old age was considered to be a sign of favor from God. Regard for the aged seems to have declined as the number of elderly people in the population increased.

Lee Guemple

GROWING OLD IN INUIT SOCIETY

Typical stereotypes of Eskimo attitudes toward aging and death present us with a paradox. How could these people who seem so full of the joy of life and who lavish much love and concern on one another, "savagely" set old granny out to perish on an ice flow? Lee Guemple in analyzing the process of aging and dying among the Inuit helps lift the veil of ethnocentrism from our eyes. He demonstrates that in order to comprehend the compatibility between love of an elder parent and the practice of gericide, we must comprehend how Eskimo cosmology constructs a view of the life cycle that links generations together in a timeless system. Recent comparative studies of "death-hastening" practices directed toward the elderly confirm that such behavior is more related to cultural definitions of aging, rather than being a simple response to the problems of a nomadic life style in a harsh environment (Glascock and Braden, 1981; Maxwell and Silverman, 1981).

THE TREATMENT THE INUIT (Eskimo) traditionally accorded their old people during the precontact period has been a source of some consternation to members of the Euro–North American cultural tradition because of a seeming paradox. We know that Inuit lavished care and concern on their old people and invested considerable interest in them. But we also know that they sometimes abandoned them on the trail (Freuchen, 1961: 194–203) and that they stood ready at times even to help them to dispose of themselves by drowning or strangulation (Rasmussen, 1908: 127). Our own notion of what people are like makes it difficult for us to see how they could be so affectionate in one context and cold hearted in another, when the chips were down.

The aim of this article is to try to resolve the paradox, to show how the attitude of love and affection is not incompatible with the idea of killing one's own parents or helping them to kill themselves. To do so we must make a brief foray into the cognitive universe of the Inuit—into their own notion of how the world (of people and things) works. Only then can we fathom how they manage to mix sentiment with seeming cruelty without a sense of contradiction.

First, however, it will be useful to offer some

background material on aging in Inuit society. Inuit have no generic term for "senior citizen." Instead, they use one term for an old man, *ituq*, and another for an old woman, *ningiuq*. These terms are used mainly while speaking about the old people, seldom when speaking to them.

It is difficult to establish the age in years at which people are consigned to old age. Like us, Inuit associate adulthood with work status, and old age constitutes a kind of "retirement" from full participation in community affairs. But Inuit do not keep vital statistics like we do so we cannot reckon an age of retirement for them. Besides, everyone is encouraged to continue working for as long as possible so that retirement comes not by convention, but by the gradual process of biological aging. While doing research in the Belcher Islands Inuit community, I was able to calculate the mean age at which men acquire the label of *ituq* at about 50 years of age (Guemple, 1969). Women seem to maintain the status of adult somewhat longer, but will ordinarily pass over into being classed as *ningiuq* at age 60 or so.

Men become old when they can no longer hunt on a year-round basis but pass on the task of routine hunting to younger members of the

© 1979 by Lee Guemple. Reprinted by permission of Lee Guemple. To appear in V. Marshall (ed.), *Aging in Canada: Social Perspectives* (Toronto: Fitzhenry and Whiteside).

household—generally a mature son or son-in-law. Hunting in winter is very demanding and because of its importance to the maintenance of life is the crucial determinant of male status. At somewhere around 50 years a man can no longer sustain the strength and stamina to perform this task on a regular basis and will "retire." His withdrawal can be gradual but is often dramatic.

Women's allocated tasks are both more varied and less strenuous with the result that advancing age does not limit their effectiveness nearly as much as it does men's. Women routinely share work among themselves and the heavy work is often passed along to mature girls even in early adulthood while the older women tend to younger children and infants. Loss of strength and agility will not quickly be noticed in a woman. She will simply spend more time at home, performing other routine tasks such as cooking or sewing. The transition to old age is thus more gradual and comes later in the life cycle than it does for men.

The onset of old age is hastened by debilitating diseases and may be slowed by what I have elsewhere (Guemple, 1969) called "renewal." The major forms of physical impairment that affect premature entry into old age are arthritis and blindness. The cold, damp character of the traditional igloo and tent tend to promote arthritis; and the incidence of blindness due to trachoma and glaucoma is relatively high. Men also suffer a relatively high incidence of corneal abrasion and snow blindness which can often lead to partial impairments of sight. In the recent past tuberculosis has also taken a considerable toll, particularly in those people who have been sent out to a hospital to have portions of lungs or bones removed to rid them of infection.

Old age can also be delayed in some instances. Men often accomplish this by extraordinary effort in hunting during the spring and summer seasons when the demands of production are not so great; and they sometimes undergo symbolic renewal by taking younger women as wives in their maturity. Women cannot aspire to marry younger men in their later years; but they can and frequently do assert they are still able to perform their primary functions by seeking to adopt children. It is said that adopting a child makes an old woman feel young again; and while the primary aim of adoption is not stated to be renewal, it is the only

reason given that makes very much sense.[1]

Old people are well cared for in Inuit society because they can draw upon two interlocking social institutions as sources of support: the household and the community at large. Members of a household share equitably; and so long as there are younger workers in the household to work on behalf of their elders their interests are seen to with great care and devotion (Gubser, 1965:122; Hawkes, 1916:117). The rules of residence stipulate that young hunters stay home until they marry, and so an aging elder can expect to have his son do much of his hunting for him. When a daughter marries, the husband will come to live in her household, and he is answerable to the father-in-law, at least until after the first child is born. Husbands may also remain in the household of an in-law if there is need, and relations between the son-in-law and other household members are cordial.

Old people can expect some support from the community at large so long as they are able to contribute to the fund of resources from which others draw. Inuit rules of sharing enjoin that successful hunters share a portion of their catch with those who were less successful; and mature hunters are generally only too happy to be able to offer support to other community members, since it is the most important source of prestige in the local hunting community. In return, the old people offer the produce of the hunting of their sons or sons-in-law as circumstances permit, they offer the help in sewing and gathering wood by their daughters, and they themselves will pitch in to help in any way they can to the general good. Men often offer work in repair jobs, executing technically difficult parts of various pieces of technology where knowledge and patience are particularly needed. They go for short hunting trips around camp, and often school young hunters on how to set snares, stalk land animals, etc. Women contribute their domestic labor for sewing, cooking, cleaning, baby tending, and so on. In the evenings, the old people as keepers of the sacred and secular lore of this nonliterate society maintain a sense of tradition by telling stories and offering advice which experience shows to be particularly applicable to some predicament.

This system seems to work well so long as old people have someone to rely on to make their contribution to the community pool; and the institutional structure appears to break down only when the old people are left stranded by the departure of their children from the household and the community for one reason or another for an extended period of time. In that context, members of the community at large gradually come to view the old couple as parasitic and begin to complain about their dependency. So far as I am aware, community members would not flatly refuse to feed old people in such a situation; but they often receive a lesser share or the least desirable portion. And they may from time to time suffer the indignity of being gossiped about or verbally abused for their failure to contribute adequately.

As the couple grows into old age, one or the other will die, leaving the survivor to move in with a son or a daughter or with some more distant relative. The children generally accept the added burden gracefully; though more distant relatives may find it a bit inconvenient to be saddled with a sibling or a cousin in old age. The Inuit of the Canadian North never collect material possessions as a form of wealth. The need to be continually on the move prevents the accumulation of luxuries. But men with ambition often collect people as a kind of "wealth"; and old men or women who are not too feeble are generally welcome in the household of an influential hunter if they have no children to care for them. Seldom are old people to be found in utterly desperate straits unless the entire community is impoverished.

If old people are well treated and cared for by their fellows in the traditional culture, they appear also to be the objects of startling cruelties. For Inuit are known to abandon their old people on the trail from time to time with very little ceremony; and there are even cases where the children have stood ready to help them end their lives if asked to do so. Such behavior strikes us as terribly inconsistent and begs for an explanation.

The well-documented facts are that Inuit sometimes abandon their old people. This is generally done either by leaving them behind while on the trail or by allowing them to go off on their own to make an end to themselves. When old people were abandoned, it was most often done out of necessity, seldom out of

indifference to the old (Burch, 1975:148–50; Gubser, 1965:122; Jenness, 1922:236; Low, 1906:165; Spencer, 1959:252), though cases of apparently cruel treatment are known (Stefánsson, 1914:130).

Freuchen (1961:200–203) describes a typical case with his usual dramatic flair: A couple is traveling from one community to another accompanied by their immature children and an old woman, the wife's mother. Sometime during the night, the old lady, having faced an arduous day on the trail, decides the burden of living is too heavy for her to carry any longer, that she has become a millstone to her children and grandchildren and should now end the struggle to survive. She tells the two adults that she can go on no longer. They try to dissuade her, but she persists. Finally they agree, and in the morning they pack their gear and depart with only a word or two of farewell, leaving the old lady behind in the igloo, alone with her thoughts and her few meager possessions.

Other examples appear to be even more infathomable. An old man, perhaps nettled over some incident which has led to a quarrel or an insult to his sense of dignity, calls his two sons to him and tells them that he is old and useless, the butt of community jokes. Because of this, he has decided that with their help, he will do away with himself. The sons encourage him to think positively, to remember the joys of playing with his grandchildren, and so on, but he insists that he has seen enough of life and wishes to be rid of it. Eventually, they leave off pleading, and under his direction, fetch a sealskin line and wrapping the middle around his neck a couple of turns, take the ends and strangle him.

The conventional explanation of these situations is that the old are stoic about death and embrace the notion of their dying fearlessly and with resignation, when they feel they are no longer useful. So the sons or daughters accept the old person's decision with but very little coaxing.

There are a number of problems with this formulation of their reaction to the possibility of death. For one thing, it assumes that life in the Arctic is a continuous struggle for survival which people perceive and respond to by a sort of stoic resignation. While this notion is one of *our* favorite themes, it is certainly not part of the Inuit repertoire. They do not see their lives as endangered by their marginal situation. They know its hazards well and have what are to them adequate means for coping with them. It is strangeness that creates a sense of threat, not familiarity; so their situation strikes us as threatening. The Inuit do not perceive it to be so.

How then are we to explain their casual acceptance of the death of loved ones, particularly the old? The answer is that old people do not, in Inuit cosmology, really die. In order to understand this statement, it will be necessary to set aside momentarily our consideration of old age as such and examine briefly the Inuit conception of the underlying character of people, whether old or young. That inquiry will provide us with the basis for solving the riddle of their indifference to death.

Inuit believe that the essential ingredient of a human being is its name. The name embodies a mystical substance which includes the personality, special skills, and basic character which the individual will exhibit in life. Without that substance he will die; and should he exchange his name substance for another through a ritualized renaming process, he will become a different person.

The name substance is derived from other humans, but is not thought of as biological in character; and it bears little resemblance to units of heredity such as genes or of some more metaphorical analogue of biological inheritance such as "blood." The name substance is induced into the body within three or four days after birth; and the process of naming a child is viewed by Inuit as one in which a ritual specialist divines what particular name substance has entered its body. Often the name is that of some recently deceased community member, frequently a relative of the child. But it is never the substance of a parent or a sibling of the child, and the most frequent "choices" of names are those belonging to members of the grandparental generation. The names of children who are sickly are sometimes changed shortly after birth, and shamans and a few others change their names in adulthood and thus become different persons; but most people keep their names throughout their lifetimes. At death, the name separates from the body but remains in the vicinity of the body or of the place of death for three or four days during which time it is thought to be dangerous to living humans.

After that time, it is thought to return to the underworld to wait till it can enter the body of a newborn child. Names thus cycle as do the social identities which are attached to them.

Names are never exclusively held by individuals in Inuit society. Three or sometimes four individuals may bear the same name and thus be the same person in principle. We might express this idea in a different way and say that from the standpoint of the Inuit community at large, the society consists of a limited number of names, each having its own social identity—personal history, personality, work skills, attributes and attitudes, etc.—attached to it. The identities are shared out in the community among its members on roughly a one-for-four basis, and cycle.

At birth, individuals step into one of these well-established identities and bear them in latent form until they come to full expression in adulthood. During their lifetimes, they may contribute to their shape; and at death, they pass their part of the identities on to the next generation fully formed. These identities are indestructible; they neither die nor dissipate, but instead go on endlessly cycling through one generation after another.

Since the name substance is not inherited from the parents and not passed on to one's own biological posterity, parents contribute little to the children's identities except body substance which, to Inuit, is of little significance. And, since the social identity comes to the individual fully formed, it is not something the individual or the community is believed to be able to change in any major way, though in special cases it is possible to actually change identities.

We are now in a position to see why Inuit are relatively casual about the death of old people even if they are bound tightly to them in life. Children permit their parents to do away with themselves because they are not attached to them as we are to our parents. Every individual shares a community of spirit with others; but in Inuit society, that community is with those who bear the same name, not those who share the same blood or some metaphorical analogue. Sentiments bind parents and children together, but these can never be compelling because parents and children share nothing more vital than those sentiments.

A more compelling reason for the seeming indifference to the death of the parents is related to their understandings about the fate of the person concerned. In our cosmology, the death of an individual means at best his departure to another place, at worst the end of all being, the end of all subjective experience of self. In either case, it is a mystery that makes life precious, that makes us rather bear those ills we have than fly to others. In Inuit cosmology, the persona is the one enduring, immutable substance. Whatever else may happen, Inuit know that their personas live on, not in consciousness, but certainly as fully formed social entities. It is this fact of their existence, and not a resigned stoicism, that makes them indifferent to death when the body becomes infirm and the will to live weakens.

The treatment of the old we have described in this paper and the cosmological order we have explored to explain what gives them confidence and courage in facing old age and death are part of a tradition that is now on the verge of extinction across the Arctic as conversion to Christianity and the transition to modern living conditions have gradually replaced the aboriginal customs and beliefs. Modern-day old people of the North live in prefab homes, draw old age and disability pensions, take their sustenance from the shelf at the store, and receive their medical care from the local nursing station or hospital. These benefits have done much to make old age comfortable materially; and old men and women alike are quick to express their gratitude for these amenities. That the cosmological explanations we offer serve them as well in death as the material comforts we lavish on them in life is a little more difficult to assert with confidence.

NOTE

1. The principal reason given for adoption by older women is that the adoption will provide someone to take care of the adopter "when they are old." But this same reason is given when the prospective adopter is in her sixties and the child is but one or two years of age. Further, the same reason is given by older women who have numerous children of their own, in some cases children already grown to maturity and ready to care for the parent.

James Dowd

SOCIAL EXCHANGE, CLASS, AND OLD PEOPLE

In this selection from his book *Stratification among the Aged*, sociologist James Dowd uses the perspective of exchange theory to examine, in the context of class stratification, the position of our country's aged and to discuss alternative routes toward improving their status. In this framework aging is viewed as a process of social exchange whereby the available behavioral responses at a given time in the life cycle are shaped by the resources available and the power dependence relationships that bind generations together. Dowd applies this type of analysis to questions of social policy and points to varied means of using extant resources possessed by the aged in order to enhance their power in cross-generational interaction.

POWER AND DEFERENCE: BASIS OF RAPPROCHEMENT BETWEEN AGE AND CLASS

AGING, AS ARGUED BY de Beauvoir (1972), is a class struggle. When this thesis was first argued, the concept was difficult to understand; it remains difficult today. The reason we resist thinking of old people as a social class is largely terminological: Age and class, as most writers have told us, are separate systems. The need to keep these concepts separate has, in my view, curtailed the utility of each. In order to achieve any integration of the two, we must first look for one factor that is of concern to both systems: One such factor is power.

Power, viewed from the perspective of the stratification theorist, involves the ability to get what one wants and "to influence others in ways that further one's own interests" (Parenti, 1978: 12). . . . This use of the term *power* differs somewhat from the way exchange theorists use the term; according to exchange theorists, power is the state of relative independence that results from having a greater share of valued resources than one's exchange partner. However, the two uses are actually complementary rather than contradictory: One is intended to describe the relations among groups (the stratification definition), whereas the other applies to the relations among individuals (the exchange definition). Although definitions of social class vary from writer to writer, the factor of access to power underlies all of them. This factor gives significance to the concepts of class and stratification. Rothman (1978), for example, although he made a point of distinguishing between the terms *inequality* and *stratification*, was unable to define either without referring to power: Inequality is the uneven distribution of any resource, including power, whereas stratification means the relatively permanent "power arrangements" (as well as the values, beliefs, and ideas) that both underlie and result from structured inequalities.

I would suggest that, just as class and stratification resist being defined without a similar reference, definitions of age stratification are not complete without reference to power. The meaning of de Beauvoir's bold assertion that "aging is a class struggle" becomes clear when one begins to think of both aging and class in terms of power. Although neo-Marxist writers may disagree with any use of the word *class* that fails to specify a group's relationship to the means of

From *Stratification among the Aged* by James Dowd. © 1980 by Wadsworth, Inc. Reprinted by permission of Brooks/Cole Publishing Company, Monterey, California.

economic production in a society, I concur with Dahrendorf's more pragmatic argument that "there is no reason why we should not call quasigroups and interest groups classes or anything else" (1959: 201). Clearly the aged are not a social class if we take the "realist" position regarding their existence. Such a view holds social classes to be "groups possessed both of real and vital common economic interests and of a group-consciousness of their general position in the social scale" (Marshall, quoted in Wrong, 1964). Aging may be viewed as a class struggle, however, if one holds the opposing "nominalist" view of social classes. According to this position, class refers to a group of individuals who share certain attributes (the individuals do not need to be aware of their common bonds, however). Paraphrasing Dahrendorf's much quoted definition of social classes, we can state that age strata are essentially "social conflict groups, the determinant of which can be found in the participation in or exclusion from the exercise of authority" (1959: 138). I would modify this definition by adding "and the exercise of *power* and control of *power resources.*"

Although it departs from the neo-Marxists' strict definition of class, the view of social class and aging proposed here does share conflict theory's concern with the ways in which unequal access to power resources determines social status and life chances. Unlike the functionalists, who insist that the distribution of rewards in society is a function of individual abilities, the conflict theorists recognize that rewards are distributed as a function of power. This theme is elaborated in Lenski's monograph, *Power and Privilege.*[1] Lenski argued that both cooperation and conflict are present in all societies to varying degrees. However, in societies that have a large economic surplus (modern industrial societies), it is conflict, or power, that largely determines the distribution of the surplus.

An economic surplus may be defined as what a group produces "in excess of what is needed to keep the producers healthy and productive" (Lenski and Lenski, 1978: 153). Until the discovery of the basic techniques of animal domestication and farming around 10,000 B.C. (the Neolithic Revolution), economic production was limited to hunting and gathering. With the development of horticulture, the first economic

surplus was created. This is an important consideration since it was only with the creation of economic surplus that an extensive system of social stratification came into being. Inequality in the distribution of the goods and services of a society first appeared on a large scale during the Bronze Age, when the more powerful group members began to use their strength to obtain larger shares of the surplus. With the emergence of private ownership and the related concept of inheritance, the way was opened for the development of a relatively permanent division of the society into social classes. As Bottomore notes, social classes "originated with the first historical expansion of productive forces beyond the level needed for mere subsistence, involving the extension of the division of labor outside the family, the accumulation of surplus wealth, and the emergence of private ownership of economic resources" (1968: 15).

Although not considered to be a Marxist sociologist, Lenski argued that *privilege,* or control over a portion of the surplus wealth, has its basis in power. Prestige, or one's esteem in the eyes of others, is a function of both power (that which enables a person to claim privilege) and privilege (actual possession of resources or rewards, such as income, wealth, land, and so forth). These concepts are relevant to the present analysis of age and stratification for, if we want to understand the position of old people in contemporary society, it is necessary that we investigate the sources of power that old people possess, the mechanisms by which this power is converted into privilege, and the role of both power and privilege in determining the prestige (or status) ascribed to old people as a group.

However, in order to proceed in this direction, we must move beyond Lenski's analysis, since it is incomplete in several important areas. First and most important, although Lenski uses the term *power* throughout his discussion, he never makes clear how people gain or exercise this precious commodity. Second, as Lenski himself points out, his theory predicts that the greatest inequality among social classes will be found in modern industrial societies—a prediction clearly not confirmed by empirical evidence. It is Lenski's ambiguous use of the term *power,* however, that is most problematic for the present analysis. How do people "get" power and, once obtained, how does power beget privilege and prestige? The answers to these questions have long preoccupied stratification theorists, and it is not likely that the answers offered here will prevent continued analysis. However, I believe that these questions, particularly the question how one acquires power, can be answered through application of the concepts of *dependence* and *deference*. . . . Let it suffice to say here that power is acquired through the ability to satisfy one's needs without having to depend upon or become indebted to other people. The reader may recognize this as a central assumption underlying the exchange theories of Emerson (1962) and Blau (1964).

The concept of *deference* may help in answering the question of how power is used to acquire privilege and prestige. Shils (1975) refers to deference as the tendency for a social actor to "appreciate" or "derogate" the partner with whom social interaction occurs. In face-to-face interaction, deference is "often but not always accorded primarily with respect to status in the larger society" (Shils, 1975: 277). Shils's use of the term *deference* is consistent with exchange theorists' use of the word *power;* that is, both terms are used in connection with social interaction, rather than with single individuals. A person's privilege and prestige, for example, does not come automatically from power or "the possession of certain entitlements" but is instead "an element in a relationship between the person deferred to and the deferent person" (Shils, 1975: 287). Without social interaction, the power of an individual cannot be translated into privilege or prestige. Indeed, power itself cannot be conceptualized apart from the interaction of at least two people. So, to suggest that a person or group of people (say, the aged) lacks power is to suggest that, with respect to a second individual or group (for example, the middle-aged), the person or group generally is deferent and, therefore, subordinate.

One may question Shils's assertion that *all* social interaction involves deference, since so many of the daily encounters among people seem fairly routinized and not at all like the drama suggested by the phrase "acts of appreciation and derogation." Deference is present nonetheless, according to Shils. It is readily apparent, for instance, when the aged widow accedes to her child's suggestion that she enter a nursing home.

It is present as well, however, in the *routine* conversation between members of different generations. Indeed, deference never is totally absent from any of our conversations or encounters with others in our social world. In other words, although it may not be recognized in every act or utterance, it is always there, near the surface, ready to be shown at the appropriate time. Deference is, as Shils notes, sometimes concentrated (evident) and sometimes not. When not concentrated, deference "survives in attenuation, in a pervasive, intangible form that enters into all sorts of relationships through tone of speech, demeanor, precedence in speaking, frequency and mode of contradiction, and so forth" (1975: 288–89).

Whether one receives or shows deference, which generally is directed upward from lower-status to higher-status individuals, depends on the relative positions of the social actors involved. This fact underlies many of the transition problems faced by older persons upon retirement, the death of a spouse, relocation to a nursing home, or other similar life changes. The routine showing of deference brings with it a degree of predictability to social relations that most people find satisfying, and it also gives an indication of how the actors view themselves and their status relative to other people. When one of the actors involved undergoes a transition in his or her *social* identity (a worker becomes a retiree, for example), deference relationships must be renegotiated to reflect the shift in power. Shils goes so far as to suggest that deference may even become *extinct.* If a person loses power, Shils argues that, "in the course of time," the person will also lose the deference that the power (Shils uses the term *entitlements*) brought him or her.

An individual's power is derived from the ability to satisfy perceived needs or to achieve goals with a minimum amount of dependence upon other persons. In satisfying perceived needs, the individual accumulates *privilege,* or a share of a society's surplus (Lenski, 1966): The resources that enable the person to remain independent— that is, not dependent upon the resources of another person—are also used as credit that the person uses to claim a "legitimate" share of the group's goods. Privilege is then converted into prestige during social interaction. In this process, deference is the link between privilege and prestige; it is manifested through conversation and other communication media, and it serves to signal any change in the relative power structure among the participants.

Before we move on to a discussion of the relationship of power, stratification, and the aged, two additional points must be made concerning the relationship between power and privilege. First, the relationship is reciprocal; that is, although power is the basis of privilege, an increase in privilege serves to increase power as well (see Figure 1). For example, an increase in wealth is a goal that may be reached by the use of power. On the one hand, therefore, an increase in wealth increases privilege; on the other hand, however, an increase in wealth also increases the actor's independence, or power.

The second point concerns the basis of power, about which Lenski unfortunately says very little. I have already suggested that power involves independence or autonomy, but independence itself is relative; it is not a constant characteristic of individuals. To say that a person has power is to say that, in the process of achieving a goal, he or she has remained relatively independent of other people. But how does an actor remain relatively independent? The answer is through *resources*. Through the possession of objects, traits, or qualities defined by a group as desirable (and, therefore, desired), the individual is able to exert power in a social relationship.

Resources can be classified into five categories:

1. *Personal Characteristics*, such as strength, beauty, charm, integrity, courage, intelligence, knowledge, and so forth
2. *Material Possessions*, such as money or property
3. *Relational Characteristics*, such as influential friends or relatives or caring children
4. *Authority*, such as that associated with political office, position in a formal organization, or status within a group (such as the status of parent in the family)
5. *Generalized Reinforcers*, such as respect, approval, recognition, support, and other rewards

Of these five types of power resources, *material possessions* is the category that is also an aspect of *privilege*. We all know that money can be used to make more money; so, money can be defined as both a resource of power and an aspect of privilege.

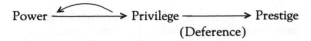

Figure 1. The Reciprocal Relationship between Power and Privilege

POWER, STRATIFICATION, AND OLD PEOPLE

The system of age stratification, because it involves "class," is also a system in which power is exercised. Age cohorts, although they don't constitute social classes according to most definitions, have certain elements in common with social classes. Most important to the present analysis, privilege and prestige are found in unequal measure among different age groups, just as they are among different social classes. Since the surplus of a society is inherently limited, and since the distribution of a surplus is based on power, age relations are power relations. The relationship between a retired worker and his or her middle-aged landlord, for example, is a power relationship. So, too, is the relationship between a widow and her middle-aged daughter. All that is meant by the term *power relationship* is that the social interaction between two individuals or groups involves the exchange of power resources. Thus, the greater the number and/or quality (desirability) of resources, the more power the individual is able to exercise.

Old people in modern society, because of their exclusion from labor markets, are disadvantaged in their intergenerational relations. Of the five types of resources, material possessions, particularly money, are the most widely accepted and easily transferred. Since the principal means by which most people acquire money is participation in labor markets, old people are limited in their access to material possessions as well as their access to positions of authority, since they are not usually active in the labor market. In old age, it is often necessary to rely upon those possessions previously accumulated, because material resources rarely accrue significantly after occupational retirement.

Old people are further disadvantaged in intergenerational relations, because their access to other power resources, including both personal and relational characteristics, is also limited. For example, aging brings with it a decline in strength and beauty (as generally defined); thus, these two power resources become inaccessible for the aged. Beauty is, of course, in the eye of the beholder; yet, physical beauty is generally associated with youth, not old age. This is not to suggest that old people lack beauty. Indeed, in the interaction among old people, beauty again becomes a power resource, because some old people are certainly more beautiful than others. It is in cross-age interaction that the aged usually cannot rely on beauty as a power resource. This difference serves to illustrate how power is relative (cf. Lehman, 1977): The value of a power resource such as beauty is greatest when the resource is combined with other resources, such as money. The value of being wealthy *and* attractive is obvious; the liquidity of beauty without wealth, however, is limited. The fact that power is relative suggests that those who view power as inevitably linked with *force*—for example, Bierstedt (1950: 202), who suggests that "power is latent force"—are defining the concept in an unnecessarily restrictive way.

Another illustration of the relativity of power is the increasing probability that death will steal from aging people the friends and relatives who serve as important sources of power. In fact, the only major source of power left untouched by the aging process is the category of generalized reinforcers. Yet, since respect or approval are universally available, they are also less valued than other types of power resources. In any case, the mere fact that aging does not *decrease* one's access to power resources does not constitute an advantage; aging does not *increase* one's access to them either.

When one considers how power resources for old people dwindle, it is somewhat incongruous to read stratification theorists' accounts of old age. Lenski (1966) and Abrams (1970), for example, claim that aging brings *increased*, not fewer, resources. Their apparent disregard of the fact that most old people are not members of the ruling elite is suggested by the following quote:

The key fact with respect to age stratification in all advanced industrial societies is the economic, political, and general organizational dominance of

the older segments of the population. (1966: 406)

Lenski goes on to list the average ages of United States senators, American military leaders, members of the property and managerial elites, and others. Such an aanalysis makes a serious error by both confusing the middle-aged with the aged and analyzing the distribution of resources by age only for the dominant classes (ruling elites) and not for the working classes. Lenski shows how age favors the old within a small proportion of the population. Certainly among the majority of the lower and working classes (to which almost half of all Americans belong),[2] resources do *not* increase past middle age.

Although some argue that resources are greatest among the older segments of the population, others insist that, although resources do decline in old age, the decline is not particularly problematic. This is the fallacy of the argument called *The Old Need Less*. An example of this argument is the observation that most old people seem quite able to get along with reduced income. They are probably able to make do, according to some, because of disengagement. Streib (1976: 164), for example, argues that the "elderly often voluntarily curtail their needs, activities, and consumption patterns in accord with their declining energy, declining interests, and declining income." In addition, Streib states that "a person with an older self-image may manage comfortably on a smaller income because he has 'disengaged from consumerism,' so to speak." The notion of a voluntary curtailment of life style, however, is speculation—a conclusion with no basis in evidence. The only conclusion from Streib's observations that appears warranted is that when the income of a group is reduced, people make do with less income. What other choice does a person have? If one excludes suicide, theft, or loans, there remains little to do when a person's income is reduced but struggle to make do. To suggest this is voluntary is beside the point; it is, for most old people, the *only* viable option.

The argument of disengagement theorists that old people voluntarily disengage in order to prepare for death and attain the new "equilibrium" characteristic of "successful aging" simply has no factual basis. Although aspects of the disengagement theory do retain significance for current work in aging, the voluntary-withdrawal notion is not one of them. Thus, for some, it may be "one of the paradoxes in later life . . . that persons can suffer severe declines in income, yet still retain essentially the same style of life" (Streib, 1976: 165). For others, however, including the present writer, there is no paradox: Old age is associated with a decline in resources that serves to drastically alter the old person's social interactions and self-concept.[3] If "style of life" refers to the tendency of many old people to live in their homes for as long as possible, then it is true that style of life is unchanged. Yet, if one considers the change in the number and quality of old people's social interactions (as well as the fact that their house still requires maintenance and takes up a greater part of their income), one realizes that the style of life *changes* in old age (cf. Alberoni, 1971). Thus, there is no paradox.

The aged are, in fact, similar to the unemployed, the destitute, and others in the subordinate classes of industrial societies in that they are the people who "get least of what there is to get" (Miliband, 1969, quoted in Parenti, 1978). The lack of resources available to old people is described in the following passage:

Class position becomes an important factor in shaping life conditions of the elderly. Like the very young, the very old suffer from natural disabilities when attempting to compete for social outputs. In a society that places a premium on beauty, youth, energy, speed, earning power, aggressive drive, and productivity, the old and infirm are easily deprived of their place in the sun. When one's status and security is determined by one's ability either to control wealth or sell one's labor on the market, the superannuated are a surplus people of little use to the productive system, to their families and, as often happens, to themselves. The deference accorded a person of years in more traditional societies is replaced with impatience, patronization, neglect, and finally incarceration in a nursing home. As the elderly are given more years to live, they are given less reason to live. (Parenti, 1978: 68)

Other sources of power, in addition to money, that are unequally distributed among age groups are *time* and *charisma*. These are *personal* characteristics that tend to favor the young. I say "tend" to favor the young since the relationship between age and charisma—although not the relationship between age and time, which always

favors the young—varies by level of societal modernization. Time is, of course, a precious resource because it is nonreplaceable and finite. Young people, more so than old people, have time "on their side." Time, in this sense, may be difficult to employ as a power resource in any single or nonreoccurring situation. However, in the long run, young people generally outlast the aged and, therefore, can strike a tougher bargain in their intergenerational relationships.

In particular, charisma tends to favor the young in industrial, or modern, societies. For example, the heroes of our popular culture, whether in music, athletics, or politics, are, almost without exception, young. In Shils's (1975) terms, charisma adheres to those closest to the "center" of society; the center reflects a society's core values, those that "legitimate or withhold legitimacy from the earthly powers or that dominate earthly existence" (Shils, 1975: 279).

Although in contemporary society, charisma attaches more readily to youthful persons than to old, this is not true of other societies or other times. In times past, when the center of a society was dominated by religion, superstition, or magic, the aged were viewed as having a great deal of charisma because of their control over the exercise of rituals, their knowledge of the past and magical things, and their closeness to death and, therefore, to the deities (cf. Goody, 1976). Among the Kiwai Papuans, for example, children stood in awe of old people because of their magical powers. Landtman (1938) describes Papuan youth crouching in a stooped position when passing a group of elders, since boys were "afraid of rousing the angry attention of some elder who could easily harm (them) by means of sorcery at the slightest cause of displeasure" (p. 21). Also, charisma as a characteristic of old people is generally found in predominantly agrarian societies. Among the Yahgan of Tierra del Fuego, to cite another example, it is reported that "almost every elderly man is said to be a wizard" (Landtman, 1938: 143).

In modern society, the supernatural plays a peripheral, rather than central, role. The roles that do have authority and control society—and that, therefore, represent the center of modern life—are the secular positions of judge, governor, scientist, and technocrat. The charisma of the aged in modern society, as a result, is diminished to almost nothing, save for the exceptional few who, like George Meany, Bertrand Russell, or Pablo Casals, were able to maintain a valuable skill or office.

THE PERSISTENCE OF STRATIFICATION HIERARCHIES: THE PROBLEM OF LEGITIMATION

Stratification on the basis of age, like methods of distributing the excess goods of a society, persists because those who suffer or derive only minimum benefits from the system either accept it as legitimate or are powerless to change it. Obviously, those who benefit most from any institutional arrangement are mostly likely to prefer maintenance of the status quo.

Old people have, for the most part, accepted their subordinate position in the age-stratification system. There have been occasional indications of organized anger on the part of the aged, such as the Townsend Movement during the 1930s, the McLain Movement following World War II, and, most recently, the Gray Panthers. Most studies indicate, however, that the number of old people who are "age conscious" remains relatively small (Dowd, 1978). The reasons for this are similar to the reasons why many workers are decidedly not class conscious. First, the aged are relatively unorganized and, as a consequence, powerless when pitted against the myriad laws and policies that mandate age as a legal basis of discrimination and exclusion. Second, many old people have internalized and accepted as legitimate the continued use of age as a criterion for stratification. Like the young, old people tend to prefer what is familiar, and they fear and dislike the unknown or uncertain. (Studies, for example, on the attitudinal effect of "mere exposure" to certain words and categories of objects demonstrate that subjects consistently demonstrate a preference for those words that appear frequently in common usage.)[4] Third, many people tend to view existing institutional structures as just and appropriate. The accumulated "tradition" of

existing structures renders them very resistant to change. This fact is recognized by politicians as part of the advantage of the incumbent in an election.

In the case of retirement policies, many people—including the aged—if they ever think about the matter at all, tend to take for granted that retirement will occur at a specified age. These policies have been in existence long enough to be almost invisible. Like sexism prior to the women's liberation movement, ageism is an unconscious ideology. Forced retirement and other manifestations of age stratification have been institutionalized in our society and have become, with time, legitimated; they are examples of our tendency to perceive what "is" as what, therefore, "has to be."

At this point . . . I want to point out that, in spite of one's dissatisfaction with society's callous treatment of many old people, in order to analyze stratification one must recognize that no system of distribution will ever eliminate inequality within a society. This is, as Dahrendorf cogently argues, the dynamic element of history. There will always be conflict among groups in capitalist economies for a greater share of society's surplus. Regardless of the morality of such behavior, all members of a class or stratum "have a vested interest in protecting or increasing the value of their common resources and in reducing the value of competitive resources that constitute the bases of other classes" (Lenski, 1966: 76). This applies to the aged no less than to other groups within society. The reluctance of old people in preindustrialized societies to share their "privilege" with younger age groups supports the proposition that to possess power is to use it.

One mechanism for protecting resources and power . . . is *ideology*—a system of beliefs that supports the dominant class by legitimating its exploitation of subordinate groups. It is apparent that any effort to effect a redistribution of societal resources must first identify the society's ideologies and demonstrate their pervasive effect, because such legitimating myths—what Weber calls *status-legends*—serve to maintain the conditions that allow continued operation of existing institutional arrangements. In capitalist society, the ideology of private control of free enterprise serves the interests of the business and political elites who reap the major profits from the system. So, too, the "myth of the Golden Years" (Gubrium, 1973), which posits a notion of successful aging that includes retirement from active participation in labor markets, serves the interests of younger age groups. This is another example of the ironic tendency of those groups who benefit least from existing structures to become some of the staunchest supporters of the structures. Although belying the market assumption of rational behavior, this tendency does suggest that dominant groups in capitalist societies have been very successful in achieving a major goal of dominant groups everywhere—the ability to keep others subordinate without using overt coercion (Collins, 1975). As Rousseau (as quoted in Parenti, 1978: 83) observed in the *Social Contract*: The "strongest is never strong enough to be always master, unless he transforms his strength into right and obedience into duty."

THE DELIVERY OF SERVICES TO THE AGED

The state of the world, as Bertrand Russell noted, is a difficult matter to dismiss. Society may wish to abandon old people, and old people may wish to disengage themselves from the world, but neither occurrence is either completely possible or desirable. Although complete disengagement would have undesirable consequences for old people, I do not mean to suggest that disengagement should be combatted by legions of geriactivists, whose function it would be to persuade—indeed require—old people to *participate*. Although they are well intentioned, such activists usually do not care about the *mode* of participation; they usually care only that old people keep themselves *busy*. Although it is not particularly innovative, their message is clear: STAY ACTIVE!

I am of the opinion that we could use less, not more, of the paternalistic pigheadedness that spawns such notions. The "state of the world" that infiltrates most corners of the everyday lives of the aged is a bureaucratized, service-providing, help-delivering, problem-solving, "jointly sponsored" program managed by a growing network of agencies and institutions, both governmental and private. The product delivered in many cases is, to be sure, welcomed by the old person, because it is truly needed. At the same time, however, the mode of delivery often serves to produce a continued state of dependency and sense of ineffectiveness on the part of old people.

This complaint about the delivery of services to the aged bears repetition, because the conditions that originally caused it have not improved. I refer specifically to the misguided belief among professionals in the field of gerontology that our "knowledge" of aging processes renders us fit to prescribe for old people what behaviors are for their "own good." Although this "paternalistic assertion" (Halper, 1978) may, in some cases, be justified, its net effect in the large majority of cases is deleterious. Even if paternalistic intervention "solves" some short-term problems, it also serves to further increase the dependency of old people, which, in the long run, will damage their morale and self-esteem.

SOCIAL POLICY AND THE INDEPENDENCE OF THE AGED

The origins of the "paternalistic assertion" that the aged are in "need of substantial outside help, whether they know it or not" (Halper, 1978: 323), probably lie in the modernity syndrome and, specifically, in the faith of modern technocrats in bureaucratic procedures and scientific "human engineering." The emphasis, as Weber pointed out several decades ago, is on total administrative control. The lives of old people in institutionalized settings are especially vulnerable to the workings of this philosophy. It has been noted by Halper, for example, that "the bureaucratic imperative of manageability is often sought through such products of science as the drug thorazine, which facilitates custodial care by numbing the elders. . . ." One particularly unnerving aspect of the bureaucratic perspective is its "catch-22" clause, which presumes that all those who resist the help or refuse the services of the geriactivist are, ipso facto, in the greatest need of all.

This perspective fails to realize, of course, that

disengagement or preference for solitary activities may constitute the most rational course of action under the circumstances. Rather than suggesting the possibility of psychological malfunctioning (paranoia, for example), such behavior may indicate the older person's firm resolve to retain his or her independence for as long as possible. In her excellent analysis of the behavior of old people who attended one particular senior center, Matthews (1977) argues that the decision of many of the participants to withdraw from the center was a tactic they employed to remain autonomous. Those who disengaged were not merely ''giving up'' or leaving because they were the ''poor performers'' in an active society and could no longer bear the burden of ''performance.'' Rather, Matthews argues, the decision to leave was calculated—that is, based on a serious evaluation of the rewards and costs involved. Instead of enduring the costs of continued interaction with the center's middle-aged staff—who viewed them primarily as ''old'' and, therefore, dependent—these old people decided to eliminate the costs altogether (and the rewards as well) by ''leaving the field.'' Matthews observes that the strategy of ''negotiation by default'' was ''one way for the old to protect their self-images,'' a means ''to avoid interaction with others who will respond to their oldness as pivotal.''

From an exchange theory perspective, the behavior described by Matthews is rational, since the older person who ''defaults'' recognizes the fact of declining profits and takes steps to rebalance the exchange. Blau (1964) includes the strategy of withdrawal as one of the options available to the dependent exchange partner to rebalance a particular relationship. Although this option is chosen only very infrequently because of the actor's continued need for rewards, the decision to withdraw or disengage is probably the best alternative, given an understanding of the critical importance of independence in most people's lives. It is a decision, in any case, that old people themselves are in the best position to make. The wishes of the geriactivist that old people remain active notwithstanding, the old person who decides to withdraw *must* be granted this right without being labeled ''disorganized'' or ''irrational.'' Researchers have documented this point in recent studies. Lowenthal and Robinson

(1976), for example, state that ''ranking low in network involvement at any life-stage does not necessarily result in low morale or poor mental health or whatever measure we wish to use.''

Once we establish the essential importance of autonomy in the lives of old people, much of their behavior can be understood as a continuing effort to maintain their independence in the face of a world intent upon total administration. In fact, one might argue (as I would) that old people—indeed, people of all ages—live out their everyday lives with an implicit understanding of the rules of social exchange, particularly the inverse relationship between power and dependence. Although academicians attempting to build reliable theories may frame their explanations in words that occasionally confuse more than clarify, the reality their words intend to convey is understood only too well by most old people.

Consequently, our gerontological literature is filled with disparate studies pointing to a similar conclusion that are without a unifying framework to focus their common concerns. We know, for example, that the aged in rural areas are reluctant to accept help, particularly if it requires a public declaration of poverty (Moen, 1978). We also know that the concern with death that characterizes older women is not necessarily a *fear* of death; rather, it is a fear of the dying *process* that ''centers on 'suffering' and 'being a burden,' both of which fall under the category of losing control over self-identity'' (Matthews, 1975: 108). The ''intimacy-at-a-distance'' style of intergenerational family contact is another pertinent example of the aged's struggle to maintain control over their lives. So, too, is Blenkner's observation that:

Most older persons under 75 are quite capable of taking care of themselves and their affairs. They neither want nor need to be ''dependent,'' but they do want and need someone to depend on, should illness or other crisis arise. (1965: 53)

This central fact of life in old age—the struggle to remain independent—must become the guiding principle of future policies and plans regarding old people. This does not mean that we should adopt a plan whereby the old person is cut off from social support and forced to rely upon what social workers euphemistically refer to as ''personal support systems.'' Rather, it means that we should attempt to maximize the autonomy of old people by carefully considering the two themes implicit in the preceding quote from Blenkner: individualism and community support (*gemeinschaft* or primary group could easily be substituted for "community"). Although individualism may appear inconsistent with the concept of *gemeinschaft* a group-oriented social organization characterized by small size, face-to-face contact, and personal ties), the two concepts need not be mutually exclusive. They are, rather, two principles, neither one of which should be disregarded in the planning of policy.

Individualism is not used here as a code word for a reactionary policy of governmental laissez-faire. An investigation of the historical uses of the term reveals that the basic ideas of individualism include notions of the *dignity of man, autonomy, privacy,* and *self-development.*[5] Each of these components of individualism, however, is threatened by bureaucratic control and the cultural hegemony of modern capitalism. They are also sadly missing in our prevailing policies regarding the aged and our everyday social interactions with them. If we want to prevent a future escalation of generational conflict as our economic growth rate stabilizes and/or declines, we must become committed to the principle of individual autonomy. This commitment requires that we view old people not as a group defined as needing *our* help, but as active agents in the management of their own lives.

Saying that we must make this commitment is, of course, much easier than doing it. The task of altering the prevailing view of the aged will be difficult, because our stratified social structure relegates old people to a subordinate position in the hierarchy. Consequently, if we are seriously concerned with the independence of our old people, we must be committed at the same time to reducing the inequalities among age groups in our society. The difficulties this entails are noted by Lukes:

Thus, for example, one will need to look very closely at the structural determinants of status ranking, if one is concerned to increase quality, or at the deeper influences (for example, through language and perception) of the agencies of socialization, if one is concerned to

maximize autonomy and self-development (1973: 157)[6]

One thing that we can do to increase the independence of the aged in American society is to abolish mandatory retirement policies. Although the age of mandatory retirement has changed recently from 65 to 70, any predetermined judgment of the occupational competence of a worker that is based on age is discriminatory, pure and simple. Evaluation of competence should be based on performance, not age. Those who present arguments *for* mandatory retirement tend to disregard the economic burdens imposed on old people in particular, and families in general, by inflation, the moral problems involved in any form of systematic discrimination, and the problems such a policy would impose on individuals attempting to negotiate equitable exchange rates.[7] Sheppard (1976) accounts for recent signs of a trend toward late retirement in terms of the high inflation rate of the 1970s and the prospects for its continuation.

Old people themselves can aid their cause through the recognition—and greater appreciation—of the power they *do* possess. It has been frequently observed, for example, that old people oftentimes contribute more to their adult children than they receive (Streib and Streib, 1978). And Shanas (1968) notes that middle- and working-class older men report that they have helped their children more often than the reverse. In the context of exchange theory, this pattern of giving more than receiving indicates that the power advantage in the relationship favors the middle-aged receiver. The exchange rate, in this case, may be something like two or three units of help from the aged parent for every one unit of help from the middle-aged child. The old person in this case is obviously more dependent on the rewards he or she obtains from the exchange than is the younger exchange partner—hence, the unbalanced rate of exchange. Rosenmayr (1977) similarly notes this unbalanced state when he writes (p. 135): "There is some evidence that parent/adult-child relations are not fully reciprocal; inasmuch as aged parents seem more attached to their children than children to parents."

Old people need to recognize the inherent value

of the resources they exchange in their relations with their children. In unbalanced exchanges, it would be a mistake for old people to assume that a gift or loan to an adult child necessarily builds an account that they may "call in" when they are in need of assistance (cf. Streib and Streib, 1978). Instead, the gift may be defined (in the context of an unbalanced exchange) as the middle-aged child's privilege—a commodity that is *expected* under the implicit rules governing the exchange.

Understanding this, old people would be in a better position to realize that their exchange partners are also—to a degree—*dependent* on rewards. Older partners must learn, in effect, the importance of negotiating from strength (Komorita, 1977), and they must recognize that they do have the power and ability to influence exchange outcomes. Consequently, if an old person perceives that an unbalanced exchange is becoming less profitable (either costs increase, or rewards decrease, or both), he or she may *change* the situation by *withholding* rewards anticipated by the other person. This strategy carries with it the risk of dissolving the relationship, but, in most cases, this risk is very small. A more likely outcome would be an increase in the rewards provided by the younger partner; in order to obtain whatever resource is controlled by the older parent, the middle-aged child will be required to *offer* more. In other words, by withholding a resource, the older person may change the exchange rate. . . .

The subject of power resources in general is an intriguing area of research because of the many possible "possessions" that people define as resources. Leggett (1972), for example, notes that old people "earn prestige partially on the basis of the class and racial content of the community." When a town comprises mostly white-collar and skilled workers, it acquires medium to high prestige. Its residents, according to Leggett, "identify with the area and acquire honor themselves, especially when they compare themselves invidiously with those living in communities with less honor" (p. 123). "Town honor" would probably constitute more of a resource in the interaction among old people than in cross-generational interaction (unless, of course, the younger person lives in a neighborhood with less prestige).

Another tactic that people use to maximize whatever power resources they have—one that applies to large groups of old people in their relations with other age groups qua political interest groups—is the mobilization of an age-based social movement. This form of collective behavior requires, in order to be effective, strong leadership and an effective organizational structure. Other conditions, such as the structural prerequisites identified by Smelser (1963), must also be present, however, before an old-age social movement can be postulated with any certainty. A more effective first step than the development of a social movement (which is unlikely for old people in the 1980s) toward maximizing power resources would be the development of a sense of political efficacy and age consciousness. An age-based class consciousness is not only possible, but likely, given the numbers of people aged 65 and over by the year 2020 and the prospects of a slow-growth or "managed" economy in the years ahead. As in all social movements, participation entails a loss of individual power (time and resources spent in achieving movement objectives) but promises at the same time "the greater power of combined resources" (Coleman, 1973).

THE FUTURE OF OLD-AGE SOCIAL POLICY

Although some writers view the last 20 years as a period of tremendous progress for the aged, it is still too early for optimism concerning the future of the aged in American society. Status gaps between the old and the non-old remain large, and existing evidence suggests that they will remain at least as large in the foreseeable future. In exchange terms, this suggests that the power of old people to influence exchange rates will continue to be minimal. Of course, this may change, given the possibility of future old-age cohorts that may possess considerably higher levels of power resources (greater education, for example) than previous old-age cohorts. One should not be misled, however, to make optimistic conclusions about the status of old people just because existing data show some improvement over the last few decades in the life situations of the population over 65. In making such conclusions one is really comparing quite different populations; a person aged 65 in 1940 was "older" than a person aged 65 today. In contemporary American society, the entry into old age for most people—judged in terms of physical functioning and activity levels—is not at age 65 but much later. Consequently, to address the issues relating to *old* age one must recognize that the age group in question consists of people in their seventies and older.

Although I am usually optimistic, I have great difficulty agreeing with those who root their optimism about the future of the aged in existing structural arrangements. Cameron (1974: 153), for example, argues that "the tremendous strides made by the elderly . . . their political visibility and power, have developed largely as a result of the activities of their special interest groups." She also notes that, "largely through the two White House Conferences on Aging," there has been "a renewed respect for the last stage of the life cycle." The accuracy of both statements, in my view, is dubious. Although old-age interest groups did have some impact on the 1971 White House Conference, the Conference itself had no meaningful impact and so, I would argue, dashed any hopes that were raised during conference preparation.

One wonders, however, whether the *bargaining position* of old people could be significantly improved. The answer is a qualified "yes." The status of old people *can* be improved, but it will require a modification of existing behaviors that may not be possible. The key to all of this is *engagement*. In order for old people to improve their negotiating positions vis-à-vis younger partners they must remain engaged in exchange networks. This is because exchange relations tend toward balance; however, in order for the balanced state to evolve, the exchange relationship must endure. Consequently, even though a strategy of negotiation by default may be a rational response to an unbalanced exchange *in the short run*, the long-term solution requires old people to remain active and engaged. The withdrawal into private life, which is characteristic not only of old people but of many in the working class as well, runs counter to the best

interests of these groups. Older people must strive to resist the "interiority" that presumably accompanies the entry into old age. The aged must join other outcasts and outsiders—"the exploited and persecuted of other races and colors, the unemployed and the unemployable"— who exist outside the democratic process (Marcuse, 1964: 265).

Engagement and activity may be difficult achievements for old people. *Increased* costs are the major reason why many people choose to disengage in old age; if they remain *active* exchange partners, they certainly will accrue even *greater* costs. Engagement is, however, the only means by which old-age status will improve. Old people must engage themselves in the course of their everyday social interactions. They must begin to appreciate the substantial degree of power they do possess.

This strategy is made more difficult to follow by the fact that age-segregated environments seem to produce considerably more primary-group ties among old people than settings in which there are actors of all ages. Hochschild's (1973) study of the occupants of Merrill Court and Rosow's (1967) earlier research on social integration each arrive at this conclusion. The reason for this is relatively straightforward. In our age-stratified society, old age is devalued and so, too, as a consequence, are old people. In cross-age social exchanges, then, age becomes a pivotal status characteristic, the criterion used to determine the going rates of exchange. Old people invariably are disadvantaged in such relationships. In settings comprised solely of old people, however, age stratification is largely eliminated. (I say "largely" eliminated because there is still the possibility that invidious distinctions may emerge between younger and older groups of old people.) The status differences that do emerge are based more on "achieved" criteria. Personality characteristics and other personal resources become the bases underlying the distribution of prestige. Ross (1977) observed this to be true in her study of a French retirement complex: "Common in communities of older people is a shared understanding that material differences, with their origin in the past, are to be muted. New signals of status distinction are just as often part of these emerging shared understandings" (p. 181).

Given the higher probability of primary-group relationships among age peers in an age-homogeneous environment, it is with serious reservations that I recommend the continued engagement of old people in cross-age exchange networks. The alternative course of social withdrawal (or restriction of interactions, to the maximum extent feasible, to those with age peers) does nothing to change the underlying problem. The status of old people will *not* improve through reliance upon the good will of younger people or the good intentions of concerned organizations. Such interventions may alleviate certain conditions but, by not addressing the central issue of power and dependence, they offer no real solution.

Present policies can assist old people to remain engaged in society by providing whatever benefits they are entitled to *directly to* the old people themselves; that is, wherever possible, rather than develop services *for* old people, these people should be allowed the freedom to decide whether this service or a similar service provided by a different supplier (or even a completely different product or service) will be purchased. In addition to actively engaging old people in society, this would have the benefit of increasing the likelihood that the services will be used to enlarge the older person's exchange networks and enhance his or her position within existing relationships. As Suttles and Street (1970: 753) note, "in this way, each recipient could become a benefactor within his own horizon or strata."[8]

The central issue in resolving the problems of the aged, as we discussed earlier, is individual autonomy. Our social policies must reflect a respect for individual freedom. This respect requires that we consider old people in all their diversity and resist categorizing old people according to the stereotypes of "sick," "useless," or "senile." Perhaps the single most damaging conception of old age is that old age is a period of life without significant *potential*. We tend to perceive old people as a group without a future, without the potential for continued growth and change. Old age is viewed as a period in which time stops. People cease to look to the future; they stop anticipating and planning for future events. Old age is, in a word, superfluous.[9]

This conception, irrespective of any prior validity it might have had, no longer fairly characterizes old age. Old people have a tremendous potential for societal contribution and self-growth that is currently not being exercised. Our stereotypes about old age, which are learned and internalized by old people themselves, violate the principle of respect for the individual person. To the extent that each of us tends to perceive old age in the same fashion, we become part of the problem. Since we are all growing old, we all have a vested interest in improving the status of old people. The necessary first step is the development of an appreciation of individual differences among old people. In concordance with the principle of respect, we must, as Lukes cogently argues:

. . . *regard and act toward individuals in their concrete specificity, that we take full account of their (social) situations. . . . This means in practice, among other things, that we see them as the (actually or potentially) autonomous sources of decisions and choices, as engaging in activities and involvements that they value highly and that require protection from public interference, and as capable of realizing certain potentialities, which will take a distinctive form in each specific individual's case. . . . It requires us to see each of them as an actually or potentially autonomous centre of choice . . . able to choose between, and on occasion transcend, socially given activities and involvements, and to develop his or her respective potentialities. (1973: 148–49)*

Although I recognize that most of us will continue to interact with old people in stereotypical fashion, I also believe that the inequality among age groups in our society will persist as long as we continue to discount the importance of autonomy in daily life. The status of the aged (and our *perceptions* of old people) is undeniably rooted in the nature of modern, postindustrial society. It would be a mistake, however, to argue that a change in political economy is, then, the only means by which the relative status of old people can be improved. Remembering that social structure exists ultimately in the countless social interactions of individuals, one can see how structural arrangements can indeed be modified as a result of changes in the interactions among social actors.

Since each of us, as an individual, is powerless

to affect directly the nature of our political economy, we must use social interaction as an indirect—but the most viable—avenue of approach. Age status will change if social actors no longer accept age as a legitimate reason for determining shares of privilege in society. Although the elimination of age as a relevant status characteristic in the negotiation of exchange rates may work against the short-term interests of the younger exchange partner, we all stand to benefit in the long run. Since each of us will, in time, become old, the conduct of social exchange that is "blind" to age is in the best interests of us all.

NOTES

1. Insightful analyses of the theories of Lenski, as well as the functionalists and conflict theorists, can be found in Duberman (1976) and Parenti (1978).

2. The numbers of working-class and middle-class citizens may be calculated in a variety of ways, thus leading to some confusion over the relative size of each class. Our estimate of "almost half" (48 percent) is taken from Giddens (1973). Levison (1975) estimates that, if only males were considered, the working class would actually be larger than the middle class (57 percent to 42 percent).

3. For an excellent article suggesting an interesting application of disengagement theory, see Streib (1968).

4. The social psychologist Zajonc is most closely associated with the "mere exposure" literature. See, for example, Zajonc (1968).

5. According to Lukes's (1973) careful analysis, the historical referents for these ideas range widely from the New Testament to Kant, Luther, Calvin, Spinoza, St. Thomas Aquinas, Herbert Marcuse, 19th century German Romanticists, and Karl Marx.

6. This and all other quotations from this source are from *Individualism* by S. Lukes. Copyright © by Basil Blackwell Publisher Ltd.

7. The case for mandatory retirement has been argued many times by academicians and businesspersons. One recent attempt, unsuccessful in my view, is by Creighton (1978).

8. Sussman's proposal that old people be provided cash sums that could be used to contract services from their adult children is consistent with this principle.

9. Mizruchi makes a similar point in his analysis of time and aging (1977).

Philip Silverman and Robert J. Maxwell

THE SIGNIFICANCE OF INFORMATION AND POWER IN THE COMPARATIVE STUDY OF THE AGED

Ironically, although holocultural research was the first approach anthropologists used in speculating about old age, only in the last decade has it been seriously employed for this purpose. Some of this holocultural research, such as that by Glascock and Feinman (1980, 1981), has been largely definitional, establishing the variety of criteria for defining old age and types of treatment elders receive. Work of a more theoretical nature has provided quantitative data showing that, among nonindustrialized societies, societal support or status is positively associated with the complexity of social structures (T. Sheehan, 1976); the value of activities performed by the aged (McArdle and Yeracaris, 1979); the availability of kin networks (Maxwell and Maxwell, 1980); and the control of information (Maxwell and Silverman, 1970).

The following holocultural study by Silverman and Maxwell is an elaboration of their earlier work that strongly indicated that "the esteem in which the aged are held in a given society varies directly with the degree of control they maintain over the society's information resources" (Maxwell and Silverman, 1970). The authors' research builds upon the other articles in this section in statistically relating the power resources the elderly can control to the behavioral aspects of prestige that Silverman and Maxwell define by a "deference index."

A QUITE DISTINCT CONCERN of anthropology in the study of the aged and the aging process is the development of cross-cultural generalizations. There are, however, a variety of approaches pursued in achieving this goal and these reflect the eclecticism typifying the broad concerns of the discipline. As a consequence, some rather sharp differences of opinion exist as to which approach provides the most reliable data and the most valid generalizations. We should be clear about what is meant by a cross-cultural study. It may consist of a sample as few as two or as many as 200 or more cultures. The crucial element is that there are comparisons made among and conclusions drawn from some plurality of cases.

SMALL-SCALE CROSS-CULTURAL COMPARISONS

It is useful to distinguish two types of cross-cultural studies. First, there are studies involving small-scale comparisons, based on the presentation of ethnographic data from relatively few cultures. Usually the material from any one case is written by the person(s) who did field work in the culture, but with some attempt by one or more of the organizers of the study to draw conclusions based on the descriptive data of each contributor. These studies attempt to preserve the

This essay was specially prepared for this book by the authors. Permission to reprint must be obtained from the authors and publisher.

The research was supported by National Institute on Aging Grant #AG-00482. We wish to thank Mary Allen and Dwight B. Read for advice on the analytic techniques employed, and Eleanor K. Maxwell for suggestions on all aspects of this article. They are not responsible for any deficiencies.

detail of the holistic approach by providing the "thick description" (Geertz, 1973) preferred by those who pursue a qualitative and interpretive mode of analysis.

An important exemplar of this approach in the anthropology of aging is the volume edited by Cowgill and Holmes on *Aging and Modernization*. Their theoretical statement links variations in the treatment and status of the aged ". . . to an independent variable which may be roughly identified as the degree of modernization" (1972:2). Then follow 17 chapters dealing with aging, or with certain aspects of aging, in 14 societies. Cowgill and Holmes list a large number of generalizations, which they refer to as 8 "universals" and 22 "variations" (1972: 321–23), which are supported by the data presented in the book. But the editors make little attempt to conceptually integrate these wide-ranging generalizations into a coherent theoretical framework. Cowgill elsewhere examines in more detail the relationship between these theoretical elements and speculates about future trends, retaining the emphasis on rather highly developed nation-states (Cowgill, 1974b).

Within the limits of their sample, the theory works rather well. But were certain other societies to be taken into account, the conceptual system might be called into question. If the status of the aged declines with modernization, then how do we explain the Chinese, with their legendary veneration of old people? And, indeed, several scholars have questioned a simple, direct relationship between modernization and the declining status of the aged (Arth, 1968; Haynes, 1963; Bengtson et al., 1975). It is all too easy, of course, to cite exceptions to any generalization. In the end, this procedure is neither fair nor useful unless the exceptional cases suggest directions for the further refinement of the theory.

Some of the recognized elements of modernization are no doubt more important in determining the role of the aged than other elements. Furthermore, perhaps the most important factor of all in determining their status is the amount of useful information controlled by the aged and only selectively shared with other members of the community. It may be that most of the other elements of modernization, to the extent that they affect the status of the aged, exert much of their influence through this one variable. We return to

this point in the theoretical discussion preceding the presentation of our data.

HOLOCULTURAL STUDIES

The holocultural approach represents the second type of cross-cultural study. This type involves large-scale comparisons, with samples sufficient to represent ideally the full range of cultures known in the literature and for which there is adequate information. The data extracted from these sources must be highly selective, otherwise the procedure becomes rapidly unmanageable. The studies should clearly specify how relevant information is to be recognized, and, ideally, allow for replication. The conclusions can be, and usually are, supported by appropriate statistical or other formal modes of analysis.

In this paper we shall report results obtained from a holocultural study. There have been relatively few such studies concerned with the aged. Although it must be considered a borderline example, Koty's book (1933) may be viewed as the first large-scale cross-cultural treatment of the aged. Koty isolates two main categories of motives which explain the poor treatment received by the elderly: objective reasons, based on material necessities, such as famine, or the requirements of a nomadic life; and subjective reasons, based on ideological or emotional factors, such as a high value placed on characteristics less likely to be found among the aged, as physical strength and stamina.

Koty compiled his data prior to the time that modern data banks were available, but he nevertheless covered an impressive range of cultures, especially from sources in Russian and German. His exclusive concern with the decrepit and dying limits the usefulness of his work for a full understanding of the treatment of all old people, and there are no formal analytic tools employed, except for the development of typologies. Yet, he ably demonstrated the great diversity of beliefs concerning the aged and the treatment they are likely to receive as death approaches.

With the creation of the Cross-Cultural Survey at Yale University in the 1930s, which later became the Human Relations Area File, researchers had available for the first time a data bank of descriptive materials on an increasingly expanding number of cultures. The data are organized according to a large number of categories so that the written context of the material is maintained, yet the relevant information is easily retrievable. Among the very first cross-cultural studies completed with the use of this research tool was Leo Simmons's *The Role of the Aged in Primitive Society* (1945).

Simmons's sample was reasonably large, 71 cases, but he included a number of closely related cultures, such as the Dieri and Aranda of Australia. Unless greater independence can be assumed among the cases, statistical procedures are inappropriate, but even in modern samples the degree of independence of cases remains only relatively achieved. With the 240 culture traits coded in this study, Simmons proceeds to generate over a thousand correlations, without employing any tests of significance. In some cases there do not exist explicit and operational definitions of his "traits"; for example, we cannot be sure what people must do in order to have the culture trait of "phallicism."

Despite the limitations and the virtual absence of a conceptual framework, the study does provide a number of useful generalizations about the role and treatment of the aged. Of particular interest to our own study is the discussion of general respect for the aged. Simmons concludes that respect is accorded on the basis of some particular asset possessed by old people, such as knowledge, skill, experience, control of property, or exercise of supernatural or expressive functions. General respect for the aged is treated as one of four categories falling under prestige. The others are: social taboos favorable to old age, glorification of aged in legends and stories, and deification of them in religion. If these seem a rather curiously selective array of categories, we can easily sympathize with the technical problems he faced in dealing with this protean variable. He writes: "Prestige in old age is a complex subject involving many aspects of culture, and this has made it difficult to formulate any clear-cut plan of analysis" (Simmons, 1945:30).

It was not until the 1970s that holocultural research on the aged continued where Simmons left it. By this time carefully constructed samples and an improved tool kit of methodological techniques were available. Our first paper was published at the beginning of the decade (Maxwell and Silverman, 1970) and will be discussed with other papers shortly. More recently Glascock and Feinman (1980) have been working with primarily descriptive, rather than relational, hypotheses regarding the definition of old age and the treatment of the aged. So far their most convincing results revolve around the various categories used cross-culturally for defining old age. They have been able to substantiate that the predominant means of defining old age is a change in the social role occupied by individuals as they progress through the life cycle.

INFORMATION AS A DETERMINANT OF ESTEEM: A THEORETICAL FRAMEWORK

In 1970 we conducted a preliminary test of the proposition that "societies can be arrayed along a continuum, the basis of which is the amount of useful information controlled by the aged. This informational control will be reflected in the participation of the aged in community affairs, and their participation will in turn determine the degree of esteem or prestige in which they are held by the other members of the community" (Maxwell and Silverman, 1970: 363). We defined "information" broadly, rather than in any mathematical sense, as having to do with the constraint imposed on someone or some group by virtue of the relations with other persons linked by a communication channel. If communication were to occur, the participants in the exchange must have corresponding constraints internally mapped or coded. We also observed that information could be of varying utility to the sociocultural system and that, to the extent that it was useful, it could be either instrumental information—relating to the exchange of matter and energy with the environment—or expressive—ideological, justifying a set of subsistence techniques, enhancing solidarity, or otherwise indirectly promoting the welfare of the group.

We examined a sample of 26 societies to assess the involvement of old people in various activities that could be considered information processing. We identified six such processes: (1) participation in collective situations such as feasts, games, or visiting groups; (2) consulting; (3) making decisions; (4) entertaining; (5) arbitrating; and (6) teaching. These six categories were found to form a Guttman scale, which allows for the ordering of the information-processing items in a cumulative, unidimensional series. To measure the treatment of old people, we developed a protocol of 24 items, some positive and some negative. The items were coded as either present or absent and a score for each society was obtained by subtracting the number of negative items from the number of positive ones and dividing by the total number of items. The higher the score, the more esteem in which the aged were held. The range of scores was from –.12 (a value attained by Western Tibet and the Kaska Indians of Canada) to .79 (China, not surprisingly). A measure of association was calculated between the two scales and was found to be significant, supporting the hypothesis.

We paused after completing about one-third of the sample for the present study and examined what appeared to be a basic contrast between elderly men and women. We found substantial differences by sex in the esteem in which old people were held, with elderly males being accorded more deference in most cases than elderly females (Silverman and Maxwell, 1978). The only kind of deference in which elderly females were treated at least as well as males involved younger members of the community doing household chores and other kinds of drudgery for them.

The present investigation continues to explore the usefulness of this informational perspective. In an important theoretical statement Schwartz (1978) refers to this approach as a "distributive model," in that it focuses on the transmission, storage, and distribution of information within some definable system. The relevant system here is the community and the various subsystems thereof. The position of the aged is thus a reflection of the informational structures within the system and its receptivity to external influences. In a preliminary way we have established that the involvement of old people in information processing leads to their being treated with greater respect. We turn now to an examination of the relative importance of the various ways in which information may be processed, and the relative importance of the ways in which the resultant esteem may be expressed. We then look at two informational variables reflecting the structure of the community as a whole, one involving external influences and the other internal relationships, which explain the involvement of old people in their capacity as conveyors of information.

RESEARCH DESIGN

Before turning to the major hypothesis, we will summarize the sampling and data collection procedures employed in this study. We began by choosing a 55 percent random subsample from Murdock and White's Standard Cross-Cultural Sample. This is a sampling frame of 186 societies, each one of which is selected with minor modification from a "sampling province" (Murdock and White, 1969) of societies whose similarities are sufficient to preclude the inclusion of more than one in the same sample. In addition, the material for each society is pinpointed according to time and place as one control on data reliability. Since our previous work (Maxwell and Silverman, 1970) had alerted us to the difficulties of finding systematic information on the elderly in the ethnographic literature, we selected 5 percent above the total number of societies considered necessary for the analysis. As anticipated, we had to eliminate seven societies either for lack of data or inaccessibility of the sources, thus allowing the completion of the sample with data on 95 societies.[1] In five cases, we were forced to substitute another society in the same sampling province in order to make use of more adequate information, a procedure consistent with using the Standard Cross-Cultural Sample.[2]

In order to test the relationship between information and esteem, as called for in our major hypothesis, it is necessary to transform these broad, complex variables into a set of researchable procedures. Of course, the particular items of information that a given society considers relevant will vary in ways far too numerous for cross-cultural analysis. To allow comparison we have developed from our earlier studies a limited set of categories based on the differing *modes* by which information may be processed. This approach does not measure the *amount* of information processed by elderly people; such a task does not seem technically feasible given the data base with which we must work. But it does provide a means of specifying the nature of the social encounter and the manner in which the information is conveyed. Perhaps the simplest way to make clear what is implied empirically by the differing modes of communication is to present the categories and briefly discuss how they were operationalized. In each society we attempted to determine if the old people did something for the others in the community which reflected one or more of the following information-processing categories.[3]

The Information-Processing Variables

1. *Reinforcement:* This involves the provision of information to prevent deviations from culturally prescribed behavior. It can occur in many different settings, but basically reinforcement describes the unscheduled volunteering of advice about another's performance, either in the form of compliments or warnings, which attempts to shape people's behavior to conform to the prevailing norms. Frequently, we have found elders admonishing young people to avoid doing or saying something considered inappropriate.[4] Among the Lozi of South-Central Africa, for example, elders protest when a young man wishes to marry a woman considered related to the family, a not unlikely possibility given bilateral descent is recognized frequently through five or more generations. If the couple decides to marry despite such warnings, elders will curse such a marriage (Gluckman, 1950; Turner, 1952).

2. *Consultation:* The provision of information to other community members when actively sought by them. Such practices as divination and fortune telling are included in this category. In Russia, for example, "younger persons, including adults, pay special heed to the advice and council of the elderly. Major family decisions almost always

require the council of years but the suggestions and comments of grandparents are also solicited for the most ordinary family problems" (McKain, 1972: 155).

3. *Administration:* The use of authority in coordinating the concerted action of people. This kind of information processing is ordinarily thought of as the exercise of leadership. Some items that conveniently fall into this category include instances of an elder organizing a hunting party, determining how food will be distributed, or directing the performance of a ceremony. In the residential compounds of the Igbo of Nigeria, for example, "the oldest male is the compound head and administers political, legal, and moral obligations and rights to household members" (Uchendu, 1965: 85).

In order to insure that administration, as an information-processing modality, was kept conceptually distinct from the notion of control over resources (to be discussed), we defined it as resulting in benefits to other community members, whether or not it benefited the older person directly. All instances were noted of administration of larger groups which resulted in deference, and in benefits accruing *exclusively* to the old person or his immediate family. Examples were infrequent indeed, and tended to occur in communities in which the elderly administrator acted for the welfare of some larger segment of the community as well.

4. *Arbitration:* The use of authority in resolving conflict between people or groups. This item is concerned with the role played by the aged in settling quarrels, feuds, or wars. It is precisely what Service (1966: 54–61) means by adjudication. An example of arbitration is found among the !Kung Bushmen of Southern Africa, in which an old man intervenes when two people of different bands are about to fight over hunting territories, telling them no one should fight over food (Schapera, 1930: 334).

5. *Entertainment:* The involvement of the aged in expressive performances in public, such as telling stories, reciting myths and legends, and making music. This gives recognition to the imparting of information by means of some affective or dramatic quality. Among the Mbuti Pygmies, for example, the old men often entertain children by imitating the behavior of various animals, and

thus prepare them for the crucial adult task of hunting (Turnbull, 1965: 120).

6. *Teaching:* The deliberate conveying of information to an assembly of younger community members in a setting that is more or less scheduled periodically. We can perhaps recognize this activity most easily as occurring in classrooms among those peoples who have not discovered a more humane setting for the passing on of information. Also, among the Aleuts, "every village had one or two old men at least, who considered it their especial business to educate the children; thereupon, in the morning or the evening, when all were at home, these aged teachers would seat themselves in the center of one of the largest village yourts or 'oolagmuh': the young folks surrounded them, and listened attentively to what they said" (Elliott, 1886: 170-71).

7. *Instruction:* Unlike teaching, the provision of some form of instruction need not be scheduled or provided on a group level. It may simply occur as a result of individual requests. We include here the passing on of knowledge in the context of status-passage ceremonies, and the teaching of skills and techniques related to the performance of instrumental and expressive activities, such as the manufacture of artifacts or the carrying out of curing practices. For example, during the initiation ceremonies of Nyakyusa (Tanzania) girls, elderly women instruct the girls regarding their future duties as wives (Wilson, 1957: 96).

All the preceding categories taken together represent the major independent variable, a measure that characterizes the differing modes through which the aged may exercise informational control. While this variable is concerned with activities they perform, the dependent variable, i.e., the esteem in which the aged are held, is concerned with the activities other members of the community direct towards them. By esteem, we refer to any activity of community members which enhances the physical well-being of old people, or is designed to maximize their self-image, or to dramatize in some fashion the respect and appreciation they enjoy from others. Since the expression of this sentiment may occur in varied and subtle ways, it has proven a more elusive variable to index. In a previous article (Silverman and Maxwell, 1978), we discussed in

greater detail the treatment of esteem for cross-cultural purposes. Here we can only describe briefly the various categories developed to index the ways in which esteem may be accorded to the elderly (or anyone else for the matter). We refer to this as a deference index[5] in the hope that eventually it will be possible to develop a composite measure of the degree of esteem enjoyed by the aged in a given society. The following items are included in the index.

The Deference Index

1. *Spatial Deference:* Any prerogatives held by the aged with respect to territory, individual distance, or relative position in a group. This may involve giving them the most valued position in a setting, such as nearest the fire, or exclusive occupancy of the most treasured room in a household, as is found among the rural Irish: "Ireland is in many ways an old person's country . . . their room is semi-sacred in the fairylore; it is the best in the house. The chair by the fire, the seat of honour and most comfort is theirs" (Arensburg, 1968: 110).

2. *Victual Deference:* Any prerogatives held by the aged with respect to the consumption of food and drink. Old people may be served first at feasts, receive the choicest portions of the meat, or have food specially prepared for them. Thus, for instance, in Samoa the majority of chiefs are older men. Since chiefs are serv   first at public gatherings, old Samoan men *de facto* receive victual deference (Grattan, 1948: 48-49).

3. *Linguistic Deference:* Any behavior directed towards old people which conveys a sense of esteem through speech or writing. Typically this can be found in the terms of reference or address used for the elderly which communicate in some manner their social worth, e.g., "the honored ones." It also may involve younger people deferring to their elders by the avoidance of certain linguistic expressions or topics of conversation in the latter's presence. One example of unusual elaboration of linguistic deference occurs among the Japanese: "Perhaps the most pervasive form of respect for elders in the family (as well as outside the family) is the honorific language used in speaking to or about elders. . . . Differential respect is reflected not only in different nouns, verbs, prefixes, suffixes, and other parts of speech, but also in the basic grammar

and syntax of the language" (Palmore, 1975: 92).

4. *Presentational Deference:* Any deference behavior that requires modifications of appearance or bodily presentation in the presence of the elderly. The Lozi again provide an apt example: In the presence of an elder, a younger person is expected to remain kneeling and show respect by clapping hands whenever addressed by the elder. A similar custom prevails among the Baganda, East Africa. "In the more traditional households young, and even grown, men still sometimes crouch at the threshold of their father's house when they greet him after an absence and they address him kneeling" (Nahemow and Adams, 1974: 157).

5. *Service Deference:* Any kind of work performed for the benefit of old people. It includes such chores as housekeeping, property maintenance, grooming, special medical treatment, or performing any kind of menial task no longer required of the aged. Here we have attempted to distinguish between such services undertaken only because of infirmity or decrepitude and similar services rendered to old people as a signal of esteem. We found that most service deference involved household chores: cooking, mending clothes, preparing food, cleaning, and so on, as among some North American Indians like the Pawnee (Weltfish, 1965: 319).

6. *Prestative [Gift-giving] Deference:* The bestowing of gifts or other favors on old people, but excluding instances where there is an exchange of more or less equal value. This includes both gifts of material value, such as artifacts, goods, or money, and also those of symbolic value, such as the exclusive privilege to sing particular songs, or utter certain prayers. Thus among the Huron, on the Canadian shores of the Great Lakes, old men are given gifts during festivities following a battle, and old women receive gifts during the performance of a curing ritual (Tooker, 1964: 107).

7. *Celebrative Deference:* Any display through ritual or ceremony which is undertaken to dramatize the social worth of elder status. In a few societies entrance into old age is marked by an elaborate ceremony which denotes the changed place of the elderly within the social order. Among the Japanese, a society rich in displays of deference, senior citizens enjoy annually a national holiday held in their honor (Beardsley, Hall, and Ward, 1959).

The foregoing categories of deference do not exhaust the various means employed to operationalize social esteem, the primary dependent variable in this study. In addition, we have also coded material which represents negative deference, that is, evidence of neglect, disparagement, or contempt suffered by the elderly. Because of the dismal ingenuity of humans to discover mechanisms by which this sentiment may be conveyed, detailed consideration of this variable must await further analysis. However, an initial analysis indicated that the most important reason given for contemptible treatment of elderly people is the lack of a family support system (Maxwell and Maxwell, 1980).

METHOD OF ANALYSIS

In attempting to submit the proposition stated earlier to an adequate test, we have treated each of the categories within the major variables as independently making some contribution to the relationship that is hypothesized. This requires a multivariate analytic technique that is designed to relate a set of predictor (independent) variables to a theoretically relevant set of criterion (dependent) variables. The technique that appears most appropriate for this task is canonical correlation analysis, which is similar to multiple regression analysis except it is also able to handle multiple dependent variables. To our knowledge, this technique has been used little in anthropology and not at all in cross-cultural studies. Thus, we remain cautious about, but encouraged by, the present results.

In the tables that follow, the canonical correlation values represent a coefficient which indicates the extent to which the composite sets of variables are correlated, based on the contribution of each variable in the set.[6] The proportion of variance in the dependent variables that can be explained by the combined effect of all the independent variables is stated as an "eigenvalue." This procedure generates a listing of the two sets of variables, and gives the individual contribution of each variable in terms of its relationship to all the variables in the other set. Thus, we are not only able to determine some overall relationship, but also what each has contributed into the bargain.

We can now turn to the results of this analysis. Table 1 shows a statistically significant relationship between information processing and the kinds of deference accorded the aged. The variables in each set are listed according to the positive contribution they make to the relationship. As can be seen, the canonical correlation is .64. Since the eigenvalue, which is simply the square of the canonical correlation, indicates the proportion of variance in the dependent variable accounted for by the independent variable, its value in this case can be interpreted to mean that 41 percent of the variance in deference behavior is explained by the involvement of the aged in information-processing activities. Administration is clearly the most important contributor to the information-processing variate, and there are two variables whose contributions are not relevant, teaching and arbitration, both of which occur relatively rarely. We shall come back to these variables after dealing with another important theoretical issue.

We now turn to one of the test variables which has been incorporated into our research design. A possible criticism of our argument could be made from a cultural materialist perspective, which might suggest that factors other than control over information are more important in determining the status of the aged. Information, according to this view, is but one of a series of resources and there is no *a priori* reason to expect that one is a more powerful predictor of status than another. Indeed, it might be argued that control over material resources by individuals or groups offers more persuasive inducements for evoking compliance and esteem from others, regardless of any recognized informational capacities. We called this argument "the Rockefeller objection." Here we are involved in the complex notion of "power," its sources and its consequences; thus information, goods of economic value, and other resources may be viewed as the basis upon which the behavior of others may be affected, manipulated, or even totally controlled.

Not surprisingly, there were few guidelines for handling this pervasive variable in a cross-cultural context. Nevertheless, we eventually settled upon the following set of categories as delineating control over resources, other than information, which could have some effect on the esteem enjoyed by the aged:

1. *Material resources of economic value:* The ownership of real and movable property or money by the aged.
2. *Material resources of symbolic value:* The ownership of articles and goods that are valued for their ritual and ceremonial significance.
3. *Social resources:* Any rights held by the aged to acquire children through adoption or purchase, and /or to be given priority over the choice of spouses.

TABLE 1
Canonical Variates for Involvement of the Aged in Information-processing Activities Correlated with the Deference Accorded Them by Others

Information Processing: Coefficients for Predictor Variables		Deference: Coefficients for Criterion Variables	
Administration	.71	Prestative	.65
Consultation	.37	Linguistic	.33
Reinforcement	.20	Presentational	.22
Entertainment	.10	Service	.19
Teaching	−.02	Victual	.08
Arbitration	−.04	Spatial	.05
Instruction	−.10	Celebrative	.04
Canonical Correlation	.64	Chi-Square	83.10
Eigenvalue	.41	Significance	< .002

(All of the remaining categories involve control over some kind of supernatural resource.)

4. *Human misfortune:* The ability to cure or cause the misfortune of others. Typically they can affect the welfare of others by means of witchcraft, sorcery, or the manipulation of some spiritual force.

5. *Natural misfortune:* The ability to bring about or relieve misfortunes caused by weather and natural upheavals.

6. *Transformational:* The power to change into animals or supernatural creatures.

7. *Communicational:* The ability to communicate with spirits and ancestors through means unavailable to others.

It is now possible to introduce into the analysis the categories of resource control. Table 2 presents the canonical variates for the relationship between the control of resources by the aged and the deference they are given. As may be seen, this relationship is also significant, achieving a canonical correlation of .59. Not surprisingly, material resources of economic value contribute most to the predictor variables. More interesting is the fact that the contribution of the categories of supernatural resource control is preponderately negative. This may be partly a function of our coding procedures in that we did not distinguish between helpful uses of particular supernatural

resources and harmful ones, which might differentially have affected esteem.

It is also interesting to note that the three deference variables with the highest positive coefficients are not the same as is found when the independent variable is information processing. Information processing is associated strongly with prestative deference, which suggests ceremonial displays that are more private and intimate. This kind of display is also evidenced by the relatively important contribution made by the linguistic and presentational deference items in Table 1. Indeed, celebrative deference, which is listed last in Table 1, is extraordinarily high in Table 2. This suggests that control by the elderly over resources, at least as they appear in this linear combination, is associated with the more public forms of deference implied by the ceremonial occasions coded under celebrative and many forms of spatial deference.[7] This proposition is complemented by the rather strong negative coefficient for presentational deference, which tends to be expressed more often in intimate, informal settings. Thus, the rich may receive more public acclaim than the kind of deference usually expressed in everyday circumstances.

Finally, Table 3 presents the data for the combined effects of both the information-processing and resource-control categories on deference. The canonical correlation for this relationship is .67, accounting for 45 percent of

TABLE 2
Canonical Variates for Involvement of the Aged in Control over Resources Correlated with the Deference Accorded Them by Others

Control over Resources: Coefficients for Predictor Variables		Deference: Coefficients for Criterion Variables	
Material resources/economic	.61	Celebrative	.97
Social resources	.50	Spatial	.30
Material resources/symbolic	.25	Service	.20
Natural misfortune	.04	Linguistic	.06
Human misfortune	.00	Victual	.01
Communicational	−.03	Prestative	−.14
Transformational	−.33	Presentational	−.31
Canonical Correlation	.59	Chi-Square	69.78
Eigenvalue	.35	Significance	< .03

the variance in the dependent variables. Although variables from both subsets of the independent variables contribute to the correlation, it is clear from the ordering in Table 3 that several of the information-processing categories make a predominant contribution to this variate, especially administration. Furthermore, we have determined that there is a very low correlation when each of the information-processing items is run individually against the resource-control items, although among themselves many of the items correlate quite highly.

ANTECEDENT SOCIAL CONDITIONS

Now that the links between information processing and deference have become clearer, we can turn our attention to variables that are antecedent to information processing. That is, we wish to discover the social conditions that promote the

involvement of old people in information processing. Two factors seemed particularly good candidates for examination since they implied systematic differences in the nature of information and its management in each society. The first was *community isolation,* by which we mean a relative paucity of information entering a community as a result of its weak bonds with external groups and institutions, a condition which is obviously a component of the multidimensional concept of modernization. The second was *social rigidity,* which refers to the way information is distributed within a particular system and denotes a relative paucity of intercommunication among community subgroups or social categories because of the presence of social or physical barriers hindering contact, as between castes, different religious groups, or men and women.[8]

As for their effects on information processing, we proposed that isolation would promote the involvement of old people in information processing because an isolated community would be characterized by a low rate of informational turnover. That is, things would change slowly.

TABLE 3
Canonical Variates for Involvement of the Aged in Information-Processing Activities and Control over Resources Correlated with the Deference Accorded Them by Others

Information Processing/Control over Resources: Coefficients for Predictor Variables		Deference: Coefficients for Criterion Variables	
Administration	.61	Prestative	.52
Consultation	.28	Celebrative	.33
Reinforcement	.26	Service	.30
Social resources	.22	Linguistic	.26
Material resources/economic	.17	Presentational	.13
Material resources/symbolic	.13	Victual	.10
Entertainment	.05	Spatial	.10
Human misfortune	.01		
Communicational	–.02		
Arbitration	–.03		
Teaching	–.07		
Instruction	–.07		
Natural misfortune	–.20		
Transformational	–.20		
Canonical Correlation	.67	Chi-Square	144.61
Eigenvalue	.45	Significance	< .001

Under such conditions the knowledge that old people have acquired during their lifetime is likely to remain useful for a longer period. Rigidity, on the other hand, suggests a set of conditions in which the elderly are liable to provide the least threatening channel for information to penetrate existing barriers. Furthermore, as Cool (1980) has suggested, the aged can best reflect a sense of continuity with the past and contribute information considered relevant for maintaining solidarity among group members who wish to differentiate themselves from a larger sociocultural context. In summary then we suggest that communities high in isolation and rigidity would be communities in which the involvement of old people in information-processing activities would also be high.

We may now briefly summarize the preliminary results of our investigation of the two antecedent variables: community isolation and social rigidity. In dealing first with community isolation, we employed additive scales of various items from four broadly construed groups of variables that could impact on the information entering a community. These include: (1) frequency of contacts with other communities, such as inter-community rituals or trading relationships; (2) presence in the community of representatives from superordinate institutions, such as government officials; (3) infrastructural characteristics, such as the presence of mass transportation; and (4) presence of mass media. When all these variables together are related to information processing among the elderly, no significant relationship is found.

However, if only the mass media items are extracted and related to information processing, the results are quite surprising. According to the hypothesis, mass media should displace older people as significant information sources; thus there should be an inverse relationship between the two. However, we found just the opposite! The following items were taken: (1) newspapers; (2) books or pamphlets; (3) movies; (4) radio; and (5) television. The media were coded as simply present or absent, yielding a score for each society from zero to five. The results show that the presence of mass media is significantly and *positively* associated as determined by the value of chi-square (p < .03) with the involvement of old people in information processing.

Evidently the relationship is not a simple one.

For an explanation we looked to the nature of our sample, which contains several truly nomadic hunters and gatherers, who must constitute the lower end of any scale of modernization, but no thoroughly industrialized communities on the order of, say, Gary, Indiana. At best, our sample has a few relatively traditional agrarian communities which were part of nation-states with some segments in process of industrialization, such as the rural Irish in the 1930s and the rural Japanese in the 1950s. Thus it may be that within a certain range, up to and including traditional agrarian communities, modernization is not at all incompatible with information processing by old people. Our sample contains no communities so thoroughly modernized as to render the activities of old people obsolete. In other words, the relationship between modernization and information processing by the aged may be curvilinear, rather than linear.[9]

Turning to the second of the antecedent variables, social rigidity was indexed by a number of items representing four categories of variables: (1) endogamous subcommunities; (2) group activities organized at the family or subcommunity level, including economic, political, and religious activities; (3) exclusive male or female activities or associations; and (4) restrictions on the movement and/or behavior of women. Again, a simple additive scale of all these items was employed to calculate a score and then related to the extent of information processing among the aged. As we proposed, we found social rigidity and information processing to be significantly and positively related (rho = .25; p < .01). As mentioned earlier, the nature of the sample does not permit us to say anything about the effects of social rigidity in urban, industrialized communities. But we believe that social rigidity deserves consideration, along with the well-recognized processes of modernization, as a key variable in understanding the role of the aged in any society.

SUMMARY

The results presented here indicate a complex relationship between broad-scale, social structural variables and the context in which the aged differentially participate in their communities. We have found that information processing is positively related to the social esteem enjoyed by the aged, and that this independent variable has an effect which is quite distinct from one of our test variables, the control over resources. Further, the elderly tend to have an increasing role to play as relevant sources of information until, perhaps, the more advanced stages of modernization. And finally, various internal barriers to communication in a community also tend to maximize the participation of old people. The more complicated interplay between community isolation and social rigidity still requires investigation.

The informational, or distributive, model which provides the conceptual basis for this study may be viewed as an aspect of exchange theory as discussed by Dowd in this volume. Within the context of certain cultures, interaction with the elderly is valued by other members of the society because of the possession of recognized resources. To the extent that these resources are considered useful, the contribution of the aged is maximized and they are rewarded with the appropriate prestige from those who value the exchanges with them. Precisely what is valued, and under what conditions, depends on the rich fabric of cultural contexts found throughout the world.

NOTES

1. Societies in sample: !Kung Bushmen, Lozi, Bakongo, Yao, Kikuyu, Mbuti, Bamileke, Ibo, Fon, Mende, Bambara, Songhai, Hausa, Massa, Fur, Shilluk, Lango, Amhara, Teda, Riffians, Hebrews, Rwala, Turks, Irish, Samoyed, Abkhaz, Kurds, Basseri, Gond, Santal, Burusho, Mongols, Lepcha, Garo, N. Vietnamese, Khmer, Semang, Andamanese, Tanala, Negri Sembilan, Balinese, Badjau, Tobelorese, Tiwi, Orokaiva, Kimam, Kwoma, Lesu, Siaui, Tikopia, Fiji, Maori, Samoans, Marshallese, Yapese, Ifugao, Manchu, Japanese, Gilyak, Chukchee, Ingalik, Copper Eskimo, Micmac, Slave, Eyak, Bellacoola, Twana, Pomo, Ute, Kutenai, Hidatsa, Pawnee, Huron, Natchez, Apache, Havasupai, Huichol, Aztec, Quiche, Bribri, Goajiro, Callinago, Yanomamo, Carib, Mundurucu, Cayapa, Amahuaca, Aymara, Siriono, Trumai, Tupinamba, Shavante, Abipone, Mapuche, Yahgan.

2. The Human Relations Area File was not an adequate data bank for our purposes. Many of our variables crosscut the categories into which the file is divided, and we discovered that much of the data relevant to the aged were not filed under the appropriate categories. As a result of the difficulties we encountered with the HRAF, coders were forced to read the original sources. This, however, added immeasurably to the richness of our data. As one check on the reliability of the coding procedures, 25 percent of the societies were coded independently by two coders, and 10 percent of the sample by three coders. The data for these and other reliability measures that we have developed have not yet been analyzed.

3. For detailed treatment of the operational procedures used for this and all other variables employed in this study, consult our *Manual for Coders* (Maxwell, Krassen-Maxwell, and Silverman, 1978).

4. This category is derived from the work of Service (1966).

5. We consider the terms *prestige, esteem* and *respect* as referring to essentially the same concept. When dealing with the operational categories of this concept, we speak of *deference*. Our use of these terms should not be confused with how they are employed elsewhere. For example, in an article on prestige among both rural and urban aged in Portugal, Lipman (1970) isolates by means of factor analysis a dimension he calls "ritual deference," a positive view of the aged found to be high among his rural sample. His variable is a cognitive one, based on responses to a series of opinion statements. Our use of *deference* is a behavioral one, based on activities performed for the benefit of the elderly.

6. Canonical correlation analysis assumes that the relationship between any two sets of variables is such that an increase in the predictor variables brings about an equivalent increase in the criterion variables. Its procedures combine separately the various predictor and criterion variables into composite variables so that the correlation between the two composite variables is maximized.

7. In a holocultural study of female status, Sanday (1974) indicates that power and esteem are two distinct variables which don't necessarily vary together. However, she does not operationalize the respect and deferential treatment concepts, concentrating instead on power. For further discussions of prestige/esteem, see also Eisenstadt (1971) and Goode (1978).

8. The concept of social rigidity and some of the items used to index it a e taken from Young and Bacdayan (1965).

9. The study by Palmore and Manton (1974) is complementary to our findings. Using national, aggregate data, they found that the status of the aged, as measured by their equality to the nonaged with respect to employment, occupation, and education, declines with increasing modernization of the country, but begins to move up slightly in the most advanced, industrial countries. Thus, their findings extend the curve beyond the limits of our sampling frame.

Linda Cool and Justine McCabe

THE "SCHEMING HAG" AND THE "DEAR OLD THING": THE ANTHROPOLOGY OF AGING WOMEN

There is indeed no one entity we can call the "aged." This is due to sociocultural as well as sexual variation. In this first article of its kind, anthropologists Cool and McCabe cross-culturally explore late adulthood from the female perspective. In doing so they attempt to go beyond the simplistic view of older women as either malevolent "scheming hags" or kindly "dear old things." They contrast the U.S. themes of the depressed middle-aged or older woman and the leveling of sex-role differences with the themes of growing dominance and power and role reversal of older women in many nonindustrial societies. Using their research experience in two Mediterranean societies known for their ideal of female subordination, the authors illustrate the paths by which women gain power and satisfaction in later life.

ONE OF THE MOST salient features in the research now available on human aging is that there is no *one* entity that can be termed the "aged." Yet, in spite of a call for its recognition (Maddox, 1969b: 7–8), the issue of the heterogeneity of experiences and interests among older people has been largely preempted by an apparent desire to focus on homogeneity in the aging process. As a case in point, although there are obvious and universally recognized differences in the biological endowment and in the social, cultural, and psychological experiences of men and women, surprisingly little attention has been devoted to the question of whether and/or how women and men differ in the aging process. In fact, the attention that has been focused on the condition of older women has tended to center on two stereotypes that appear at opposite ends of a power/weakness continuum. On the one hand, many societies (and the anthropologists who study them) represent older women as scheming manipulators of personal and magical powers— powers over which they may not have full control. At the opposite extreme lie the representations of older women as smiling, kindly grandmothers whose main interest in life is

amusing and spoiling grandchildren. In actuality, the experiences of older women may lie somewhere between these extremes, and, as for most people, the differences that do appear among them are the result of psychological, social, and cultural variables. Often the particular representation of a society's older women is as much a cultural myth and even a creation of the anthropologist's expectations as it is a depiction of a "social reality."

The implicit challenge to anthropology in the area of gerontology is to question existing theories of aging by putting them to the cross-cultural test and to formulate cross-cultural models of aging as a universal phenomenon which transcends the immediate sociopolitical situations of industrialized nations. As Shanas et al. have observed, we must seek both to ask and answer ". . . the basic question: can a hypothesis about social behavior be considered proved by a study carried out within a single culture?" (1968:7). This present work attempts to review, integrate, and evaluate the theories and data that do exist concerning female and male responses to aging. More importantly, this chapter provides, by means of detailed examples, a useful method of

---

This essay was specially prepared for this book by the authors. Permission to reprint must be obtained from the authors and publisher.

analyzing the aging process of men and women in the hope that new interest and dialogues may be kindled in this area.

WOMEN AND AGING: THE COMPARATIVE APPROACH

Prior to the 1960s, Leo Simmons's (1945) monograph was the only anthropological work devoted to the subject of aging (Clark, 1973:79). As one facet of his study, Simmons compared sex-role related differences in the aging experience. He concluded by denying the existence of any "feminine patriarchy" in later life, at least in terms of *formal* office holding. In fact, only two of the societies which Simmons examined yielded examples of women (young or old) who held office. Based on such findings concerning formal office holding by women, Simmons dismisses women's ability to exercise control functions in society. However, in pursuing this argument, he overlooks very important areas of potential control and dominance for women, namely informal networks and *de facto* power: gossip groups which control others' actions by their negative and public commentary, self-help groups, communications networks for the sharing of information, and private dominance in the households.

In a later attempt to estimate the extent of possible matriarchy among older women, Gold (1960) questioned 24 anthropologists about their observations of age variations in the sex-role patterns of the various cultures they had studied: 13 reported a matriarchal shift; 11 reported no change; no one reported an increase in dominance among older men. Gold only partly concurs with Simmons's earlier generalizations:

Like him, I find that matrilineality coincides with old women being dominant over old men. There is also some support of his finding that women tend to be dominant over old men in hunting-gathering societies, since two of the three examples in my sample [of 24] manifest the pattern (Blackfoot and Mohave versus the Pilaga). . . . The peasant communities (and urban middle class America), with their strong emphasis on ideal male supremacy but actual pattern of old women

dominating old men, conflict with his observation that where there is settled agriculture, old men tend to be dominant; if the people are peasants, the old women get the upper hand. (1960:11)

In a more recent attempt to study sex-role differences in aging by means of a large-scale, cross-cultural comparison, Bart (1969) selected 30 societies representing the eight culture areas of the world from data contained in the Human Relations Area Files. From these societies, she gathered information on the presence of "six post-child-rearing roles available to women" (1969:2): grandmother, mother or mother-in-law, economic producer, participator in government, performer of religious or magical rites, and daughter of aged parents. Working from the belief that in American society women lose one of their most important identity-giving roles (namely mother) which results in a "mutilated self" (Rose, 1962), Bart sought to document the relationship between changes in status and the availability of important roles. In general, she found that when society has a multiplicity of roles available for older women their status ". . . not only does not drop necessarily at this stage of the life cycle, but in most cases also rises . . ." (1969:15). According to Bart, only two of the six roles she examined are *not* associated with higher status for women, namely economic producer (". . . it cannot be concluded that the mere presence of an economic role will keep women's status from declining" [Bart, 1969:4]) and daughter of aged parents (a role found only rarely).

One obvious problem with studies of this kind involves definitions. For example, Bart says that she did not include housekeeping and food preparation as economic producer roles for they are so common. But, might not a woman's *control* and leadership in these activities in the context of her household or family be considered such a producer role, or at least provide the woman with a positive self-image? In a similar vein, Simmons, Gold, and Bart all include consideration of some formal aspect of control (Bart talks of "participator in government" and Simmons of "formal office holding") and conclude that women (of any age) rarely are allowed to fill such roles. Rather than focusing on *public* control through formalized offices, it seems that studies ought to deal with areas where women in a variety of cultures do seem to have some power: informal networks, the domestic situation, and personal attributes. These, of course, are difficult to recognize and code in nomothetic studies.

Finally, like so much of this nomothetic research, Bart's work has illuminated certain structural features of society which seem to be associated with a particular aspect of life. But she is unable to prove a causal relationship or deal effectively with individual manipulations of these structural features. For example, Bart has suggested that a woman's status does not remain static throughout the life cycle. However, she cannot illustrate *how* a woman undergoes such status variations. Is the change abrupt or gradual, is the woman able to control the timing of the status change or is she at the mercy of external forces? Even though Bart does examine six societies in more detail, the reader is not particularly enlightened in the dynamics of *how* and *why* the status changes come about. The remainder of this article will attempt to resolve these questions by examining structural and cultural factors which influence the female response to aging in a variety of cultures.

THE PARADOX OF THE AGING AMERICAN WOMAN

Studies carried out in the United States have not only failed to provide clear-cut answers to questions concerning gender differences in the aging process, but have produced confusing and often contradictory results. This becomes evident in the kinds of portraits painted of older women by a variety of researchers.

The Ignored Older Woman

Some studies characterize older American women as members of a minority group who see themselves as a social problem: a group of people who have been excluded from full participation in society, accorded an inferior position within it, and denied access to power and authority (Bell, 1970; Lopata, 1971; Palmore, 1971; Sommers, 1974; Sontag, 1972). In this perspective, women seem particularly disadvantaged as they age since

the roles that are allowed them in American society either are never accorded real power or are rendered obsolete by time, for example childbearer or sex object. Older women's lack of power and status is reflected in their invisibility in American society and their absence as subjects in research endeavors. Lewis and Butler (1972) have pointed out that even the women's liberation movement has largely ignored the problems of older women by focusing on issues of special concern to younger women such as abortion and day care facilities. In all fairness, however, it must be stated that the social sciences are not the only area to render women invisible. Nancy Sheehan (1976:59), for example, notes that most historical studies of women are written by men who seem to be bent on preserving the status quo and that ". . . while histories of men are written concerning their relationship to the environment, histories of women are written concerning their relationship to men."

The Depressed Older Woman

An indication of the difficulties that American women face in growing older is reflected in the incidence of middle-age depression among women. Although American folk wisdom (and often science) attributes such depression to biological changes occurring during "the change of life," Bart found no cross-cultural correlation between the biological fact of the menopause and depression: "Depressions in middle-aged women are due to their lack of important roles and subsequent loss of self-esteem rather than hormonal changes of menopause" (1972:139). The roles that women are allowed to play in America (wife and mother) are such that a woman's sense of worth comes not from her own accomplishments but from the lives of others, namely her husband and children. As these people change or depart, a woman must be able to change her self-concept or face debilitating psychological stress.

Other social scientists (e.g., Davis, 1979; Dowty, 1971; Flint, 1975; Neugarten and Kraines, 1965; Neugarten et al., 1963; Silverman, 1967; Vatuk, 1975) have also attempted to distinguish culturally determined responses to menopause from those biological imperatives shared by women in all societies. Like Bart, Flint

(1975, 1976) links a woman's status from midlife on to the attitudes and symptoms that characterize menopause. In contrast to the experiences of American postmenopausal women, Flint describes the situation of Indian Rajput women for whom menopause marks the end of *purdah* and the beginning of a freedom and power previously unknown to them:

When these women were asked if they had any problems associated with the menopause, a most unusual response was forthcoming. Few women were found who had other than menstrual cycle changes—there were no depression migraines, no incapacitations, nor any of the classical symptoms associated with what we call the "menopausal syndrome." Furthermore, these women informed the author that they were eagerly looking forward to achieving this event in their lives, if they had not yet achieved it, and if they had already reached the menopause, they were also most positive about this fact. (Flint, 1976:48)

In general, the aforementioned studies have all suggested that high or unchanging female status in middle age will be related to a positive attitude toward and/or the absence of difficulty with menopause. In contrast, Davis (1979) emphasizes the emic perceptions of menopause and the *total* biosocial self of the Anglican women she interviewed in a Newfoundland fishing village. These women were found to have a very high status and positive self-image *throughout* adulthood. Furthermore, this high status persisted in the face of the negative physical symptoms and attitudes that the *majority* of women experienced in menopause. Davis (1979:7) explains this by three factors: (1) that bodily, psychological, and sociocultural processes are not compartmentalized, (2) that menopause is viewed as a normal process, and (3) that the major symptoms of menopause are not considered unique to midlife or cessation of the menses. Within the anthropological literature on the menopause, Davis's study is unique in its treatment of the menopause as one more biosocial phenomenon—no more or less significant—within the context of *all* biosocial events of the culture in question:

Newfoundland women do not distinguish among biological, psychological, and social realms of experience. The folk notions of nerves and blood act in the conceptual integration of these realms throughout adult life. They have a folk system which explains what is happening to their minds and bodies at menopause and provides a female support system for those who experience difficulty. This effective support system reflects the continual high status of Newfoundland women which is characterized by extensive social networks, open communication channels, and a varied range of meaningful activities. (Davis, 1979:13–14)

What about the Men?

While Bart and Davis have approached the study of menopause differently, both researchers' data suggest a similar theory to explain some depression among middle-aged men. Typically, those older American men who suffer depression, according to Bart (1972:142), have immersed themselves in their jobs just as the "feminine" women have immersed themselves in their children and husbands. And, like the women whose children leave home, these men face depression upon retirement when all the public "props" to their self-esteem are removed. The severity (and disastrous consequences) of such depression is evidenced by the fact that in the urban American setting men die earlier than their female counterparts and also are more likely to commit suicide (Gutmann, 1980:442). Similarly, Davis (1979:5) indicates that because of the relentlessly strenuous physical life endured by the Newfoundland fishermen she observed, many of these men at middle age must relinquish the high status role of fisherman for the alien one of a land-based worker, supported by disability or unemployment insurance or work at the local fish plant. Thus it appears that in this case too, without the "props" to his self-esteem, and threatened by a loss of status, the middle-aged Newfoundland man—not the woman—is apt to become depressed.

The Older Woman as a Success Story

One general attitude fostered by some gerontological literature (see especially Cumming, 1964) in comparing female and male reactions to the aging process is that personal adjustment to later stages of the life cycle is somehow easier for women than for men because of the women's "smoother life cycle." The argument here is that from girlhood to death, a woman's key roles (wife and mother) remain essentially unchanged, while men suffer the sudden and complete loss of their core roles (worker and provider) when they reach retirement age. Although this situation is particularly dramatic in industrialized nations like the United States which have artificially created mandatory retirement ages, Cumming's implication is that women universally face fewer age-related social and personal adjustment problems than do their male counterparts because of this "smooth," continuous social development.

While apparently agreeing with Cumming that women are more successful at adjusting to age changes, Kline (1975) suggests that this success may be due *not* to social role continuity (the "smooth" life cycle), but rather to women's socialization to repeated role loss and to their ensuing adaptability to role change. Thus, according to this argument, women experience fewer adjustment problems as they grow older because they are more accustomed to dealing with status and role variations, of which aging is merely one more example.

Age, the Great Leveler of Sex-Role Differences

The research of Lipman (1961) and Cameron (1967, 1968) among aging populations in the United States generally provides a different outlook on the experience of aging. Their studies suggest that old age is in fact a greater leveler of sex-role differences, for men and women become increasingly more alike as they grow older. Specifically, Lipman (1961:271) finds that the retirement of the husband contributes to the apparent egalitarian character of the observed marriages, and that, consequently, such marriages appear to be happier. According to Lipman, this egalitarian state is fostered by the sharing of household tasks, which are no longer defined as the wife's duties, and by the emphasis on the expressive aspects of marriage, such as love, companionship, and affection. These trends lead Lipman to conclude that in such happy, older marriages, ". . . apparently role differentiation by sex is reduced with increased age and retirement" (1961:271).

In a similar vein, Cameron's data indicate that the *interests* of the aged may be typed as feminine,

while their basic personality is more typically masculine than that of a comparison group of young people (1968:64). Although his data actually seem to support the concept that older men and women have convergent interests, Cameron interprets this tendency as a reflection of socioeconomic status rather than old age per se:

. . . *accessibility to and success in various kinds of endeavors also determine interests. The lower SES and general physical weakening of the aged often preclude participation in the relatively expensive and vigorous masculine activities. One often has to be content with what one can do, and what one does is generally what one professes to desire.* (1968:65)

Unfortunately, Cameron provides no examples of these "expensive and vigorous" interests.

Sex Role Reversal in Old Age—The Dominant Older Woman

The research of Cumming and Henry (1961), Kerckhoff (1966), Lowenthal et al. (1975), Neugarten (1968), and Neugarten and Gutmann (1968) contrasts with the position of Lipman. For example, Lowenthal et al. find that middle-aged and older women become more dominant in the family, and Kerckhoff (1966:179–80) believes that he has found data indicating

. . . *a greater sensitivity to interpersonal relationships in the conjugal unit on the part of the husband and a greater concern with the practical activities of daily living on the part of the wife. If such an interpretation is acceptable, it would indicate a kind of role reversal from the presumed model of husband-wife relationship in our society which calls for the husband to emphasize an instrumental orientation and the wife to have more of an expressive orientation.*

In attempting to make a comparison with non-American populations, one finds a relative dearth of cross-cultural gerontological literature with regard to gender differences in aging. For example, this possible "role reversal" among aging American men and women has been only alluded to in studies of other cultures.[1] In one of the more detailed comparisons, Kardiner et al. (1945:65) describe the older Comanche women:

Women, with few exceptions, had no power before the menopause. After the menopause a woman could acquire power as readily as a man. It was common for a medicine man to have his wife assist him, teaching her everything that was required for curing, except rituals for the actual transfer of power. Immediately after the menopause, the husband gave power to her. . . . After the menopause, the distinction between the sexes, as far as medicine power went, was largely disregarded. . . . As she grows older her security becomes greater. . . . In comparison with the male, therefore, the woman starts with initial disadvantage, but she has greater mobility as she gets older.

Similarly, Borgese (1964) and Gutmann (1974, 1977) note that over the life cycle women who had earlier been subordinate to men with regard to authority (Rosaldo, 1974), become quite dominant and powerful vis-à-vis men. In Gutmann's terms, men begin with active mastery of their biosocial environment and move toward passive mastery (characterized by dependence and passivity) with increasing age and lessening physical capabilities. Women, on the other hand, move from passive mastery (cultural deference to and resulting personal dependence on fathers and husbands) to active mastery of their social environments in later life. Gutmann argues that such inner subjective shifts together with their overt behavioral indicators are universal for men and women.

The Older Woman as Witch

A traditional context in which older women are seen as dominant and aggressive within the anthropological literature is the recurrent theme of the older woman as witch or sorcerer (for example, Evans-Pritchard, 1937; Fortes, 1962; Fuller, 1961; Harper, 1969; Kluckhohn, 1967; LeVine, 1963; and Nadel, 1952). In these cases, even implicit recognition by men of the power of senescent women can often be made only by ascribing evil motivations to their hegemony. Fuller (1961:51) confirms this in her description of the Lebanese villagers she studied: "Men sense this invisible power of women. To older women, in particular, is attributed the power of witchcraft or of the evil eye, both signs of an uncanny force."

One possible explanation for this malevolent characterization of older women is a correlation suggested by Douglas (1966:120):

. . . where the social system recognizes positions of authority, those holding such positions are endowed with explicit spiritual power, controlled, conscious, external, and approved—powers to bless or curse. Where the social system requires people to hold dangerously ambiguous roles, these persons are credited with uncontrolled, unconscious, dangerous, disapproved powers—such as witchcraft and evil eye.

Nadel's work among the Nupe of Northern Nigeria appears to support this viewpoint: older Nupe women occupy an ambiguous position in their society. They are female and therefore normatively inferior to men; yet, they resemble the male cultural ideal by possessing power (albeit de facto power). In other words, in these situations, because women are, in men's eyes, usurping what is "rightfully" male (i.e., the exercise of power), men "punish" older women by accusing them of witchcraft and other acts of malevolence.

The general picture is that of a sharp sex-antagonism, which assigns the evil intentions to the female, and to the male, a benevolent and ideally decisive—if somewhat utopian role. . . . Men are never blamed or accused of witchcraft, and the main collective weapon against witchcraft lies in the activities of a male secret society which, by threats and torture, "cleanses" the villages of witchcraft. . . . In the majority of cases the alleged witch is a woman, usually an older and domineering female, who would attack a younger man who somehow fell under her dominance. . . . The men, though on the utopian or fantasy plane the masters of the female witchcraft, are, on the plane of "real" incidents and fears, its main victims.

A second possible explanation is that this pervasive ascription of evil motivation to older women is related to their actual powerlessness and low status position. This reasoning is pursued by Harper (1969) in his study of the belief system of the Havik Brahmins of South India. In this situation, Harper (1969:81) proposes that the dangerous nature attributed to Havik widows may be the result of guilt on the part of those who occupy high status positions (men) toward those who formally lack power and prestige and occupy the lowest positions (widows) in this social system.

Despite their explicitly inferior and powerless status, Havik women are, in fact, rather powerful, at least in a negative sense: They influence and affect the lives and behavior of others—especially men. In keeping with Havik men's attitudes toward all women, it is possible that widows, who are mainly older females, are feared simply because they are believed to possess the ultimately powerful weapon—death through witchcraft. However, Harper's explanation of guilt on the part of high status Havik men could be made even more compelling. At present, it merely emphasizes projections of *recent* resentment of Havik widows, and their *currently* intolerable status; instead, this explanation could be extended to attribute males' fears to projections of *long-hidden*, accumulated anger which men could expect these mainly older women to feel and express in response to a lifelong inferior position.

CULTURE AND WOMEN'S STATUS

An increasingly significant source of data with regard to women's power in society is found in anthropological studies of women's status. This growing body of literature (e.g., Collier, 1974; Friedl, 1975; Lamphere, 1974; Murphy and Murphy, 1974; Quinn, 1977; Wolf, 1972) indicates that female solidarity, flexibility, and a keen perception of male-female relationships characterize women with age, and enable them to adapt with increasing success to situations normally controlled by men. One emphasis of this literature is that, although the power of women—old and young—increases most dramatically in informal, domestic settings, its expression is felt throughout the societies in question.

For example, Wolf (1972:40) describes the influence that older Taiwanese women have on men's behavior in a family of which they are never a member but to which they are essential:

Taiwanese women can and do make use of their collective power to lose face for their menfolk in order to influence decisions that ostensibly are not theirs to

make. Although young women may have little or no influence over their husbands and would not dare express an unsolicited opinion . . . to their fathers-in-law, older women who have raised their sons properly retain considerable influence over their sons' actions, even in activities exclusive to men. . . . When a man behaves in a way that they consider wrong, they talk about it—not only among themselves, but to their sons and husbands.

By banding together in informal gossip and work groups, these Taiwanese women have gained a great deal of power to effect changes and maintain some independence in their lives—an ability unavailable to a lone woman living in the "foreign" territory of her husband's patriclan. Without such an informal control mechanism, the Taiwanese woman would be as powerless and unsupported as the stereotyped image predicts.

We could continue to cite references to the increasing power of senescent women in many dissimilar societies. However, it becomes increasingly clear that two themes regarding gender differences in adaptation to aging that have been reported in research carried out in the United States are not apparent in the literature concerning the aging experience in other cultures. The first is the theme of the older woman becoming depressed with increasing age, and the second concerns age as the great leveler of sex-role differences. This latter theme emphasizes the male loss of power to bring him down to the level of women, while much of the cross-cultural literature emphasizes the increased status of older women. This is not to say that these themes are "wrong." These situations may hold in the United States because of specific social and cultural features which must be determined. Whatever their cultural sources, these adaptations to the aging process are not a universal or biological fact of life to be faced by all older men and women.

Two conclusions appear from the cross-cultural evidence cited so far: (1) Women in many disparate societies become increasingly dominant and powerful as they age, and (2) with such a transition in female power and status, there may be a concomitant decline in the power and dominance of the older men in these societies. The remainder of this article will focus on a detailed analysis of two distinct cultures in an effort to determine the bases of self-perceived success in adjustment to growing older among men and women. In particular, we will focus on two of the adaptive strategies employed by women which were delineated earlier: (1) the self-assessed success of older women as based on the continuity of the core role throughout life *or* on their socialization throughout the life cycle to role changes, and (2) the question of the increasing dominance (both in terms of personality and social roles) of older women.

AGING WOMEN IN MEDITERRANEAN SOCIETY

Following the anthropological principle that researchers can best discover the operation of a variable when its functions are observed in extreme cases, the ethnographic foci in the following analyses are two locales within the Mediterranean culture area: (1) the Niolo, a mountainous region composed of five autonomous villages in the center of the island of Corsica, and (2) Bayt al-'asir, a modernizing peasant community of about 600 people in southern Lebanon. These are "extreme" environments compared to the urban United States in several ways. First, the informants presented in the following analyses live in small towns where the traditional economy is based on transhumant pastoralism (the Niolo) or wage laboring with small-scale agriculture (Bayt al-'asir). In addition, both these locales are firmly entrenched in the Mediterranean culture area where one of the defining cultural characteristics is a seemingly obsessive (at least to Western eyes) concern with female modesty and submission, for male and familial honor is embodied in the chastity of kinswomen, especially wives. In this manner, it appears that these societies offer valuable cross-cultural checks on the general validity of some of the findings concerning the adaptive success and growing domination of women as they age.

In both societies, women perceive themselves (and are also considered by the men) to be aging successfully and to be better off than their male counterparts in old age. For example, aged Niolan men say that women adapt better to old age

"because they have less desire to get out" and "because they are less independent." Older women are of the same opinion, but for different reasons: "Men find it harder to grow old well because they are not accustomed to resignation." The anthropologists' data agree with their informants' perception of the women's relative success in aging. However, in analyzing the perception of greater life satisfaction on the part of their female informants, Cool and McCabe tend to focus on different factors. Cool emphasizes the *individual* manipulations of a Niolan woman as she undergoes socialization to role change and personal adaptability in her move from timid bride to domineering older mother-in-law. McCabe stresses that this life-satisfying situation for older Lebanese women is the result of an accumulation of several cultural factors which are differentially emphasized at various points in the life cycle. With increasing age, Lebanese women become relatively more competent and confident in their roles than do men. There is a sense of *control* in their lives, which is absent in those of men.

THE NIOLO

Successful aging depends on the developmental cycle of the traditional Niolan household. It demands that a woman learn to adapt to changing roles and statuses.[2] Such socialization begins early for Niolan girls, for they learn the basic skills while helping their mother and sisters. The ideal was for all daughters to marry; but financial limitations of all but the wealthiest families sometimes prevented this realization. In the past, even the unmarried daughter who remained at home had important roles to perform: she first helped her parents and later her brother (the heir) and his wife. As a "blood" relative of the patricentric family, she had an important standing even though she would never be a "housewife," and often she developed a close, confidante relationship with her sister-in-law as the two women worked to increase the reputation of the household.

In the Niolo, a bride is expected to be fully capable of running a household upon marriage.

This is the case even if the new couple is to live patrilocally. For upon arriving in her new home, the first person the young bride meets is her mother-in-law, the woman under whose authority she will live and work for the next several years. In this sort of patricentric household, the young bride's most important roles become those of wife and daughter-in-law, both of subservient status in traditional Niolan society. The young woman must work hard to establish herself in her new household and to win even grudging approval from the mother-in-law who is convinced that no one can care for her beloved son as well as his own mother.

A period of expansion in the developmental cycle of the household arrives with the pregnancy and birth of the young wife's first child. Although she continues in her submission to her mother-in-law's authority, the young mother finally is recognized as having personal value other than that of "another worker." In the role of mother, the young woman creates emotional bonds and achieves positive status in her husband's household. From her, the infant receives the emotional ties and support of which the young wife must herself feel deprived, especially when her husband is away with the animals. In this regard, some old women mentioned that the most important part of their lives was giving birth to a son and then raising him so that they would be assured of affection and care in their old age.

The peak stage (arriving eight to ten years after the marriage) for the Niolan household begins when the young wife has several children, for she begins to prove her own ability as a housewife and domestic decision maker. Her husband begins to appreciate her more as a partner, and the complementarity of the roles of wife and husband become clearer in the young couple's intense activity to support a nuclear family and a household. When she has reached 35 and has had five, six, or more children, her family may continue to expand but the older children have reached an age and a developmental stage where they can make useful contributions to the group. And in spite of the fact that this is the busiest period of her life, the housewife might have attained some peace. For by now, the mother-in-law, although still the privileged head housewife, begins to entrust her younger counterpart with more responsibilities in the household's management.

When the wife is aged 45 to 50 years, her first child usually leaves the home to emigrate or prepares to marry. Although the household still includes children, the wife's childbearing years are over and the remaining children are her youngest and last. Gerontologists predict that this shrinking circle stage is the most difficult for urban women: The urban housewife loses prestige as she ceases to perform the housewife role at its peak. The Niolan housewife, however, does not seem to experience this letdown as she herself acquires a new status and role, that of mother-in-law, as she welcomes her own son's wife into *her* household.

Finally, when most of the children are either married or away from home, the Niolan wife faces the likely prospect of widowhood. In spite of the loss of her role as wife, she continues as mother, grandmother, and organizer of the home. Child care which was once just another burden among other tasks becomes a pleasure since grandchildren need only be loved, not trained. Although her knowledge of house and children may be common to younger women, her advice in an emergency can be vital. Such advice includes the ability to diagnose illness as to whether it was caused by the evil eye and to effect cures. Although younger women may also perform this role (*signadore*), older women are more sought after since they have more experience and, probably, more successful cures about which they can boast. An older woman's knowledge of the community and its inhabitants is unique, and she often is skilled in problem solving. In this manner, the elder female in the Niolo is in a position not only to maintain her prestige, but to actually improve her status as well.

Thus we have traced the developmental cycle of the housewife from the timid, subservient bride to the respected and confident head of the domestic unit. The basic role concept remained the same. However, the woman constantly underwent modifications in the characteristics of each assigned role. These variations occurred as the woman entered different stages of the life cycle and correspondingly changed her definitions of her roles. Having reached old age, the housewife can look at her children and her home with a sense of pride in accomplishment. Women are not the submissive, powerless creatures which are often portrayed in the Mediterranean. Rather they are manipulators of people, events, and the rules themselves.

What about the life cycle of Niolan men? The young man selected as his father's heir is under the older man's domination. The young man acquires the role of father upon the birth of his first child, but his relationship to his children is remote due to his frequent and prolonged absences from the home while caring for the animals. In fact, the most commonly given description of a traditional Niolan father emphasizes his rigidity and distance:

The mother is the person the child loves. The father has little significance. He commands the children, but he is less important to them than the mother. (62-year-old man)

In time, a man's failing health requires him to delegate more and more responsibility to his son, and the old man must watch his role as the household's chief provider disappear. Some old men are able to assume the respected roles of advisor, arbitrator, or adjudicator in their later years. But, for the most part, the old men seem to be left with ephemeral authority as they tell their sons how best to manage the household's affairs. In changing from the aggressor to the negotiator, the aging Niolan male begins to show behavior that is less stereotypically masculine while his wife assumes more and more control within her own domain.

In analyzing such age-based changes in roles, Cottrell (1942) suggested that an individual will make an easy adjustment to a role change to the extent that he has undergone anticipatory preparation for the role. Kline attempted to pursue this viewpoint with regard to aging American women:

Women have had considerable experience in adjusting to age-linked changes (children leaving home, menopause) and have therefore become accustomed to change and impermanence. Thus, women are not as devastated as men are likely to be when old age, another impermanence, separates them from the productive, involved . . . world of middle age. (Kline, 1975:490)

From the analysis of the life cycle of a Niolan

housewife, it appears that Niolan women do undergo role changes throughout the life cycle to a greater extent than do their male counterparts. It is suggested that this is one reason for the apparent privileges of women in successful aging.

BAYT AL-'ASIR, LEBANON

By the time a woman in Bayt al-'asir has reached her sixth decade of life, her ever increasing air of confidence has emerged with a rather bold and assertive countenance. Earlier, as a middle-aged woman, for instance, it is likely that she had already become a controller of her household budget and appropriator of its funds; these responsibilities were earned through deference paid, services rendered, and the manipulation of her various cultural assets (e.g., her sexuality, kinsmen, and children). However, as an even older woman, she fills her influential position with increasingly less dependence upon and consultation with her husband.

Thus, it is this older woman—not her husband—whom grown and dependent children and kin approach with requests for new clothing or other material (and emotional) needs. Indeed, where a younger, middle-aged woman would still *ask* her husband for money when the local peddler came around, the (healthy) woman approaching old age would often *tell* her husband to give her the money or use funds which she herself has put aside.[3]

The manifestation of the power of female sexuality changes as a woman ages: Before menopause, she influences male honor largely by her own sexual behavior; after menopause, she influences younger women's status and reputations (and male honor) by what she chooses to say about them in the community. Older village women have the credibility in the eyes of both men and women and can effectively pass judgment on another woman's virtue; moreover, their advice, and especially their approval, are sought by their sons and other young men who are contemplating marriage. To vital older women, respect and a kind of homage accrue: from younger women, an empathetic recognition for their having weathered a hard life, raised children, and contended (usually successfully) with a normatively second-class, powerless status; from men (especially sons) there is a gratitude and emotional dependency, and some recognition of the wise, prophetic, and mediating qualities of older women who are at the center of the community's daily social, cultural, economic, and political activities.

The first half of the life cycle of these Lebanese women is largely characterized by nurturance and attendance to the needs of others—husbands and children—rather than to personal needs and wants. As young wives and mothers, these women are so occupied with raising their children and maintaining their households that they virtually have no free time to devote to "frivolities" such as their own pleasure or interests. Although women of all ages extolled the virtues of "country" living, they wistfully spoke of the easier life or urban women or those depicted in Western television. By contrast, young husbands spent little time around their homes, coming and going with their male friends during nonworking hours.

With increasing age, village women realize that their strength, satisfaction, security, and influence ultimately derive from the very source of their hardships and struggle: marriage and motherhood. Nonetheless, some women express resentment and frustration at having to remain at home with so much work while their menfolk are able to move about—like children—unfettered by the demands of housework, children, etc. However, as the children mature and become independent and helpful, village women, too, have more time for themselves. Young and older women espouse the prevalent attitude of "better late than never" found among women in late middle age.

Accordingly, the psychological aging of the women of Bayt al-'asir is characterized by the Arab "masculine" qualities of self-assertiveness and confidence, at least partially replacing the "feminine" traits of self-denial and passivity. They not only approach equality with men, but appear also to surpass them at least with regard to the personal satisfaction of life task achievement (i.e., as mothers and homemakers).

Able older women in this community begin to be conspicuously more mobile, even going visiting or on errands out of the village. For example, some of the numerous visits by older women to the doctor in another community are regarded as

"legitimate" desires for personal attention and/or simply for going on an outing. A village woman at this stage of life is even more candid in telling others that she does or does not like something that affects her personally, whether it is a kind of food, her child's spouse, or visitors. One 62-year-old matron rather eloquently expressed her perceptions of growing old:

As I grow older, I have more confidence in myself, more faith in only my ability to make myself happy. I find that there is a greater sensitivity and listening to my feelings, thoughts, and even to my body.

Also, societal norms (i.e., with regard to modesty) have a decidedly lesser influence on old women's behavior, although they may still pay them lip service where *other* women are concerned. Moreover, because an old woman is no longer able to bear children or menstruate, she is perceived as having moved from the realm of women and nature (to which "femaleness" is likened) toward that of men and culture, an analogy which Ortner (1974) has duly elaborated. It is the perception of this symbolic shift that at least partly permits the often audaciously bawdy and otherwise inappropriate behavior of older women to occur without societal sanctions.

This bawdy, sometimes brash behavior of old women was amply illustrated during the research period. For example, one summer day, McCabe was standing near her village home speaking with an elderly neighbor, Zayna, a very vivacious grandmother of 72 years, in the presence of a few young, unmarried women and men. The conversation touched on several topics, including her opinions on the scandalous type of clothing young women were wearing (a subject she raised). In so speaking, Zayna unabashedly hoisted her skirt a considerable distance above her knees to expose her bloomerlike underpants, all the while disapproving the skimpy panties she knew the young girls were wearing. The onlookers' obvious embarrassment did not seem to disturb her in the slightest; she eventually pulled her skirt down and acted as if nothing extraordinary had happened. McCabe later asked the young people whether such behavior was considered shameful. They stammered a bit and said yes, it was, but that it really did not matter because ". . . she is an old woman."

In sum, an older woman's public behavior and

attitude acquires the stereotypically Arab masculine dimensions of self-indulgence and assertiveness. According to McCabe's observations, an older woman spends more time visiting her cronies for the sake of socialization and not just under the guise of doing work with them or going on an errand. She is more likely to get around to preparing her husband's meals or fulfilling his requests when or if she feels like it, rather than automatically kowtowing to him as before.

Simultaneously, a man of the same age acquires the stereotypically Arab feminine dimensions of passivity and patience. As his job retirement approaches, he begins to gravitate toward home more and more, sitting there alone or with a few friends. According to older village women, these men just seem to get tired of cavorting and always trying to have fun. In his home—his wife's domain—an older man's feminine side is most evident. McCabe observed older women telling their husbands to do this or that. The old men complied and obviously did not care enough about the issue to disagree, preferring instead to avoid any potentially hostile situation. In the face of his often vivacious, but sometimes irascible wife, an older man stays out of her way or tries to mollify her in an argument—just as she often did as a younger woman.

Therefore, over the lifetime of these Lebanese women, there occurs a transition from a feminine influence that is implicit, covert, and marked by subterfuge, to one that is increasingly overt, and recognized by at least those in an older woman's immediate environment. Essentially this transition involves a change from *de facto* to *de jure* control; that is, feminine power in older women acquires an aspect of authority. By contrast, the power enjoyed by men in this society is *de jure*; they have authority over women. However, due to certain psycho-socioeconomic components, this masculine power is tenuous. As men age, the fragile nature of the foundations of their authority is increasingly exposed and eroded.

In conclusion, among the several ways by which these life cycle changes in the hegemony and concomitant life satisfaction of women and men occur in this society are the following:

1. There is little incongruity between the ideal and real life task of a Lebanese village woman. In one form or another, *mothering* (of children and even husbands) is still the role not only idealized by society and a woman herself, but also the one actually attained by her. By contrast, for a Lebanese man there is considerably less consonance between what his society expects him to be, and what it actually allows him to be. Generally, the men of this community are not wealthy, important, or powerful in the public marketplace—the sphere to which they have been assigned by society. Consequently, by middle age, men perceive themselves as unsuccessful, women perceive them as unsuccessful, and men perceive women's perceptions of them as unsuccessful. Hence, they become increasingly impotent vis-à-vis the successful and confident older women.

2. Female solidarity and support are great sources of comfort and power for women individually and as a group. By contrast, the divisiveness of men and their perception of one another as competitors and exploiters of one another's kinswomen allow them to become increasingly isolated as individuals in their later years.

3. Finally, the locus and source of female power and satisfaction over time are a woman's home and her children. With increasing age, she becomes the focal point of the lives of her husband, her children, and their own young families. The support of children for their mother, even in opposition to their father, cannot be overemphasized. Moreover, this locus of power (the home) for a village woman in the first half of her life continues to be such in the latter half. Her expertise and confidence in the performance of her life tasks are manifest in the same place over time. By contrast, the working life of a man in this wage-laboring community is characterized by absence from village, family, and other men. When he retires, a village man retires to his wife's domain of influence and expertise. Also, he is without benefit of the equality-enhancing symbols of the skills and seniority he may have acquired in his own work place—one which is still separate from where he will live out his old age.

CONCLUSION

Based on the cross-cultural evidence presented here, it does appear that women, especially in the later life cycle stages, are not the powerless, submissive creatures that have often been portrayed in the literature. Rather, some sources of power are available to women in all societies, and women's ability to manipulate their own lives and the lives of others around them increases with the passage of years. This emphasis on women as capable, energetic members (and sometimes the recognized leaders) of society has typically been overlooked. Most studies focus on *de jure* power (or authority, the publicly recognized right to exercise control) which is typically a male domain. Therefore, most cultural descriptions fail to examine the full range of social interactions in a society, focusing mainly on the more active, public, and dominant relationships. As Hammond and Jablow point out, ". . . descriptions of curing concentrate on the medicine man, not the patient; accounts of government focus on rulers, not the ruled; we are told a great deal about parental behavior to children and little of children's responses" (1976:132). When anthropologists turn their attention to *de facto* power and control that is exercised in the private rather than the public sphere, the strengths of women begin to appear. Thus, we find today that cross-cultural analyses of sex roles such as Rosaldo and Lamphere's *Woman, Culture, and Society* (1974) and Schlegel's *Sexual Stratification* (1977), to name but two, are pointing to the relative power of women.

This article has focused on a cross-cultural analysis of women's greater adaptability and success in growing old and has indicated the sources of this success: women's socialization to continued changes in their roles and self-concept, their increasing expertise and confidence in their domain (the home), their move from covert use of power (in their manipulations of their children's affection) to overt and recognized control in the eyes of the larger community, and the strength and comfort they draw from female solidarity. Such an emphasis seems particularly compelling because the detailed ethnographic examples are drawn from the Mediterranean, an area of the world commonly thought to represent one of the extreme cases of the domination of men and the subordination of women. The message is clear. There is no biological imperative for a submissive (or powerful) female role. Women, like men, are products (and producers) of the particular culture in which they are socialized and live out their lives.

NOTES

1. As just a few examples from the anthropological literature, see Fortes, 1962 (Tallensi of Kenya); LeVine, 1963 (Gusii of Kenya); Nadel, 1952 (Nupe); Spencer, 1965 (Samburu); Leonard, 1967 (Mexican-Americans); and Yap, 1962 (Chinese).
2. The stages of the life cycle of the Niolan housewife are adapted from the stages developed for an American housewife by Lopata (1966:5–22).
3. With regard to the latter, McCabe discovered that from a younger age, some village women in the constant struggle for economic security and independence had found one way to put money aside. Having paid for the article or service, they would then tell their husbands that it cost twice as much as it actually did, and they then would pocket half of the amount for themselves.

AGE BOUNDARIES AND INTERGENERATIONAL LINKS

> *"Man is the only animal that can be induced, willy-nilly, to provide amply for his grandfather."*
> —Leo Simmons (1962:37)

AGE AS A SOCIAL BOUNDARY

Age is a universal basis by which humans make social distinctions. In the terms of Neugarten and Datan (1973:56–58) *lifetime* (chronological time), representing the flow of human populations through the life span, is translated into some notion of *social time*, generated by passage through successive age-based statuses that culturally demarcate the major segments of the life cycle. The concepts of child, adult, and elder become social boundaries, creating generational borders. Such borders not only separate categories of persons on the basis of expected behavioral norms but also express rules for entering and exiting the categories. Everyday expressions of these boundaries may be marked by simple variations in dress (for example, compare the shoe styles of the old and the young in our society) or may be more sharply underlined by a formal complex of appropriate appearances, modes of speech, permitted behaviors, and deferential gestures. An actual physical border can be involved—Scheper-Hughes in Section III discusses the Irish peasant tradition of

elders moving into the sacred west room of the family house, which younger persons could not enter without permission. There are even a small number of societies such as the Nyakyusa-Ngonde peoples of Tanzania and Malawi where the "retired" elder generation live in separate age-villages (Wilson, 1951, 1977). A parallel to this is found in the retirement communities now becoming commonplace in certain industrialized nations (see Keith's article in Section V).

The actual building blocks of social time and age boundaries show a bewildering variation from diffuse categories (child, teen-ager, middle-aged), entered into as a matter of individual biological and social transition, to highly ascribed *age grades* that are collectively attained by *age sets* when, through elaborate ritual, members of one grade make the transition to the next highest grade (see Eisenstadt, 1956; Stewart, 1977; Foner and Kertzer, 1978; Legesse, 1979; Hinnant, 1980; Keith, 1981; Fry and Keith, 1982; and Kertzer, 1982, for comparative analyses of age differentiation). In the latter instance, age not only is a highly visible symbolic border; it may also provide the basis for distinct social groups with special solidarity, goals, and organization. Such social groups may even include ancestors who can be called upon, especially by the eldest community members, to sanction through supernatural means inappropriate behavior by the younger generation. This can sometimes provide the framework for the development of gerontocracies (from *gerontes*, old men) where authority and esteem accumulate with age and reside most potently in the hands of the eldest community members (see especially Warner, 1937; P. Spencer, 1965; Lansing, 1980; Werner, 1981). However, as van den Berghe points out in the first article of this section, rule by the most elderly is quite unusual. Many so-called gerontocratic societies vest maximum power with men of late middle age.

In fact, societies using age as a significant basis for group organization throughout the life cycle are relatively rare. Such comprehensive age-set systems have been best described for East African pastoralists, where the lives of men especially are marked by successive age-graded roles as herders, warriors, and elders (see Kertzer and Madison, 1981, for the rarer case of women's age sets). The specific elements of such a system among the Masai people of Kenya and Tanzania are described in this section's first article, by van den Berghe.

GENERATIONAL TIES IN THE FAMILY

Even in age-set societies, the strong bonds among age mates and the ritual ties across the social generations created by the different age sets do not obliterate the importance of links between what Baxter and Almagor (1978) call "genealogical generations"—created by ties of kinship. Indeed, family organization, at least in the preindustrial world, appears to be one of the most important factors influencing the nature of one's survival into late adulthood. As Simmons has observed:

Throughout human history the family has been the safest haven for the aged. Its ties have been the most intimate and longlasting, and on them the aged have relied for greatest security. When other supports have crumbled and disappeared, the aged have clung to kith and kin as their last saviors; . . Indeed, many individuals have been able to find in family relationships opportunities for effective social participation well into senility, and even to exploit some rights which have outlasted life itself. (1945:176)

One must note, however, that living in a small-scale society with an extended family organization does not assure tranquil relations among generations (Levine, 1965). As Simić and Myerhoff remark, in many traditional agrarian societies "one of the salient aspects of group engagement and dynamics consists of dissatisfaction (or potential dissatisfaction), veiled competitive hostility, and open conflict" (1978:16). Nonetheless, kin-based societies such as in Samoa (see Holmes and Rhoads's article in Section III) offer the elderly a great continuity in access to essential resources derived from their membership in powerful kinship groups. This can be contrasted to the discontinuity in capitalist industrial societies where access to resources is justified by productive participation in a nonhousehold work force and sharply diminishes upon retirement (Keith, 1980b).

Yet predictions about the isolation of the grandparental generation from the rest of the family in our society appear exaggerated. Much of the research on this subject over the last 15 years has shown the persistence of a "modified extended family" composed of partially independent nuclear families that do exchange some services, goods, and emotional support (Sussman, 1965b; Shanas, 1968, 1979a; Treas, 1977; Shanas and Sussman, 1981). Certainly in the United States the *potential* exists for high levels of intergenerational family contact. Consider these two facts: (1) During the period 1920 to 1970, the likelihood of a 10-year-old youngster having two living grandparents increased from 40 to 75 percent (Butler, 1981). (2) Although elderly postparental couples generally reside independently (fewer than one in ten live in three-generation households), about 80 percent live within one hour's drive of one of their children and see them frequently (Federal Council on the Aging, 1981).

From the perspective of the elderly, then, are there important differences to be found in comparing family organization and intergenerational ties in different cultural traditions or within our nation's own divergent ethnic background? The final three selections in this section deal with various aspects of this question. Simić argues that in order to really understand the differences between U. S. family organization and that in Yugoslavia, one must concentrate on the cultural model each society has for developing intergenerational ties. Similarly, Johnson shows that the support generated for elders in Italian-American families cannot be readily comprehended solely by consideration of statistical measures of social contact. Finally, Nahemow studies the role of grandparenthood in an agrarian African society and makes insightful comparisons to the way that role functions in the United States.

Pierre van den Berghe

AGE DIFFERENTIATION IN HUMAN SOCIETIES

In this selection from his book Age and Sex in Human Societies, *van den Berghe details some elements of how societies use age as a basis for social differentiation. Important variables influencing the relevance of age to a community include: the extent of total social differentiation, the degree to which age recruits people into corporate groups, and the stress put on relative versus absolute age. In many preindustrial societies age is shown not only to significantly order relationships in the family but also to form the basis of bonds that crosscut kinship ties and form a wider level of communal solidarity.*

BECAUSE AGE DIFFERENCES ARE biologically based, they are recognized in all human societies. There is not only an obvious cognitive awareness of age and aging, but there are also social differences linked with role expectations and status. That is, age is *put to social use* in creating differentiated social structures. The biological constraints of age are obvious and are, of course, reflected in social structure: A two-year-old and an 80-year-old would both make poor warriors or wet nurses. There are age constraints also on the physiological maturity necessary for an infant to learn to walk, talk, and acquire other skills basic to all societies. Even as late as puberty, there might be a biological basis to the acquisition or nonacquisition of cultural skills. For example, until puberty, the majority of people are able to learn to speak new languages without noticeable foreign accents, whereas after puberty, full phonetic mastery is exceptional (Lenneberg, 1967).

However, the social use of age extends well beyond these obvious constraints. In all societies, birth, puberty, and death are important social events marked by *rites of passage*. Infants are given few responsibilities, but gradually they are trained, consciously and unconsciously, to behave according to their particular position in society (especially, according to their age and sex roles). As the infant becomes a young child—a stage achieved in most societies when the child is fully

mobile, weaned, toilet trained, and perhaps most importantly, when he has mastered his language well enough to communicate with other members of his society—he is initiated into social responsibilities commensurate with his skills and strength.[1] At or near puberty, a ritual typically marks the social recognition of adult status, which means reasonableness and responsibility. Often, this recognition precedes by a few years marriageability or full civic status. Young adulthood is devoted to economic production, warfare, and procreating and nurturing infants. For some males, older adulthood is a time for political leadership. Even death does not put an individual's social role to an end: Through some conception of immortality, he becomes a silent partner in a continuing ritual relationship.

Beyond the broad similarities in the social recognition of maturation and aging, including the attendant abilities and disabilities, the plasticity of human behavior is wide, unlike that of any other animal. One variable is the relative importance of age compared to other aspects of social differentiation. Naturally, this is inversely related to the total degree of differentiation in a given society. In many of the "simpler" societies, social organization is clearly defined by the types of differentiated relationships based respectively on kinship, marriage, age, and sex. Any one of these necessarily looms large, but even among these

From *Age and Sex in Human Societies: A Biosocial Perspective* by Pierre L. van den Berghe.© 1973 by Wadsworth Publishing Company, Inc. Reprinted by permission of Wadsworth Publishing Company, Belmont, California 94002.

societies there is a considerable range in the importance of age. In the more complexly differentiated societies, especially in industrial societies, age loses in relative importance partly because there are more competing bases of social organization, such as class, ethnicity, religion, occupation, voluntary associations, and the like, and partly because technology emancipates man from age-specific disabilities.

A second important age-linked variable is the degree to which, in a given society, age forms the basis of a corporate social grouping. To be sure, in all societies, age labels are used to refer to such broad social categories as "children," "young men," or "the elders." But, societies differ widely depending on whether age labels refer to ill-defined aggregates of people covering a wide age span (for example, terms such as *senior citizen* or *my generation* in American society) or to a self-conscious, precisely defined group of close coevals (for example, "the Harvard class of 1970"). Some societies, especially in Africa, stress heavily the importance of the latter type of age grouping. For these precisely defined, self-conscious, corporate age groups, we shall use the terms *age grades* and *age sets*. The former term we shall use when the emphasis is on the position of that age category in relation to similar others, for example, "The sophomore class at Harvard" is in our terms an *age grade*. We shall reserve the term *age set* for the specific group of individuals who move up as a group through an age grade system. For example, "the Harvard class of 1970" is an age *set* until its last member dies; in 1966, it entered the freshman age *grade*, in 1967, the sophomore one, and so on, until, in 1970, its successful members superannuated themselves out of the four-grade system and became lifelong elders or *alumni*. Entire societies are principally organized around such age sets and age grades, as we shall see.

A third dimension of age differentiation is the stress put on *relative versus absolute age*. Is the sociologically important question that A is 55 years old and B, 67, or simply that B is A's senior? In Western societies, an unusual stress is put on absolute age, a concomitant of an almost compulsively elaborate and precise system of timekeeping. There are relatively few societies in which being born on April 15, 1945, for example, is a matter of any social consequence. In

fact, many societies manage quite happily not keeping track at all of the year, much less the month and day of birth of their members. In those societies, the sociologically important fact is *relative seniority*. Nor must it be thought, as ethnocentric Westerners often have, that lack of concern for one's absolute age is merely a reflection of ignorance or of the society's inability to keep a calendar. In many traditional societies of Africa, for example, in which people do not "know their age," they time their agricultural activities precisely according to a lunar calendar.

At the other end of the spectrum, we find Western societies in which a person's birthday is, next to his name, the most socially important fact concerning him—a fact that needs to be officially certified, failing which he will have difficulty in enrolling in a school, obtaining a passport to travel abroad, getting married, obtaining a driver's license, purchasing liquor, qualifying for retirement, and so on. Western man is almost unthinkable without a birth certificate. As might be expected, the consequences of European countries trying to enforce on African societies an absolute conception of age and a mania for timekeeping have often been ludicrous. Some African bureaucracies have taken over from their former colonial masters the worship of the birth certificate, and people simply choose a date of birth at random within the plausible range. The only limitation is that once you have chosen an age, you have to stick with it. The state has learned to accept one fictional date of birth per person, but it still balks at two.

Relative age is of far more widespread significance. Indeed, it is of some importance in all cultures, and of paramount consequence in a good many. Perhaps one of the most widespread and general concepts of relative age is *generation*, which links age to the kinship system, both laterally and linearly. In systems of bilateral descent, in which lineages and clans are absent, such as in Western societies, the concept of generation has been extended to mean one's approximate coevals, the narrowness of the age limits varying according to the circumstances. Thus, a "student generation" at a university covers roughly four or five years, that is, the people who were there synchronously with ego. In the broader societal context, a generation spans 20 to 25 years, but since the reference is to an ego placed in the middle of that span, it means, in effect people born within 10 or 12 years of ego, that is, those not old enough to be ego's parents nor young enough to be his children.

In the far more common type of society characterized by unilineal descent, whether matri-lineal or patrilineal, the concept of generation becomes more specific. Where there are clearly defined lineages and clans, it becomes possible to order all of one's relatives by generation in relation to oneself. Thus, in one's parental generation belong his parents, his grandparents' children, his great-grandparents' children's chil-dren, and so on. Often, the same kin term may be used for father and father's brother, or for mother and mother's sister, or for brother and father's brother's son. Naturally, when the concept of generation is so closely linked to kin ties, it correlates less closely with age—over three generations, and especially with a polygynous system, there is typically some overlap in age between a man's younger children and his older grandchildren.

This leads us to the distinction between what we may call *sociological versus chronological age.* If the generational criterion of seniority is para-mount, then it may happen that the chronological junior becomes the sociological senior, for example, the junior uncle outranks the senior nephew. The same situation can also arise in age-grade systems in which there is often some overlap in chronological age between sets. Some college sophomores are younger than some freshmen, yet, sociologically, in the college age-grade system sophomores are sociologically senior to freshmen, irrespective of birth order. Seniority is relative, but in this case, not to individuals' birth order, a mere biological accident in this context; rather, it is relative to two *groups* in an age-hierarchized system.

An extremely important aspect of age differen-tiation is hierarchy. Age is almost by definition a hierarchical criterion causing *asymmetrical relations,* at least between adults and children. All societies are ruled by adults, despite the observation that the behavior of American children sometimes gives the impression that the United States is an exception to the rule. However, societies vary considerably in the extent to which age is a pervasive and significant criterion of hierarchy outside the family, schools, and other child

socialization agencies. Some societies are relatively egalitarian on the age dimension, whereas, on others, age is the paramount criterion of differentiation in power, wealth, status, inheri-tance, and other scarce resources.

By and large, age stratification seems most pronounced in those societies in which other bases of invidious status distinction (class, caste, race, ethnicity) are absent or undeveloped. Conversely, Western industrial societies are less prominently age-stratified and have become decreasingly so over time, except for their educational systems, which are rigidly stratified and segregated by age. Privileges of primogeniture, once so important in several parts of Europe in preventing the breakup of landed estates and the outbreak of fratricidal civil wars, whenever the throne became vacant, are only vestigial today (mainly, in the inheritance of the crown in the few remaining constitutional monarchies). Rank, of course, is correlated with age and "seniority" in most modern bureaucracies, but other criteria take precedence. Typically, modern bureaucracies are stratified into two or three educational and class levels (officers versus noncommissioned ranks in the army, for example), so that the lower ranks of the upper stratum are much younger than the upper ranks of the lower group.

In most Western societies, parents lose legal rights and responsibilities over their children at age 21, and there is a tendency toward lowering the age of political and legal responsibility to 18. There are still some vestiges of age deference in forms of speech and etiquette, but status, power, and income drop sharply after retirement age (usually 60 to 65 for men, and even earlier for women). Allowing for differences from occupa-tion to occupation, positions of greatest power and wealth are typically held by men in their late forties, fifties, or early sixties, but such hierarchy as exists is only incidentally correlated, rather than causally linked, with age. Promotion by seniority is seldom the paramount principle, and, even then, years of service matter more than chronological age.

In European languages that differentiate be-tween a "polite" and a "familiar" form (for example, French: *tu-vous;* German: *Du-Sie;* and Spanish: *tu-usted*), the forms are often used asymmetrically between adults and children who are unrelated to each other, but reciprocally between parents and children. Furthermore, the etiquette across age lines often applies across class lines as well, and class etiquette may even supersede age etiquette. Thus, as we see in nineteenth-century European novels, a social superior may address his chronologically senior subordinate in the familiar form, and expect him to reply in the polite form.

Another negative correlate of age stratification is associated with the rate of change, especially technological change. The increasingly rapid obsolescence of skills makes it difficult for older workers to vindicate their claims to higher status in an industrial economy that stresses productivity and efficiency (whether under capitalism or socialism). Beyond the "prime of life"—the thirties for women, the forties for men—increasing age is, by and large, a social liability in Western societies. To some extent, the professional elite is shielded from the adverse effects of advancing age, but, for the majority, the advantages of growing old are few. Although by no means all older people are poor, for example, the aged, along with the blacks, are among the most impoverished strata of the American population.

In the sphere of kinship, also, the principle of seniority plays a minimal role in Western societies. In the absence of any large corporate kin units, such as lineages and clans, seniority does not have any collateral extension: Older siblings have little authority over their younger brothers and sisters, much less over younger siblings' children. Parents can, with mixed success, impose their will upon their minor children, but any legal authority is extinguished when children reach 21. Grandparents exercise only limited authority over grandchildren, and then, largely *in loco parentis*. In short, since the nuclear family is by far the most meaningful kinship group in industrialized Western societies, it is not surprising that seniority in the kinship system operates almost solely within the nuclear family, and only until children reach adult status. Even within the nuclear family, there is a clear tendency, at least in the urbanized middle classes, toward more age-egalitarian relationships.

The contrast in age stratification with most nonindustrial non-Western societies is striking. The prototypical social organization of a great many non-Western societies is the local unilineal descent group, including the in-marrying spouses from other lineages and clans. For the sake of illustration, let us take a common form of kinship organization in nonindustrial societies—the extended, polygynous, virilocal family with exogamous clans and lineages based on patrilineal descent. Under such a system, all the descendants of a putative ancestor form a clan, itself subdivided into lineages of varying generational depth, descent being traced only in the single male line. The male members of a lineage or segment thereof live in physical proximity to each other, together with the unmarried female members of the lineage, and with wives who have come from other lineages. The residential kin group is an extended family spanning three or four generations, and including collateral branches. As such systems are frequently polygynous, these localized lineages may include hundreds of persons.

With few exceptions, and with provisions made for senility and other forms of mental incapacity, the authority structure of such large kin groups is based on seniority, the simplest and most universal way of solving the authority problem with a minimum of contention and argument. Authority passes from father to oldest son, then through the line of sons until the last member of the generation dies, then to the oldest son of the oldest son, and so on. There are, of course, numerous variants on this basic pattern, and localized lineages typically break up. The segments establish a new residence as the group becomes too large, or as conflict develops between brothers and half-brothers after the death of their father. In principle, however, the oldest male in the lineage holds legal authority over all members of the lineage, including the descendants of his brothers and brothers' sons.

The seniority principle is typically symbolized (as are other forms of inequality) through a distinct etiquette regulating formal interaction between age unequals. Among the Yoruba of southwestern Nigeria, for example, who, in common with many other African peoples, have an elaborate age deference etiquette, the language prescribes two forms of address, one familiar, one deferential, which are used nonreciprocally between juniors and seniors, and even between siblings who are no more than a year apart. Furthermore, the junior upon meeting a senior must prostrate himself to the ground if male, and kneel with bowed head if female. In the contemporary urban context, these age deference patterns become somewhat attenuated, but the principle is still powerful enough to create acutely embarrassing situations when it comes into conflict with other nontraditional forms of inequality. Thus, relations between master and servant, or between superior and subordinate in the civil service become tense if the person superior in class or rank is junior in age. Frequently, such situations are either avoided altogether (for example, by not hiring a domestic servant who is one's senior), or various evasive techniques are used to minimize the embarrassment, such as speaking English to sidestep the Yoruba spoken age deference.

In a number of societies, the seniority principle among siblings, so crucial in establishing lines of succession and authority in kin groups, is entrenched in the kinship terminology. There may be, for example, two entirely different kin terms to designate "junior brother" and "senior brother," as among some Maya languages. This senior-junior brother relationship may be considered so basic that its absence is inconceivable. Once, as I was doing field work in the Chiapas highlands of southeastern Mexico, a Maya area in which religion is a combination of Catholicism and indigenous beliefs, I noticed a statue of the Virgin Mary, but she had two children on her lap, one larger than the other. When I asked a Maya Indian for an explanation, he told me that one infant was "Jesus-older-brother" and the other "Jesus-younger-brother."

Since authority is mainly exercised by men, seniority is generally more developed among males; it is not, however, restricted to them. In many polygynous societies, the principle of seniority among wives of the same husband is resorted to in order to reduce conflict among them. Typically, the first wife is senior over the others and exercises a measure of authority over them. The first wife is nearly always the oldest, since polygyny is normally serial (a man marries his first wife when he is 25, his second one 10 or 12 years later, and there is a steeply increasing age disparity between husband and wife with each successive marriage).

In most societies, even the relatively undifferentiated ones, ties of solidarity link kin groups together into larger political units. A common arrangement is one in which the lineage heads (determined by seniority within the descent group) collectively constitute a "council of elders." This may take the form of a decentralized village political structure, in which the elders, acting as a body, exercise judicial, executive, and legislative functions. Or, such a council of elders may act as a representative body of their respective kin groups to a centralized authority. Often, the elders function as a body of councilors to the king, representing the mass of commoners. The elders are ineligible for the kingship, but they are not uncommonly the kingmakers, choosing the sovereign from the eligible princes in the royal clan. Thus, within unilineal descent groups, a seniority principle for the transmission and legitimation of authority may become generalized and furnish the basis of political integration for societies of hundreds of thousands of people.

Another interesting generalization of the principle of seniority occurs when the concept of age ranking is extended from individuals to groups. It is one thing to say that A is senior to his brother B, and thus has authority over B and his children so long as A lives. When A dies, B then assumes authority over A's children, and no segment of the lineage is permanently under the authority of someone who is not a direct ascendant. It is quite another thing, however, to claim that because A is senior to his brother B, his *segment of the lineage* has collective authority over B's. Such a claim, that a whole branch is senior to the others, establishes a permanent hierarchy among *groups of people*. Yet, ethnographic evidence suggests that such a claim has frequently been made, and, along with military conquest, constitutes perhaps one of the two most common ways of establishing in one stroke a system of centralized government and a genuine class system. In effect, when such a claim of collective seniority is successfully made (that is, when the claim becomes accepted by "junior" descent groups), the "senior" group has the potential of turning itself into a ruling aristocracy. The senior group becomes a royal clan from which the king is chosen, and the other clans or lineages are reduced to the status of commoners. A number of centralized African kingdoms may have developed out of what anthropologists call *acephalous* or *segmentary lineage* societies in the way just sketched. What were originally societies segmented into unranked unilineal descent groups and devoid of centralized authority (that is, stateless) may have grown into stratified, politically centralized states through a seniority claim of one of its component lineages or clans.

Interestingly, within the royal clan of many African kingdoms, there is no rule of primogeniture. Quite often, *any* son of the previous king is eligible. Combined with extensive royal polygyny, this rule frequently creates a class of several scores or even hundreds of eligible princes. Not uncommonly, the choice from among the potential claimants is made by a council of elders drawn by seniority from commoner lineages.

The concept of *group seniority* may operate within an aristocracy also, as it did in Europe, where primogeniture was well established. A kin or nobleman could pass on his title only to his first son, his younger sons receiving a title one rung lower in the noble hierarchy. Thus, the brothers of a reigning king would be princes or grand dukes, and the younger brothers of a duke would be earls or marquis. Descendants of several brothers would be referred to as the "senior" or "junior" branches of the family, even though European societies had already moved away from unilateral to bilateral descent.

So far, in dealing with age in nonindustrial and non-Western societies, we have stressed its linkages with the family and the kinship system. Perhaps the most creative and extensive use of age as a criterion for social differentiation, however, has been achieved by *emancipating* age from kinship. The principle of age sets and age grades is not unique to Africa; it has had some limited applications in other societies, as illustrated by our Western age-graded educational system. However, an age-grade system as a primary basis of society-wide integration is indeed characteristic of Africa. This is not to say that all African societies have age grades, nor even that most of them attribute age grades overwhelming importance. Within Africa, the functions and importance attributed to age grades and age sets vary greatly (Eisenstadt, 1956, 1965). But, the "classical" age-grade societies of East Africa such as the Nandi, Kipsigi, Masai, Kamba, Kikuyu, Meru, and others are uniquely African. Even though the details of the system vary among these, a general pattern clearly emerges.

In summary, the system works as follows. Every few years, a group of boys born within a few years of each other are initiated together into adult society, thereby bringing into existence a new age set occupying the most junior age-grade position. That age set, usually named, remains in existence until its last member dies. After the period of initiation, the age set is typically closed, and no initiations take place for a few years, until a new batch of initiates forms the next age set. When that happens, all previous age sets move up by one age grade. That is, the creation of a new age set through initiation of the next group of boys is the signal for a massive promotion exercise in which all previous age sets assume the age grade position hitherto occupied by their immediately senior age set.

The time interval between age sets varies from society to society, typically ranging from seven to fifteen years; the number of age sets in existence at a given time varies also. The functions of age sets differ, ranging from recreational clubs to the basis of military organization and government. In some societies, each age set enjoys a great deal of autonomy (freedom from control from seniors), whereas in others, this autonomy is much more restricted. Overriding these differences, however, age-set systems exhibit common characteristics: They cut across kin groups; they establish society-wide ties of solidarity among coevals; and, they establish a stratification that, though resulting in the differential distribution of status and power, is nevertheless democratic and universal for men. In short, age sets both stratify and integrate societies on a basis other than kinship, and in a way that, for men, is as uninvidious as possible. Every boy gets initiated, and, once in the system, a man need only survive to be promoted.

Let us look more closely at a stateless society like the Masai, in which age sets are maximally important. The Masai are a pastoralist, seminomadic people, numbering around 300,000, and occupying a vast area of southern Kenya and northern Tanzania, which they conquered in a series of military raids in the late nineteenth century, just before the British and German conquests. They herd cattle, sheep, and goats, and use donkeys as beasts of burden, but engage in no agriculture, and despise their peasant neighbors. Their diet consists mostly of the meat, milk, and blood of their herds. Slaughtering cattle is uncommon and done mostly on ritual occasions, but cows are milked, and the Masai, like many other African pastoralists, periodically bleed their cattle by carefully puncturing a neck vein. Cattle are not simply an economic asset, but also a social one, being essential in the payment of the bridewealth, without which no marriage or parenthood is legal. Like most African peoples, the Masai are patrilineal and their kinship system is organized on the basis of the extended, polygynous, virilocal family. The Masai have lineages and clans, but these kin groups do not have the overwhelming importance that they assume in a number of stateless societies, such as the Nuer, in which they constitute the principal social organization.

Unlike the many politically centralized societies of Africa, the Masai have no state, in the sense of clearly distinct political institutions (like a bureaucracy, a police force, tax-collecting machinery, tribunals) and a group of officials (king, ministers, army officers, spies, judges, executioners) specializing in wielding power over their fellow men. As do all societies, the Masai have a government—that is, a system of rules of conduct to regulate internal conflict and maintain internal peace. The term *acephalous* applied to stateless societies, in which power is diffuse and there is no king or chief, is misleading, for such societies are anything but "headless" or anarchical. They are rather polycephalous, that is, ruled collectively by councils of elders, often with a considerable measure of democracy for adult men.

The Masai, in common with many other East African pastoralists, and indeed some agriculturalists as well, have made age the paramount principle of social integration, ritual activity, government, and military organization. Prior to the "pacification" imposed by the European conquest, these societies were extremely bellicose; they were efficiently organized as permanent cattle-raiding machines that had universal military service for young adult men. The Masai, whose spectacular military successes against the Kikuyu and other groups have become a legend and an East African embodiment of the romantic Noble Savage theme, have been extensively studied by anthropologists. Bernardi (1955) gives us the best and most extensive account of their age-set system.

Around adolescence, boys undergo a long series of initiation rituals, during which they are segregated from the rest of the society for several months, are circumcised, have their heads shaved by their mother, and are presented by their father with a spear, sword, and shield, the weapons of the Masai warrior. After circumcision, boys are said to have "become men," but, in fact, they are still several years away from full adult status. They are not allowed to marry or own cattle, they are subjected to food taboos, and they are under the supervision of elders. Boys are initiated during the rainy season, a time of abundance, and initiations take place in cycles of roughly four successive years. Starting at time X, the boys initiated during the time interval of $X + 4$ years are referred to as the "right-hand circumcision" and become the senior subset within the age grade of warriors. For the time being, they are still regarded as apprentices, and, though allowed to take part in raids, they are expected to accompany more senior warriors. The batch of boys initiated during a single rainy season constitutes a subdivision within that four-year subset, but these smaller groupings are of minor significance, though they do establish an order of seniority within the subset.

After usually four years, the subset is closed and no initiations take place for three years or so. Then, at time $X + 7$ years, initiations start anew, and a second subset is opened, referred to as "left-hand circumcision." By this time the older warriors in the senior subset assume their full status as senior warriors, and the new initiates make up the junior subset between the times of $X + 7$ and $X + 11$ years. Then again the subset is closed for about three years, until time $X + 15$ years, when the total age set is promoted, and a new set is opened, repeating the fifteen-year cycle.

Thus, all the young men initiated between times X and $X + 15$ years make up the age grade of warriors on active duty, internally subdivided into a senior and a junior subgrade. The young men range in age from around fourteen to thirty. A pattern of rivalry, including mock combat, exists between the senior and the junior subsets, sometimes resulting in wounds. These conflicts, far from being condemned, are looked upon with favor.

The entire age set of warriors, made up of unmarried men, remains under the supervision of a special group of senior elders known as *piron*, who control and perform the initiation ceremonies, institute the new age sets, assist the initiates, and sponsor them. The warriors live in segregated villages, known as *manyatta*, where food is cooked by their mothers, and where young girls are present for their sexual diversion.[2] They are, however, strictly forbidden to marry and own cattle, and are still economically under the control of their fathers, who own the cattle necessary for bridewealth payment, and socially under the collective control of the senior elders. When a subset of "right-hand circumcision" warriors accedes to senior warrior status through the opening of a "left-hand circumcision" subset below them, a ceremony takes place and a leader of the subset is chosen by consultation between the elders and the members of the subset. That post, though highly honored, is not considered as desirable because the leader or *aunoni* is expected to start behaving as an elder, and to marry and settle down before his time. The *aunoni* is a link between the warriors and the elders, being granted elder status despite his membership in the warrior age grade. He is obeyed by his age mates, but he is, in fact, under the control of the *piron* elders, and is not in any strict sense an executive head. There are other officers of the age set, but these too have ritual and honorific rather than executive functions, and the age set is an internally egalitarian institution despite finer age gradings within it. Within the age set there is a small group of opinion leaders and decision makers, often made up of the older members of the set, but also open to individual skills. These leaders have very limited freedom of action, and they can be demoted by a council of their age mates.

The group of young men living in a given warrior village or *manyatta* constitutes a *sirit* of 50 to 100 people. Common residence establishes a close bond among age mates, and is also the foundation of military organization. Members of a *sirit* fight shoulder to shoulder. Thus, there are two main principles of age-set solidarity: contemporaneity of initiation and commonality of residence in the *manyatta*. This powerful solidarity is reflected in several aspects of life besides military organization. Members of the same age set throughout Masailand are expected to extend each other automatic hospitality, including sexual: Visiting age mates may sleep with their host's wife. Conversely, the incest taboo is extended on an age-set basis: Under penalty of severe beating,

the burning of his homestead, and the slaughtering of his cattle, no person is allowed to marry or fornicate with a daughter of a member of his age set nor with any wife of a member of his father's age set. Age sets are named, and these age-set names are the principal historical milestones in Masai oral tradition.

When a new age set is opened at time X_1, the previous warrior age set goes through a series of rituals by which the warriors accede to junior elder status. They exchange their long-bladed warrior spears for short-bladed ones, they are allowed to own cattle, to marry, and to establish their own homestead, and they are freed from dietary taboos. The prior distinctions between the subsets of junior and senior warrior lose their significance, and for the rest of their lives, the set forms a unified whole. For the 15-year duration of the X_1 initiation cycle, the age set initiated during the X cycle belongs to the age grade of junior elders, a position they hold while roughly 30 to 45 years of age. In the prime of their middle age, men are primarily concerned with marrying, procreating, raising boys who will be initiated in the X_2 cycle, and accumulating cattle (as the primary mark of wealth and status, and the means to become polygynous). Junior elders constitute an army reserve during raids, but they are relieved from the brunt of the fighting, which falls to the senior warriors. Junior eldership is thus a time devoted primarily to private domestic concerns, sandwiched between two long periods of civic duties, first as warriors, then as ruling class.

Fifteen years later, with the opening of the X_2 initiation cycle, every age set is again promoted into the next most senior age grade. The surviving junior elders now become the senior elders, with again a marked change in their status and functions. Senior elders, aged 45 to 60, are in their late middle age; they are experienced but not senile. They constitute the ruling age grade and their lives are devoted principally to public affairs, notably to running the entire initiation system with its multiple ritual and pedagogical tasks, and, hence, controlling the whole age-grade system, which forms the basis for Masai social organization. Naturally, age attrition in a society that has a high mortality rate through disease, war, and accidents (as occur in lion hunting, a test of manly courage) insures that senior elders are far fewer than warriors and junior elders; however, in keeping with the democratic conception of the Masai political order, power is decentralized, and leadership is shared and hemmed in by custom. There is no arbitrary use of power, and all adult men have some say in the collective decision making. Thus, the system cannot really be called oligarchic, because executive functions are not centralized enough to allow the use of a concept of state. Nor, interestingly enough, is it gerontocratic, for it is not the oldest men who are in positions of authority, but the ones in late middle age. True gerontocracy, as practiced, for example, in the College of Cardinals of the Roman Catholic Church, is a very exceptional political arrangement anywhere in the world. Power is typically vested in men in their late middle age, but far short of senility.

When, after another 15 or 16 years, the time comes for the opening of the X3 initiation cycle, the surviving senior elders gracefully retire from active political life and become respected old men, consulted in matters of tradition, but otherwise without any direct ritual or political role. At any given time, there are typically a few surviving members of three superannuated age sets living in such esteemed retirement.

The central role of age stratification for Masai males, then, is in allocating social roles. In the simplest and most schematic terms, Masai males are stratified into five broad age categories: uninitiated children; initiated warriors (junior and senior); early middle-aged men concerned with procreation and domestic affairs; late middle-aged men devoted to public affairs; and old men in retirement. This age stratification system cuts completely across lineage membership, but it is integrated with the kinship system, since incest

prohibitions and other constraints based on generation (for example, that fathers and sons may not belong to adjacent age sets) are extended to the age-grade system.

Perhaps most interestingly, this elaborate age-stratification system is probably the most democratic way of integrating large numbers of people (several hundred thousands) into a single, identifiable, self-conscious nation. Of course, as in all human societies, the democracy is limited by sex: For all intents and purposes, women are excluded from public life, except as wives and bearers of children. But the male Masai is indeed a free man. Neither tyrant nor slave, he earned the respect and admiration even of colonial administrators, and indeed became a colonial legend. It is ironic that now, as citizens of one of the more progressive African states (Tanzania), devoted to notions of freedom (*uhuru*) and egalitarian communalism (*ujamma*), the proud Masai are subjected to the assualts of a misguided neocolonial bureaucracy eager to "civilize" them and to make them till the soil. In 1968, a puritanical Area Commissioner, with the approval of President Julius Nyerere, even attempted to force Masai men to wear pants because he was afraid that camera-happy tourists might perpetuate stereotypes about Africa's being inhabited by naked savages. The same bureaucrat, incidentally, also banned on moral grounds emancipated urban women's wearing miniskirts in his district. The fate of the Masai at the hands of the neocolonial black bureaucracy is all the more ironic, since the Masai represent in purest form the ideal of African Socialism propounded by Nyerere, indeed in much purer form than the more "civilized" and "progressive" ethnic groups from which their new overlords come.

NOTES

1. With the full realization that English syntax (and that of many other languages besides) reflects the male bias of the society that produced it, I shall nevertheless continue to use masculine pronouns to refer to members of both sexes until such time as we manage to get new ones accepted into standard English.

2. Residential segregation by age is by no means unique to the Masai, nor even to stateless, pastoralist societies. For example, the Nyakyusa of southern Tanzania (described by Wilson, 1951) are an agricultural society organized in small chieftainships. There, groups of coevals establish

separate residence for the duration of their lifetimes. There results a pattern of quasi-neolocal residence and nuclear (but polygynous) families, very uncommon in Africa. Adolescent boys leave their parents to establish age villages, where their wives will later join them. Unlike the far more common African arrangement of the extended virilocal family, in which three or four generations of the male descendants of a man and their wives share a common residence, the Nyakyusa are sharply segregated by generation. As Wilson (1951: 31–32) describes the arrangement: "There are always villages of three generations in existence—those of contemporaries of the late chief, the headmen of which have ritual functions; those of mature men, contemporaries of the ruling chief, whose headmen have administration and military functions; and those of boys and young men, contemporaries of the heir, who have not yet 'come out' and who fight under the leadership of their fathers' senior headman . . . . Each age-grade, or generation, covers a span of 5 to 8 years." As in most societies, the ruling generation are the men in mature middle age (roughly between 35 and 65), and not the oldest. Among the Nyakyusa, as among the Masai and many other societies, corporate age groupings play a key role in political, military, religious, and economic organization.

Andrei Simić

AGING IN THE UNITED STATES
AND YUGOSLAVIA: CONTRASTING MODELS OF
INTERGENERATIONAL RELATIONSHIPS

While many gerontologists have recently marveled at the "discovery" that our system of urban industrialism has not totally destroyed extended family contact and intergenerational exchange, little attention has been given to the cultural factors shaping these bonds. In this example of small-scale cross-cultural comparison, Simić contrasts intergenerational relationships in the United States and Yugoslavia in terms of two opposing models: an American (white, upper–middle class) model stressing self-realization, independence, and generational replication; and a Yugoslav context characterized by kinship corporacy, interdependence, and generational symbiosis. These distinctions cannot be simply attributed to situational factors stimulating familial coresidence and economic cooperation in Yugoslav cities. Rather, differences in the role of the aged in these two societies are explained in terms of underlying systems of values and basic assumptions that are reflected in family structure and process.

A STEREOTYPE AT LEAST as old as the Classic civilizations of the Mediterranean has characterized urban life as a negative force undermining the traditional basis of social relationships (*cf.* Caro Baroja, 1963). These ideas are still with us and, indeed, much of our experience in highly industrialized and urbanized Western countries such as the United States tends to substantiate the view that modernization leads to the disruption of family life, the alienation of the individual, and other forms of social pathology (*cf.* Wirth, 1938). Similar viewpoints can be observed in the field of social gerontology. For example, in a study of aging among a largely white middle-class sample from Kansas City, Cumming and Henry (1961) propose a direct correlation between aging and decreased interaction within a social system, a concept they label *disengagement.* In another American study, Anderson (1972) suggests the idea of *deculturation,* a process by which the aged gradually assume a "cultureless"

position, one in which they live outside the body of tradition that constitutes the daily pattern of younger persons.

Clearly, *disengagement* and *deculturation* models are the product of a segment of American experience, and as such should not be elevated to a universality they may not merit. On the one hand, even a cursory perusal of worldwide ethnographic literature reveals that aging assumes a variety of forms and meanings corresponding to the social and cultural contexts in which it occurs (see among others: Cowgill and Holmes, 1972; Simmons, 1960). On the other hand, culturally specific theories such as those of disengagement and deculturation can provide a valuable contrasting framework for viewing aging in other societies. In this respect, anthropologists have typically assumed that an examination of their own uncritical behavior is essential to the understanding of that of others, and that only in such a comparative context can perceptual

From *Anthropological Quarterly*, April 1977. Reprinted by permission of The Catholic University of America Press. This research was funded by Grant #G1-ERP 72-03496 under the Exploratory Research and Problem Assessment Component, part of the Research Applied to National Needs program of the National Science Foundation.

distortions be avoided. In other words, the greatest risk in the study of exotic sociocultural systems is the natural tendency to interpret them in the light of one's own matrix of values and assumptions, that is, on the basis of the observer's own set of "common-sense" under-standings of which he may have little or no conscious analytical knowledge.

In this paper opposing patterns of American and Yugoslav intergenerational relationships will be explored in terms of their relevance for the understanding of the role of the aged in urban and urbanizing societies. In the first case, a largely impressionistic model consistent with theories of disengagement and deculturation will be suggested as typifying what I believe to be a common, but not necessarily universal, complex of behavior and belief among the Anglo and Anglicized urban upper–middle class in contemporary America—a pattern which, however, appears to be diffusing rapidly among other segments of our population as well. A contrasting model of familial and interpersonal relations in Yugoslavia has been derived principally from field materials collected on four occasions since 1966 in both rural and urban Yugoslavia. The data upon which these findings are based were gathered in the following areas: the Orthodox village of Borina in the Jadar region of western Serbia; the Bosnian market town of Zvornik and the industrializing city of Tuzla, both with mixed Christian and Moslem populations; in Serbia, the predominantly Ortho-dox cities of Belgrade, Šabac, and Kragujevac; and on the Catholic Croatian Littoral (Hrvatsko Primorje), the villages of Njivice, Hlapa, and Sveti Vid on the Island of Krk, and the port city of Rijeka and its nearby suburb of Matulji. Field work was carried out in Belgrade on three separate occasions, and more than 200 individuals spanning the social spectrum from newly arrived peasant migrants to highly educated professionals were interviewed. The most recent field work was conducted over a six-month period during 1973 and 1974, and focused exclusively on gerontologi-cal concerns and intergenerational relations. Older persons were studied in both familial contexts and in institutional settings in four homes for the aged.

The methodology employed in Yugoslavia included a variety of informal and formal techniques: structured interviews, the taking of life and family histories, the compilation of genealogies, censuses of household composition and age structure, and the usual ethnographic participant observation. This of course points to a methodological problem in that the American materials are drawn mainly from literary sources and my own casual, rather unstructured observa-tions as a native. Nevertheless, as I have previously noted, anthropology is a comparative discipline, and its comparative basis has most frequently been the implicit knowledge of the ethnologist of his own cultural milieu, a basic premise that this paper attempts to make overt. Also, the author recognizes the methodological and theoretical problems inherent in such broad societal comparisons, and the tentative nature of the emergent generalizations. This is especially true since the societies under consideration are of the so-called "complex" type, and one, the United States, is of a vastly greater magnitude and heterogeneity than the other. In this respect I would like to emphasize that undoubtedly there coexists a variety of differing cultural patterns in America and a wide range of individual and familial responses in the areas with which this paper deals. Therefore, I have deliberately restricted myself to those elements which I (and some other observers of the American scene) judge to be relatively widespread, and that stand out in high relief when contrasted with prevailing custom in Yugoslavia and surely elsewhere. In the case of Yugoslavia, generalization is easier and more certain since both the anthropological literature and my own field data drawn from the three major ethnic groups forming the majority of the country's population give evidence of a high degree of homogeneity in terms of the basic norms that govern familial and other social relationships.

As valuable as a broader understanding of the aging process in cross-cultural perspective may be, this comparison of intergenerational relations in America and Yugoslavia also strives to shed light on the more pervasive and as yet unresolved theoretical problem in the social sciences regard-ing the fit between overarching values on the one hand, and social structure and real behavior on the other. Thus, I have attempted to demonstrate a rough correlation between certain abstract, diffuse, transcendental ideas and specific behavioral manifestations in two contrasting social settings. However, it is not my intent simply to echo Ruth Benedict's (1934) contention that integration occurs in each culture within the matrix of a single theme that permeates the entire fabric of social life. In contrast, this essay proposes that culture is simply one of a number of imperatives present in the environment, and as such it has a tendency to channel behavior rather than to determine it absolutely (*cf.* Barth, 1966). Though this study has tended to focus on cultural and processual regularities distinguishing American from South Slav society, this should not be taken as a negation of the individual as an active and frequently unpredictable force in the interplay between relatively static mores and everchanging social situations.

AN AMERICAN PROTOTYPE

Disengagement and deculturation are essentially the social and cultural sides of the same coin of personal alienation. They are explained as the end result of a gradual process of separation in later life from significant interpersonal contacts and the shared symbolic system underlying them. Thus, the isolation and normlessness that many elderly Americans experience are considered a necessary concomitant of the aging process *per se.* However, it is my contention that these characteristics, though undoubtedly accentuated by old age, are not simply the product of seniority itself, but rather reflect a more generalized age-nonspecific ideology of atomistic individualism which permeates a large segment of American thought. In this regard, individuals do not suddenly find themselves isolated in their declining years, but are socialized for this role almost from the time of conception in the context of the family and community.

Independence, unencumbered freedom of decision making, self-determination, and individuality are among the most widely enunciated values in contemporary North American society (*cf.* Clark, 1972). This ideology is mirrored in family life with its deemphasis of corporacy, and the

outward orientation of individual members toward the external world, each with his own focus. Such centrifugal forces within the family have been frequently noted; for example, Riesman (1972: 38), in a study of American character in the twentieth century, observes that "in large measure the home directs children away from home and early provides them with direct access, through their peers, through school, and through the mass media, to moods and imperatives which may not be in harmony with the parental ones." Similarly, in a novelistic description of a young Frenchman's reaction to American family life, Lindbergh (1963: 97) writes: "They were all individuals . . . loosely but reluctantly tied together into a family group." Noting the same tendencies, Yugoslav anthropologist Vera Erlich (1972: 55), who spent a number of years in the United States, comments:

The desire for complete independence has become so strong during the past few decades that it has emerged as one of the principal causes for the isolation of older people, and although the entire American life style from its incipiency placed personal independence on a high rung of the value scale, the desire for independence has become so absolute in recent times that it is threatening family life. (my translation)

Bronfenbrenner (1974: 53) places this phenomenon in an even broader context, and notes in a recent article regarding the origins of alienation in contemporary America that "the degree of estrangement between young people and adults in the U. S. is currently higher than it has been in other times." He attributes this to the failure of both the family and the larger society to maintain mechanisms which had formerly integrated young people into meaningful sets of intergenerational relationships.[1]

If self-fulfillment and individual realization are indeed prime American values, what then are some of their underlying premises, correlates, and behavioral expressions? In part, this question can be elucidated with reference to the family developmental cycle, the socialization process, lines of authority and affect within the family, basic assumptions about interpersonal relationships, and ideas regarding the function of work.

By world standards the developmental cycle of the American family is rather short, spanning the period from premarital neolocality until a couple's youngest child reaches his late teens. The almost universal expectation is that from about the age of 18 all adults, married or single, will maintain autonomous households, that is, separate from that of their parents. Facilitated by the ready availability of housing and relative material prosperity, independence in the spatial, economic, and psychological sense has been transformed into a tenet of American ethos. Thus, the abandonment of their natal homes of young adults, whether for work, education, or marriage, constitutes a sharp and permanent disengagement in both their lives and those of their parents. These parents nevertheless share the same expectations, and either overtly or tacitly encourage this phenomenon.

American children are socialized from their earliest years toward the goal of independence. A key element in this process is the concept of *privacy* (one notably lacking in many other cultures) with its connotation of the *right* and *pleasure* of being alone as expressed in the exclusive control of space and material objects, and the freedom from the intrusion of others. Ideally, each child, even a baby in the crib, is provided with a room separate from that of his parents so as to respect the mutual need for privacy. In the same way, wherever possible, siblings are similarly isolated from each other, both because of the presumed requirement for individual private space, and the belief that each child's principal interests will lie not with his older or younger brothers and sisters, but rather with his extrafamilial age mates.

Underlying the entire socialization process is the assumption of peer group solidarity and communality. This is reflected in the realization of such crisis rites as birthday parties where family members remain discreetly behind the scenes while active participation is limited to the child and his extrafamilial age mates. Such behavior reaches its apex during the teens when children freely exile their parents from the home during age-specific social gatherings. The orientation of American children is further directed away from the household commencing at an early age through participation in a myriad of voluntary associations, organized sporting events, and extracurricular activities. Moreover, in general, children are not expected to spend a significant amount of their leisure time interacting with family members, and if they do, they are regarded as "odd," and corrective measures are taken to assure greater participation in the peer group. Such extrafamilial orientation continues into later life, and adults, in association with their peers, frequently immerse themselves in a frantic and frenetic round of benevolent, "self-improvement," and recreational activities that bear no relationship to the specific interests and welfare of their households as a whole. The distinctness of generational interests has in fact become such a commonly accepted idea in the United States that there is a widespread presumption that there are corresponding age-specific cultural matrices, one of which has even been graced with the formal designation, "youth culture."

Within many American families, rather than an emphasis on hierarchal principles based on age and sex, there is an ideological stress on equal rights and equal participation in the decision-making process, though practical considerations and the nature of individual personalities often make the realization of this ideal fall short of expectations. Thus, not only are the rights of parents vis-a'-vis children vaguely defined, and almost all formal forms of deference for those of ascending generations lacking, but those parental prerogatives that do exist are rapidly eroded as children approach adulthood. Similarly, older siblings are not ordinarily given extensive authority over, or responsibility for, their younger brothers and sisters. In fact, while attempts by older children to dominate younger ones are regarded as a natural tendency, they are nevertheless considered as an unfortunate form of antisocial behavior to be actively discouraged.

Just as dominance within the family group is regarded as antithetical to the democratic ideal, so too is "excessive" affect threatening to the principle of autonomy. Overt displays of affection are limited, for the most part, to the conjugal pair and interaction with very young children. With the incipience of adolescence there is a firm expectation of diminishing affect between parents and children, and upon marriage there occurs an almost total transfer of sentiment from the natal family to that of procreation. Thus, it is assumed that the most enduring ties will bind husband and wife who comprise the only really corporate unit within the family (and now there are also strong currents of thought suggesting that they too should be "free," each to follow his, or her, own star).

Neither in its internal dimensions nor its external relations can the American family be said to constitute for most purposes a truly corporate group. Nowhere is this more evident than in the area of economics where children are encouraged to earn, control, and "learn the value of" money, while at the same time they are not usually expected to contribute their earnings, which are regarded as "private property," to a common coffer. Though parents often extend financial aid to their children after they have left home, it is almost always with the overt rationale of helping them get established as independent units, rather than creating a binding reciprocity of mutual dependence between the two generations. In later life this same ideology also prevails, and among the aged, economic independence has become such a widespread value so as to comprise a cultural imperative whose manifest function is the avoidance of "demeaning" dependency upon one's children or other family members. Though inheritance continues to descend from generation to generation, among the living the redistribution of wealth within the family is generally limited by the moral concerns of individual accomplishment and the need to remain "one's own man."

In its relations with the external world the solidarity of the American family is limited by a commonly held antipathy toward personalism, and a concomitant predisposition toward universal standards which by their very definition transcend the boundaries of the familial group. In this respect, the family is not the intense focus of a highly differentiated moral double standard, and even such basic and traditional ideas as a parent's responsibility for the actions of his children have been questioned. Thus, the weak corporate image of the family fails to generate a compelling rationale for a continuing reciprocal concern linking the generations in the maintenance of a common reputation.

If the family is not the primary arena for individual engagement, then what is? The answer, I believe, is to be found in a concept whose origins are commonly attributed to Calvinism (*cf.* Weber, 1958), the ideology of work as a personal moral commitment containing its own intrinsic rewards. Probably nowhere is this idea more evident than in the contemporary United States where it has assumed for many the character of an admonition overshadowing all other imperatives. The reputed American preoccupation with productivity has become a cliche' of national character, but nevertheless merits restatement in the context of family relationships. In this respect, one's occupational status has become his primary marker of social identification rather than his position in a matrix of kinship and familial relationships. In contrasting the American and Hindu world views, an Indian anthropologist (Triloki N. Pandey, personal communication) once commented that upon meeting a stranger in India one does not first ask his personal name and occupation as in the United States, but rather the identity of his kinship group. His observation underscores the primacy of individualism and work in America, and one may well conclude that the contemporary family exists as a logistic mechanism for supporting its individual members in their various occupational statuses. In other words, work is not regarded as a symbiotic effort uniting family members in the maintenance of the corporate whole, but rather as a set of individual moral obligations carried out to assure personal spiritual well-being and emotional fulfillment. Thus, the question considered here is not whether work is valued in a particular society, but rather the particular value that is attributed to it, and the relationship it bears to other activities and social processes.

It seems inevitable that the aged, caught up in a system stressing individual psychological and socioeconomic independence, and in which excellency is judged in terms of dedication and virtuosity in the performance of occupational tasks, deprived of their work statuses, and lacking a system of intense interdependence with children and kin, are left in a state of cultural and social semi-isolation in their declining years. It is not coincidental that the rallying cries of the retired echo the values of the society as a whole: "Be independent" and "Stay active."[2]

A YUGOSLAV PROTOTYPE

Some knowledge of traditional Yugoslav social organization is essential to the understanding of the contemporary South Slav family. Not only have archaic forms of household organization persisted in many rural areas, but more generally, even in urban centers, the ideology of kinship solidarity has survived almost intact.

Prior to World War II the overwhelming majority of the Yugoslav population was rural. The society was strongly kinship-oriented, and though there had been some erosion of traditional social forms in the interwar period, the extended family remained the primary unit of production and social identification. In Serbia, Macedonia, and much of central Yugoslavia the basic model of the family was the *zadruga,* a patrilocally extended household holding land, stock, agricultural equipment, and other material and ritual property as a corporate unit. In some cases they consisted of as many as 80 or more coresident members (*cf.* Hammel, 1968: 14–15). In the period prior to World War I, a closely related and probably more ancient form of social organization occurred in the rugged Dinaric highlands of western Yugoslavia. Here, smaller economically independent households were organized into patrilineal clans which were not only maximal units of social identity, but also organs of political power articulated through the blood feud (*cf.* Djilas, 1958: Simić, 1967). Both systems reckoned descent and inheritance patrilineally, and although there were elements of political and economic democracy within the kinship group (*cf.* Burić, 1976), family organization was basically hierarchal in nature with the male principle and seniority dominant.[3]

In the more Westernized areas of Yugoslavia, in the far north and on the Dalmatian and Croatian littorals, family structure more closely resembled the bilateral forms found in the Western Mediterranean and Central Europe, though here too existed a strong patrilineal bias, and a tendency toward kinship solidarity beyond the confines of the nuclear family.

In regions characterized by the zadruga, since the beginning of the twentieth century, there has been a decline in both the size and economic significance of extended households, though the change has been less one of function than form with a tendency toward lineal, rather than lateral extension (Halpern and Anderson, 1970). Similarly, highland tribal society, though it has maintained its emphasis on kinship solidarity, has gradually lost its political functions due to the encroachment of central government.

In spite of the tremendous social and demographic dislocations resulting from World War II, the subsequent socialist revolution, the industrialization of Yugoslavia, and the massive peasant migration from the countryside to urban areas, South Slav traditional culture has shown great vitality (Simić, 1974). Thus, while kinship has been generally viewed by social scientists as more important in primitive than in contemporary societies, the evidence from Yugoslavia indicates that urbanization and modernization do not necessarily result in the demise of the family (*cf.* Hammel, 1969).

The model of the contemporary Yugoslav family suggested in this paper is one which endeavors to elucidate those characteristics which transcend both regional differences and the rural-urban dichotomy. By way of introduction, I would like to suggest that the cultivation of social ties with kin and nonkin alike can be said to constitute a Yugoslav national vice. The interest in interpersonal relationships is an all-absorbing one, one which frequently goes so far as to inhibit the rationalization of administrative and economic functions, a phenomenon that is recognized by many Yugoslavs themselves as an impediment to development (*cf.* Burić, 1976: 117–18). Of all arenas of interaction, family and kinship are the most compelling.

The developmental cycle of the South Slav family contrasts sharply with that in the United States which is typified by a number of sharp breaks or discontinuities marking new periods of development. The Yugoslav family often spans a number of generations without total cleavages in composition, and even in death constituent members continue to exert their aura in the context of the living. It is difficult to place temporal boundaries on the family developmental cycle since, in many cases, one generation flows almost imperceptibly into the familial roles occupied by the previous one; thus, replication takes place, not in the context of newly formed units, but rather through the medium of gradual replacement of personnel within the same social entities.

Postmarital neolocality, though it occurs, is neither in tune with the values of traditional South Slav society nor the exigencies of modern Yugoslav urban life. In the Serbian countryside patrilocality is still the rule, with the bride most often initially joining her husband in his parents' home, or in other cases, in a house newly constructed on a plot adjoining the groom's father's or grandfather's farmyard, and still forming an integral part of the paternal estate. Frequently, some child will remain with his parents until their death, and then continue to live in the same house with his own family of procreation, working the same land which he sometimes shares with his brothers as an undivided patrimony. Thus, though there is some sloughing off of members through death or other forms of separation such as migration or the establishment of new loci of residence, households tend to evidence continuity over a number of generations. In other words, the cyclical process of fission and fusion within the family is not generally characterized by abrupt and relatively complete separations as appears to be the common case in the United States; rather the transition from one generation to the next tends to be more often a gradual one.

The situation is similar in urban Yugoslavia where intergenerational relationships are also characterized by high levels of continuity and reciprocity engendered by both the survival of a mentality of kinship corporacy and the exigencies of city life in a newly industrializing nation. Thus, a critically short supply of urban housing, and the realities of a cash-poor economy reinforced by tradition and ideology compel young married couples to take up residence, where feasible, with parents or other kin. Moreover, these same economic forces in the city have significantly contributed to later marriage and the limitation of family size in terms of children. In the case of

unmarried individuals of whatever age, in city and village alike, the expectation is that whenever possible they will live with parents or kin. Though the economic potential for premarital neolocality is generally lacking, cultural considerations are perhaps paramount. For example, the response of a 22-year-old university student was typical of the attitudes of 56 young adults interviewed in Belgrade in 1968 and 1969. When questioned as to whether she would like to have "her own apartment," after some perturbation, she replied, "What a strange idea! It would be so lonely without my parents."

Even the eventual physical separation of household members does not necessarily signify the psychological and economic diminishment of family ties. For instance, dual or even multiple residence on the part of the elderly and young is not uncommon. Older people frequently spend the pleasant spring and summer months in their village homes, and winters in the relative comfort of their children's urban apartments, though perhaps the most common pattern is the exchange of rural and urban children during school holidays. Another indicator of the psychological ties binding recently separated households is to be found in behavior surrounding the Serbian custom of the celebration of the lineage patron saint, the *slava*.[4] Many adult males do not hold an official commemoration as long as their fathers are still alive even though they may reside separately. The explanation offered for this is simply, "one household, one celebration."

Economic behavior also reflects continuing family corporacy, though members may be scattered in a number of locations, even as distant as West Germany or the United States. This is particularly true in the case of rural migrants who continue to be tied to their village homes through intense material reciprocity even decades or generations after having established households in the city (*cf.* Simić, 1973b):

I left my village when I was only three, but I still have roots there. My three grandparents live in Rosići and I have visited them all my life. This year I have been there five or six times with my parents—and people from the village are always visiting us in the city. When we go to Rosići, we take presents and money to pay the taxes—when we return to the city we are loaded with cheese, rakija *(fruit brandy), sausages, and sometimes even a pig. (22-year-old informant)*

When distance or other considerations limit the substantive nature of such exchange, other types of reciprocity that are essentially symbolic and ritualistic fulfill the same function of perpetuating family ties:

Milan's 74-year-old father and stepmother live far from Belgrade on the shores of Lake Plav in the high mountains of Montenegro. Once a week, during the warm months, his father sends him trout freshly caught that morning via a cooperative bus driver whom the informant meets in the late afternoon at the Belgrade bus station. Subsequently, there is a madcap dash around the city to distribute the fish to various relatives and in-laws before it spoils in the heat. In exchange, Milan regularly sends medicine and presents of inexpensive manufactured goods via the same driver to his parents as well as scrupulously attending all family weddings, funerals, and the yearly patriline Saint's Day (slava) in the village. (33-year-old informant)

Visiting patterns are a good indicator of familial sentiment, and Hammel and Yarbrough (1973: 132) found, in the study of a sample of 326 males living in Belgrade who were not coresiding with their fathers or brothers, that there was a mean frequency of contact between fathers and sons living in the same city of approximately every other day; and a mean of 159 yearly personal contacts between brothers under similar conditions. In the case of fathers and sons, and brothers, separated by residence in different communities, there was a compensatingly high incidence of written communication.

Though death is the ultimate physical separation, in Yugoslavia the deceased exert a strong psychological presence among the living. Generational continuity is assured through elaborate funerary practices, the erection of imposing monuments, regular visits to the grave, feasting on the Days of the Dead, yearly religious or secular observations on the anniversary of death, and an eventual place of honor for the deceased in the kinship pantheon celebrated in family history and myth. Death does, however, signify the assumption of fully adult statuses by the descending generation since children remain emotionally tied to their parents far into adulthood.

The continuity of intergenerational relationships and the strong collective spirit of the Yugoslav family can be explained in part with reference to child-rearing practices. The socialization of children accentuates the reciprocal roles they will play throughout their life with other family members and kin. For instance, the concept of *privacy*, described as a key to interaction within the American household, is notably lacking, and the need to be alone and to control personal space is not culturally recognized in terms of the family group. Such tendencies, whether in adults or children, are regarded as antisocial or signs of personal rejection or emotional imbalance.

The Yugoslav child is expected to identify more strongly with other members of the household than with an external peer group. Consequently, children spend (what would be considered by American standards) an inordinately large proportion of their leisure time at home. While there is a firm expectation of age-specific role behavior, these roles are seen as symbiotic rather than autonomous in the context of intergenerational relationships. Thus, while there are activities thought appropriate to youth, these are not conceived of as divisive but simply part of a familial solidarity based on a sexual and generational division of labor. This ideology is reflected in crisis rites where family members and more distant kin of all ages participate in their preparation and execution. For example, birthday parties are not regarded as an opportunity for the child to interact exclusively with his extrafamilial peers, but rather, as an occasion to strengthen and reaffirm kinship ties.

Within the household the principle of age is dominant, and most forms of independence are discouraged in children. Childrearing and discipline are shared by all senior household members including older brothers and sisters who are given responsibility for, and authority over, younger ones. Outside the home, even unrelated and unfamiliar adults feel free to reprimand children. Though individualism and self-determination are deemphasized, nevertheless, children are encouraged to perfect their talents and to perform tasks assigned to them with excellence as fulfillment of their part of a set of reciprocal obligations, as signs of filial respect, and out of concern for family reputation. Economic individualism is likewise antithetical to the family ideal, and in most cases even adult children contribute their earnings to a common household fund. On a more general level, there is a high expectation that among close kin good fortune will be shared as an equalizing mechanism reflecting corporate rather than individual interests.

Affect within the family also tends to link generations, and there is a concomitant deemphasis on the communicative aspects of the conjugal relationship, perhaps reflecting an earlier state where marriage was an alliance between potentially hostile lineages. Even today the union is regarded principally as an economic and procreative one, and in most cases husbands and wives do not look to each other for their main source of companionship (cf. Burić, 1976: 135). However, on the one hand, parents are linked by mutual concern for their children, and are drawn together through the medium of their progeny (cf. Hammel, 1967: 57). On the other hand, intense affection and respect typifies the relationship of children of all ages toward their parents, and this positive affect is reciprocated within the bounds of the authoritative roles assigned to mothers, and particularly fathers. For example, public demonstrations of affection between parents and adolescent or adult children are commonplace, while similar manifestations between husbands and wives are very rare, and at best considered "odd" or "indecent." Thus, the minimalization of the affectual characteristics of the conjugal bond tends to strengthen intergenerational relationships and to assure the integrity of the extended family group:

A 28-year-old Moslem woman was greeted by her father, mother, aunt, and husband as she left the hospital after a prolonged stay. She rushed up to her parents embracing them warmly with obvious joy, she hugged her aunt, kissing her on both cheeks, then formally shook hands with her husband. (Tuzla, Bosnia)

The Yugoslav family is the focus of a double standard in a society that functions to a great extent in terms of particularism and personalism rather than universal standards. Thus, in the context of the external world a family member is expected, as his first obligation, to use his position or influence to aid his kin. While intrafamily relationships are characterized by cooperation, reciprocity, and corporacy, the external world is seen as an amoral social field in which (with the exception of close friends and those related through fictive kinship), behavior is essentially exploitive: "Everyone is out for himself and his kin—without connections (veze) you are lost—those with big families are ahead of the game" (17-year-old student from Belgrade).

In Yugoslavia there are few transcendental values which can vie with those associated with the family. For example, work is not regarded as a value unto itself, but rather as a means to support and enhance familial and other significant social relationships. Thus, work statuses can be seen as subordinate to those of kinship. Even the strong nationalistic passions which typify the various Yugoslav peoples are closely associated with familial origins, and in turn religion and politics are inseparable from nationality.

As the process of aging takes place in the South Slav family the individual progresses from one age and sex-specific role to another, each with its firm behavioral referents. Nevertheless, these roles are parts of a collective mosaic, and are behaviorally operative on the basis of a dominant principle stressing mutual dependence and reciprocity. Moreover, it would appear that the actors carry out their roles in the unselfconscious manner so typical of much of culturally generated behavior everywhere. As Yugoslav family sociologist Olivera Burić notes (1976:131):

Such obligations are regarded as part of the "natural order," and people uncritically strive to fulfill them. As in the normal course of events in other societies, most parents attempt to rear their children to the best of their ability. In return, Yugoslav children also consider it their duty to care for their parents in old age and infirmity, wherever they live and whether or not social services and help are available.

Clearly, the evidence points to the mutual expectation of reciprocity between parents and children regardless of their stages in the life cycle. Thus, not only do children regard their filial obligations as continuing moral imperatives, but parents also appear to accept these prestations without feelings of debilitating or degrading dependency. Rather, both parties view these intense relationships as further opportunity to engage in the kind of exchanges that have typified their entire lives.

Conclusions

This paper has suggested two opposing stereotypes of intergenerational relationships, each consistent with certain sets of values. However, it should not be inferred from these generalizations that the contrast is an absolute one, that familial solidarity is utterly lacking in America or that atomistic individualism is unknown among the South Slavs. Clearly the difference between the two societies is not totally qualitative, but also one of degree. Moreover, it is evident that even small, relatively homogeneous communities are not entirely consistent in terms of values, and choices must be made in every society between often paradoxically conflicting assumptions and imperatives. In this respect, long-range goals are frequently interrupted by concern for short-term gratification and advantage. People commonly make choices which are not in key with their society's overall consensus as to what is valued. Each man is further limited by his ascribed characteristics, psychological make-up, and the vagaries of historic accident. Thus, these suggested paradigms are abstractions, and as such idealizations from which real life experiences will vary considerably. Nevertheless, in spite of these reservations, I believe that the United States and Yugoslavia can be effectively opposed in terms of two very different patterns of belief regarding man's social and personal life objectives. In turn, these values generate distinct models of family organization and intergenerational relationships: in America, one stressing individualism and generational replication; and among the South Slavs, one focusing on kinship corporacy and generational symbiosis.

NOTES

1. It should be noted that there are also those in the social sciences who do not entirely concur with the "generation-gap" model of American society—see, among others, Bengtson (1970: 19–22).

2. See Bengtson (1973: 42–43) regarding the activity theory of aging.

3. For more detailed summaries of South Slav social organization see Hammel (1968: 13–37) and Simić (1973a: 44–52).

4. Among the Serbs the *slava* (krsna slava) is a Saint's Day celebrated by all those who recognize common patrilineal descent from an eponymic ancestor. Observances take the form of rituals and feasting in each economically independent patriline household, while clan solidarity is recognized by the veneration of a common sacred occasion.

Colleen Leahy Johnson

INTERDEPENDENCE AND AGING IN ITALIAN FAMILIES

Despite our society's pervasive general model of intergenerational relations (described in the previous article), cultural plurality expressed in ethnic family structures still persists. Even among European immigrant groups, often portrayed as totally assimilated into the American mainstream, there are distinct varieties of family organization. Fully understanding the salience of such differences to the elderly requires a *cultural* approach, stressing values and their expression in family interaction, in addition to a strictly *structural* approach dependent on the statistical analysis of demographic variables. Applying the former approach to a study of Italian-American families in Syracuse, New York, Johnson sees that their values of interdependence, age-hierarchy respect, and free emotional expression contribute to intense family centrality and high status given to elderly parents. In contrast to a sample of Protestant non-Italians, these ethnic-based values not only contribute to higher levels of intergenerational contact and material exchange but also are associated with a significantly decreased willingness to send elderly parents to nursing homes.

THIS PAPER EXAMINES THE position of the elderly in Italian-American families, a position in part distinctive to this ethnic group and in part similar to the wider elderly population. On one hand, there is a commonality with other European groups who have their origin in Old World family systems and similar immigrant situations in this country. From this perspective, one finds a paradox of uniformity among European groups. For example, the articles in a book on ethnic families by Mindel and Habenstein (1976) convey a sameness which comes under the rubric of traditionalism: The old are treated with respect; kinship solidarity is prominent; families are hierarchical with old over young and males over females, *ad infinitum*. Because of the processes of assimilation and acculturation, however, sociologists often assume European groups are changing from traditional family structures to modern ones. According to this view, these families are not "ethnic" but rather exhibit variation on the basis of social class (Horowitz, 1975; Patterson, 1979; Stein and Hill, 1977).

Elderly in immigrant groups, on the other hand, usually face some specific problems not experienced, or experienced to a lesser degree, among longer-established groups. The low educational and occupational levels of most foreign-born elderly can create social differences between them and their children. However, since large-scale surveys of social contact and mutual aid among the aged do not usually report findings by ethnicity of European groups, we do not know with certainty the degree of differences even though popular views assume that groups like Italian Americans have closer families. Thus, except for a few recent reports (Fandetti and Gelfand, 1976; Gelfand and Kutzik, 1979; Siemaszko, 1980), a review of the literature leaves us with some uncertainty as to the degree to which ethnicity acts as a determinant of the family status of the aged among those of European origins. As Trela and Sokolovsky conclude, "One finds a research wasteland dotted now and then with statistical demonstration of ethnic nonsalience" (1979:127).

This essay was specially prepared for this book by the author. Permission to reprint must be obtained from the author and publisher.
The research reported was funded by NIMH (1 RO1 MH31907).

One source of these discrepant views possibly stems from the conceptual approaches used to study European groups. Until recently most of the research has been done by sociologists who study social structural variables such as social and geographic mobility (Yancey et al., 1976) or patterns of intermarriage (Alba, 1976). Since there have been structural realignments with advancement to middle-class status, residential mobility from old urban neighborhoods to the suburbs, and high rates of intermarriage, it is often assumed that assimilation has been virtually complete. Any Old World traits are then seen as devoid of social content and lacking social significance (Parsons, 1975). Sociologists, when addressing the vocal protests of these "new ethnics," dismiss their statements of ethnic pride as largely sentimental or as political strategies to advance group interests (Glazer and Moynihan, 1975).

In contrast, the *cultural* approach, usually used by anthropologists, studies the norms and values, the less institutionalized forms of behavior expressed in day-to-day interaction, and the meanings individuals attach to them. Since behaviors and norms associated with ethnic membership are commonly observed in such settings, and are an important dimension of individual experience, the endurance of ethnicity is usually found. One can conclude from this disparity that the factors which can tap ethnicity today might be more amenable to study by anthropological rather than standard sociological techniques. Furthermore, since ethnic neighborhoods are dispersing and ethnic languages and customs have fallen into disuse, a collection of traits linked to the country of origin is no longer a vehicle for the expression of ethnic membership (Barth, 1969). In other words, more subjective elements of ethnicity have possibly replaced objective indicators.

Attempting to understand ethnic group differences usually devolves upon a conceptual choice between what Wallace (1970) describes as the *social structuring of uniformity* versus the *cultural organization of diversity*. The former approach tends to overlook group diversity and the more dynamic interpersonal facets of ethnic experience, and the latter can neglect structural conditions which are reliable indicators of change. As a result we have little understanding of the contemporary ethnic group as a new but identifiable social form (Glazer and Moynihan, 1963) and the factors associated with its varying significance among different ethnic groups. The problems are compounded by the great variation among groups in the structural conditions at the time of immigration and the degree to which prejudice and discrimination limited their opportunity structures. The cultural dimension also was differentiated in the degree of compatibility between the culture of origin and American culture.

Given these background variables which create diversity, the study of immigrants or children of early immigrants is certainly relevant to an analysis of adaptation in old age because of the high percentage of today's elderly who are foreign born. Gerontological research has also largely overlooked the tremendous ethnic and social class differences within each cohort of elderly. James Dowd (1980) points out that two images of the elderly emerge from this research, one of the elderly as mainly middle class, and a second as the very poor and the "social problem" elderly. He concludes that both are biased views which neglect the numerous variables which differentially affect individuals. Certainly Italian-American elderly fit into neither category, and as will be described below, the antecedents to their current situation can be obscured by this narrow focus on structural variables such as stratification.

In the following, I will examine the social situation of Italian elderly within the context of their subculture. The research reported here was conducted in Syracuse, New York. It explored both structural and cultural dimensions of interdependence in Italian-American families which were associated with the status of elderly parents. Seventy-six families in which both spouses were Italian Americans were interviewed and compared with 98 families where intermarriage had taken place and only one spouse was Italian American. These groups were then compared with a control group of Protestant non-Italians. These families were in the midstages of the family cycle, where their parents were generally in old age and their children in adolescence or early adulthood. Sixty-six elderly Italian Americans were also interviewed, and their reports of supports from their children were compared to those of respondents in middle age.

Based on the assumption that one's family position in old age stems from long-standing family processes, data were also collected on various areas of family life such as kinship activities, patterns of socialization, and family responses to illness and other stressful life events. Focused interviews provided relatively open-ended data which were then "blind" coded and subject to statistical analysis.

In all comparisons between Italians and non-Italians, the older Italians were found to have an elevated status in their families (Johnson, 1979) as measured by the frequent contact with their children and other relatives, the concrete assistance they received, and the respect and esteem given them. In searching for the factors associated with this favored status, both statistical procedures and a content analysis helped to reveal patterns in Italian families which remain distinctive of that group and serve to distinguish them from other elderly.

First, interdependence governs their relationships. By interdependence, I mean the sources of integration which create intimacy, need satisfaction, and group allegiance. It refers to a reciprocal, ongoing *quid pro quo* in family relationships. In contrast to dependence, interdependence connotes a gratification of needs which is not accompanied by guilt or resentment, on one hand, or inordinate passivity or regression, on the other.

Second, authority and power in the family lies in the hands of old over young and males over females. This hierarchy tends to enforce social conformity to family goals and limit the options of its members to seek nonfamilial allegiances. A more absolute value system espousing *respect* reinforces the existing hierarchy.

Third, affect and emotions expansively expressed tend to act as an escape valve to balance out the costs imposed by the authority structure. These feeling states function as oppositional forces between expectations for conformity (the Italian way) versus the need to pursue personal interests (the American way). Thus ambivalence between the traditional and the modern and the "ethnic" and the American can be channeled through socially approved behaviors within the family, making the rejection of the family and its elders less likely.

Before I describe these processes, a brief review of the cultural background of the Italian immigrants is useful in understanding their position today.

BACKGROUND

The antecedents to family solidarity can be traced to the culture of southern Italy, the origin of at least 90 percent of the elderly. In research in Italy, the family is depicted as the core of the social structure and the source of an all-pervading influence over its members. While Banfield's concept of *amoral familism* (1958) has created some confusion in the significance of the extended family vis-à-vis the nuclear family, all literature on the family system in southern Italy points to the conclusion that the family is the fundamental unit of social structure. The important concept of *onore della famiglia* (honor of the family) refers to family solidarity and maintenance of traditions through service, respect, and devotion (Covello, 1972). According to Cronin (1970), the mandate of service to family means "the extent to which the individual—his desires, plans, and ambitions—is subjugated to the interest of the family." Within this cohesive unit, there is little individuality apart from the family, and members are expected to support male authority, sacrifice for the family, respect parents, and avoid bringing shame on the family (Moss and Thompson, 1959). Consequently, there is widespread agreement on the supreme importance of family, the submersion of the individual within the family, limited options for nonfamilial interests, and well-defined means to enforce conformity to family goals.

In the immigrant setting, the family of origin was rarely transplanted in total to this country, yet the tendency of Italians to confine their relationships to primary ones led them to create familylike groupings to buffer the initial hardships. Where few family members were available, the immigrants created fictive kin relations (*compari*) out of *paesani*, fellow townspeople (Juliano, 1973). Hence, their early years in this country were noted for insularity. Virtually all of them were enclosed in the "Little Italies" of urban areas in the Northeast. In this setting, their world was divided into the Italians and the Americans (or "merigans" as their children remember them saying it). Most would agree with Ianni's (1975) father's advice: "Trust family first, relatives second, Sicilians third, and after that, forget it." Probably the only allegiances other than family were the *paesani* and the *compari*. This primary social network provided most immigrants economic, social, and psychological support in place of American institutions, making the effects of assimilation of minimal importance.

Historically, the largest immigration took place after 1890 with the largest numbers arriving in the early years of this century. A large majority, over 80 percent, came from southern Italy; over half were illiterate and few had job skills for urban America where they settled (Lopreato, 1970). The characteristics of the elderly today reflect this background. In a sample of 67 elderly with a mean age of 70 years, 56 percent were born in Italy but the majority of these had immigrated before adulthood. Even though a majority had spent much of their childhood in this country, 70 percent had fewer than eight years education and 20 percent were illiterate. All but four men retired from blue-collar jobs.

Poverty and discrimination characterized the young adulthood of many elderly, for Italian immigrants generally got the hardest, lowest-paying jobs. Our respondents remember the rigorous work well. "We had the dirtiest jobs—the pick and shovel type—we dug your ditches." "We had to fight for everything. Nothing was handed us on a silver platter." "We Italians suffered to make America great. We built your railroads, bridges, highways. We worked like animals and earned very little money." Since the average wages of the day were too low to support a family, women and children had to work as well. Work histories of mothers, however, were sporadic, and as children matured, their earnings replaced those of the mother. Interestingly, Italian women rarely worked as domestics, an occupational choice typical of other immigrant groups (McLaughlin, 1971). In general, when Italian women worked, the jobs available to them were closely identified with their traditional activities, and they rarely went far from home or the watchful eye of the family.

While most men now in old age stayed in blue-collar jobs, their occupational histories show a progressive acquisition of skills. Even with serious setbacks during the depression, today most live in a modest but comfortable retirement. The stories of heroic struggle and hardship are frequently recounted to their children and grandchildren, offering a subtle reminder of the many sacrifices made for the family.

The situation of their children has notably changed when one confines an examination to these structural varibles. The insularity from the larger society is much less prominent. For example, the second-generation offspring who are now in middle age have experienced considerable social mobility with a majority having graduated from high school and over 40 percent in white-collar occupations. Of even greater importance is the high rate of intermarriage where over half of the marriages in the 1950s were with non-Italians. Marital patterns as well as occupational and friendship relationships are as likely to include non-Italians as well as those within the group. The one point of persistence of "Italianness" has to do with the resistance to moving far from the family of origin. Two-thirds of the Italians in middle age still remain within the old Italian neighborhood or adjacent suburbs, making their distance from their parents no more than a short drive away. In this context, the relationship between parent and offspring has the potential to be functionally important, in terms of comprehensive support, as well as socially rewarding.

INTERDEPENDENCE

In the above, I defined interdependence as a style of interpersonal relations where primacy is given to cohesiveness and mutual support within the primary group. It results in a social integration which creates structured intimacy (Kiefer, 1971), need satisfaction, and group allegiances. Within this context, dependence is less likely to be negatively sanctioned at any age, for the family has a socially active group with built-in mechanisms to take care of individuals in need of help. The functioning of such a primary group rests upon high levels of social contact and reciprocity. For example, if a middle-aged man rejects his firm's offer to move to another city and take on a better, higher-paying job because he wants to be able to see relatives often, that is interdependence. If a woman quits her job without complaints to have more time for a sick mother, that is interdependence. If a young adult gives up a peer group activity to attend a family gathering, that is also interdependence.

The Italian elderly are recipients of the benefits, for to them the centrality of family and primary relationships within the ethnic community and insularity from the larger society have changed little over the years. The daily lives of the elderly are filled with interaction with numerous relatives who live nearby and continue long-term patterns of sociability. The mean number of children is 2.6, and a large majority of these children live near the parents. Only two of our respondents or 3 percent have no children in the city or the surrounding suburbs in comparison to 25 percent in Shanas's national study (1973, 1979a, 1979b). In fact, 21 percent share the household with an offspring, while another 34 percent have a child within walking distance (see Table 1). Predictably,

TABLE 1
Percentage of Elderly with at Least One Child in Area (within 30 Minutes by Car)

Italian Americans (n=59)	97%
Polish Americans (n=43)*	82%
National Sample (n=2002)†	73%

*Siemaszko, 1980
†Shanas, 1973

the proximity of children leads to frequent interaction: 76 percent have contact with children within a given 24-hour period, and another 21 percent within the past week. It is really only those who have no children and the two individuals with no children in the area who are deprived of sustained contact and support (Table 2).

Grandchildren are almost as important as children to most of our respondents. In fact, three individuals had a grandchild living with them while the parents lived elsewhere. Thirty

percent of these elderly see a grandchild daily while 89 percent see one at least weekly. The relationship among siblings is also more important than is generally found (Johnson, 1981; Shanas et al., 1968). Sixty-eight percent have at least one brother or sister nearby, and 61 percent see that sibling at least weekly. The elderly see other relatives besides siblings and offspring quite frequently as well. Two-thirds see these other relatives in the area at least weekly. Another source of social contact for the elderly are godchildren, their fictive relatives of long standing. Here it deserves mention that this role remains one of importance for 69 percent of our sample. In fact, godchildren can assume a significance equal to one's own children if one has no children or has children who fail in their duties (Table 2).

A comparison with a national sample (Shanas, 1973, 1979a, 1979b) and a small sample of Polish elderly in Chicago (Siemaszko, 1980) indicates that the link of proximity and frequent contact are characteristic of all elderly. Nevertheless, Italian Americans are considerably more likely to have at least one child in the area and to see that child daily (see Table 2). Several other findings point to the family centrality of Italian Americans. For one thing, almost twice as many Italians than the other groups are likely to see a sibling weekly. Additionally, contact with grandchildren is almost as frequent as that with children. Both incidences point to the breadth of the kinship network where resources extend beyond the parent-child relationship.

Since a majority of our interviews were with middle-aged offspring, it is also possible to determine ethnic differences in their relationships to the elderly parents. Prominent differences were found in several measures which focus on the qualitiative aspects of family interaction (see Table 3).

First, the propensity for an offspring to include elderly parents in the activities of his or her nuclear family indicates not only the frequency but the quality of the social contact. In this respect, in-married Italian Americans are significantly more likely to include elderly parents than are out-married Italian or Protestant families.

Second, attitudes toward the use of a nursing home for a parent are a good indicator of what one would do if faced with the possibility. Almost one-half of both in-married and out-

TABLE 2
Percentage of Contact with Relatives

	Italian Americans (n = 59)	Polish Americans* (n = 43)		National Sample† (n = 2002)	
Children					
Yesterday or today	75.9%	55.8%		65.4%	
2–7 days	20.7	23.3		18.6	
8–30 days	1.7	11.6		6.7	
31 days–one year	1.7	7.0		6.9	
Not in last year	—	2.3		2.4	
	100.0%	100.0%		100.0%	
Sibling	All	Men	Women	Men	Women
In past week	62%	31%	35%	34%	43%
Grandchildren					
In past week	89%	—	—	—	—

*Siemaszko, 1980
†Shanas, 1973

TABLE 3
Family Centrality of Middle-aged Children by Percentage

	In-married Italians (n = 76)	Out-married Italians (n = 98)	Protestant non-Italians (n = 56)	*Significance*
1. Usually incorporate parents in leisure activities	36%	18%	7%	Chi square = 30.782 df6, < .0001
2. Unqualified rejection of nursing home	44%	41%	6%	Chi square = 30.082 df6, < .0001
3. High amount of aid to parents	38%	23%	15%	Chi square = 26.678 df12 < .009

married Italians reject this option outright with no qualification in comparison to 6 percent of the Protestants.

Third, the character and extent of assistance to a parent indicates what one actually does for a parent and by this measure Italian Americans are more than twice as likely to extend more aid frequently.

Table 3 not only indicates significant group differences but also shows how the offsprings' filial behaviors changed with intermarriage, in terms of the propensity to include parents in social activities and to extend aid to them. Clearly, Italian Americans who intermarry decline in the frequency of these measures but nevertheless are significantly more active than the

Protestants. However, intermarried Italians retain those features of the ethnic family which have to do with attitudes toward nursing home placement. They, like their in-married counterparts, are likely to reject the possibility of resorting to such an option. Although we do not know what options these three groups might choose when faced with the actual situation, the value system remains unchanged with intermarriage even though the social involvement with parents diminishes somewhat. These findings suggest that the cultural dimension is an important one to include along with the usual measures of social contact that elderly have with their children.

Although the engagement in activities with family and relatives is higher for Italians than others, there is still considerable variation among our respondents. Examining variables associated with the level of interaction allows us to make several interesting conclusions. For one thing, Italian males and females participate in like fashion in the family networks and do not differ in the degree of isolation or morale. Generally, the greater isolation of men from family over their work life often can have a cumulative effect by retirement and result in an inability to reenter the lives of children and other kin once time becomes available. The evidence indicates that this pattern does not apply to Italian-American men, which suggests that their lifelong activity pattern has focused on family, a situation that continues in old age. Although the Italian father is often a somewhat distant authority figure in his younger years, his power and authority become eroded in old age, probably much to his own advantage in terms of his relationships within the family.

Another significant variable is that of age itself. Those over 75 are more socially isolated even though no one is without any major person to provide supports (t=2.22, p < .05). These "old old" Italians are more likely to be widowed, a factor also associated with increased social isolation. Evidently, the lifelong activity pattern of avoiding social contacts outside the family and circle of primary relationships has made it more difficult to compensate for role losses when a spouse dies. Forming new friendships or devising new activities outside the family in order to keep involved are alien activities to these elderly. Hence, even when one remains actively involved with children, grandchildren, and siblings, there is shrinkage in the social environment because of a decline in other contacts.

Measures of acculturation are also important variables affecting the life situation of Italian elderly. Place of birth or the designation of generation level significantly affects the situation of the elderly but not in the predicted direction. Those who were born in this country and had greater exposure to American institutions have a more active family life than the immigrants (t=2.45, p < .02). This social involvement was particularly evident in kinship measures where American-born Italians report more contact. Language usage, or the level of fluency in English,

likewise also indicates acculturation. Those who are fluent in English have more social contact with relatives than those who speak only Italian (t=2.64, p < .02). Thus, ease of communication with children and kin apparently increases their integration into family activities, just as the second-generation elderly Italians are likely to hold values more compatible to those of their children. In other words, some acculturation appears to enhance rather than detract from the status of the elderly. I shall return to this point in a later section.

With this family centrality of most older Italians, there is continuity in old age. For elderly women, motherhood and attendant domestic roles change in intensity, but do not lose their centrality, for as grandmothers, their nurturing functions continue. For the men, usually patriarchal immigrants, the loss of the work role does not usually mean the loss of the central role, since family was always considered more important. Instead, the absence of the work role allows for the intensification of family involvement. An elderly Italian-American man with a small pension, social security, and perhaps an apartment upstairs, can easily provide for his wife and have enough resources remaining to make gifts to his children and grandchildren. If he is healthy, he continues to work for his family in some capacity such as gardening, carpentry, or odd jobs, which makes him feel important and useful and increases family interdependence. Hence, the Italian family has relatively flexible boundaries around the various age strata. Since parenting roles continue well into adult life, they are more readily blurred into grandparenting roles without sharp breaks and discontinuity as one moves from middle to old age.

The typical day of a highly engaged 68-year-old woman illustrates a fairly typical life situation. Mrs. Lansini has been widowed for 36 years and retired for eight years as a clerk in her father-in-law's fruit stand. At the time of the interview, she worked for a few hours daily in her sister's grocery store. Although she lives alone, her daughter and family live in an upstairs apartment, and they share their meals with her. Her other three children are within a five-minute ride. She sees them all almost daily. Her seven grandchildren are continually dropping by. Her eleven siblings live in the city, and she sees most of them weekly. She also spends time each day "babysitting" for a neighbor who is ill.

Another example, Mr. Corsello, a retired carpenter, said his days are completely taken up with family involvement. Since retirement, he "takes care of" 13 members of his family, meaning that he makes rounds from nine in the morning until nine at night, touching base with all close kin. When he mentioned the possibility of a son leaving the area, he described how he would handle it:

There's no reason why I won't see him. As long as I have two legs, two arms, and two eyes. With two legs, I can go to him. With two eyes, I can see him. If I ain't got eyes, I can feel him, so I know he's there.

All these examples indicate that long-standing supports extended in old age cannot be suddenly developed when the need arises. Instead, the long tradition of help patterns more readily provides continuity in social support in the last stage of the life cycle. Townsend comes to a similar conclusion, "Once weakened, family relationships are difficult to renew or repair; they need to be regularly reinforced—like conditioned reflexes" (Shanas et al., 1968: 173). The evidence is clear that Italian Americans do have the mechanisms to reinforce the bond between family members.

AUTHORITY AND POWER: COVERT AND OVERT CONTROLS

A convincing argument can be made that those families which place a high value on hierarchical arrangements are in a position to exert more influence over their members. Where high priority is placed upon family interests, the controls over individuals can be geared to family interests and goals. Such family systems, however, are incongruent with the American value system, so exerting such controls runs the risk of rebellion by the younger members and possibly rejection of the family. Since rejection of traditional hierarchies receives high consensus by the wider society, young members would be

rewarded by external standards and in the process establish a wider reference group with values possibly incongruent to their family.

Italian elderly seem to have solved this problem by using both overt and covert systems of control. The overt system of control begins in early childhood when physical punishment was the primary means to enforce parental wishes. Many middle-aged offspring recount techniques which by modern judgment border upon cruelty. In their childhood, infractions were addressed swiftly and directly by physical means as well as by strict supervision. From the perspective of middle age, however, their memories are not always negative; in fact discipline techniques are often linked to family solidarity.

Respondents identified *respect* as the value most descriptive of the Italian family at its best. The term connotes a hierarchy where egalitarian norms, although sometimes given lip service, are not often translated into behaviors. The parents, especially the father, are in a superior position from which they demand obedience from their children. These clearly demarcated roles call for parents to be parents and not to act like brothers, sisters, or friends to their children. Although there has been an erosion of patriarchal values which give the men and the elderly considerable power over women and children, there remain well-developed patterns of authority which continue to regulate behavior. Since respect within a family is linked to discipline by traditional "old-fashioned ways," physical punishment remains today a major means of instilling respect, particularly with small children.

Respect is used as a catch-all term to conceptualize family responsibilities. This directive includes duty and service to family at the expense of personal interests. Respect is also equated with love, in that one cannot extend or receive love without the accompaniment of respect. Generally respect is viewed as an ascribed component of family roles; it does not have to be earned. Furthermore, it has a reciprocal aspect; one respects parents in order to gain their respect in turn. At the behavioral level, respect colors most relationships within the family and is seen as the underpinning of countless favors and services one extends and the esteem one conveys to others.

By the time they are in old age, the parents' reminders to children of their obligations can take the form of extolling the value of *respect* rather than through explicit exhortations. Since the hierarchy in the family has always been explicitly defined and usually advocated by their offspring, the parents in old age can turn to less direct, covert means to reinforce family interdependence.

SELF-SACRIFICE AS A CONTROL DEVICE

One covert technique centers upon the mechanism of *self-sacrifice*, which can be an effective device to exert control over children. Repeated storytelling of the early years with their many struggles and hardships has entertained family gatherings for years. Feeding a family for a few cents a day, fathers walking to work to save a few pennies, mothers doing piecework for the "needle trades" well past midnight are among the innumerable examples mentioned. The point is usually made that despite almost impossible odds, the offspring realize that the family remained intact through heroic struggles of their parents and thus was not subject to the disorganization characteristic of other immigrant groups (Johnson, 1978).

Parents then are assigned an elevated status in a major sense because of these past sacrifices. The ultimate sacrifice was bringing one into the world. Repayment for one's existence is only one link in a long line of sacrifices:

My mother brought us into the world and cared for us. She was only concerned with our good. She never spoiled us, but told us what was right. She always said, "Please don't disgrace me." We never did and now we lead good lives. She was an important part of our lives. How could we put her in a nursing home when she sacrificed for us?

Very few Italian-American offspring cited explicit norms to describe the relationship. Many objected to our use of the term *obligation*, because it meant "having to do it," rather than "wanting to do it." One common identification of the source of their filial behavior was the continuation of a process that had never been put into words.

"Italians have been programmed for it," said a respondent. While they might also mention the idea of sacrifice, a few admitted to their devotion as a means of avoiding guilt. "It's the old-fashioned way of Mama and all she's done for me." "It's easier to sleep nights knowing that I'm doing all I can." "They never ordered us to do anything, but you can see the hurt in their eyes if you don't." "My parents are so good to us that I have to hold my tongue." "How can I reject her when she cries if I don't call her every day?"

A DUAL VALUE SYSTEM

While elderly parents extoll the virtues of traditionalism, for all practical purposes they also express a set of values more congruent with American culture. This dichotomy indicates that they have made many concessions to American culture and in doing so are using indirect means to retain their status. When asked, "What do you expect from your children?" only one respondent reported having expectations for total care and support from their children. Almost one-half expected only companionship or help in the event of an emergency while a surprising 34 percent stated that they expected nothing from their children. As we will see below, however, the espousal of the value of independence does not mean that in actuality expectations for children are absent, or for that matter that parents live independent lives.

Sharing a household with a child is also not widely endorsed; 78 percent of the respondents not currently living with an offspring said they would not consider such an alternative. To most of our respondents, the ideal situation was to maintain one's own home near one's children, but not to be in the same household. Most older Italians do not see the need to voice explicit expectations, because they know they will not be forgotten by well-reared children.

I don't expect a thing from them. What they do for me and their father they do because they have love and respect for us. They know how we have worked hard all our lives to give them the best we could.

Essentially, the assurance that one has raised

children to show respect and affection allows elderly parents to be staunch defenders of their own independence, even though most elderly were dependent upon their children for at least some of their social needs.

I explained earlier that the measures of acculturation, generation level, and language usage are important factors affecting the life situation of the elderly Italian Americans. The more acculturated have significantly more interaction with relatives. However, like good Americans, they highly value their independence; they do not want to be a burden on anyone. One respondent described the process as "bending a little," which means making concessions to new values and behaviors however much they are at odds with the old-fashioned way. If younger members of the family have rejected the code, the elderly, of course, disapprove, but they usually place the blame on an outside force in society, a fatelike force that no one can control. Obviously, such a moderate stance minimizes conflict and assures them a continued position in the family.

Such commendable behaviors, however, do not mean that other expectations do not operate at the covert level. The absence of explicit expectations—"you are duty-bound to take care of me"—does not mean that these expectations are absent. Lifelong socialization patterns have been geared to produce filial offspring. If sons or daughters forgot, mothers were frequently reported to use nonverbal techniques such as sighs of despair. Elderly parents have also been known to dwell upon friends who were "abandoned" by their children. "Look at them—they can't even take care of their own parents." "What did she do to raise such ungrateful children?" Probably half of the respondents asked rhetorically, "How is it that one mother can raise eight (or 10 or 12) children and these eight children can't take care of one mother?" Another comment frequently heard over a lifetime is, "A child is your cane in old age." Tears could flow when one was recounting the abuses of ungrateful children.

It is evident that those who modify traditional values of southern Italy do so to their own advantage in retaining a good relationship with their children. The combination of the factors already discussed facilitate a cohesive bond: Respect has been thoroughly instilled; parental sacrifices define an implicit set of expectations;

and compromises to American culture ameliorate some of the costs of filial responsibilities. Such techniques go hand in hand with an active extended family system which functions for the purposes of sociability irrespective of the instrumental functions it must serve. In other words, the cohesiveness between the elderly and their children is repeatedly reinforced through frequent social contact.

EMOTIONAL ESCAPE VALVES

The preceding discussion emphasized the strong pressures on individuals to conform to family interests. Certainly, the middle-aged children of today's elderly Italians are also products of American culture and thus cannot ignore its major values which are at odds with the ones described here (Stone, 1978). As a result, the traditional values of their parents are viewed with some ambivalence, for they are considered incongruent with achievement in the larger society. Many interviews prominently featured these inconsistencies: "The parents smother us— they won't let go" or "They cling to us—we would have made more of ourselves if it weren't for our attachment to them." These same interviews, however, also extoll the virtues of the Italian family and the security and support it provides.

These contradictions center upon what Yanigasako (1978) calls a dual conceptual scheme: duty versus feeling, constriction versus freedom, group interests versus personal interests, and dependence upon family versus independence. Although potentially conflictual, the resolution of these contradictions and the ambivalence stemming from it appear to be facilitated by the management of emotions in Italian families. Pressures can be reduced through the tolerance for, or even encouragement to express one's feelings; venting feelings of love and attachment as well as rage and anger is quite acceptable (Vicoli, 1979). For most Italians neutrality in regard to family is considered an American characteristic when contrasted to the Italian style of interpersonal relationships. The fact that the expression of both negative and positive feelings is quite acceptable gives individuals considerable leeway at the behavioral level no matter how absolute the values are on respect and social conformity. In fact, criticisms can be a source of humor and comic relief where one can poke fun at practices in which all are deeply involved. Such practices can function as an escape valve when family responsibilities become too much.

The resulting ideology of the families is a study of opposites, often in basic contradiction. These opposites are examined and filtered through a dual normative system. The paradoxes are recognized and accepted, and choices are made which usually give precedence to one without totally suppressing the other. If choices are made which are at odds with family values, these can be justified on the basis of emotions as long as they are only temporary infractions.

For example, respect has been described as a catch-all concept usually used to explain the positive features of the family: "Italian families work well because there is respect." However valued, respect does not mean one must suffer silently in the face of some personal affront. One can even challenge a parent and freely ventilate feelings. Yet the respect is not seen as being diluted, because the parent understands it is merely a show of emotions which does not change the quality of the relationship.

A second theme is that of forgiveness. Despite clearly defined values on family obligations, most Italian Americans accept another family member irrespective of his or her behavior. They might complain and argue with the deviant member and hope for the desired result; however, if that fails, they are more likely to eventually desist and live with the consequences. For example, Mrs. Nappa's brother had been in trouble with the police and had never completely reformed, yet he was never rejected for he is not to blame. "He has always had bad friends," she explained.

In other words, Italians are pragmatic when dealing with the personalities of individuals. In this ideology, behavior is traced to the uncontrollable forces of emotion. Consequently, this expression of what are initially viewed as absolute values, such as respect, sacrifice, and devotion to the family, actually is juxtaposed with their polar opposites. Because of the vagaries of human nature, idealized conceptions of family are modulated by realistic assessment of the situation.

This duality provides a hedge against acting upon these values; an "out" is provided if idealistic goals cannot be fulfilled. The result of this pragmatic orientation essentially means that family expectations are generally met, because there is a sliding scale of expectations where individuals should strive to meet family goals. If he or she fails, the individual is accepted as he or she is, and any blame to be assigned is traced to the uncontrollable forces of emotions or to the immutable elements of the environment.

CONCLUSION

This paper has broadly outlined those dimensions of the Italian-American family which enhance the position of its elderly members. I have attempted to draw a distinction between a structural analysis and a cultural analysis. In the former, one finds many points of similarity between Italian families and others where traditional values are being eroded by assimilation and acculturation. On the contrary, a cultural analysis centering on values and how they are expressed in the day-to-day interaction within the family indicates the preservation of some features of the Italian family which most likely are ethnically determined. The evidence is convincing that the elderly occupy a high status in their family both in the high regard they receive and the frequent involvement they have with their children and other relatives. In comparisons to other groups (Shanas, 1973; Bengtson and Morgan, this volume), they are more embedded in family life. Since the family has occupied a central place in their lives at the expense of other associations, continuities in roles in old age are the prominent pattern. The pervasive interdependence among family members provides a setting which confers status even when middle-age determinants of status are no longer available to these elderly.

In an explanation of this impressive evidence of familism, I have turned to the value system for some insight into the sources of this solidarity. One set of values, mainly traditional ones, center upon the tight rein of authority and the enforcement of conformity through a strong emphasis upon respect, altruism, and self-sacrifice. These values can act in contradiction to the American culture, creating ambivalence. As an ameliorating mechanism, however, much flexibility in behavior is tolerated through socially approved means in the freedom of emotional expression.

From a cross-cultural perspective it seems apparent that a hierarchy which confers authority and power to the elderly is an important prerequisite for an elevated status in old age (Cowgill and Holmes, 1972). However, when this situation is incongruent with a parallel value system, as it is in American culture, some mechanisms must resolve the ambivalence. We have seen that Italian Americans use the management of emotions to grant individuals some leeway while still retaining expectations for family cohesiveness.

Other ethnic groups might exhibit different mechanisms to maintain family cohesiveness. For example, Japanese Americans resemble Italians in their allegiances to their parents, their family interdependence, and their hierarchical authority structure (Johnson, 1977; Osako, 1979). They differ markedly, however, in the management of emotion through suppression rather than expression of its overt form. Nevertheless, family bonds do not necessarily diminish with later generations (Johnson, 1976), for acculturation in the form of value change among both Japanese and Italians appears to create a greater consensus between generations, a situation which makes family membership less conflictual. Perhaps rather than associating change in ethnic groups with the American family model, it is time to examine how some acculturation facilitates rather than impedes family centrality. This paper points to the importance of the cultural dimension where selected factors are singled out as principles of organization, the net results of which are significant group differences. Such distinctions can perhaps give us new insights on the status of the elderly in various subgroups and in the process tell us much in regard to the sources of ethnic revivalism so prominent today.

Nina Nahemow

GRANDPARENTHOOD AMONG THE BAGANDA: ROLE OPTION IN OLD AGE?

With the use of a large-scale questionnaire survey, Nahemow examines how a particular family role, that of grandparent, affects the status and perception of the aged among the Baganda of Africa (in Uganda). In other preindustrial African societies residential concentration and control of scarce resources by the elders fosters high levels of interdependence and power-laden roles for the grandparental generation. In contrast, Baganda values stress independence and individual achievement over familism. Their practices of neolocal residence and a type of agriculture requiring little labor beyond the nuclear family do not particularly favor older people in high status roles. Nahemow makes the important point that while such traits are thought to be concomitant with the transition to highly industrialized, urban societies, they are *traditional* features of the Baganda sociocultural system.

The resultant grandparental roles among the Baganda are consistent with those found in societies where the aged do not retain an authoritarian and dominant role in the family or the community. The Baganda practice a "formal-distant" style of grandparenting, which combines a lack of concern for being a "parent surrogate" with a desire to gain emotional joy without the burdens of child care. Thus, the Baganda grandparental roles are found to be similar to those reported for the United States.

IN WESTERN INDUSTRIAL SOCIETIES old people seldom play dominant roles in the major social institutions. This lack of power and status has been interpreted as resulting from the modernization process which undermined those traditional roles and sources of status not tied to specific economic functions. It is becoming apparent, however, that there have been preindustrial societies in which the aged did not enjoy great official authority and high status merely as a function of their age (Haynes, 1962; Levine, 1965; Harlan, 1968; Arth, 1972; Cowgill, 1972; Press and McKool, 1972). Regardless of the impact of modernization on the position of the aged in the past, it is clear that today older people generally do not have high status. As the population in the United States ages and the problems of the aged multiply, gerontologists are increasingly looking to familial roles as a source of both social participation and status.

This article will examine the extent to which one such family role, grandparenthood, affects participation and status of the elderly. Since there is confusion in the literature concerning the impact of industrialization on both societal and family roles, it is instructive to compare the position of the aged in societies at different levels of development. Specifically we will examine the role of the aged in a traditional society, the Baganda of Uganda, with that of a more industrialized society, the United States. This will increase our understanding of both the impact of modernization and the function of the grandparent role.

Although little systematic work has been done in the area of grandparenthood in traditional societies, Radcliffe-Brown's discussion of social structure based on relations between the generations provides us with a good starting point. He notes that "between two proximate generations

This essay was specially prepared for this book by the author. Permission to reprint must be obtained from the author and publisher.

the relationship is normally one of essential inequality, authority and protective care on the one side, respect and dependence on the other. But between the two generations of grandparents and grandchildren the relation is a contrasting one of 'friendly familiarity' and near equality" (Radcliffe-Brown, 1967:30). This pattern, which he says applies to the Baganda, suggests that respect and obedience are not solely a matter of relative age. It also underscores the absence of institutionalized authority relations between grandparent and grandchild as well as the presence of the indulgent grandparent role.

Sweetser's study of preindustrial and traditional societies (1956) confirmed the hypothesis that friendly familiarity between grandparents and grandchildren was associated with the absence of grandparental authority within the family and the society as a whole. She found that old people performed one of two roles in the family power structure depending on their status in the larger society: Where the aged remained in control of scarce resources in the larger society, they continued to play a dominant and authoritarian role in the family; where they no longer had control over such resources, they retained little formal authority within the family and played a more indulgent, easygoing role. The role of the aged in industrial societies such as the United States follows the latter pattern in that the elderly in America generally do not have a monopoly over scarce resources and they seldom exercise direct authority within the family.

These structural conditions in the United States foster a situation in which the content of family roles may take on added meaning, especially in terms of continued social integration. In fact, there is considerable evidence that the quality of life for the aged is in large part dependent on the nature of their relations with kin. As their social world shrinks and their mobility becomes somewhat circumscribed, there is increased reliance on kin as a source of emotional and, in some cases, economic support. Based on a review of the research on kinship, Adams (1980) characterizes the relationship between parents and their adult offspring as one of "positive concern." This is manifested by frequent contact—at least weekly where kin are proximate. A second aspect is substantial mutual aid which flows generally

from parents to offspring though the direction may change as aged parents become physically and/or financially dependent. Lastly, it is characterized by a strong affectional tie and a secondary obligatory element. These and other studies throughout the 1960s and 1970s have failed to support the thesis that the isolated nuclear family is normative (Shanas, 1979a; Adams, 1971; Sussman, 1965a). It is generally accepted that the nuclear unit is integrated with some members of the larger kin network. This modified extended family, based on choice rather than obligation, typifies family structure in the United States today. The frequency and content of the active parent role has, in turn, implications for relations with grandchildren. Gilford and Black (1972) report that the grandparent-grandchild relationship is contingent on the intervening parent-child bond, especially when they are residentially distant. However, regardless of separation, if grandparents and their adult offspring have close ties, they and their grandchildren are likely to be important to each other. Along these lines, Kahana and Kahana (1971) argue that one of the few social roles potentially available to American aged is that of grandparenthood, and they point out that approximately 75 percent of older Americans do have living grandchildren.

Having noted the potential importance of the grandparental role in the United States, we will now examine the nature of this role among the aged Baganda, a traditional society albeit influenced by the modern world, and comparisons will be made with grandparenthood in the United States. Our goal is to ascertain the viability of grandparenthood as a source of interaction and gratification in the lives of the aged and specify whether the level of societal development has any major effect on the structure of this role.

METHODOLOGY

To describe the significance of grandparenthood in traditional Baganda society we have relied on ethnographic materials from a variety of sources and data from two social surveys carried out in 1971 as a part of a larger Ugandan study. The data consist of a questionnaire study of secondary school students and intensive interviews with 115 Baganda between the ages of 60 and 90. The student subsample dealt with in the present analysis comprised the 1,699 Baganda secondary school students between the ages of 12 and 21 (1,015 males and 684 females). Each was asked to recall when he or she was in the fifth grade (P5) and to discuss relations with one grandmother and one grandfather who were living at that time. The rationale is that since we were dealing with students of different ages it was necessary to establish some common baseline to which they would all refer.

The interviews with elderly Baganda themselves introduced several problems: establishing the respondent's age, determining chronological and role parameters for the term *elderly*, using a tribal language, and assuring a representative sample. Although Ugandans have not traditionally kept track of years or of people's ages, the recorded reigns of rulers allowed us to calculate the respondents' approximate ages.

More troublesome was the lack of a common definition about who the elderly are. There is a tendency for the aged to define old age as somewhat older than they believe themselves to be. Thus an elderly respondent who believes herself to be 67 is likely to consider old age as 75 or older; if she is—or thinks she is—80, she is likely to say that old age begins when one reaches 90. A substantial proportion of the sample chose, however, to define old age not in terms of the number of years lived but rather cited physical attributes such as baldness, grey hair, wrinkles, poor eyesight, walking with a stick, bent over, and generally those changes which are commonly associated with aging. In determining old age the respondents also included the assuming of a broad range of roles, such as grandparent and retired person, as well as rights, obligations, and duties such as "no longer paying taxes" and "being respected" and weaknesses such as "can only do menial work," "forgetful," "doing childish things," and "useless talk."

Our definition thus evolved into a composite of age (on which many aged respondents were quite vague), being a grandparent, and certain physical manifestations. The latter, however, was used only when the prospective respondent did not know his or her age and was omitted as

"looking too young." Notwithstanding the shortcomings of age measurements, we estimated that the average age of the 66 males was 67 while that of the 49 females was 73. Within broad limits very old age to these people is around 70 with the actual onset of old age beginning some 15 or more years earlier.

Language was a problem because few of the respondents spoke English. The interviews were therefore conducted in Luganda. This entailed translating the schedule from English to Luganda and then translating the responses back into English. Such translations were checked for accuracy and equivalence by two university graduate students who were fluent in both languages. In addition, it was deemed preferable to have Baganda interviewers to minimize any possibility of reserve or ethnic rivalry.

Assuring a representative sample of older Baganda was less difficult because the predominantly rural character of Ugandan society makes it relatively homogenous. According to the 1969 Ugandan census, of the country's 9½ million people only 5 percent lived in urban centers and many of these retained rural ties. Furthermore, although relatively few Baganda live in towns, most travel to and from the towns with enough regularity to be familiar with urban conditions (M. Fallers, 1960). The occupational distribution of elderly respondents is as follows: 38 percent cultivators, 19 percent housewives, 19 percent skilled workers, 12 percent white-collar, and 12 percent unskilled workers. The majority of respondents, however, included cultivating as a component of their work even if it was not the primary aspect. Thus the sample is more occupationally homogeneous than the figures suggest. Of the 97 who responded only 9 percent are retired or report doing nothing now. The remainder are either doing the same work they have always done (65 percent) or some light cultivating, trading, or housework (26 percent).

Thus, in our description of Baganda society we are working with three data sources: ethnographic reports, questionnaires from students, and interviews with the elderly. Where they diverge we cannot be sure that the results are not a function of differing techniques of collection. However, where they are consistent our confidence in the results is heightened by the very diversity of sources.

CULTURAL BACKGROUND

The ethnic group under investigation is the Baganda who comprise 25 percent of the Ugandan population and traditionally have been dominant politically. They live in the fertile south central region of Uganda and enjoy both an ideal climate and a dependable food supply. These factors have especially important implications for the status of the aged because it means that as long as they are physically able to care for themselves they can remain independent and self-sufficient. A Bantu-speaking people, the Baganda are eclectic and for centuries have adapted their way of life to changing conditions. While they have a patrilineal kinship system, they generally maintain nuclear family households and the generations are often residentially segregated by considerable distances.

The flexibility of the Baganda is not unique among preindustrial societies. The Ibo of Nigeria have a similar value structure. According to Shelton (1972:31), they are hard working, intelligent, ambitious, value individual achievements, and have a ready acceptance of social and cultural change. Like the Baganda, they are agricultural, but the social organizations of these two peoples differ markedly. The Ibo lack a centralized government, and political power is solely in the hands of village elders. Patrilineal descent and patrilocal residence serve to underscore both the control that older men have over property and their generally higher social status.

The gerontocracy of the Sidamo of Ethiopia (Hamer, 1972) offers another interesting contrast. Patrilineal clans linked together by generational classes make them more similar in their social organization to the Ibo. The Sidamo conceive of power in terms of control over land and cattle, and the aged hold a monopoly over these resources. While all three have a norm associating venerable old age with prestige, the actual status and power which accrue to the aged appear more a function of control over property than age per se. The aged among the Ibo and the Sidamo have that control as well as the status and power which go with it. Since aged Baganda tend not to exercise such control, their position vis-à-vis other aged groups is not as secure.

Baganda values and norms "fit" fairly easily into the modern world. They have traditionally emphasized independence and individual achievement above familism, a value structure similar to that of the United States. An important cultural factor to be emphasized is the Baganda identification with progress; their traditions value and foster change. The dominant features of their social organization—which include (1) a weak patrilinealism, (2) individualism, (3) achievement orientation, (4) neolocality, and (5) political hierarchy—facilitate this adaptation to external changes. Gibbs (1965) notes that Baganda agriculture does not require the cooperation of people outside the single household, and as cash crops become increasingly important, the Baganda tend to hire tenants rather than relying on kin. L. Fallers (1965:142) reports that, in the modern world, the Baganda continue to be on the "cutting edge" of achievement and change. The Baganda, he says, "do, of course, participate in a money economy to a degree which is relatively unusual for East Africans and they generally value the goods and services which this participation provides. But the incentive for most is the 'carrot' of the essentially luxury goods which the proceeds from their cotton and coffee will buy, not the 'goad' of actual privation or landlessness . . . ." Another reason for the acceptance of change may be the lack of an abrupt shift between rural and urban values in Baganda society. Even in Kampala, the major urban area and capital of Uganda, those who enter the wage labor force are able to maintain ties with their rural roots by either commuting daily or weekend visiting (M. Fallers, 1960).

Similar to most traditional societies, the division of labor among the Baganda has been on the basis of sex and to a lesser extent on age. With regard to the sexual division of labor, Gibbs reports that:

In the old days men took little part in agriculture, since their only task was the clearing of new land, not frequently required; men built houses, made bark clothes, hunted and in some places fished. But much of their time was spent in attendance on the chief and waiting for the call to go to war, or to labor on public works. Today men are considered responsible for earning cash, usually by cultivating cash crops . . . . Most men put in an average of about four hours work a day, and spend much of their free time in drinking banana beer, or even brewing it. Women, with their domestic duties as well as their work in the food gardens, have less free time (Gibbs, 1965:106).

In terms of the division of labor based on age, the pattern is not nearly as clear-cut. According to all the ethnographic reports, old people played ceremonial roles with births and marriage, but while these roles reflected some status little or no power accrued to them. Their daily activities, like those of the Ibo, can best be described as continuity from the past at a reduced level (Arth, 1972). An earlier paper (Nahemow and Adams, 1974) sought to confirm whether the Baganda aged had any specific roles to play. When asked, "Do old people have any special position or do different things *just because they are old?*" Fifty-one percent of the students and 56 percent of the aged responded that old people do not hold any special position. When students see the aged as playing a specific role, they often see it as a weak one. That is, more students speak of the old as doing only light work, sitting around smoking or drinking or behaviorally manifesting senility, rather than acting in a positive way as adviser, storyteller, official, or object of respect. Among our respondents, it appears that expectations with regard to the position of the aged are consistent across the generations, the majority seeing them as having no speical position at all and a sizable minority of these viewing them negatively. Only a few see the aged as either officials or advisers. The license for increased leisure pursuits and lighter work loads, while important from the student's perspective, is seen as less of a boon by the old people themselves. Both samples view respect and obedience as a component of old age, but this is more the case among the aged respondents. Based on Arth's analysis, it seems that like the Ibo, the Baganda pay lip service to the ideal of respect for old people but it is in reality of less salience to the young.

While preconceptions based on the bulk of literature dealing with the position of the aged in traditional societies would have led us to expect the aged Baganda to hold a variety of lineage and administrative positions, as well as ceremonial roles, this is not borne out by either the data or the specific ethnographic reports. That is, given their infrequent official involvement as clan

leaders in the past and the devaluation of their advising and storytelling skills for the challenges of contemporary life, the position of the aged Baganda *vis-à-vis* other age groups in society has come to be even further reduced. The most significant difference, then, in terms of how each generation views the special status of the aged is in the area of respect. Already we see emerging among the young a divergent view of old age even from what was portrayed in the literature, though there is reason to believe that the ethnographies reported ideal-type behavior especially in this realm. It appears that the young did not automatically associate advanced years with respect and high status. In a society where a merit system has traditionally operated, and success is rewarded, one must always be able to prove oneself. Rewards did not accrue solely for past accomplishments, they hinged on future achievements as well; this was and continues to be part of the culture. Apparently the young see their elders' potential in this area as considerably foreshortened. This does not necessarily imply that old people are estranged from the larger community, but it seems that the age-based division of labor does not particularly favor older people in terms of high status roles in the larger society. It now remains to be seen whether they play significant roles in the family sphere.

FINDINGS AND RESULTS

In an attempt to assess the salience of grandparenthood as a role alternative in old age we will begin by looking at the way in which the young view their grandparents and then examine the implications of this for intergenerational relations. We will examine some of the constraints and limitations on interaction that are a function of traditional residence patterns and then turn to network involvement with kin, focusing on the daily activities of the aged grandparents. Finally, the analysis will focus on the behavioral manifestations of the grandparent-grandchild relationship with special emphasis on the activities and tasks the two do with each other as well as the manner in which respect is demonstrated.

Grandparents were viewed by the majority (90

percent) of the student sample as kind, calm, loving, and gentle. This nurturant role was perceived as existing for both sexes equally. In addition, about 60 percent of the students said that their grandparents, particularly their grandfathers, were funny and/or talkative. This was certainly consistent with the storytelling function performed by many grandparents. Also, 62 percent of the students reported that their grandparents were friends. We have, then, a picture of a warm, close relationship between the respondents and the grandparents they chose to discuss.

Before developing this picture of the grandparent-grandchild relationship, it is necessary to specify the geographical constraints on interaction. Older people did not live as near their children as one might have expected in a still predominantly rural society. Asked about their grandparents' residence, the secondary school students indicated that they were slightly more likely to live close to their fathers' rather than their mothers' parents. The magnitude of differences, however, was not significant. Of more importance is the fact that the majority of both sets of grandparents lived in a different village, generally over 15 miles away. This was not a great distance in areas where public transportation was available at a modest cost, but the journeys were nevertheless time-consuming and were therefore not undertaken too frequently.

Old people, asked whether or not such residential separation was customary, indicated that the ideal living arrangement was separate from their children. In fact, 99 percent of the aged said that it is wrong and/or untraditional to live with one's children. Asked why one might live with a son or daughter, approximately 43 percent of the old people stated that extenuating circumstances such as illness, danger, or helplessness might make it necessary to live on the same homestead or next door to one's adult offspring. This could not be in the same house with a married daughter, owing to the rules of avoidance (Mair, 1934:92–93). It should be noted that in the United States independent living is also normative. But aged Americans, similar to their Baganda counterparts, seem willing to violate this norm when illness and/or economic necessity make it unfeasible to live separately.

In examining the daily tasks performed by the elderly, we find that housekeeping and cultivating are largely managed by the older couples, with the woman carrying a heavier burden in both cases. Consistent with the Baganda system of residential separation, kin provide little household labor. For example, 55 percent of the grandmothers clean their own homes and 61 percent do the cultivating, though kin and/or servants do help.

In most households when grandchildren are present (n = 460), they are called on to perform minor tasks and run errands for their grandparents, though grandmothers tend to rely on them somewhat more than do grandfathers. For example, shopping involves the tedium of long walks to purchase a pound of sugar or a loaf of bread, and for the most part grandchildren are sent on such errands. Thus, while the adult offspring often provide the money, the grandchildren frequently do the actual purchasing. Another case in point involves the fetching of water. Though the water supply is sometimes close at hand, it often has to be hauled from communal boreholes or wells, and this task, usually in the female realm, also falls largely to the grandchildren.

The pattern that emerges, then, is fairly clear: Roles are essentially sex-segregated with women handling domestic affairs and men being dominant in the cash-economic realm; this division of labor is further defined on the basis of age. The aged couple tend, whenever possible, to do for themselves in day-to-day household activities. The modal pattern for tasks which require money or leaving home is largely one of assistance by adult offspring in the more important areas, followed by dependence on grandchildren for errands such as shopping and fetching water, when the latter are nearby. Thus, grandchildren assist grandparents with menial tasks which demand some endurance yet have little intrinsic reward. Where their assistance is not available, servants and female relatives fill the void for the least interesting chores, and male relatives play a somewhat more active role for the others.

In looking at the specific relationship between the student when he was in the fifth grade and his grandparents (see Table 1), we find that about 80 percent of the grandchildren shared common activities with their grandparents. A sizable portion of both grandparents seem to serve as companions in leisure activities, such as storytell-

TABLE 1
Activities Performed by Males and Females with Each Grandparent

	Grandfather		Grandmother	
	Males (n=430)	Females (n=303)	Males (n=525)	Females (n=362)
Nothing	20.5%	22.8%	26.5%	14.4%
Hunting	23.5	12.5	20.0	22.1
Storytelling	21.6	31.4	12.4	21.0
Presents	17.2	15.8	15.2	16.9
Duties	2.6	4.0	11.6	12.4
Advice	4.4	3.3	4.2	3.9
Talked	2.6	3.0	3.2	2.8
Comfort	1.4	.3	2.3	—
Other	6.3	6.9	4.6	6.6
Total	100.1%	100.0%	100.0%	100.1%

ing and singing, or in subsistence activities, such as food collecting, hunting, and cattle herding. Specifically, the grandfather is both storyteller and food collector with his grandsons, but he is rarely more than storyteller with his granddaughters. The grandmother is sometimes a food-collecting companion for grandsons and granddaughters and, while grandmothers are less often storytellers than their spouses, they still tend to perform this role with granddaughters and to a lesser extent with grandsons. Of all the cross-sex relationships, males and their grandmothers tended to have the least to do with each other.

While it was clear that duties and tasks done around the house are not the primary activities shared, it should be noted that grandchildren are almost four times as likely to do such things with or for their grandmothers as with or for their grandfathers. This supports the finding reported earlier that grandmothers tend to rely slightly more heavily than do grandfathers on their grandchildren for assistance and underscores the greater burden women carry in this society.

When the sample of old people were asked about their activity pattern with their grandchildren, we found that grandparenthood is not an option for a sizable minority. Twenty-nine percent report no living children (15 percent of the males and 39 percent of the females) as compared to one-quarter of aged Americans. Of those Baganda who have grandchildren, fully 60

percent do nothing with them, but more than half of the grandparents attributed this to their grandchildren either living too far away or being too young. Of those with living offspring, 30 percent are still in the active parent stage of the family life cycle with adult unmarried children at home. Hence the relatively low level of shared activities reported by the aged sample does not necessarily preclude subsequent interaction. In fact, data from the young people's sample would suggest that indeed when children are older there can be considerable interaction.

Since interaction with grandchildren, especially when they are young, is often a function of interaction with adult offspring, the aged sample were also asked, "Are you able to do anything to help your children and grandchildren, even small things?" About 30 percent say they do nothing. The remaining 70 percent cite gift giving and, to a lesser extent, services. Comparing the two samples, the content of shared activities is seen to be alike. Whether they live in the same house or in a different village, grandparents and grandchildren report doing the same kind of things—when they are together. The interaction which does exist seems more a flow of tangible resources than a teaching and/or sharing of activities. This flow of resources, it should be noted, is a reciprocal one. A majority of aged respondents do report that their children give them gifts of sugar and other small things including money; at the same time aged parents continue to assist their offspring. A 66-year-old male reports that he helps "with money because I have more money than my children have." This pattern of resource flow is very similar to that found in the United States. Generally the flow is downward in generation. However, as parents age, if the descending generation is in a better position financially, the direction of flow reverses.

In examining patterns of respect between grandchildren and grandparents, we find traditional values have not changed. Ninety-nine percent of the aged sample agree with the statement, "One of the most important things I want my grandchildren to learn is to respect their elders." Only a few of the student respondents say that there is a grandparent whom they do not respect, and the vast majority of both grandsons and granddaughters believe they are obedient and respectful.

Grandchildren in Baganda society demonstrate respect in various ways. Grandsons show respect primarily by doing things instead of by a particular demeanor: 50 percent indicated they showed respect by doing tasks they are asked to do while only 28 percent said they did so by talking or acting in a respectful manner (or kneeling) when addressing their grandparents (see Table 2). For granddaughters the pattern is reversed: 50 percent said they showed respect by kneeling or speaking and acting in a subdued

manner in their grandparents' presence while 35 percent said they did so by obeying them or doing things for them. These differences, i.e., the grandson as "obeyer" and "doer" and the granddaughter as showing respect by demeanor, are clearest in the cross-sex relationship (grandson with grandmother and granddaughter with grandfather). This is consistent with the more general societal status distinction based on sex, i.e., the male is more an object of respect than the female. In relative terms, this puts the young male closer to equal status with his grandmother than the female is in relation to her grandfather.

Keeping in mind the sex differences on the part of the grandchildren in demeanor versus obedience, we note once again that grandchildren show respect to their grandmothers to a greater extent by obedience or service and to their grandfathers by their manner. Respect is demonstrated along sex lines following the traditional sexual division of labor, with aged females being the object of "task help" and aged males objects of respectful demeanor. Women tend throughout the life cycle to bear a heavier work burden, and this, coupled with the generally lower position of women in Baganda society, has taken the form of greater assistance in daily activities as a sign of respect. Overall, the data suggest that the grandmother is not approached in a respectful manner as often as the grandfather, but is rather defined as worthy of and in need of services. The

TABLE 2
Signs of Respect Demonstrated by Grandchildren toward Grandparents by Sex of Student

| | Signs of Respect for Grandfather | | | | Signs of Respect for Grandmother | | | |
| | Males | | Females | | Males | | Females | |
	n	Per-centage	n	Per-centage	n	Per-centage	n	Per-centage
Didn't respect	5	.9%	2	.5%	16	2.4%	7	1.5%
Obeyed/did tasks	270	48.0	127	33.1	380	56.5	196	40.6
Respectful manner	186	33.1	219	57.0	159	23.6	218	45.1
Didn't laugh at	3	.5	1	.3	5	.7	2	.4
Didn't argue	24	4.3	1	.3	22	3.3	11	2.3
Bought presents	4	.7	7	1.8	10	1.5	6	1.2
Other	70	12.5	27	7.0	81	12.0	43	8.9
Total	562	100.0%	384	100.0%	673	100.0%	483	100.0%

data indicate respect for her but not commensurate with that for him.

Although students tended to cite specific activities as the primary aspect of their relationships with their grandparents, they and the grandparents view each other with warmth and affection. These relationships are characterized by friendship but are not perceived as a substitute for the parent-child tie. In fact, few student respondents claim that a grandparent is more like a parent to them, and few grandparents appear to take over major parental roles *vis-à-vis* their grandchildren. Grandparents appear, for the most part, to steer clear of intense involvement and/or participation in rearing and disciplining grandchildren.

Since grandparents are objects of respect for their grandchildren, is it also the case that their grandchildren are unlikely to argue with them? Students were asked, "When you were in P5 did you talk back to or argue with your grandfather?" While slightly over half did not argue, there are some interesting variations among those who did. Few argued really frequently with grandparents, but about 30 percent did get involved in arguments with some regularity. Females tended to argue considerably more with grandmothers than is true of any other cross-generational combination. This is not surprising since grandmothers and granddaughters tend to have more intense and frequent contact.

Proximity serves to increase markedly the probability of intergenerational conflict between grandparents and their grandchildren for both sexes and each grandparent. Grandparents and their grandchildren who have greater exposure and do more things together are found to come into conflict. This is not inconsistent with the notion developed earlier of a warm, loving relationship. In fact, it supports it in that in those societies where intergenerational interaction is structured around clearly demarcated authority relations, we would expect conflict to be held to a minimum because it threatens the foundations of the social structure. On the other hand, where there is a "friendly-equality" ethos operating, we expect more open conflict to arise and to be smoothly resolved. Tasks performed and arguing, it should be noted, are both related to proximity. As increasing residential separation diminished the frequency of task performance, it also seemed

to reduce the relationship to its "warm and loving" aspects because there was neither as much instrumental contact nor the kind of intensity which makes for conflict.

For the most part, grandparents try not to interfere in situations involving their adult offspring and their grandchildren. When encounters do occur between the first and third generations, a majority of these grandparents fight their own battles; students, for their part, also take a stand. The general thrust of these encounters is intimately tied to an involvement by older people in the rearing of their grandchildren, especially when they are nearby. The discussion of conflict leads us, therefore, to the following point. The notion that old people exercise authority in the family and thereby direct control over their offspring and grandchildren has been rejected, but it does not necessarily follow that they relinquish all decision-making roles or influence on their kin.

Since there is neither a pattern of joint residence nor extensive interaction between generations within most families, as reported by our aged respondents, it is of interest to ask to what extent these grandparents think they share in the responsibility for how their grandchildren turn out. That is, do they perceive their role as integral, complementary, or extraneous to that of parents? Although about a quarter of the grandparent sample say that the parents must take full responsibility for their children, it is clear that to the majority of these old people, being a good grandparent nevertheless means being responsible for teaching right and proper behavior as well as traditions. Given this understanding on the part of the aged Baganda, it is of interest to construct an "ideal-type" relationship to bring some of these factors into better focus. Who is a good grandparent? Elderly men and women agree that a good grandparent is defined as one who teaches, loves, and cares for his or her grandchildren (Nahemow and Adams, 1974).

While teaching is the principal "ingredient" of the grandparent-grandchild relationship, it seems somewhat more important to the grandmother role. This is a function and reflection of the existing division of labor in the larger society where females are concerned with activities centered around the household, while males are more involved in economic or leisure affairs.

Since young children and especially girls are expected to do tasks around the house, this serves to strengthen ties with grandmothers or at least increase the frequency of interaction between them. This tie is analagous to that found in the United States, presumably for the same reason. Atchley (1980) notes that grandmothers have a better chance of developing close ties with granddaughters because they are more often in contact with them. And, owing to the relative stability of the housewife role, grandmothers have more to offer to their granddaughters that is and will continue to be relevant to their daily lives.

Specifically, with regard to the role of the grandparent, what remains is a respected and affectionate role limited in its expression by neolocality. Grandparents feel that there is a contribution they can make first in manifesting love and also in directly teaching and encouraging appropriate behavior to their grandchildren. The elderly have assumed a small but complementary share of the responsibility in the child-rearing process and perceive their contribution as important, though bounded by both traditional and modern limitations on the role of the aged in Baganda society and by cultural emphases on achievement and change.

CONCLUSION AND DISCUSSION

It is apparent that grandparenthood among the Baganda is generally viewed favorably although it is not that significant in the daily lives of the aged. Having ascertained this general picture of the content and meaning of grandparenthood among the Baganda, it is instructive to compare our results with what is known about grandparents in American society. The advantage of looking at grandparenthood in cross-cultural perspective is that it increases our base of knowledge about other societies as well as heightens our understanding of both our own uniqueness and universality.

Until recently there has been little systematic research on grandparenthood in the United States and the picture which emerges is at best inconclusive. Troll et al. (1979:119) conclude

that "the research findings to date suggest that the grandparent role is not a highly significant one for most older people but that for a few older people it is very meaningful and a great source of personal satisfaction."

The meaning of grandparenthood has changed dramatically in the United States since the turn of the century. The quickening of the stages of the family life cycle has meant that grandparenthood has become a middle-age phenomenon. Further, increased life expectancy means there are a growing number of four-generation families, which makes grandparenting a second—rather than a first—generation phenomenon. That is, grandparents are no longer the oldest generation. In addition, many grandfathers and grandmothers are still employed (Troll et al., 1979:108). In Uganda the picture is very different since the time lapse between generations is greater and the average life expectancy is lower. Thus, the position of American grandparents is structurally quite different from that of Baganda grandparents who tend to be older, first generation, and closer to the end of their life cycle, though probably also still employed.

One must be cautious in attempting to draw cross-cultural conclusions from comparisons of societies at widely different stages of modernization. The greater prevalence of older people in the United States, as well as increased life expectancy, means that while like age groups are compatible, the age structure and the social significance of age diverge considerably (Nahemow, 1979). There are, however, a number of similarities between grandparenting among the Baganda and in the United States. Neugarten and Weinstein (1964), in their pioneer work on the meaning of the grandparent role in the United States, report that only a small proportion of their sample were reservoirs of family wisdom. Also, the "parent surrogate" role, which was played by some grandmothers, was not normative. They further report that the style for the majority of grandparents was "formal" or "distant," though a quarter of the sample were categorized as "fun seeking" which is equivalent to the friendly-familiarity style posited by Sweetser.

The "formal" style emphasizes the "proper" role of grandparent as continuing interest in the grandchildren without the parental surrogate function. The "distant" style is similar to this, but with less frequent interaction. Both styles are remarkably similar to the Baganda pattern. Within the limits set by residential distance, Baganda grandparents do take an active interest in their grandchildren and, as noted above, are concerned with teaching them appropriate behavior. Thus, while authority lines are basically irrelevant in terms of direct intergenerational control, the informality and playfulness which epitomize the fun-seeking style does not typify the Baganda case either. This is partially a result of the strong element of respect which continues to separate the generations. It is also noteworthy that Neugarten and Weinstein found the "fun-seeking" style more typical of younger grandparents. Presumably, this will become a more characteristic style in the United States as the average age of grandparents continues to decline. Perhaps the Baganda pattern will be similar; it is as yet unclear what the impact of these demographic changes will be on the cultural expression of family roles.

In terms of perceptions of and satisfaction with the grandparent role, Robertson's findings for the United States have broader applicability. She reports that 80 percent of her sample of grandmothers actively enjoyed the role as a source of joy and pleasure without the socialization responsibilities generally associated with parenthood (1977:165). Thus, like the Baganda who view socialization of grandchildren as outside their domain, American grandparents also seem content with a less active role in the child-rearing process.

Robertson (1976) also presents data from young adult grandchildren which indicates that grandchildren do not view grandparents as old-fashioned. Indeed, they report that their grandparents are an important source of influence on them. However, while they espouse positive attitudes, ". . . it is interesting to note that they do not choose to use grandparents as companions, advice givers, liaisons between them and their parents, role models, or somebody who financially supports them. Thus there is an incongruence between what grandchildren think and feel about the significance of grandparenthood and the behaviors they expect from grandparents" (Robertson, 1976:140).

There is a similar contradiction found among the Baganda. The student sample describe their relations with their grandparents as warm and loving. However, in a series of unstructured questions they do not characterize grandparents in terms of these roles. Neither do they select these roles when they are presented as forced-choice responses. Furthermore, the vast majority of students report that old people's advice should be asked for, but there is little belief that what they have to say is worth very much or that they are wise. The student sample was evenly divided in agreeing with the statement, "Men are considered wise when they grow old." Thus age and wisdom were not automatically viewed as synonymous. Considering the statement, "I do not value the advice of old people as much now as when I was young," over half of the students agreed with this. In fact older students were even less likely to value the advice of the aged. This suggests a growing devaluation of the elderly on the part of the young. Finally the aged sample were asked a more age-consistent question, with the same intent: "Young people do not value the advice of old people as much now as when I was young." Fully 90 percent of them agree with this. At least from their perspective there has been a change; they are on the short end and seem to know it. In Baganda society, it appears one has the obligation to clear or check things out with elders, but little responsibility to take their advice seriously or act on it in any way. Perhaps old people should be consulted because of their age, but beyond that there is little commitment to following through.

This seeming contradiction underscores a prevalent problem in social research. Normative statements about the way things should be oftentimes are not reflective of the way they actually are. In the United States today there is a norm against premarital sex, yet many young people are sexually active. Unfortunately the researcher is not always able to separate the real from the ideal. However, using a number of different items to tap these dimensions helps increase their validity. From the student survey we found that advice from elders is sought. Yet using other items from both samples it became apparent that this was the ideal; in practice most young people do not conform to the wishes of their elders. However, given what we learned about the position of the aged among the Baganda and the significance and meaning of grandparenthood, it appears that the future of the aged Baganda is not that grim. They are not falling from great heights as did aged in some other societies, if indeed that ever was the case for any sizable portion of old people. In the familial context grandparenthood is a viable and rewarding role option for some aged, although for others it is a largely inactive role which does not assure continuing interaction. Thus, despite the diversity in social organization and societal complexity between the United States and Baganda, the expression of grandparenthood is remarkably similar.

AGING, MODERNIZATION,
AND SOCIETAL
TRANSFORMATION

"When social conditions become unstable and the rate of change reaches a galloping pace, the aged are riding for a fall . . . change is the crux of the problem of aging."

—Leo Simmons (1960:88)

With very few exceptions social scientists today cannot hope to study the aged in unchanged, "pristine," traditional societies. Virtually all human groups have been altered in some way by the expansion of economic, political, and communication links on a global scale. Indeed, concern for studying the aging process as a societal problem is now a worldwide issue, no longer a special dilemma of Western industrialized societies. In the period from 1970 to 2000, the number of persons in the world age 65 and older is expected to double from 190 million to 396 million, with 58 percent of these elderly living in economically less developed nations. By the year 2000, the less developed regions of the world will still have about one-half (7 percent) of the percentage of aged in their populations that the more developed regions have (Decker, 1980:75). But increasing poverty, rapid overurbanization, a rural exodus of the young, and change in ideological systems may create the greatest problem for the elderly in what are now considered traditional societies (Goldstein and Beall, 1981).

The type of massive social change that has drawn the most attention from gerontologists has

been labeled "modernization." Donald Cowgill defines this process as:

The transformation of a total society from a relatively rural way of life based on animate power, limited technology, relatively undifferentiated institutions, parochial and traditional outlook and values, toward a predominantly urban way of life based on inanimate sources of power, highly developed scientific technology, highly differentiated institutions matched by segmented individual roles, and a cosmopolitan outlook which emphasizes efficiency and progress. (1974b:127)

Various writers, expecially Cowgill (1974b), have suggested a very strong inverse relationship between modernization and the social status of the aged. Cowgill suggests that four factors—(1) modern health technology, (2) economies based on scientific technology, (3) urbanization, (4) mass education and literacy—shape a decrease in roles, resources, and respect available to older people in modern societies. The first factor, improving health care and sanitation, leads to increased life expectancy and an eventual rise in the numbers and proportion of the aged, thereby triggering generational competition over positions in the labor force. Retirement programs develop to "substitute for death as the means of exit from the labor force" (Cowgill, 1974b:12). In a related manner, age segments are further differentiated by technical developments in the economic sector. Such changes create new and highly valued occupations that can make obsolete the skills acquired in youth by the older generation.

The reputed impact of urbanization on the aged is linked to the effects of increased social mobility and migration of the young to cities. This residential separation and the taking of new urban occupations by the young foster the breakup of functional extended families. The isolated nuclear family becomes the norm, marked by a diminished dependence on parental support and a lessening of obligations to the elder generation. Finally, urbanization is accompanied by the establishment of public educational institutions that not only promote literacy but train the young for jobs created by technological innovations and emerging industries. The greater "formal" education of the younger group gives them a "power-resource," as Dowd would describe it, with which to compete for prestigious occupations (see Dowd's article in Section I). Concomitantly, the increase in literacy and mass education can destroy the function of the elderly as unique repositories of wisdom and knowledge acquired over a lifetime (see Silverman and Maxwell's article in Section I).

How does such a model fare in the light of comparative research? A study by Palmore and Manton (1974) used an index of relative resource equality between generations in comparing 31 nations. They found that while economic development generally corresponded with relative decrement in resources held by the aged, the relationship appeared to be curvilinear. That is, in the most economically modern nations new institutions and entitlements (such as pension plans) have begun to redress the losses caused by the transformation of family and community organization.*

Another study by Bengtson et al. (1975) surveyed—in Argentina, Chile, India, Pakistan, Israel, and Nigeria—young men's perceptions of the educational value of old people, the young men's attitudes toward their own aging, and their obligations toward the aged. The data showed only weak and inconsistent evidence that the most modernized countries had the most negative attitudes toward aging. However, there was also some evidence that within some developing countries, *increasing* individual modernity (for instance, exposure to urban factory work) was associated with more *positive* perceptions of aging. For example, in four of the six nations examined, rural cultivators were the *least* likely to look forward to old age.

A different approach is taken in *Aging and Modernization* (Cowgill and Holmes, 1972), the only major qualitative cross-cultural study on the subject. In-depth studies of 14 different societies were used to examine the impact of industrialization, urbanization, and Westernization on the aged. Based on these data the authors propose 22 "variations" in the status of the aged that relate directly to the impact of modernization. Among these hypotheses are:

1. Longevity is directly and significantly related to the degree of modernization.
2. Modernized societies have older populations, that is, higher proportions of old people.
3. Modern societies have higher proportions of women, especially of widows.
4. The status of the aged is high in societies in which there is a high reverence for or worship of ancestors.
5. With modernization the responsibility for the provision of economic security for dependent aged tends to be shifted from the family to the state.
6. The individualistic value system of Western society tends to reduce the security and status of older people.
7. The status of the aged is inversely proportional to the rate of social change.
8. The status of the aged tends to be high in agricultural societies and lower in urbanized societies.
9. Stability of residence favors high status of the aged.
10. The proportion of the aged who are able to maintain leadership roles declines with modernization.

The general implication of these 10 propositions is that modernization tends to lower and make more ambiguous the status of the elderly.

---

*In an analysis of the changing positions of America's elderly population, Palmore (1976) suggests that the year 1967 represents a watershed after which " . . . relative status of the aged in health, income, occupation, and education is rising and probably will continue to rise for the rest of this century" (p. 301).

Yet Holmes (1972) recognized that cultural and historical differences might strongly mitigate the negative effects of such change for the aged:

How a society develops and changes under the impact of modernizing forces depends to a great extent upon the values it held previously. A society whose major religion is Buddhism may be quite differently affected by industrialization and urbanization than one operating under a Judeo-Christian tradition. The same is true for traditional differences in political or economic philosophy. (p. 87)

Indeed the issue is far from settled.* This section's first two articles show two quite different results from the impact of modernizing forces. In one case, that of Samoa, the cultural system has been flexible enough to maintain the aged as a quite viable part of the society, even in urban areas. Just the opposite has occured in rural western Ireland where Nancy Scheper-Hughes documents not only the destruction of a traditional culture but also the alienation of the elderly from a society that no longer sees their value.

In the final selection, David Plath examines how respect for the elders has fared in modern Japan. This highly industrialized society, with its traditions stressing vertical hierarchy and filial piety, provides an ideal social laboratory for exploring the mediating effects of culture on social change and modernization.

---

*See Finley (forthcoming) for a comprehensive discussion of the complex issues involved in aging and modernization studies.

Lowell Holmes and Ellen Rhoads

AGING AND CHANGE IN SAMOA

In undertaking a study of aging and social change in American Samoa, anthropologists Lowell Holmes and Ellen Rhoads had the unusual advantage of being able to build upon Dr. Holmes's previous ethnographic work there in 1954 and 1962 as well as the insights contained in Margaret Mead's classic research *Coming of Age in Samoa* (1928b). Despite a crash program of U.S. aid, the influx of several industries, and Western-style education programs begun in the 1960s, the authors found that adjustments to change have been made without destroying key social institutions linked to the high status of the aged. Most crucial is the *matai* family system involving leadership roles within large bilateral kinship groups and a village council that accords the aged not only respect but a considerable amount of power. The *matai* system, combined with open-air housing and a lack of age-segregated work activities, has made it almost impossible for the aged to disengage from Samoan society.

THE SETTING

THE SAMOAN ARCHIPELAGO CONSISTS of nine inhabited South Sea islands in a culture area of the central Pacific known as western Polynesia. A plane flying on a direct course from Hawaii to New Zealand would pass over Samoa about midway in its journey at a point 14° south latitude by 170° west longitude. The group is divided politically into American Samoa, a territory of the United States (since 1900), and Western Samoa, an independent country since 1962. American Samoa consists of the island of Tutuila, where the port town of Pago Pago is located, and the Manu'a group of smaller islands lying 60 miles to the east. Western Samoa's capital and largest port is Apia on the island of Upolu. A few miles west, and well in sight of Upolu, lie two islets, Apolima and Manono, and the largest of the Western Samoan islands, Savai'i. Throughout the entire archipelago Samoans are remarkably homogeneous culturally, linguistically, and racially. Ninety percent of the 185,000 inhabitants of this island chain can be classified as full-blooded Polynesians, and the

majority of them still practice the traditional economic activities of subsistence agriculture and periodic reef and deep water fishing.

Culturally Samoa is much more conservative than most island groups in Polynesia. In 1928 Margaret Mead wrote that Samoans possessed "all the strength of the tough willows, which bend and swing to every passing breeze, but do not break" (1928a:495). Several decades later Douglas Oliver (1951) also remarked on the Samoan capacity to retain traditional culture, and even in 1980 there are great numbers of individuals in both American Samoa and Western Samoa who primarily operate in terms of a traditional system known as *fa'asamoa* (the Samoan way). Conservative strongholds of *fa'asamoa* are to be found in the Manu'a group of American Samoa and on the islands of Manono and Savai'i in Western Samoa.

THE TRADITIONAL SOCIAL ORDER

With the exception of those who reside around the Apia or Pago Pago areas, most of the

This essay was specially prepared for this book by the authors. Permission to reprint must be obtained from the authors and publisher.

inhabitants of Samoa live in traditional villages located near the sea. These consist of a long string of thatch-roofed *fales* and European-styled dwellings that front on beaches of white coral sand. The average village contains about 300 individuals living in household units headed by a titled chief, or *matai*. Household units vary in size from about 6 to 24 people, all of whom are related either through the bilateral kinship system, through marriage or adoption. The household head (*matai*) is elected to his (or in a very few cases, her)[1] position of authority by the members of the household plus any other interested members of the extended family whose title he will hold. *Matai* are elected on the basis of service to the family, intelligence, knowledge of Samoan tradition, and in recent years, also on the basis of education, wealth, or knowledge of the Western world. Once elected, the *matai* holds the position for life unless he voluntarily steps down in very old age to allow a deserving younger family member the honor and responsibiltiy.

As holder of the family title the *matai* administers family lands and other property, settles domestic disputes, coordinates the efforts of the household labor force, and promotes family unity and prestige. In addition to directing the day-to-day affairs of his household, the *matai* represents them in the village council (*fono*), where he functions in accord with his relative rank in the village hierarchy of chiefly titles and in accord with his expected role as either a chief (*ali'i*) or a talking chief (*tulafale*), depending upon the nature of the title he holds.

The *matai* system, as the Samoan family arrangement is known, is also seen as important for all family members, even those who will never have an opportunity to function as its head. Since every Samoan can, through the kinship system, trace descent to at least one high title and possibly even to a king, the system serves as a major source of personal prestige and identity. Unless Western culture provides avenues for acquiring status greater than is now available through the *matai* system, it will continue to receive the support of the Samoan people.

The *matai* system is a contributing factor in maintenance of respect and status for the aged. The fact that *matai* hold lifetime tenure reveals the faith that Samoan families place in the ability of the elderly to deal with family and village

social and political problems. *Matai* are by definition "old men" although most are elected to their positions in middle age. On rare occasions when fairly young men are chosen to head a family, they feel constrained to emulate the behavior and attitudes of the men of more advanced years. Mead quotes a 27-year-old chief who found his age a problem:

I have been a chief only four years and look, my hair is grey, although in Samoa grey hair comes very slowly, not in youth, as it comes to the white man. But always, I must act as if I were old. I must walk gravely and with measured step . . . . Old men of sixty are my companions and watch my every word, lest I make a mistake. Thirty-one people live in my household. For them I must plan. I must find them food and clothing, settle their disputes, arrange their marriages. There is no one in my whole family who dares to scold me or even to address me familiarly by my first name. It is hard to be so young and yet to be a chief. (Mead, 1928b:536)

Although the *matai* system continues to represent an institution which values the experience and wisdom of men who have lived long and experienced much, it is flexible and can adjust to the needs of the younger, more educated elements of Samoan society. The Keesings observed that "minor titles . . . go to young or younger middle-aged persons, who then may move up the rank of titles with age as they prove themselves and are chosen for such honor" (1956:41). As the man proves himself capable of handling the lesser family titles he will be considered for more important and responsible ones. He may finally receive a paramount chief title and in that capacity not only represent a very powerful household group but function as the head of the village council, as a representative to the district council, or even be appointed to an advisory position for the government of American Samoa. This prospect of advancing to more and more prestigious positions is also a powerful force in maintaining the system.

Not only does Samoan social organization respect age by placing major responsibility in those of advanced age, but the kinship terminology itself confers special honor on those who can claim seniority. Siblings are always required to defer to older brothers and sisters in a variety of situations ranging from who can receive gifts first to the matter of who should be obeyed in work details.

The importance of age is documented by the use of special terms to acknowledge those to whom special respect is due. Male relatives, for example, who are 15 or more years older than the speaker must be addressed as *tamā* (father) while those less than 15 years older are addressed as *uso* (brother). And a man more than 15 years senior would call his younger relative *atali'i* (son). The phenomenon also holds true among female relatives but they would of course substitute the terms *tinā* (mother), *uso* or *tuafafine* (sister), and *afafine* (daughter). It should further be pointed out that *tamā* is not only a kinship term but that it is also a term of respect which is used to refer to a family head (*matai*) regardless of his kinship relationship to the household member addressing him.

DEFINITION OF OLD AGE

Old age is a well-recognized and highly revered status in Samoa. In 1962 when we did our first study of Samoan aging it was generally agreed that old age begins about 50 years of age. It should be stated, however, that Samoans do not think of aging in chronological terms and they do not normally categorize age. They did state, however, that at about the half-century mark people begin to refer to you as *toeaina* or *matuaali'i* (old man) or *lo'omatua* or *olomatua* (old woman), and that sometime between 60 and 70 the word *vaivai* (weak in the body) may be added even if that does not accurately describe the physical conditions. Samoans maintained that there is great variation in individuals and generally they thought people old when they were unable to care for themselves or contribute to the welfare of the household. By 1976 many Samoans had become more chronologically oriented and changed their notions of when old age began. They stated that old age started at 60 or 65. As societies become more modern there is a tendency for the threshold of old age to be pushed upward (Cowgill and Holmes, 1972). Since the Territorial Administration on Aging collects data on everyone 60 and older, and there are also a fair

number of individuals receiving Social Security, these factors may tend to focus the onset of old age on the 60–65 age period.

ATTITUDES TOWARD OLD AGE

In 1962 old age was universally referred to as the "best time of life" by both old and young Samoans. In 1976 folks of all ages were having second thoughts about what period is best, although they still did not complain about old age. Traditionally old age has been viewed as a period of maximum security when one could cash in on one's "annuities," i.e., they could, if they wished, sit back and let children and relatives support them. Samoans, however, have never believed that old age is for rest and leisure. In fact, most elderly explain their longevity by the fact that they work hard every day.

SOCIAL PARTICIPATION

Samoa is not an unpleasant place in which to grow old. The climate, which greatly resembles that of some retirement areas in the United States, is mild and therefore permits maximum social contact and community participation. There is no time of year when the weather would make it difficult for an old person to get out of the house. Elderly Samoan men and women spend a great deal of their day visiting and socializing with friends and relatives in various parts of the village. The aged are fully integrated into their society and they perceive themselves as valuable, participating members in all family and village activities. It was repeatedly observed that while the aged enjoy the company of others of their age set, they also participate in activities and events involving relatives and neighbors of all ages. They enjoy being with younger people, and it is not unusual to see elderly women working and gossiping with a group of young women at a mat-weaving bee or some other coordinated work project for women. In like manner, old men may be observed among a group of village youths engaged in trap or line fishing on the reef. Old folks in Samoa probably know the latest happenings in the village as well as anyone. They experience no disengagement.

Even the architecture of Samoa contributes to a positive attitude toward aging. The traditional Samoan *fale*, with its open sides, permits even invalid elders to see who is going by on the village path and to convey a greeting. Although the new style houses are made of lumber and often somewhat more enclosed, this has not interfered with this pattern of communication and participation. Elders cannot be isolated in this kind of housing as they can in the SRO hotels and the boardinghouse rooms or the small flats of America. In the small Samoan villages there is none of the anonymity characteristic of many urban communities in our country. It would be difficult for Samoan aged to withdraw from social participation even if they wanted to.

The later years of life are also pleasant because they are accompanied by a softening of taboos and an easing of the rigid code of etiquette that governs much of Samoan social and ceremonial interaction. One of the prohibitions which disappears is the brother-sister avoidance pattern. This restriction normally applies not only to siblings of the opposite sex but to all relatives of one's own generation who are, by the nature of the Samoan classificatory kinship terminology, referred to as "brother" or "sister." The brother-sister avoidance norm takes effect at about age 9 or 10 when actual siblings and cousins of the opposite sex may not touch each other, sit in close proximity, eat together, be in the same house alone, or address each other familiarly, or mention salacious matter in one another's presence. It is a prohibition undoubtedly instituted to discourage incest. After Samoans have reached old age, brothers and sisters (real or by virtue of terminology) may disregard these prohibitions and may sit together for long periods of time enjoying each other's company without feelings of guilt or embarrassment for having violated the mores of the society.

In village council meetings special deference is shown to old chiefs, and even the most boring or intemperate of speeches is tolerated. The aged also appear to feel less constrained to maintain a dignified image on ceremonial or social occasions. Oldsters are occasionally observed carrying this to

such a limit that they make comic objects of themselves by performing ludicrous dances or by making witty remarks at village social gatherings. The general impression is that since their status is not in jeopardy, the aged feel free to behave in any manner they choose without the threat of social disapproval.

TRADITIONAL ROLES AND ACTIVITIES OF THE AGED

We learn a great deal about Samoan attitudes toward the aged by observing the division of labor and the way in which responsibility is assigned. While there are certain kinds of work considered more appropriate for older men or women, Samoans feel that the aged should be permitted to engage in any form of labor which they are capable of performing. There are not definite categories of "children's work," "adults' work," or "old people's work." This is because there is a smoothly flowing continuity to the life cycle and a tendency to allow people to perform day-to-day tasks according to their ability and interests.

Samoa, with its lack of emphasis on individual, as opposed to situational, status and with its comfortable ideological environment allowing a smooth and unrestricted maturation process, seems to have been able to promote a positive attitude toward its elders and an atmosphere of freedom in which they can participate fully in their society.

As we have noted earlier, old age in Samoa is not viewed as a period of retirement from work (although that is not disparaged) but merely a time when work activities are different, i.e., adjusted to match the strength and interests of the aged. It is not a time, however, when Samoans are relegated to doing jobs of little value.

Since Samoans generally believe that patience increases with age, the elderly are often asked to do jobs which involve tedium but which are also important jobs, vital to the economy. These are often tasks which can be accomplished sitting down and with a minimum outlay of energy. For old men such jobs would be the preparation of coconut fibers and the twisting and braiding of them into a stout twine. The production of this valuable commodity—needed in the construction of traditional houses and canoes—is almost solely the responsibility of old men. To carry a bundle of coconut fiber is as typical of aged males in Samoa as carrying one's fancy work or knitting was for elderly women in America. A traditional guest house (and every village still has at least one) requires thousands of fathoms of twine for lashing together the myriad components which make up the roof structure.

House building also provides the aged male with another important role—that of the *tapuaiga*, "the one who prays for the work." The presence of a *tapuaiga* (even when European-style houses are being built) is considered an important ingredient in successful construction. The *tapuaiga* does not actually pray but merely sits and serves as a conversationalist to the carpenters. He is not permitted to be critical of the work but his mere presence probably helps eliminate a lot of shoddy work. There is supposed to be something magical in his presence which will insure good luck.

Old men also contribute to the education of young men, particularly young orator chiefs through the traditional institution known as the *fa'asausauga*. These are gatherings that take place in the evening when old men assemble to discuss Samoan myths, legends, and customs and young men sit outside the house and listen. Similar discussions are held within the family with the elders communicating family genealogical information and family history. The aged are generally considered storehouses of traditional knowledge and they are frequently consulted as experts on bush medicines and on matters of traditional religious lore. While Samoans are Christian, there is still a viable mythology dealing with the god Tagaloa and other traditional anthropomorphic deities. It is said that the aged are the only ones who can sense when the spirit of a traditional deity is visiting the village. One such spirit is said to walk with the aid of an orator's staff, and it is believed that only old men can hear the sound of his staff on the village path. In old Samoa and even today in some outlying rural parts of Samoa, elderly males performed many of the ceremonial operations ranging from the tattooing of young adults to the circumcision of adolescents.

Perhaps the most important role reserved for an elderly chief is that of *tu'ua*, elder statesman. F. J. H. Grattan describes the role as follows:

As a mark of respect and dignity, the village may choose one of their orators to fill a position known as tu'ua. Not every village chooses a tu'ua. Such a person must enjoy high personal rank as an orator and have a degree of knowledge relating to village and perhaps district affairs which fits him for the position. Considerable deference is paid to him and it is to him that the village looks thereafter for pronouncements on any disputed point. The tu'ua is the one entitled to sit in the middle post of the front of a house and if he should arrive late or unexpectedly at the village meeting and that post is already occupied, the place will be vacated at once and left open to him. (Grattan, 1948:19)

Although old women often play a ceremonial role and are consulted on political issues in the Women's Committee,[2] an organization like the village council in structure and family representation, the major contribution of elderly women is economic. Women in general produce goods categorized as *toga*. This includes all classes of weaving—floor and sleeping mats, baskets, fans, house blinds, bark cloth tapestries, fine mats. While all women contribute to the production of *toga*, the bulk of the production is in the hands of elderly women who can devote longer hours to these tedious labors since they no longer are required to engage in other types of female labor such as plantation cultivation and reef scavenging. Much as elderly Western women engage in quilting and "fancy work," Samoan oldsters produce the heirlooms of the future while they tend the small children left behind by the young mothers who must assist their men in work on the plantations. Often they are joined by elderly men who seem to recognize no stigma in assisting their wives or female relatives in the preparation of mat or bark cloth materials. One job completely reserved for aged women has been the burning of candlenut and collecting the soot which is used for pigment in tattooing. With the resurgence of the tattooer's art in Samoa in recent years, this activity has taken on new importance. What is disappearing, however, is the profession of midwifery. Once this was the exclusive function of older women but today the responsibility of assisting with the birth of village children falls almost entirely upon the village nurse or the Samoan medical practitioner. At least 90 percent of Samoa's babies are now delivered at the hospital (American Samoa Health Coordinating Council, 1979). The old women of the village continue to serve as repositories of knowledge concerning the medicinal properties of herbs, however, and many of the specialists in tradition-al therapeutic massage belong to the senior age group.

Elderly females often prepare the dead for burial and serve as caretakers of family graves—keeping them free of weeds and well supplied with cut flowers. Yard work is generally a primary concern of old women and they often sit for hours weeding and chatting with their age peers and never seem to regard such work as either too difficult or too menial for anyone of their station in life.

THE SIXTIES—A DECADE OF CHANGE

The era of radical cultural change began in the early 1960s. In 1954 we found an idyllic South Sea culture only slightly modified by Western influences, but in 1962 we found that there was a movement of considerable force to move Ameri-can Samoa into the modern world, culturally and particularly economically. In 1962 an editor of *Reader's Digest*, Clarence Hall, visited American Samoa and, not finding it like the movies had always portrayed South Sea island societies, he wrote an article titled "Samoa: America's Shame in the South Seas." This precipitated a consider-able volume of mail to congressmen, resulting in the Department of Interior inaugurating a special crash program to rectify its sins of omission. Govenor Rex Lee was charged with the responsi-bility of bringing American Samoa into this brave new world, and Congress tripled its appropria-tions for the island territory's budget.

When we arrived to do a study of Samoan aged in 1962, we found a number of changes. A new high school had recently been built on the shores of Pago Pago Bay, making it possible for all island children to have secondary education. Plans were

also underway for the construction of 26 elementary schools, and the government had contracted for the installation of a very costly educational television system. Construction was soon to begin on a grand new hotel, for the air strip had been lengthened and the harbor facilities improved, and it was believed that American Samoa would soon become a tourist mecca. Many new cottages and apartments had been built to accommodate a host of new American teachers who would handle the television programming and the expanded secondary curriculum.

Prosperity was mounting in American Samoa in the early 1960s. There were new jobs in a variety of island government agencies and in the two tuna fish canneries, and many Samoans were convert-ing newly imported automobiles into taxis and jitney buses to accommodate the new demand for island transportation over the newly paved roads stretching to all the villages in the territory. Even in isolated areas like Manu'a it was evident that there would soon be major changes in Samoan life style. It could readily be sensed that there was a general lessening of the economic and political influence of the *matai* and greater opportunity for the individual family members to control their own affairs.

However, when we conducted our study of Samoan aged in Manu'a and on the island of Tutuila we found that things had changed very little for the elderly. Family support was strong and in spite of new Western ideas and values coming into the society, the aged did not have a sense of being threatened nor was there any diminution of their status. Care of the elders continued to be top priority for the large household units both in outlying villages and in the Pago Pago Bay area. A considerable amount of migration to Hawaii and the United States had occurred, but there was still enough family to care for the needs and desires of the aged.

MODERNIZATION—ITS IMPACT ON THE AGED

In 1976 we spent several months in American Samoa studying the impact of the extensive change (post 1962) on the aged. The economic development in the islands had been considerable. While the Manu'a group was little affected (only 136 people—mostly teachers—engaged in wage labor), on the island of Tutuila a total of nearly 5,000 people were employed for wages in 1970. This amounted to 20 percent of the total population. In 1954 when our first research was done, most Samoans were engaged in subsistence agriculture, but by the 1970s there was so little cultivation of family lands on Tutuila that produce had to be imported from Western Samoa. Now Samoans not only worked for the government and for the Van Camp and Star Kist fish canneries, but in industries such as the Beatrice Foods dairy products plant and the Bulova watch factory. Some worked in the tourist trade or drove taxicabs. In the mid 1970s the government was trying to expand its industrial park near the airport through advertising campaigns designed to lure more industry.

There had also been great changes in the educational program of American Samoa since the early 1960s. An educational television network had been installed (to improve the use of written and spoken English) and 26 new consolidated elementary schools and two high schools had been built. The architecture of the school buildings was more European than Samoan, which meant that the children were frequently uncomfortable because of the lack of ventilation—a necessity in this humid tropical area. A television set was still a conspicuous feature in every classroom, but with budget cuts and the loss of television personnel, less and less television programming was produced.

There was also an attempt to provide programs in adult education. At first the schools were opened to the adults in the evening for television viewing but soon most homes had their own sets. Undoubtedly a great number of Samoans watched and profited from these educational offerings, but in general this programming ran a poor second to the commercial television schedule that was offered nightly. National Broadcasting Company programs complete with commercials were taped in San Francisco and the cassettes flown to Pago Pago for viewing a week after their initial presentation. Now for the first time Samoans were given an opportunity to view an alternative to the large Samoan extended family household—the suburban nuclear family as presented in situation comedies and family series.

With the new emphasis on education well underway, the government boasted that 94 percent of the children were attending school daily and 99 percent of the secondary students were graduating. A community college, founded in 1971, had an enrollment of approximately 1,000 students in 1974.

Because of the changes in Samoan education and economics there were signs that the social structure was being affected as well. Robert Maxwell had observed in 1970 that

Family heads, who previously commanded the distribution of wealth, now find themselves with a decreasing economic basis for their political authority . . . . And their moral influence, even within their own families, is waning, as more youngsters move out from under their scrutiny and control and establish themselves as wage earners elsewhere. (1970:145)

Many Pago Pago Bay area households had a very motley composition indeed, for relatives had moved in from outlying villages and from Manu'a in order to take advantage of employment opportunities in industry or government. One must also realize that the composition of Manu'an and rural Tutuilan households is also adversely affected by this migration in search of work. In the 1970s the government of American Samoa reported a growing juvenile delinquency problem in the form of property destruction, truancy, pilfering, and drunkenness.

Maxwell also reported that the attitudes of younger Samoans were not supportive of the *matai* system. For example, he quotes a young school teacher: "It seems to me that the chiefs of the clans are taking advantage of the people who don't hold titles . . . . My family has asked me several times to try to get a title, and I say: 'No.'" And another man, age 36, from the Pago Pago area is quoted as saying, "I don't want none of that chief stuff! Who cares about chief anymore?" (1970:144–45).

Maxwell (1970) believed that better transportation, both local and to the United States, better education (particularly in the use of English), the coming of a money economy, and an influx of material goods, plus an increasing desire for and capacity to acquire them, were causing Samoan traditional social institutions to break down.

In our research in 1976, we were unable to

substantiate as great a degree of change in family organization as that suggested by Maxwell (1970). The kinds of statements quoted above, which he implies were typical of young Samoans in the 1960s, were occasionally made to us, but we believe they are far from typical of the attitude of Samoan young adults. We did not find hostility among most young adults in regard to the *matai* system. Students at the community college who responded to questions about the *matai* system had varied opinions. Some think the *matai* is too powerful or is guilty of inequality in treatment of extended family members. On the other hand, many believe the *matai* does much to help his people and to continue the traditions of *fa'asamoa* (the Samoan way). Perhaps most revealing, however, are the comments of those who express criticism for the system but admit that they would like to be chiefs. A case in point is the young man who objects to the power of the *matai* but wants a title "so that I could have all my family's property. And I can rule the whole family, and let them give me things that I want."

We uncovered several cases where people who had been educated in the United States or who had been in the military service for several years had returned to Samoa at the request of their families who wanted them to hold the family title. We also found that in a few cases people had given up good jobs on the mainland and had moved all their belongings to Samoa when chosen to receive a *matai* title. Most of the derogatory remarks against the system appeared to us to be of a "sour grapes" variety emanating from people who had little chance of being chosen as a *matai* anyway.

David Pitt (1970) also wrote about the stability of Samoan social institutions after his research in the somewhat more traditional Western Samoa. It was his feeling that the *matai* system and other traditional Samoan institutions are more than adequate to support economic progress. Whether in the recruitment of labor for cash cropping, in cooperating with relatives in marketing enterprises, or in financially assisting commercially minded young Samoan businessmen, the family system appears quite capable of providing the necessary organization for future economic development. It has also been discovered that the traditional social institutions are providing support in New Zealand among Samoan migrants

who are trying to survive in a somewhat hostile European society (Pitt and MacPherson, 1974).

In order to assess the influence of modernization on the status of Samoan elders since 1962, we conducted interviews with elderly villagers (aged 60 and over) in Ta'u village in the isolated Manu'a island group and in Fagatogo, the government center on the main island of Tutuila. The Ta'u sample consisted of 35 elders (54 percent male, 46 percent female) with an average age of 69.7 years; in Fagatogo the sample was 50 elders (42 percent male, 58 percent female) with an average age of 70 years. This represented nearly the total universe in this age category for these two villages.

The roles of the aged in their families and households seem to be much the same as in earlier years. Ta'u village remains more traditional than the villages on Tutuila island, especially in terms of activities. It is still common in Ta'u to see the old folks weaving mats, braiding sennit, and even carving oars for use with the long boats. These traditional tasks for the aged were not observed in the more urban villages except at the craft houses established by the Territorial Administration on Aging. Elders on Tutuila who participate in that program are paid a minimum wage (about $1.25 per hour in 1976) to produce items which are then sold, mostly to tourists, in a retail shop.

The extended family household still prevails in American Samoa, and our aged respondents, with the exception of one couple, were all living in such households. The old couple living alone were in the urban area, and we were told by a neighbor that their children went to the United States to live and had never even written a letter back. This seems to be an atypical situation as we were unable to confirm other similar cases.

Family is very important to aged Samoans. In fact, when asked what they thought was the best thing about being old, almost all replied that having their family—children and grandchildren—to enjoy was best. Most agreed that the *aiga* (extended family) is as important now as it was 10 years ago, although some old people think family members listen to them less. They all say they are still consulted about family problems, about ceremonial events—weddings, funerals, selection and installation of a *matai* (chief)—and about church donations. These and other issues which entail family decision making and usually contributions of money and/or goods are referred to as *fa'alavelave* (trouble). Exclusion of the aged from these deliberations would imply a serious change in their status. This does not seem to have occurred.

As described earlier, the later years of life have been a time when special consideration and respect could be expected by those in that period. This means, for example, being entitled to the best food, assistance with a bath if needed, perhaps a back rub, or having someone bring a coal from the fire to light one's pipe. High school students in Samoa in 1976 still seemed very cognizant of the obligations involved in caring for the old. The general theme of their comments was "we have to help the old people and do what they say because they took care of us when we were babies."

There is other evidence that the patterns of care do indeed continue. In both Ta'u and Fagatogo, there was almost unanimous agreement by the aged that they are obeyed and respected by the young. More than 90 percent of the elderly interviewees in Ta'u said they get better food and special treatment that other family members are not entitled to. In Fagatogo, however, just over half the old people said they receive preferential treatment. This may reflect, in part, an effect of the increased economic demands on younger family members; they have less time to devote to these "extras" for anyone. There are also many entertainment opportunities outside the home in the urban area, e.g., movies, bars and nightclubs, bowling, pool, and bingo games with cash prizes. Most of these attract the young, especially men; but bingo has become a popular pastime even for the aged on Tutuila.

The aged in Samoa seem not to have experienced any serious decline in status to this point. The 1976 research data indicate that many of the customs regarding care for the aged are still operative. There are some potential problem areas, however, which if unchecked, could alter their situation in the future. As noted above, the increasing number of activities outside the home in the urban villages, which attract the younger people, is one such issue. Some of the elders in Fagatogo expressed concern about the fate of the family with people spending so much more time away from home.

Without question the emigration rate since the 1960s has had an adverse effect on individuals, families, and institutions in the islands. Motivations for leaving Samoa seem to lie in the desire for well-paying jobs which will permit acquisition of attractive material possessions, desire to obtain better education for themselves or their children, and for some, a desire to escape what they consider an oppressive traditional social system involving heavy financial obligations to *matai*. Others no doubt leave out of a desire for adventure, and some leave to make use of their island-acquired education which has often been out of step with island occupational opportunities. Some have labeled American Samoa's education as "education for export."

This emigration to the United States primarily involves young Samoan adults. This seems to represent a more serious threat to the old people of Ta'u than to the more urban villagers. The population of that island has decreased by about 29 percent since 1960 (U.S. Bureau of the Census, 1963; Marcus et al., 1974). It has become almost routine for the young to leave Ta'u following completion of high school. The depletion of this age group, which normally would form a significant component of the work/support group for the household, is probably the biggest threat to the continued high status of Ta'u's elders. While the life style of this village is still as traditional as can be found in American Samoa, there are some signs of stress. Given the distorted demographic balance that has developed, with little possibility of an economic incentive that might reverse the trend, it is not surprising that the aged of Ta'u reported psychosomatic symptoms at a level found in other studies to be indicative of mental stress (Inkeles and Smith, 1970; Murphy and Hughes, 1965).[3]

THE BUREAUCRATIC IMPACT

The presence of the Territorial Administration on Aging (TAOA) in American Samoa requires some comment. This agency, organized in 1974, administers funds made available from the federal and the local government for programs for the aged. By 1976, the major accomplishments by the agency had been a survey of all residents aged 50 and over in the territory and establishment of a craft program. The latter was developed to encourage retention of traditional skills in carving and weaving. Funds had been acquired for a nutrition program, and there were plans for providing assistance with transportation and acquistion of hearing aids. The TAOA was experiencing difficulty in implementing the nutrition program due to conflicts between government regulations and cultural values. Similar problems have been reported from Micronesia by Borthwick (1979), who makes two points that seem especially relevant for the Samoan situation. First, he suggests that old age is not viewed as a social problem in Micronesia. In the case of nutrition programs for the aged, he says that given the nature of the extended family in that area, the existence of serious nutritional deficiencies would affect an entire family and not just the aged, as these American-formulated aid programs usually assume. This also appears to be true for Samoa. The presence of this social agency for the aged, therefore, does not necessarily imply a real need for its services or failure of traditional support systems.

Whatever problems modern change may pose for the Samoan aged, few of those interviewed verbalized any real dissatisfaction with their lives. When asked if they would like to migrate to the United States to live, more than 95 percent said "no," although many have been to the states and others think they might like to visit briefly. The most common reason for wishing to remain in their homeland is preference for their familiar life style and customs. There were expressions of concern about the different climate and the expense of living in the states, fear of dying in a foreign land, and most often, of not understanding the way of life. Family ties and responsibilities seem to be crucial to the aged; many feel that they are needed to care for the young and to advise the family.

SUMMARY

American Samoa is a society which has been characterized as having a great deal of cultural stability. Adjustments to change have occurred apparently without sacrificing the integrity of the major social institutions. The cultural system has also been conducive to conferring status on the aged members of the society. However, Samoan society has been subjected to increased exposure to the forces of modernization in recent years.

Due to political circumstances a crash program designed to promote change was imposed on Samoa by the American government in the early 1960s. The major effects of this modernization effort have been: (1) increased migration from the outer islands to the government center and from Samoa to the United States; (2) a shift in the economic base from subsistence agriculture to wage labor, which takes more people out of the home; and (3) improvement of the educational system.

In spite of the undeniable impact of these changes on Samoan culture, the *matai* system remains viable. It has been modified to meet contemporary economic and social conditions, but most Samoans are loyal to the *matai* and continue to support and to receive support from the system. Since the *matai* system is inextricably associated with respect for the aged, we believe the persistence of this traditional social institution is a significant factor contributing to the retention of high status among Samoan elders.

NOTES

1. On rare occasions titles are held by women, and when this occurs, their selection is based on the same criteria as apply to men—intelligence and family service. Many villages, however, have traditional mores which prohibit the election of a woman to a *matai* position.

2. The Women's Committee is composed of the wives of chiefs, talking chiefs, and untitled men plus the village organization known as the *aualuma*. The *aualuma* at one time served as the retinue

of the village ceremonial princess, the *taupou*, and is made up of unmarried women and widows. The Women's Committee is primarily interested in public health and infant welfare projects, in civic undertakings such as raising money to furnish the home of the village pastor or to provide beds and other equipment for the dispensary. They also have ritual functions such as entertaining visiting ceremonial parties.

3. The Psychosomatic Symptoms Test (Inkeles and Smith, 1970) is similar to the Health Opinion Survey (Murphy and Hughes, 1965) and consists of questions such as "Do you have trouble sleeping?" "Are you bothered by your heart beating hard when you are not exercising?" "Are you often troubled by headaches?" The test includes 12 questions, 11 of which were used in the Samoan interviews. Anyone reporting more than half of the symptoms is judged to be suffering psychic stress (Inkeles and Smith, 1970). We found that 66 percent of the Ta'u aged reported experiencing more than half of the symptoms whereas only 38 percent of those in Fagatogo reported that symptom level.

Nancy Scheper-Hughes

DEPOSED KINGS: THE DEMISE OF THE RURAL IRISH GERONTOCRACY

Oh, how the mighty have fallen! In this sensitive article, Nancy Scheper-Hughes documents how all the reputed demons of modernization have come to roost on the heads of the aged western Irish peasant. In studying the tiny parish of Ballybran, Scheper-Hughes serves as an anthropological "keener," standing eloquent wake over the death of the Irish gerontocracy. This event, stimulated by a fourfold population decline in the last century, has been marked by a drastic reduction in support by children, the collapse of community economic cooperation, forced-retirement programs, the ridiculing of remembered Celtic lore, and even the radical transformation of customs regarding death and aging. The once dignified movement of the elderly couple to the sacred "west room" of the house, which signified high esteem, has been replaced by unceremonious "warehousing" of the elderly in old-age homes and mental institutions.

"Ca"il an sneachta bhi' comh geal anuirig?"*
—*Irish proverb*

KEEPERS OF THE DREAM: ORIGIN OF THE IRISH GERONTOCRACY

EVER SINCE THE PATH-BREAKING work of Conrad Arensberg and Solon T. Kimball (1940), based on their field research in County Clare during the 1930s, social anthropologists and folklorists have portrayed western Ireland as one of the few remaining and viable "folk cultures" in Western Europe.[1] They have attributed to the traditional coastal community a lively, unbroken tradition of calendrical festivities, open-air markets, fairs and pilgrimages, music, dance, storytelling, quaint customs and fairy beliefs, and a relatively autonomous peasant economy supported by a devout, land-worshipping, self-reliant, egalitarian class of subsistence farmers who rely as much on barter and mutual aid as on hard cash. The bond that holds this harmonious society together has been described as an overarching web of kinship relations that makes kin of friends, and "friends" of kin. At the pinnacle of the familistic kinship structure stand the "old ones"—all power, authority, privilege, and wealth vested in their venerable hands. As Arensberg has written:

Ireland is in many ways an old person's country. Where emigration carries the youth away, old age is disproportionately numerous. But that fact is not all the story, for the rural Irish are long-lived . . . . They live long because they have much to live for. In their own sphere of life, they are honored; they have power. (1937:107)

And elsewhere, according to Arensberg and Kimball:

Place of Honor and privilege within the household

This essay was specially prepared for this book by the author. Permission to reprint must be obtained from the author and publisher.
Sections of this article previously appeared in *Medical Anthropology*, 1978, 2(3); in *Marxist Perspectives*, 1979, 2(1); and in *Saints, Scholars and Schizophrenics: Mental Illness in Rural Ireland*, 1979, University of California Press.
*"Where is the snow that was so bright last year?"

belongs to the old couple. In their families they are objects of respect and a mild sort of veneration on the part of all younger members. This respect is as much folk custom as the norms of family life. (1940:163)

The traditional rural Irish family was described as the three-generational stem family, patrilocal, and to all appearances, patriarchal. The father characteristically rose to power late in life after his own father had reluctantly loosed his reins and retired with his wife to the proverbial vestibule of sanctity, the "west room" of the cottage. Fathers passed on their names, lands, and households to the favored (usually firstborn) son, while the disinherited sons were prepared for village trades or town professions or forced into emigration to England or America. Daughters were passed on like pawns in strategically arranged marriages with neighboring households. Although the daughters were theoretically entitled to a dowry or "fortune," this was nothing more than a circulating fund, which passed into the hands of the bride's father-in-law to be used as dowry money for his own daughters. The "old man" delayed both inheritance and dowry decisions for as long as possible in order to maintain control over his dependent and vulnerable sons and daughters for as long as possible. Irish sons remained disenfranchised "boys" as long as they lived at home unmarried, which not infrequently reached their fiftieth year. The stability of this system, resting on the unquestioned authority of the "old man," was maintained through the siphoning off of the "misfits" and the "rebellious" children through forced exile (emigration) and training for the clerical life.

This anthropological paradigm of "peasant" Ireland corresponds to the official version of rural society disseminated by Irish language revivalists, nativists, and nationalists, and has, as well, a long literary pedigree in the romantic writings of Douglas Hyde, Lady Gregory, W. B. Yeats, J. M. Synge, and William Carleton.[2] It is also reflected in the genre of Blasket Islands "folk" autobiographies—those of Peig Sayers, Tomas O'Crohan, and Maurice O'Sullivan.[3] Since as early as in the late nineteenth century some of these writers were already lamenting the passing

of the "real" Irish peasant along with his proverbial respect for the "old ones" (parodied in Synge's *Playboy of the Western World*), it is quite possible that we anthropologists, beginning with Arensberg and Kimball, have inherited a cherished myth, an "ideal type" that never existed save on the tips of the wily tongues of native informants. Alternatively, the dramatic changes of the past 40 years have resulted in a true realignment of power relations in rural Ireland detrimental to the elderly.

ANTHROPOLOGIST AS "KEENER"*

John Messenger (1969) began to reverse the tides of anthropological reporting with his startling description of Aran Island peasants as depressed, hypochondrical, and guilt-ridden: straining against the bit of gerontocratic authority vested in the parish priest as well as in the rural *pater familias*. Robert Cresswell (1969) followed fast with his brief discourse on the pervasive spirit of death and decay in the depopulated west, which he dramatically symbolized in the forlorn, ancient graveyard on his book's dust jacket, as well as in the photo frontispiece of a solitary and weather-beaten old farmer, staring listlessly into his half-filled pint of stout. While generally uncritical of the rural Irish gerontocracy model, Gordon Streib (1972) nonetheless suggests that the "veneration of the elderly" may be a class-linked phenomenon, characteristic of the familied, "strong" farmers of the countryside, but not applicable to the numerically more dominant solitary farmers, eeking out a rather miserable existence on their "grass of two cows" and weekly pension of four or five pounds.

Some years later, Hugh Brody (1973) described the transformation of rural Irish economics, social life, and ethos since Arensberg and Kimball's seminal work. Although Brody does not concentrate on the role and status of the aged, his discussion of the eroding effects of agrarian capitalism on rural patterns of mutual aid,

---

*Keener—paid mourner at the traditional Irish wake.

traditional values, courtship and marriage, and on the authority of the country farmer, paved the way for the following analysis, based on a year of fieldwork in a mountain parish of west Kerry ("Ballybran") during 1975. I will suggest that the collapse of the Irish "gerontocracy," witnessed in the old ones' loss of power and control over their adult children, in the specter of forced and early retirement under Common Market guidelines, in the wholesale "warehousing" of the elderly in hospitals and old-age homes, and in the radical transformation of customs regarding death and dying, is a by-product of the postwar industrialization of Ireland and the spread (even in remote areas like Ballybran) of an alien, capitalist ethos.

THE PEOPLE LEFT BEHIND: CHANGE AND DECLINE

Nellie, mother of 11 children and one of several village matriarchs, is at 92 a shut-in. She is tended to by her only child to remain in Ireland, and 68-year-old Mikey is today almost as feeble as herself. Mikey's marriage was arranged late in life, and his wife, a wealthy widow from "west o' Dingle" several years his senior, died early and childless. Nellie delights in telling visitors about her sons and daughters abroad, their gains and successes—a small square in Springfield, Massachusetts, named after her eldest and "pet" son, a city park commissioner; newspaper clippings of local elections won and occasionally lost by other sons and sons-in-law; colorful Penney's Department Store portraits of "Yankee" grandchildren in bountiful number. When urged, Nellie will tell some of the stories for which she has gained local renown—tales of the "Black Protestant" Cromwell, of the Penal Days, of the "Troubles," and of her son who was shot in error by his own companions during a local IRA skirmish. But in the midst of the telling, the animation vanishes from her voice, and she begins to stare aimlessly out her window and over the wild Atlantic coastline. "Wisha, I should have gone off to America, too," she muses. "But, Nellie," I coax, attempting to bring her back, "look at the beauty of the place: the sea, the grass, the mountains . . . ." She laughs, cutting me off. "Sure, girlie,

there's the sea and the mountains all right. But what is this miserable rock of land but a curse on us?"

The quality of social life in western Ireland today has little relationship to that so delightfully described in Arensberg's *Irish Countryman*. To be sure, the gay strains of the melodeon and the primitive beat of the goatskin bodran can still be heard on a long summer's evening. But the melodeon players are more than likely city cousins come home to visit their native turf from Liverpool or Dublin, where they now permanently reside, and the lively crowd at the pub consists largely of German or English tourists in the area for backpacking and salmon fishing. The winter "regulars"—the solitary tight-knit group of permanent parish bachelors—sit grimly in a row neither sure of how they feel about the invasion of their normally silent card-playing and round-drinking "club," nor how they should act in the presence of outsiders, some of them women.

During the first weeks in August when the hay is normally cut, raked, and stacked by a "*meitheal*" or cooperative work force of fathers and sons who attend each man's fields in turn, what can be heard today—except the repetitive lament by solitary bachelors as they watch their field of hay rot from rain: "Where are the people?" A few attempt to do alone or with the help of an aged wife the work once done by 10, 15, 20 pairs of hands. Others, with remittance money from relatives abroad, hire tractors and part-time summer help. Still others seek solace at the pub and utter, "Bad cess to the hay!" hoping the "dole" will get them through the winter and enable them to buy feed for their cows and calves.

The fabric of a social life once rooted in intense familism—a dependency upon the reciprocity within wide circles of near and "far out" kin—has been rent beyond recognition by the virtual disappearance of the necessary relations. Family farms without the labor of extended families cannot operate today, although villagers still attempt to work within the same economic model.

The origin of this demographic collapse was most certainly in the Great Famine of 1845–1849 which reduced Ballybran parish by half, from 2,772 to under 1,500 people. As in the rest of *Eire*, an initially adaptive reversal of marriage and birth patterns (toward later marriage age and smaller families) and a vigorous emigration followed. Whereas in 1965 the parish civil police census recorded a population of 645, today the community is just barely holding together at 461 souls. Only four births offset the 38 deaths and 15 emigrations during 1974–1975.

The predominant household of Ballybran in the current generation is neither the stem nor the nuclear family, but rather a nonconjugal, consanguinous domestic unit. As marriage becomes increasingly uncommon, the majority of middle-age adults live with one or more members of their family of origin, while the majority of the elderly live alone. Of 138 households that comprise the parish only 21 conform to the traditional three-generational stem family, while 63 households are comprised of varying combinations of blood kin: bachelors alone or with their unmarried brothers and sisters, widows and widowers alone or with their middle-aged unmarried children (see Table 1).

The celibacy, childlessness, and sexual imbalance of the Irish farm population have important implications for the status and welfare of the elderly. Due to successive waves of female emigration, males outnumber females in all except the over 75 age group for the County Kerry farm population (see Table 2). While the aggregate ratio of male to female farm children is approximately five to four until age 18, afterwards males outnumber females by roughly three to one.

In Ballybran parish there are today 64 bachelors over age 45 but only 27 unmarried women (nine spinsters and 18 widows). Even more dramatically, although there are more than 30 still hopeful and eligible young men between the ages of 21 and 35, there are only five young women between these years still unattached—and none seems inclined to give up her freedom. Although fleeting courtships and flirtations occur between adolescent secondary school pupils during the year, a trail of broken romances

TABLE 1
Domestic Cycles in Ballybran Household Composition

Stages (Total n = 138 households)		Classes		Percentages	
I. Simple conjugal groups; nongenerative or postgenerative (21)	A.	Husband-wife childless (by preference or sterility) (11)		A.	8.0
	B.	Husband-wife childless (by emigration of all children) (10)		B. Total	7.2 / 15.2
II. Fully conjugal and generative; parents and young or still marriageable children (41)	A.	Nuclear households (20)		A.	14.5
	B.	Extended households (21)		B. Total	15.2 / 29.7
III. Transitional households: conjugal-generative becoming nonconjugal, nongenerative (13)	A.	Husband-wife-middle-aged bachelor son(s) (11)		A.	8.0
	B.	Husband-wife-middle-aged spinster daughter (2)		B. Total	1.4 / 9.4
IV. Nonconjugal or postconjugal and nongenerative: consanguineous domestic groups (63)	A.	Solitary bachelor (16)		A.	11.6
	B.	Bachelor brothers (7)		B.	5.1
	C.	Adult brothers-sisters (12)		C.	8.7
	D.	Widow-middle-aged son (9)		D.	6.5
	E.	Widower-middle-aged son (8)		E.	5.8
	F.	Widower-middle-aged daughter (1)		F.	.7
	G.	Widower-aged mother (1)		G.	.7
	H.	Widow alone (9)		H. Total	6.6 / 45.7

Source: Hughes, 1979. Reprinted by permission of The University of California Press.

TABLE 2
Percentage Distribution of County Kerry Farm Population by Sex and Age

Years	Male	Female	Total
14 or less	14.3	13.5	27.8
15 to 19	4.6	3.8	8.4
20 to 44	14.2	8.7	22.9
45 to 64	14.0	11.2	25.2
65 to 74	5.9	4.4	10.3
Over 75	2.7	2.7	5.4
Total	55.7	44.3	100.0

Source: County Kerry Committee of Agriculture, *County Kerry Agricultural Resource Survey* (Tralee, 1972), 63.

follows each summer at graduation time, when the vivacious and mobile young women migrate. They leave behind a large proportion of their beaux who are committed, as the girls are not, to carrying on the family farm and name—a task rendered more absurd each year as these men come to recognize that they are not likely to produce any heirs of their own: The County Kerry Agricultural Resource Survey (1972) reported that 41 percent of all farmers over 50 in the county were without prospective heirs either because of celibacy, childlessness, or emigration of all prospective heirs. Nationally the picture is not quite so bleak: The Irish Farm Center Survey reported that approximately one-quarter of all farms in the Republic are without successors—a total of between 44,000 and 50,000 farms.

What have occurred in western Ireland during the intervening 40 years between Arensberg and Kimball's analysis (1940, first edition) and this study are not only a radical shift in demography, changes in technology and marketing, but, more important, changes in the consciousness and self-definition of the younger rural populace, and a reevaluation (even by elders) of the values of traditional country life. Arensberg and Kimball's vivid description of a lively farm family life in which patriarchal father delayed retirement and set son against son in the spirited competition for the "old fellow's" favor and eventual birthright of the farm has not only colored the "official" anthropological view of Irish family life, but has even dominated the Irish government's conception of the mechanics of farm succession. As

recently as 1973 the Department of Agriculture published a report (Macra na Feirme, 1973) widely distributed through small shopkeepers of the west, urging farm owners to retire early, select and name an heir as soon as feasible, and free all children for marriage at a reasonable age. The report was guided by a number of assumptions—that fathers still rule imperiously over their children, that competition over inheritance of the land is intense, that women are eager to marry into farms, that farming is valued as a priceless, if not a profitable, way of life—assumptions which, if they were once true, no longer hold today. For at least three decades the selection of an heir for the land has been governed by the process of elimination rather than by choice. That is, the last one to escape (usually the youngest son) gets stuck by default with an unproductive farm and saddled with a life of celibacy and greatly resented service to the "old people." And, as the statistics on female emigration make abundantly clear (see Kennedy, 1973:41–65), the last thing on the minds of village maidens is staying around long enough to get "hooked" into marrying into "a miserable little farm in the outback," as one girl put it. Or, as another teen-age girl sized up the situation: "Who in their right mind would ever want to stay around here and marry one of these *angashores* (worthless leftovers)?"

The consequences for the aged parents are fairly obvious: They have lost their economic power base over the younger generation. Inheritance of the family farm (often a little plot of 10 to 15 acres) and arranged marriages have become a bad joke among the young lads and upwardly mobile lasses of the village, and both are parodied in popular songs coming out of Cork City and Dublin where the "liberated" rural youth flee as soon as they are able. As the "old ones" control little that the youth want, awe and respect for the aged have, in many cases, given way to pity, contempt, and ridicule. An anecdote from my field work illustrates this radical transformation.

The summer of 1974 was particularly wet, and anxiety spread as villagers worried about saving the hay that would feed their cows and calves through the winter and part of the spring. At least three consecutive dry days and several helping hands are needed to cut, turn, and stack the hay. Less than a decade ago this task would have been done unquestioningly by cooring—by farmers taking turns in each other's fields. Children and adolescents would do lighter tasks, and women would take turns bringing the tea and fresh bread to the fields. It was an occasion for conversation, storytelling, poetry recitation, and drinking. Boundaries would be adjusted, and old disputes and hard feelings softened by the porter and spirits. But, increasingly, connotations of "low class" and "small farmer" are attached to those few "backward" farmers who participate in cooring. The more prosperous and "stronger" farmers hire tractors and pay village adolescents to help with the hay.

Tomas and Nora, an aged, childless couple who observe the older customs, sent out word that a *meitheal,* or cooperative work force, was needed for the haying. My husband, children, and I showed up at their fields the next sunny day to find the 70-year-old couple bickering about how best to do the job alone. They were surprised and grateful for our offer to help, and we worked until the sun set that evening. Later in the pub we asked the "idle" young lads of the village why they had not gone up to Ballybran to lend a "friendly" hand to their distant cousins. The boys were incredulous to think that anyone would be so "stupid" as to work for nothing. "That old pair is so backward and miserly," offered one young man, "that they expect a dinner of dry spuds and a bottle of ale is pay enough for a day's work in the fields." Other youths in the pub protested that the old farmer was pensioned and had enough to make do on. Finally, the young men pointed out the absurdity of time spent harvesting the hay needed to feed the old man's "herd" of two sick old cows kept up out of affection for the creatures rather than for profit. The consensus of the youths was that the cows should be destroyed and that the old couple should accept the inevitability of retirement. Old Tomas's face grew red with anger as I relayed the message to him, and he replied: "I helped their fathers and their grandfathers, and now they 'have right' to help me." But no such help was to be forthcoming that season, and my husband and I were ridiculed for continuing to coor.

While older villagers valiantly attempt to cling to their tried and familiar, if rapidly failing, patterns, adolescents and young adults are today only rarely motiviated by the same "friendly" (i.e., kinship-based) values. The ethos of individ-

ualism and capitalism has made steady inroads into their world view.

With the demise of traditional family farming and its values, the rural father is no longer the regal *paterfamilis* described in the early literature. Today he is, like the patriarchal culture he represents, a broken figure. At best, he is humanely tolerated; at worst he is openly ridiculed by his adult children. The shadowy, invisible presence of the rural father was brought home to me during an evening visit with Teresa, her husband Brian, and their unmarried adult children. While the children and their mother conversed animatedly with my husband and me, old Brian stood off alone in a corner of the kitchen. It grew dark and as the evening shadows began to cast themselves against the walls, my four-year-old was startled to see the dark, nearly motionless figure of the old man. "Mummy, who *is* that man?" she asked fearfully. This was met with a long pause, followed by a stifled giggle from Teresa and her daughter. Later in the evening when Teresa began to berate her husband for his careless dress and appearance, the old man responded by picking up his goatskin drum and beating out a rhythm, at first melancholy and then fierce and warlike. Such was his release. But never a word spoken.

In addition to the erosion of their economic authority, both elderly men and women are no longer cherished for their role as keepers of the ancient Celtic tradition. Although officially a "Gaeltacht" or Irish-speaking community, only the very old in Ballybran are Irish speakers "from the cradle" and use the language voluntarily, drawing on a rich store of myths, stories, proverbs, songs, and prayers. The younger generation "have" only "Christian Brother Irish," as the elders are wont to call the young people's halting, stilted "book-learned" Irish, devoid of the finer folk forms of the versatile tongue. Worse, the young people resent having to study Irish, and questioned in a high school survey, two-thirds of the students said they saw little value in perpetuating the "dead" language which was no use in commerce or other professions and would take the emigrant no further than Cork City. It is little wonder, then, at the reluctance of the few remaining Irish storytellers to share their rare gifts. Of their language the old men are wont to say: "The words are broken in my mouth." Of their music, village musicians can be heard to comment: "My spirit is broken. How can I play when there are none to listen?"

I am reminded of the occasion when my husband and I were rather formally invited to the home of Mary, a village matriarch of 93, where we were to tape her recitation of Celtic prayers, stories, and proverbs. Her granddaughter had coaxed Mary out of bed and dressed her in the traditional garb of long skirt and black shawl, and had her sitting primly by the fire. Mary proceeded dutifully, if somewhat dubiously, to recite her rich repertoire of folk culture into the recorder, while her granddaughter winked at us from across the room and shook her head in evident pity. After Mary had completed her recitation she turned rather abruptly to ask with a quiver in her thin, melodious voice:

"An' do ye understand any of it?"

"No," I replied rather guiltily.

"Not a bit?"

"No, but I can have it translated back in America."

"Pity," she said sadly, with an edge of bitterness in her voice. Others among the elderly were not so cooperative and said, in no uncertain terms, that they'd be damned before they'd commit their treasures to a ridiculous black box. As one old woman put it: "Now I have a prayer, and nobody else have it. But see if I don't die with me lips sealed before I let some strangers take off with it."

THE SEXES: SOME CONTRASTS

While the general forces eroding the Irish gerontocracy—demographic imbalance, the shift from a peasant to a capitalist ethos, and from stem to nuclear and fragmented consanguineal households—have negatively affected both sexes, elderly women (particularly widows and mothers) maintain some influence and command respect in spheres of life from which village males are generally excluded. While virtually all villagers are practicing Catholics, religious activities (including the care of sacred vessels and priest's vestments, the organization of house Masses, the preparation of children for the sacraments and of bodies for

wake and burial) are considered women's work, and work in which advancing age increases influence and participation. A curious inversion of the Mediterranean honor and shame complex limits male participation even at Sunday Mass. Where bachelors of all ages congregate outside church reverently attending a Mass they can neither see nor hear, and middle-aged and elderly married men and widowers (domesticated by their marriage ties) line the walls and aisles of the church, the village widows and ancient matriarchs command "front stage," occupying the central pews of the church. During Holy Communion the old women make their way to the altar first, often dramatically leaning on the arms of an adult son or daughter, or both. Men rarely receive Communion, save during Christmas, Easter, and at the Station Masses, because as they are wont to say when questioned on the delicate matter: "Women have right to receive; men have shame." They are referring to the relative difficulty males have remaining in a permanent "state of grace," tempted as they are by the serious sins of the flesh: drunkenness, irresponsibility and sloth, "bad thoughts and deeds." The harmless, little venial sins ("sineens") of women—gossip, lying, loss of temper—do not exclude them from approaching the altar rail daily, if they so please. The widespread guilt and what I call the "confessional conscience" of village men also result in their avoiding interactions with the parish priest, still one of the most powerful and highly esteemed members of the rural community. As a result the priest tends to both give and take counsel from the elderly women of the parish who can "make themselves bold" in his presence as the old men cannot.

Similarly, mothers control and influence the lives of their children long after they have even left home, because bonds of affection are generally speaking more effective than bonds of authority, duty, and respect. Where relations between fathers and sons in rural Ireland are characteristically distant and tense in adulthood— the son's sullenness rooted in the not too distant memory of the tyranny of rod and cane (see Scheper-Hughes, 1979:154–55)—mothers maintain warm and caring relationships to their daughters, and Oedipally intense, if somewhat ambivalent ones, to their sons (Scheper-Hughes, 1979:169–85). Adult children of both sexes are more likely to feel responsibility for, and actively care for, their elderly mothers than their fathers. Guilt about leaving one's mother behind was a dominant theme of the many emigration motif stories told by young adult villagers on the Thematic Apperception Test (Scheper-Hughes, 1979), as well as the most frequent explanation given by middle-aged or elderly bachelors for never having married. Even more significant, as will be explored later, old women (who are better able to manipulate family guilts), are less likely to be institutionalized in an old-age home or mental hospital before they die than are village men.

FORCED RETIREMENT: THE COMMON MARKET VERSUS THE KERRY FARMER

In addition to his loss of status within the home, the aged farmer is likewise viewed by county agents as a serious impediment to the government's vigorous plans for agricultural "development" and "modernization." The elderly bachelor farmers of County Kerry are a particular target of criticism as they are viewed as neither change- nor production-conscious: the former because they are old and set in their eccentric ways; the latter because they are without wife or heirs and have minimal wants and needs. Agricultural adivsors in the county seat complain that the old farmers resist adoption of modern innovations, and although they are comfortable with traditional patterns of cooperation with neighbors and extended family members, are suspicious of participating with "strangers" in development schemes or agricultural cooperatives. Hence, traditional small-scale farming appears increasingly unproductive and uneconomic, seemingly justifying the EEC (European Economic Community, the Common Market)-instigated proposal to prematurely retire all traditional and noncompetitive Irish farmers.

The small farmers of Kerry were among the last in western Europe to experience the impact of international agrarian capitalism, world marketing, and secularization. They are still smarting from the blow.

Since the period of colonization England has

blocked the economic development of Ireland. Although Ireland gained political independence in 1921, more than two-thirds of Irish foreign trade is with Great Britain. This pattern of trade has resulted in an increasing dichotomy between the urban and industrialized east and the underdeveloped and agricultural west. The west has emerged as the region devoted to the breeding of calves; the midlands as the region for fattening them; and the east as the region for the preparation of cattle for sale to British markets. The east has prospered at the expense of the west, which has gradually changed from mixed, subsistence farming (the peasant, familistic model of Arensberg and Kimball) to what Gibbon refers to as a "commodity economy" (i.e., agrarian capitalism), more responsive to England's than Ireland's needs.

Ireland's unfortunate dependency upon England, even when clearly detrimental, can be seen in its entry into the European Economic Community (EEC or Common Market) in January 1973. It entered on the coattails of England despite negative public opinion in Dublin and Cork and considerable active protest and demonstrations by the small farmers of the west. During the formal negotiations at EEC headquarters in Brussels between Great Britian and her partners (Ireland, Denmark, and Norway) and Common Market officials, the Irish representatives concluded that they must "join immediately without tears." And so the Republic opted to follow the yellow brick road of "modernized" and "competitive" agriculture.

As almost any western villager will eagerly relate over a friendly pint of ale, this fateful entry into the EEC sounded the death knell of traditional Irish family farming. Through participation in international agriculture the village farmer has been shamed and exposed—forced to measure his worth in terms of acres, head of cattle, the English pound and the American dollar. Judged in these capitalistic terms, the Kerry farmer with his "grass of three cows and six sheep" has begun to look upon his work as a failure and an embarrassment to the changing, modern image that Ireland wishes to project to the world.

The EEC soon demanded that the Kerry farmer gracefully bow out of farming altogether in order to make room for "agribusiness." One of the highest priorities on the EEC agenda is the restructuring and "modernization" of agriculture in the remaining marginal and "peasant" areas of Europe, with a view toward equalizing urban and rural incomes. The EEC's infamous Mansholt Plan proposed to reduce drastically the number of people living on the land by encouraging "nonproductive," subsistence-oriented peasant farmers to sell their land and accept an early retirement with a small pension for life. The released farm land would then be placed at the disposal of the EEC to be sold to "development-oriented" substantial farmers.

In exchange for a farmer's retiring his land, he would receive its market price plus a small weekly pension for life. In addition, each complying farmer would be allowed to keep two acres for a garden plot, but he was prohibited from ever taking up farming again as an occupation. Neither age nor successor status bore on the qualifications for retirement, and those with young heirs as well as those without them, and the young and able-bodied along with the elderly and feeble were to be pensioned off together. The Minister of Lands, Mr. Fitzpatrick, reported to the Irish Parliament that of the first thousand retirement applications received, 14 percent were from farmers under 55 years, 61 percent from those between 55 and 65, and only 25 percent from those 65 and over. One of the most vocal critics of the farm moderniza-tion scheme, Dr. Ivor Browne, Chief Psychiatrist of the Eastern Health Board, expressed his alarm on the front page of the *Irish Times* that such widespread early retirement would not only "set farmer against farmer" but could contribute to "premature senility" and add to the already staggering geriatric problems of the dispirited rural areas.

A representative of the Irish Land Commission in Tralee estimated that more than 90 percent of the farmers on the Dingle Peninsula would qualify for retirement under the scheme. The farmers had little choice since those not complying would be severed from the grants and subsidies necessary for survival. Transitional farmers would no longer qualifiy for sheep and beef premiums and would be disqualified from the grants for equipment and livestock purchase, farm buildings, and land reclamation. In all, the farm scheme was designed to facilitate the transfer of land from small to big farmers, rather than from father to son. In

Ballybran the EEC retirement scheme was interpreted as a vote of no-confidence in traditional family farming, and further undercut the already waning status of the elderly.

Throughout the long and discouraging winter Ballybran farmers gathered in clusters at the pub or at each other's homes to listen to radio or public television reports decry and deride the "backwardness" and "conservatism" of the western coastal farmers, who were characterized as living like parasites off welfare handouts, grants, and subsidies, who were opposed to progress, and who hung greedily and tenaciously onto their unproductive and miserable farms. The specter of forced and early retirement hovered over the nightly pub sessions in Ballybran, and a puritanical gloom settled like a mist into each man's pint of bitter porter. "Well, lads, 'tis we're finished up now for sure" was a commonly heard refrain. The local residents read about their lives and livelihoods, which the national press treated as so much debris.

A number of opinion surveys recorded the dissatisfaction of the western farmer with the EEC retirement scheme. The Irish Farm Center Report (Macra na Feirme, 1973) cited one in which 385 farmers over 55 were asked whether they would avail themselves of such a scheme. Only 23 percent replied that they would seriously consider it. Likewise, the small farmers of southwest Kerry united to protest forced retire-ment, and until our departure in the late spring of 1975, only one farmer in all of west Kerry had signed up to retire. And he was held up to vicious ridicule.

Traditional rural Irish society recognized no such status or role as "retired" farmer. Even after the aged farmer had eventually "signed over" legal ownership of the land to his heir, the old man usually maintained a managerial role in the affairs of the farm until death. Even the word *retired* only begins to creep into the occupational listings of the deceased in the Ballybran death register during the mid 1960s. A deep-seated and pervasive fear of idleness keeps not only young and middle-aged farmers busy at tasks that outsiders might consider unproductive, but the same Celtic work ethic drives elderly and already pensioned farmers and shepherds to keep up at least the pretenses of the daily round. The mind of the Kerryman associates inactivity with immorality ("idleness is the devil's workshop") and retirement with death. Many a rugged old shepherd attributes his longevity to a life of hard work and "no idling." Villagers are particularly fond of repeating stories of the miraculous cures of ancient farmers who struggled out of their deathbeds at the last moment in order to check up on a favorite old cow or newborn calf, only to discover that they once again felt better on their feet and could engage in the business of the farm.

ON DEATH AND DYING—OR, WHATEVER HAPPENED TO THE IRISH WAKE?

"Sing a song at a wake;
Shed a tear when a baby is born."
   —Irish proverb

The decline of the status of the old ones in western Ireland is perhaps best exemplified in the remarkable reversal over the past 40 years in attitudes and practices surrounding death and dying. Until a few decades ago virtually all village deaths took place at home and were accompanied by exacting attention to a blend of pious folk Catholic rituals and pre-Christian or "pagan" festivities.

The rural Irish preoccupation with death, wakes, and funerals is proverbial—commented upon by Irish writers, folklorists, and poets, as well as by social scientists. Although all major life events are celebrated in Ireland by a sacrament, and most accompanied by some kind of celebration, no life passage event was ever more celebrated than death. Where birth goes hardly noted at all (see Scheper-Hughes, 1979:143), and weddings are more often than not elopements or very private affairs with only the closest of kin and most intimate friends invited (and the uninvited traditionally crashing the festivities dressed as "straw boys"), a village death and burial demanded (and still does) the participation of every adult parishioner. "Every wake day a holiday" is a saying still heard in parts of west Kerry.

The old ones of the village not only dominated household relations as long as they lived, but orchestrated many details of their own death, wake, and burial, as well as controlled significant family- and farm-related decisions through their dying wishes. The village tailor commented that in the "old days" (circa 1930), he would be called on to make a new suit for three events in a man's lifetime: his First Holy Communion, his wedding, and his wake. Ordinarily, a man would order his "wake suit" well in advance of his death, and it would be hung ceremoniously on a hanger behind the bedroom door, and periodically taken out for display to, and admiration by, household callers.

Until the Catholic Church clamped down on what the clergy viewed as "pagan abuses," the traditional Irish wake (best described by Sean O'Suilleabhain, 1967) was a merry, raucous, and frolicking affair—especially if the deceased were an old person who died a "proper" death (see below). It was a time for storytelling, dancing, singing, feasting, and drinking. The corpse might be lifted out of its bed and propped up at a card table with a shot glass of whiskey placed in its hand, or even taken out on the kitchen floor to dance. The "carry-on," as wakes are called in Ballybran, lasted for at least two days for, as Brendan the shepherd explained it: "You never know for sure when the soul leaves the body, so you want to keep it company for as long as possible, and not bring it into the church when it's too fresh-like." Traditional Irish wake amusements included literally hundreds of games (see O'Suilleabhain, 1967:38–129), contests of strength, skill, and endurance, taunting and mocking, riddles and tongue twisters, mock weddings, deaths and confessions, and above all, perhaps, faction fighting. A good wake always culminated in a good fight. Sean O'Suilleabhain tells of a distressingly sedate funeral in County Kerry he attended some years back. Just as the villagers were preparing to leave the gravesite the dead man's son shouted: "'Tis a sad day when my father is put into the clay and not a single blow struck at his funeral." As he ended the complaint, the boy landed a blow squarely on the head of the man next to him, and within minutes, the rest of the procession rose to the occasion and did full justice to the memory of the old man.

A "good death" was, and still is, considered

the ultimate sign of a good life. Good or "holy" deaths are, above all, premeditated, expected, and relatively gradual events, the final moments arranged in the presence of family members and with the last sacraments and final blessing of the parish priest. As villagers say: "A death without a priest is no death at all." The final moments are the crucial time when old feuds and disputes are set straight and put to rest, when the wishes of the dying regarding inheritance, marriage, and other family decisions are made explicit, and when the individual can make his final peace with his Maker—confessing to the priest, perhaps, the one, last horrible sin, held back over the years out of shame or pride or stubbornness (and which, unconfessed, could prejudice his chances of salvation).

The old ones are expected to "know" (sense) the approach of Death, which is often personified by country people, as in the expressions: "Death hasn't left Cork on his way to meet me yet," or "He has struck me; I have his blow in my heart." This particularly strong folk belief lends an aura of supernatural power and mystery to the elderly. Many a villager tells with deep satisfaction of the moment his mother or father took to bed and sent for the priest with the words: "I will not last the night," or "Today is my dying day." Auntie Peg, a village matriarch, explained the ritual of Lon na Bais, the death meal:

Well, I hadn't been in America for a year when I received a letter from my mother saying that my father's time was drawing near, and it was best that I come home. No sooner did I step inside the door when my Da said to me: "Now that you're home, girleen, I can take to my bed and die in peace." He ate no solid food from that day on, only a cup of tea and a few drops of cognac from time to time. Then, one morning, about two weeks after I had returned home, he sent for me, and asked that I bring him a large bowl of tea and two thick slices of bread. "No, father," says I, "you must be mistaken. Our people haven't used bowls for more than a century. You must mean a large cup of tea." "It's a bowl I want, and two thick slices of bread," he replied. I offered him some cognac, but he stopped me, saying: "No, my daughter, I have no use for that anymore—I had plenty enough when I was a boy. But today I am going to see my God." I did bring him the tea and the

toast and laid it out next to his bed, but he never touched any of it at all. He just sat up in bed, smiling at it, anxiously waiting. He died that night. He didn't tell me at the time, but now I know that this is what the old folks called the Lon na Bais, the death meal. Wasn't that a beautiful death? His death has made the rest of my life happy, and God willing, my own end will be the same.

Other premonitions of death are looked for and found in: the distant sound of wailing (the banshee); the dim twinkling of lights against the window of the sick room ("fairy lights"); bird formations in the sky; a clock that has stopped ticking.

Elderly villagers to this day recite a Gaelic prayer that calls upon God to grant them a "Holy death"—a slow, gradual, even painful death, one that is met head on: alert, awake, aware, and with full faculties of sense and reason. There is no rural Irish sentiment analogous to the American wish that a loved one die peacefully dazed or unconscious in sleep. The old ones would be in control until the bitter end.

Conversely, a "bad," unholy, or untimely death is one that is sudden, unheralded, unexpected, and unprepared. These include: any "sudden" deaths by naturalistic ills (heart attacks, strokes); chaotic or accidental deaths (falls, choking, drowning); and death through inexplicable, supernaturally tinged "folk" ailments ("inwardly disease," "devil-touched-person," "shock," "the evil"). Other bad deaths are those that occur away from home and kin (while traveling or in a hospital or institution), and deaths at an early and untimely age. All these deaths hint of Divine displeasure for, as villagers gossip, if a man had led a clean, decent life surely God and the Blessed Virgin wouldn't abandon him to such an end. Much to-do, for example, was made of the "sudden death" of a foolish old man who "lost his life" while "saving the hay." A judgment was implied in the death: The old man, too stingy ("sure he had the heart of a mouse") to pay hired help, and too proud and impatient to wait for help from his busy neighbors, died instantly of a massive heart attack on the third day of haying.

Although a villager cannot always control the way in which he dies (although certain pious folk Catholic practices are said to insure a "happy death'') a proper wake and many Masses said for the repose of his soul can soften the stigma of a sudden death and aid his soul in Purgatory. Respect and veneration for the elderly demanded such care at death. From reports of villagers, as recently as the 1950s the only acceptable pattern of treatment for the elderly was a well-attended death at home followed by a "kitchen wake." Today, as will be explored in a later section, most deaths occur in the Dingle Hospital, and many occur in an old-age home or in the county mental hospital.

A death at home is a costly affair, emotionally as well as financially. The village midwife who is also called upon to wash, dress, and prepare the remains of deceased villagers for wake, estimated that the average "carry-on" (wake party) cost upwards of 120 pounds (about 300 dollars) in 1975. Villagers are reluctant to lay out the expense and go through the bother of a home wake for any other than the most intimate relation. Since Ballybran is both an aging and a dying parish, fewer and fewer survivors are called upon to wake and bury seemingly more and more distant kin. The somewhat callous but pragmatic solution to the problem is the one reached by Teresa: "When you can see that they're close to 'finishing up,' that's the time to send them off to the hospital."

Death at the nearby hospital is followed by a representation of villagers who travel over the mountain pass to claim the body and bring it home to rest. As the small procession of cars winds its way down into the village, the church bell tolls, calling parishioners to pay last respects. The closed coffin lies in state, alone, overnight in the chapel and, following a funeral Mass the next morning, is carried on the shoulders of the nearest male kin to the graveyard. After the burial the village men take to the nearest pub for several hours of drinking and "passive" mourning, and the women take to each other's homes for a "supeen" (a small taste) of sherry. All but four of the 38 village deaths in 1975 were handled in this rather brusque fashion.

While a few elderly men and women still keep a trunk with their home wake and funeral accouterments ready—white sheets, blessed candles, brown habit or wake suit—the more pragmatic, like the self-sufficient widow, Bridie, have prepared instead a traveling bag for the final trip over Connor Pass to Dingle Hospital where they can reasonably expect to die.

That many of the rural elderly do not consider this shortcut to the grave a proper or fitting tribute to their long lives is indicated by the increasingly common phenomenon of what I will call the "death pact." While the rural Irish village has always been plagued with its share of local money lenders and petty capitalists, known in the local jargon as "gombeen men,"* in the past 40 years a new class of local entrepreneurs has arisen who make their living by profiting on the growing tourist industry by gobbling up the farms of bachelors without heirs and converting good pasture land into vacation bungalows for visiting English tourists. While no old farmer in his right senses would sell his lands to a rival farmer (land equals status in western Ireland) elderly bachelors are particularly prey to the temptations offered by the socially alienated gombeen men. The entrepreneur knows the Achilles' heel of the bachelor farmers and exploits the anxiety, isolation, and status deprivation of the old men. In exchange for sale of all or part of their lands (at well under market value) the entrepreneur promises that he or his wife will regularly look in on the old man and protect him, should he become incapacitated, from institutionalization. Most seductive of all, however, the petty capitalist will sometimes promise, if not a "holy death," at least the benefit of a decent and proper burial: a death and wake at home, followed by a formal procession to the ancient graveyard. During the period of our stay at least a half-dozen old men had made such pacts, and could be seen ambling over to the homes of their patrons for a plate of spuds and boiled bacon after Sunday Mass, served not always without ill grace by the mistress of the house. Time will tell whether the gombeen man fulfills his promise *after* the death of his client, but clearly the pact was successful in keeping a

---

*From the Latin, *cambiare*, to count or change money.

few candidates for eventual institutionalization free from the dreaded threat of confinement.

ANOMIE, ALCOHOLISM, AND MENTAL ILLNESS

"I am anxious in my mind, turning it around and around, alone here in my house two weeks since my wife is dead. Cait, my daughter, has left me—gone aboard ship to America with a big crowd from Dingle.

"I am troubled and fearful in mind.

"Tomorrow I will write her on a scrap of paper.

"She will send me help and it will be bountiful.

"Flour, sugar, tobacco, tea I will have in the larder.

"Maybe I will even live to see Cait return, dressed in white silk with a purse of money and a yardful of cows.

"Many a handsome, well-built young man will want to take her home, and after I am dead and laid out in white sheets on the kitchen table, both will 'keen' me.

"Cait! Cait! Come home to me!

"Don't lay me down to sleep in the poorhouse of Dingle at the end of my days.

"Would you send me out with a beggar's pack to wander the roads like a Tinker begging bread and tea and kept in the houses of strangers?"

—Translation of a villager's "keen" or funeral lament, after the death of his wife

The most visible effect of the collapse of the traditional patriarchal and gerontocratic social structure can be witnessed in the contagious spread of despair and anomie among middle-aged and elderly villagers in western Ireland. This anomie emerges in the alcoholism, sexual devitalization, and, most tellingly, in the high prevalence of psychiatric hospitalization among bachelor farmers over 50 (see Scheper-Hughes, 1979:65–82).

Durkheim's concept of anomie is especially useful here because of its focus on the loss of a meaningful work identity and its relationship to the proliferation of such self-destructive tendencies as alcoholism, and on the primary importance of men's and women's work to their sense of self-esteem.

Although bachelors are most prone to despondency drinking during the "idle" winter months, married men also drink heavily during this time because, as one farmer confided: "I can't sit around the kitchen all day where the missus can remind me that I have nothing to do." The pub provides a sense of solidarity and community as well as spirits for the dispirited. Bachelors, isolated in their lonely stone cottages, drink heavily and largely account for the alarming statistic that the Irish are hospitalized 12 times as often as the English for alcoholism. Four of the six village pubs in Ballybran cater exclusively to single men who gather in little "clubs" most evenings of the week but in greatest number on weekends, fair days, and funeral days. Brody's poignant description of winter drinking patterns in a bilingual village of west Cork is reminiscent of pub behavior in Ballybran:

These men [village bachelors] do not stay [in winter] for the long hours which characterize their summer drinking nor do they often consume the sheer volume of alcohol drunk in summer. But when they do drink hard and the effects of the drinking begin to appear, despondency becomes more extreme and its behavioral indices more overt. A drunken man in winter leans more heavily on the bar. He often seeks to draw another drinker or two to his side. Such a group creates a tight circle of privacy around itself—a privacy physically expressed by the arms they lay across one another's shoulders. Then, with faces almost touching, they appear to join closely in evident despair. This despair is not expressed in discussion among the drinkers. Rather they exchange silence as if it were words, and words in brief expressions of the lonesomeness. (1973:32–33)

The majority of village bachelors make an adequate adjustment to the demands of their harsh existence through such strongly enforced male bonding patterns as "round drinking" at the pub. For the more psychologically vulnerable, however, a gradual withdrawal from peer activities, such as sports events, Sunday dances, cooperative turf cutting, and hay making, signals the onset of an engulfing spirit of depression and despair—sometimes climaxing in the fits of rage or violence that lead to eventual psychiatric diagnosis and hospitalization.

While single girls who rarely feel trapped by village life display little of the winter depression suffered by boys and men, married women are also prone to depression and despondency. As a category, village women are more likely to be treated for the condition that they describe as "feeling run down" or "bad nerves." Between October and March the village dispensary, located in the back kitchen of the home of the village midwife, is filled with sighing, sad-faced, middle-aged women of whom the dispensary doctor complained brusquely: "They are all nothing but a bunch of neurotic hypochondriacs. Not a thing wrong with them—just bored and feeling sorry for themselves." His blanket prescription: a mild tranquilizer and an admonition to get out and visit with the neighbors. The local folk remedies for winter despondency used by other women are prepackaged tonics and elixirs sold at village shops in large quantity. Alcohol is a refuge for many others.

The most depressed and dispirited group in the village however are the aged, many of them solitary widows, widowers, bachelors, and spinsters without family or friends to look after them. Within this group the desire for death can be strong, and I often heard the refrain: "May God spare me the cold and loneliness of another winter." With one 90-year-old bedridden woman I had a continuing dialogue about the morality of suicide in which she debated her longing to die versus her fear of God's wrath at her lack of faith. The elderly have reason to be depressed. Because of the disintegration of Irish familism, institutionalization, often in the county mental hospital, has become a common solution for dealing with troublesome and demanding old people.

WAREHOUSING OF THE ELDERLY

The laws governing temporary certification for psychiatric hospital admission in Ireland have changed in the last decade, but still appear to be in need of revision. Prior to 1945, most patients

were admitted to mental hospitals by order of a judicial authority. Under the Mental Treatment Act (1945), hospitalization was effected upon medical certification only. The act provided for three main classes of patients: voluntary patients, who enter mental hospitals of their own accord; temporary patients, who may be committed for up to six months of treatment; and persons of unsound mind, those judged likely to require more than six months of treatment. This act has been amended, and although all commitments today are nominally "voluntary," upon entrance into a hospital the patient is still asked to sign away his freedom for a stipulated amount of time. In addition, referrals for commitment are still frequently made by family and community members working with the cooperation of the local dispensary doctor or visiting psychiatric nurse. The dissenting patient may be in a vulnerable position, unable to defend himself against "helpful" family and neighbors. The forms for temporary certification to the psychiatric hospital need only be signed by the district dispensary doctor, a general practitioner. The burden of proof is skewed—weighted toward proving sanity rather than the reverse, as the forms require the doctor to state reasons for refusing to certify an individual, while they do not require him to justify the institutionalization. This makes it difficult for the doctor to refuse certification in doubtful cases—especially under pressure from influential family and community members.

In familistic rural communities where bitter disputes, petty jealousies, and envies often divide social groups into factions, vindictiveness can and does sometimes result in psychiatric certification and commitment of rival family members and neighbors. The director of a psychiatric hospital in County Cork commented in his hospital's journal that there are often times when "the real reasons behind certification are ill will in the family, land disputes, desire to be rid of the elderly relatives once they have made deeds of assignment of their property in return for care, etc." (Dunne, 1970:33).

As discussed earlier, the average rural villager can expect to spend his last months, weeks, or days not in a rocking chair by the fireplace, but in a hospital, old-age home, or mental institution. Today when most old people in the village are isolated and unattached bachelors, spinsters, and widows, they live alone rather than as a natural extension of the farm family. Sickness and death at home pose an emotional and financial burden upon relatives who no longer feel a strong responsibility to care personally for their distant kin. The proliferation of old-age pensions,[4] Gaeltacht grants,[4] free coal and electricity for the aged, and the presence of a visiting health nurse has created among younger villagers a strong feeling that the *government*, rather than family and friends, has the primary responsibility to look after the aged. Today, villagers expect to be, and are, reimbursed by the County Welfare Services for their neighborly acts of visiting the sick and elderly. And institutionalization has become— even in rural Ireland—the main solution for dealing with the troublesome and ubiquitous old people. Since spaces are considerably more difficult to arrange in old-age and nursing homes, and since the rural aged are frequently driven to eccentricities by the isolation of their lives, the county mental hospital, with its thousand-bed capacity in tiny, depopulated Kerry, has become the largest recipient of the unwanted elderly. Throughout Ireland, 30 percent of the psychiatric hospital population is elderly—65 and older (O'Hare and Walsh, 1974).

The director of the Kerry County mental hospital frequently addressed himself to this issue during our conversations. Although during his five years of directorship he reduced the resident population from its full thousand-bed capacity to 700 occupied beds, he expressed the desire for still further reduction. Of the 700 hospital residents, he said 300 "could and should be returned to their communities this very day, except they are old and have no one who will take them in."

An assistant psychiatrist attached to the county medical hospital and administering a circuit of outpatient clinics in rural Kerry, confirmed that "psychogeriatrics" was his greatest problem as well. Many of the single, isolated old people referred to him at the Dingle clinic were in his estimation not mentally ill but physically ill— suffering from malnutrition and lack of human contact and care. "Many of these old people are weak and delusional from hunger and loneliness; if they seem 'paranoid' in their accusations against kin and neighbors, their accusations are often well founded. For every single old farmer there are a host of greedy neighbors waiting to pounce on his land and possessions."

While this same doctor was a psychiatric intern some years ago at a hospital in Donegal, he was asked by the director of the hospital to do a medical and psychiatric survey on 170 chronic and "questionable" mental patients. "Of all 170 I could positively diagnose only five patients as psychotic or severely mentally handicapped," the doctor said. "The remaining were somewhat senile, withdrawn, unattached old people with nowhere else to go."

The pathogenic loneliness of the village elderly is epitomized in the case history of David, a crusty old retired seaman under treatment for a rather eccentric disorder, which was diagnosed by the hospital psychiatrist as amnesia. David complained that he could not locate his image in the mirror. His eyes would search the glass over and again, but not a trace of "himself" could he find. To the best of his recollection he lost his image soon after the death of his best—indeed only—village friend, a fishing partner. With the death of his "soul mate," David's mirror image had disappeared.

And, surely, loneliness is part and parcel of the constellation of Michael O'Brien's "madness"— Michael, the harmless old village "saint" who sits up all night with his cows, milking them, crooning to them, reciting a few decades of the rosary, or, more often than not, simply "standing the night with then" to protect them from unseen dangers; in short, serving the dumb creatures with the same devotion he once lavished on his mother.

That male psychiatric patients significantly outnumber female patients for all age groups in Ireland, increasing with age (O'Hare and Walsh, 1974), can be explained in part by the protection from designation as insane through a family claim to a husband, children, or more distant kin. Since village males throughout western Ireland are more frequently single than females, and since bachelors are less likely or able than village spinsters to attach themselves to an extended family, *their* eccentricities are less likely to go unnoticed.

The old maiden aunt Teresa, for example, spent the whole of the winter of 1974 indoors sitting passively and morosely in front of the turf range. Although normally a sociable woman, Teresa could not be coaxed into conversation with family members or neighbors. She was, in villagers' estimation, "very depressed." Although Teresa grew thin and haggard from her ordeal, the depression was interpreted within the realm of "normal" behavior given the long, uninterrupted winter rains and the woman's advanced age.

Tolerance for, and definition of, normal and abnormal behavior is determined in part by the individual's integration, or lack of it, within a strong kinship network. Although Auntie Peg is an aged, mentally handicapped, cantankerous old spinster given to episodes of rage followed by withdrawal and deep depression, she is considered "little bother" to her large extended family who owe her a lifetime of debts. Consequently, Peg will never see the dark walls of the county mental hospital. Over her lifetime, Auntie Peg had reared all of her sister's 13 children, most of whom had emigrated and "made good" in America. The few nephews remaining feel a responsibility to dote on the "old one." Explained Brendan:

We leave her free-like. She raised us up and took care of us. She would never harm anyone, so why would we put her away now? We let her have her fags when she wants, buy her a pretty ring now and then, and we make sure she takes her tablets to keep away the gloom.

CONCLUDING REMARKS

The rapid and radical loss in the status of the aged in western Ireland conforms to the prevailing social science paradigm regarding the relationship between aging, industrialization, and "modernization" (see especially William Goode, 1963; Donald Cowgill, 1974b). The combined effects of increased longevity due to medical technology, urbanization pressures and values, and higher education for the younger generation everywhere contribute to decline in gerontocratic authority. The old ones of rural Ireland are, ironically

enough, suffering from their own demographic gains—their longevity and their proportional increase in the rural population (over 20 percent of Ballybran were over 65 in 1975). The changes of the past 40 years, especially the reevaluation of small-scale familistic farming, the continuing exodus of the young and able-bodied, and the consequent disintegration of the three-generational stem family has resulted in the virtual abandonment of the elderly to a variety of impersonal and inadequate social welfare schemes and institutions.

The Irish village of the western coast today embodies a broken culture: a state of affairs most detrimental to the aged who are unable to flee or to accept new values, and who, consequently, are left to contemplate the wreckage. As village social life and institutions have constricted, and as younger villagers seek entertainments in the "singing pubs" of nearby towns, the lives of elderly villagers have become isolated and their temperaments, correspondingly, more secretive, withdrawn, and eccentric. The winter *ceilidhes*, friendly fireside chats among neighbors, presided over by the *shanachie*, the old storytellers and mythmakers of the village, have given way to "telly" watching among the few prosperous families and early bedtime among the elderly. Where parishioners once built their cottages closely nestled against each other for comfort and support, the younger generation now build regulation stucco bungalows, appropriately modern, that remove them from proximity and contact with the "old folks." Where once the irresponsible and fresh young "boy-os" of 40 protested that they were "too young" for marriage and "too inexperienced" for farm ownership, the 40-year-old bachelors of the '80s face a premature retirement and the realization that they have been left behind by the upwardly mobile village girls who already consider them "old men." The apparent ironies of the current sutuation will, no doubt, be buried along with this last generation of Irish-speaking peasants. And with them will disappear, as well, a venerable way of life, of which the old widow Mag, says, "The likes of which will never be seen again."

NOTES

1. For anthropological works on Ireland in the classical functionalist tradition *see:* Eileen Kane, "Man and Kin in Donegal," *Ethnology* 7 (1968): 245–58; Robin Fox, "Tory Island," in B. Benedict (ed.), *Problems of Small Territories* (London, 1968); A. J. Humphreys, *New Dubliners* (London, 1966). The best sources on Irish folklore and peasant traditions include: Kevin Danaher, *Gentle Places and Simple Things* (Cork, 1964) and *The Year in Ireland* (Cork, 1972); E. Estyn Evans, *Irish Folkways* (London, 1957); Robin Flower, *The Western Island* (Oxford, 1944); Marie MacNeill, *The Festival of Lughnasa* (London, 1962); Sean O'Suilleabhaian, *Irish Wake Amusements* (Cork, 1967) and *Nosanna agus Piseoga na nGael* (Dublin, n.d.).

2. *See* Douglas Hyde, *The Religious Songs of Connacht* (Dublin: M. H. Gill, n.d.); Lady Augusta Gregory, *Poets and Dreamers* (Oxford: Clarendon, 1903); William Butler Yeats, *Collected Poems* (New York: Macmillan, 1933); John Milton Synge, *Irish Folk Stories and Fairy Tales* (New York: Grosset and Dunlap, n.d.) and his *Complete Plays* (New York: Vintage, 1960); William Carleton, *Wildgoose Lodge and Other Stories* (Cork: Mercier Press, 1973).

3. *See* Peig Sayers, *An Old Woman's Reflections* (London: Oxford University Press, 1962); Tomas O'Crohan, *The Islandman* (Oxford: Clarendon, 1951); Maurice O'Sullivan, *Twenty Years a Growing* (London: Oxford University Press, 1957).

4. The Irish Gaeltacht, or Irish-speaking communities, are heavily subsidized through grants meant to encourage the use of the language.

David Plath

"ECSTASY YEARS"—OLD AGE IN JAPAN

Much has been written about the high status and prestige accorded the elderly in traditional Japanese culture (Benedict, 1945; Smith, 1961b; Plath, 1964a, 1972; Palmore, 1975a). In particular, many have focused on the Japanese version of Buddhism and its linking of the aged and even the dead to a family system emphasizing filial devotion and an elder's role infused with loving indulgence and an accepted dependence in this "second privileged period." However, demographic and economic changes have begun to alter traditional conceptions of old age. Although the percentage of elderly in Japan (8.8 percent in 1980) is one-half the figure for North European nations, the life expectancy and the rate of increase of the aged population there are among the highest in the world. Problems seem to be greatest for the very old. Their increasing dependency in the light of new demands on family caretakers has led a growing number of the aged to pray for a quick death (pokkuri) in Buddhist temples.

It should be noted that a great deal of controversy surrounds the issue of modernization and aging in contemporary Japan (see especially Sparks, 1975; O'Brien and Lind, 1976; Maeda, 1978; Plath, 1980). For a contrasting view to the one Plath presents here, consult the works of Palmore (1975a, 1975b, 1975c).

THE SCENE IS FROM Japan's best-selling novel of the past year. A middle-aged wife is commenting to her husband on the situation in their home and many homes around them. "I get the feeling," she says, "that all of a sudden every family has an old person to take care of." The novel, *A Man in Ecstasy*, by veteran authoress Sawako Ariyoshi, portrays the decline and dotage of an 84-year-old man, and his family's struggle to keep him alive. More than a million copies of the book were sold within six months, and a movie based on it already has been rushed to the theaters. "Ecstasy years" has become a fashionable euphemism for senile decay.

The story's popularity is but one indication that Japanese in the 1970s have awakened to a new concern over the "social pollution" of old age in an affluent society. Rapid growth in longevity has run parallel with rapid economic growth, and the result is a veritable "elder boom." Within the past two dozen years, average Japanese life expectancy at birth has increased by 20 years. Latest calculations put it at 70.2 for men and 75.6 for women, higher than in the U.S. and rivaling that of populations in Northern Europe. In January 1973 the Ministry of Health and Welfare forecast that by 1985 Japan will have surpassed even Sweden, and become the world's leader in human longevity.

But a high rate of increase in the life span coupled with a low birth rate spells unprecedented demographic change: in the current phrase, an aging of society. Today somewhat less than one out of every ten Japanese is over 65, in contrast to almost two out of 10 persons in Northern Europe. But the percentage of old persons in the population is expected to double by 1985. With retirement compulsory in most Japanese enterprises at age 55, and with pensions and old-age benefits at perhaps half the level provided in other industrial nations, older Japanese find themselves barred from a fair share in the very prosperity they have helped earn for their countrymen. The majority have little choice but to cling to the generosity of their younger kin. If Labor and Construction deserve their Cabinet-level ministries, the editorial writers are saying, should there not also be a Ministry of Aging?

From *Pacific Affairs*, Volume 46, No. 3, 1973, pp. 421–429. Reprinted by permission.

Signs of new popular concern over aging can be seen on all sides. If "Elder Power" still speaks with a quaver, it is beginning to find a voice. The day after Kakuei Tanaka took office as Prime Minister in July 1972, 40 members of the Tokyo area League on Aging, demanding better support for senior citizens, staged a mini-demonstration and march past the vast complex of ministerial office buildings in Kasumigaseki. The League also has at various times sat-in before the Labor and Finance ministries and the national headquarters of the ruling Liberal-Democrat party. In April 1973 it began demonstrating in front of the offices of major commodity corporations which are under fire for hoarding fuel, building materials, and foodstuffs in a speculative gamble that fans inflation. Study groups on aging also are being formed in many places, some of them enlisting support from students and housewives and even an occasional "salaryman." As yet, all this activity put together amounts to far less than a Townsend Club in the U.S.—much less a broad-based people's movement. But already the national newspaper, *Asahi Shimbun*, has suggested that old-age welfare may become the source of the next surge of popular action when the present high tide of outrage over industrial pollution starts to ebb.

In the opening minutes of the year 1973, NHK-TV, the public network, began the year by broadcasting scenes of temple bells ringing at famous locations across the country. Moments later the television showed the ringing of telephone bells from a Tokyo "tele-care" center. Middle-aged female attendants were shown dialling New Years's greetings to the elderly shut-ins whom they now contact at least twice a week under a program begun during 1972. A survey in 1970 by the Ministry of Health and Welfare had found that more than 610,000 older Japanese are living alone, and that only one in three of them had a telephone. With Ministry aid some local governments have begun to install phones for solitary old persons, and others provide at least a bell or buzzer for summoning a neighbor in an emergency. In a few parts of the country home-helper service is available, but at present Japan has one professional home-helper for each thousand persons eligible for the service. For Sweden the figure is one in sixteen, for Britian one in ten.

Mass-media fascination with geriatric topics tends to peak in mid-September—because September 15th is "Honor the Elders Day," set aside as a national holiday more than 20 years ago. But news stories and special reports on aging continue to appear frequently in the media. In the autumn of 1972 the *Asahi Shimbun* ran a serial report of some 50 installments on "Here Comes the Senior Society," and the collected series already has been issued as a book. Another *Asahi* series, still running, deals with "Medical Care from Middle Age Onward." One young woman complained to me that concern over aging already has lured the media away from the topic of women's liberation.

Plastics manufacturers have caught the mood and are advertising the "Filial Piety Toilet" as the thoughtful gift for one's elders. A slightly more elegant version of the portable camping toilet familiar to Americans, it is lightweight, odorless, and can be left right in grandma's room and emptied periodically. Unlike traditional Japanese toilets it has a seat, and it can be fitted with handrails.

Writers and scholars are taking up geriatric themes with vigor, though none has come anywhere near to Ariyoshi in terms of popular sales. Ariyoshi caught further attention late last year by offering to donate 100 million yen (US $385,000 at current rates) in royalties from the novel to homes for the aged. Existing tax regulations allowed exemption from income tax for charitable donations only up to 15 percent of one's annual income. This meant that she would have had to surrender some 80 million yen in taxes. A new ruling was issued, allowing the total amount of any such donation to be exempt from taxation.

Five years ago when I tried to collect Japanese-language materials on aging I found only a handful of novels and scholarly monographs. Today the larger bookstores devote a whole section to the topic, and only a few of the items available are translated works, Simone de Beauvoir's *La Veillesse*, or Hemingway's *The Old Man and The Sea*, for example. Most of Japan's famous, as well as lesser-known, fiction writers have recently issued works on aging. Examples are *The House of the Sleeping Beauties* by Nobel Prize-winner Yasunari Kawabata, and *Diary of a Mad Old Man* by Jun'ichurō Tanizaki, to mention two who are widely known outside Japan. Among those less known overseas are Yasushi Inoue's *The Light of the Moon,* Kazuo Ozaki's *Nonchalant Old Man,* and Tatsuō Nagai's collection of linked short stories *Bound for Cochabamba.* On the nonfiction side several do-it-yourself handbooks on how to fend off senility have been published in the past few months. And along with a number of scholarly monographs on gerontological topics there is now a three-volume compendium, *Japan's Old People,* with essays by respected psychologists, psychiatrists, and sociologists.

Mass-media interest tends to follow lines familiar in the U. S.—pensions, reemployment, "golden age" centers, or eminent elders' hints on how to dodge dotage. But there also is a secondary focus of attention, less common in the U. S., on issues that include suicide, euthanasia, and *pokkuri shinkō* (prayers for a quick and painless death). In short, if the life span is going to stretch on and on, then how and when might it properly be terminated? The premodern Japanese ethic, reaffirmed during the Imperial years down to 1945, preached an ideal of almost unlimited sacrifice for the sake of one's elders. Historically it was derived from Confucian ideals of filial piety that have become familiar to many in the West. In Japan, however, the filial ethic was counterposed by another theme that is not familiar overseas, a theme which suggested that when elders became burdensome they had an obligation to leave this world. Juniors might even assist them in doing so. This is the image of *obasute* ("discarding granny"); a mountain 90 miles west of Tokyo still bears this name. The *obasute* theme can be found in stories and dramas dating from the sixth century down to the present, and has been the subject of at least two noted short stories in the past generation. One of the two, "The Old Oak Mountain Song," won a 1956 prize for the best story of the year by a new author.

There is little evidence that *obasute* has ever been practiced in fact as much as it has been screened in fantasy. Nevertheless, judges tend to be lenient when setting punishment for a junior who has taken the life of an ailing and age-wracked kinsman. The courts have yet to accept a formal plea of euthanasia as justification for homicide, but in a celebrated case in November 1962 the Nagoya Superior Court, though declaring the defendant guilty of killing his father,

spelled out the conditions under which it might accept such a plea: (1) the person must be near death from a disease for which modern medicine offers no therapy or cure; (2) the pain must be so great that no one could bear it; (3) the person must be conscious and honestly able to request death; (4) the act must be done primarily to relieve pain; (5) a physician must perform the act unless none is available; (6) the means used must be ethical. In the Nagoya case the court said that the defendant had failed to meet conditions five and six.

In October 1972 the *Sankei* newspapers ran an opinion survey on the issue, with these results. One out of two persons said they would choose euthanasia for themselves if afflicted by a painful and incurable disease; the rest said they would try to bear the pain. What if a member of your family asked for death under similar circumstances? One in three said they would consider it an act of sympathy to help bring on a death that would end the pain, but the other two-thirds said that any such action is tantamount to manslaughter. And the response was much the same (about a third in favor and more than half opposed) when people were asked if, assuming legal conditions were met, they would regard euthanasia as "socially acceptable."

Pokkuri shinkō might be thought of as a nonmedical or religious variety of euthanasia. *Pokkuri* is a vernacular word for a sudden and decisive action, loosely translated as "to pop off." Certain temples are believed to have the power to confer a death that will take one away *pokkuri,* swiftly and without agony. Though the belief is far from new, the number of supplicants at such temples is reported to have shown a steep increase in the last few years. One such temple near Takamatsu City, Shikoku, is said to draw more than 10,000 visitors on the days of the spring and autumn equinoxes. Suicide is a common pathway to death for old people in Japan as in many countries. And if longevity forecasts call up muffled national pride, the continuing high frequency of old-age suicide brings out public dismay. Older Japanese males range among the top 10 or 20 ranks in World Health Organization tables for rates of death from "suicide and self-inflicted injury"; older Japanese females usually are in first place. In North Atlantic nations, as well as in Japan, the suicide rate for men tends to climb steadily after age 60. For women, however, the North Atlantic curves tend to level off or even decline after 60; in Japan the curve rises continuously to age 80. As one Japanese writer put it, the old women keep sending home gold medals in a discouraging kind of Olympic contest.

Like other industrial nations, Japan has been building a complex of services aimed at making old age more secure and it is hoped more worth living. Bias is difficult to avoid when comparing such configurations among nations, but in general Japan seems to do well for its old people in terms of medical care and social education, and to lag behind many North Atlantic nations in terms of employment, housing, and overall economic security.

The rapid improvement in longevity is itself evidence for the high caliber of Japanese medicine and public health. Free physical examinations are offered annually to everyone over 65; the public health insurance program covers some 70 percent of their medical expenses, and local governments are beginning to pay for most of the remainder. More than 80,000 senior citizen centers have been developed across the nation in the last two decades, and they offer an impressive array of educational and recreational programs at little cost. On the other hand, low pensions, coupled with early forced retirement, continue to elicit cries of "welfare dumping" from domestic as well as foreign critics. In North Atlantic nations only about one in ten persons over 65 is said to be completely dependent upon younger kinsmen for routine life support. In Japan the figure was six out of ten in 1970, according to a White Paper issued that year by the Ministry of Health and Welfare.

The Tanaka government's policy on the retirement issue was set forth by Labor Minister Hajime Tamura in his very first news conference upon inauguration. Compulsory retirement at age 55 is an absurd and an outdated practice, he said, and retirement age should immediately be raised to 60, and eventually to 65. (The out-at-55 rule grew into standard practice before the Pacific War, when life expectancy in Japan was less than 60 years.) Retirement age varies considerably by type of enterprise and number of employees. Small companies in almost any sector of the economy are not likely to have a fixed retirement

age; large companies do in some sectors but not in others—e.g. almost all large insurance firms but only half of the large construction corporations. From Ministry of Labor surveys one can piece together the following overview.

(a) Three out of four firms with more than 30 employees have a fixed age for retirement. (b) Half of these firms require retirement at age 55, one-fifth of them at an age between 55 and 59, and the remainder at age 60. (c) Workshops that allow retirement later than 55 usually have raised the cutoff year only since 1965, to counter the growing labor shortage that has come in the train of economic prosperity; however, the most widespread practice is for an employee to retire at 55 and then to be rehired if he wishes—at the company's pleasure; reemployment most often is by short-term contract, with no provision for increases in rank or salary. (d) Except for high-level executives and bureaucrats, those who want reemployment but are unable to obtain it from the parent company are likely to end up in jobs where pay and working conditions are far inferior; the most widely quoted average for monthly reemployment income is 55,000 yen ($210) or about what a recent high-school graduate can expect as a new employee; when the Ministry of Health and Welfare surveyed persons reaching age 60 in 1970, it found that seven out of ten of those who had taken reemployment had lost their new jobs at least once, and two out of ten had lost them more than twice. (e) More than a third of those retiring still have children in school and a smaller but growing number also have aged parents as dependents; if the majority of retirees are eager for reemployment, perhaps this is not because of some work compulsion alleged to be inherent in Japanese national character so much as because they cannot provide for dependents out of rather meagre savings and retirement benefits. (f) Women ordinarily must retire some years earlier than men, most commonly at age 50.

On February 12, 1973, the Tokyo Superior Court brought down the wrath of women's liberationists, and amazed many others, by ruling that physiological differences justify an earlier retirement age for women than for men. A woman's level of physiological functioning, said the Court, is inferior to a man's, and at age 55 it approximates that of a man of 70. Therefore a five-year differential in retirement age—as in the case in dispute—is not inherently discriminatory. Ministry of Labor officials were nonplussed to learn that the Court based its ruling on a portion of a study they had issued in 1965. That portion of the study had concluded with due caution that while evidence from physiological tests did not rule out the possibility of overall sex differences in functioning, neither did it lend any support to the possibility. The Court favored the former interpretation—even though the intent of the full study had been to discourage sex differences in employment standards. However the issue is far from resolved. In March the Tokyo District Court, hearing a similar case, ruled the opposite: that early retirement for women amounts to illegal sex discrimination.

Managers are understandably hesitant about extending the retirement age. Doing so would boost personnel expenses, since base pay, fringe benefits, pensions, and retirement allowances all are pegged to years of service. And though the labor federations periodically call for raising the retirement age to 60, their major goal in the annual *shuntō* ("spring struggle") is for higher base pay. The Ministry of Labor has drafted a plan for subsidizing firms which retain employees beyond the cutoff year, but both labor and management have snubbed the proposal as tokenism. Both sides urge instead that the government's first steps be to double the social security payment and to exempt from income tax the initial 10 million yen of an employee's retirement allowance. Social security payments currently start at age 60 and amount to the equivalent of $60 a month (at current exchange rates). Retirement allowances differ widely from company to company. One retiree in four may receive $15,000 or more but the majority get less than $9,000.

Pension programs for some categories of workers pay about $100 a month, occasionally even more, but these programs cover only one out of ten in the labor force. The rest are eligible only for the National Pension and social security programs. The National Pension plan is a contributory one begun in 1960; the most one can draw from it at present is about $20 a month. One out of four oldsters is receiving the $60 monthly social security payment, and all in all only one in two is receiving a government

annuity through one of these programs. (Comparable figures are 80 percent in the U.S. and Britian, and 100 percent in Sweden.) The Ministry of Health and Welfare has proposed raising to $190 late in 1973 the monthly maximum for payments under both the National Pension and the social security systems. Payments will be pegged to a sliding scale, and will increase proportionately whenever the consumer price index has gone up more than five percent by November 1st of any calendar year.

Opposition parties grumble that the National Pension plan returns little more than one could obtain by putting the same money into an ordinary savings account. They also are advocating a noncontributory pension program which could provide immediate benefits to ease the burden on those who already are retired. The opposition would like to see part of the fund already in reserve in the various pension programs—as of now some $25 billion—used for this purpose. However, it appears that the Tanaka government wants to tap these reserves for its ambitious plan to "remodel the archipelago" (a reference to the title of the Premier's best-selling book).

Even after a decade of massive building construction the shortage of comfortable housing still evokes resentment. Very few public projects have been built with the aged in mind, but then survey after survey turns up the same result: Japanese tend to be lukewarm towards the idea of living in retirement tracts. As yet Japan has no senior citizen communities of the sort familiar in Florida, California, and Arizona, though some are in the discussion stage. On the other hand many villages are becoming de facto rural retirement communities, abandoned by the young in their mass migration to the Pacific Coast conurbation.

Recently the Japan Public Housing Corporation promised to give priority, in new housing units, to families that include an aged or handicapped member. These families will be guaranteed a first-floor unit if they wish one. The Corporation also is building in Yodogawa ward, Osaka, its first project designed for occupancy by an elderly couple jointly with a married child and his or her family. Elder and younger households will have separate apartments, with a shared veranda. Living with or near a married child has been a time-honored part of Japan's stem-family ideal.

Where space and finances allow, the elders have been provided with a separate retirement cottage, preferably on the same lot with the junior family's home. Eight out of ten Japanese over 65 still are living with descendants. The majority of persons polled in opinion surveys in recent years tend to favor the practice, but there is a growing secondary trend in favor of separate residence.

Raw statistical comparisons can sometimes be misleading in such matters. In North Atlantic nations only four out of ten old persons are living in the same dwelling with their offspring. Japanese and Westerners alike have been tempted to interpret this as a rejection of the elders and a symptom of family collapse. But studies in the West over the past decade show that the vast majority of old persons live nearby to at least one descendant, and that elder and younger generations, though dwelling apart, come together for a goodly amount of mutual aid and interaction. After comparing Japanese and Western patterns of aid, visiting, gifting, and the like, the distinguished Japanese family sociologist, Kōkichi Masuda, came to this conclusion: The only striking difference is that when a Western married couple decide to call on their parents, the couple will have to travel a few minutes to reach them.

Law and custom in Japan still declare that children must provide support for aging parents, but fewer and fewer old people feel that they can expect this as a matter of right, much less demand it. At regular intervals for 20 years public opinion on the matter has been sampled by the Mainichi Newspaper's Population Problems Research Council. The Council's surveys find that 70 percent of the populace still believe that one should care for aging parents as a "natural duty" or as "a good custom." In 1950 half said they expected to depend on their children for support when old, and one-fifth said they did not. But by 1969 the proportions had been reversed. These days when elders do live with married children, family power and authority almost always are in the younger hands. And from the juniors' point of view it is best for the elders to live separately—close by, perhaps, but nevertheless apart. A current slogan exaggerates the point but makes it plain: The ideal husband, says the slogan, is one who comes ie-tsuki, kā-tsuki, baba-nuki (with house, with car, without granny).

Dilemmas of caring for the elderly are at the heart of Ariyoshi's novel A Man in Ecstasy. Akiko, the fortyish daughter-in-law in the Tachibana family, has been a full-time secretary as well as housewife for most of her married years. (The wife with a working career still is a somewhat uncommon figure in Japan, but one swiftly growing in numbers and gaining in approbation.) But when grandmother dies and grandfather Shigezō is found to be sinking into dotage, Akiko is expected to sacrifice her career in order to nurse him. She struggles to arrange for outside help, but with only temporary success. Shigezō wearies of being left all day at the "golden age" center. A neighbor widow comes to look after him but he is repulsed by her attempts to woo him. Old people's homes refuse to take him because he is likely to wander off and they cannot afford to provide close supervision. By reducing her work to part-time Akiko is able to see him through stage after discouraging stage of regression. Before he dies he has become like a three-year-old, gazing at flowers and caged birds by the hour, smiling inscrutably at everyone, speaking only one word moshimoshi, "hello." But his safe passage into this realm of ecstasy is Akiko's reward for her filial fidelity—and perhaps, she thinks, it is his reward for longevity.

Akiko not only must cope with the increasingly incontinent and incompetent Shigezō. She also must confront the question of what will become of her when she grows old. Watching the 72-year-old widow make overtures to the old man, as Akiko "heard the voice and saw the rejuvenated figure of the old woman in front of her, she lost the ability to predict what would happen to herself when she got old . . . . She had realized that mankind is mortal; but when she was younger it never even had occured to her that at the end of the life she was leading, and well before death, this kind of—what has to be called a fiendish snare—would be there waiting for her." Akiko's husband asks a physician if senility isn't a disease? Well, comes the reply, senile dementia is. Are the old man's hallucinations a symptom of dementia? Not necessarily, says the physician—unless the old man goes berserk one probably shouldn't call him mentally ill. "It's a sickness of civilization, like tooth decay."

Mass longevity in Japan as in other industrial nations is pressing great numbers of persons into an environment about which we know astonishingly little. No N. A. S. A. programs have sent teams to chart the territory and test the life-support systems. We are all serving as laboratory animals in the sense that mass aging is an experiment involving not only the old but all those who must help them fend off what one theory in gerontological circles calls "disengagement." Concern over "ecstasy years" is a sign that Japanese are reaching new levels in their consciousness of human welfare needs. Worried Western stereotypes about the Japanese as "Economic Animals" look more and more like ethnocentrism in a new disguise. Lacking evidence to the contrary I prefer to assume that Japanese economic dynamism can be mobilized for welfare just as it has been for productivity. However I do not look for it to happen quickly, not even in Japan.

THE ETHNIC FACTOR

IN AGING

"The combination of being old and ethnic . . . forms a distinct social category, albeit of heterogeneous individuals. They suffer from a double stigma, where they have perhaps been lifelong victims of ethnic prejudice and now are victims of ageism."
—Elizabeth Markson (1979:344)

". . . rather than providing yet one more obstacle to be overcome in the aging process, ethnicity can furnish the elderly with a source of identity and prestige which they can manipulate to make a place for themselves in society."
—Linda Cool (forthcoming)

The consideration of ethnicity as a factor affecting old age brings back home the question of sociocultural variation. Ethnicity is commonly understood as social differentiation derived from cultural criteria such as a shared history, a common place of origin, language, dress, food preferences, and values that engender a sense of exclusiveness and self-awareness of being a member of a distinct social group. This definition of ethnicity overlaps but goes beyond the concept of a minority group "whose members have been singled out for differential and inferior treatment on the basis of such characteristics as their race, sex, nationality or language" (Jackson, 1980:2). Viewing the variations of aging in our country within the context of ethnicity seems mandated by the continuing cultural plurality in our nation. As Woehrer notes, in addition to the existence of American Indian, black, Hispanic, and Asiatic groups:

. . . as of the 1970s there were estimated to be five million Polish Americans, 20 million Italian Americans, two million Greek Americans, one and a half million Puerto Rican Americans, six million Mexican Americans, five and a half million Eastern European Jewish Americans and over a half million Japanese Americans. (1978:329)

Older persons in these groups are first- and second-generation Americans and along with earlier emigrating populations—Germans, Irish, Swedes, Greeks—have spent at least a portion of their lives in distinctive ethnic enclaves.

In the emerging literature on ethnicity and aging there appear two key themes that on the surface seem contradictory.* One theme stresses how minority group membership in the context

*For general works about the ethnic aged see: Place, 1981; Gelfand, 1982. Discussion of specific ethnic groups and their aged population can be found in: Kiefer, 1974; Cuellar, 1978; Cheng, 1978; Dukepoo, 1980; Ishikawa, 1978a, 1978b; Ishizuka, 1978; Peterson, 1978; Stanford, 1978; Valle and Mendoza, 1978; Gelfand and Kutzik, 1979.

of structured inequality intensifies the problems of growing old (Federal Council on the Aging, 1981; Jackson, 1980; Stanford, 1981; Manuel, forthcoming). The other theme focuses on the benefits accruing to those elderly who remain attached to an ethnic identity and subculture (Trela and Sokolovsky, 1979; Cool, 1980, forthcoming; Weeks and Cuellar, 1981).

DOUBLE JEOPARDY VERSUS AGE AS LEVELER

The first theme concentrates on the impact of class differentiation and racial discrimination on minority groups. The notion of certain ethnic aged being a disenfranchised minority within the devalued status of elderly in our society has led to their being characterized as being in *double* (Indian and old) or even *multiple jeopardy* (black, old, female, and poor). Minority populations such as blacks, Hispanics, and American Indians contain a smaller proportion of persons over 65 (7.8 percent, 4.2 percent, and 5.7 percent respectively) as compared to whites (11.5 percent over 65). Yet the 1971 White House Conference on Aging found that in terms of education, income, housing quality, rates of chronic illness, and life expectancy, the minority aged find themselves in even harsher living conditions than do the majority of older Americans (U.S. Senate, 1971:157–201). Not only are these problems more severe but aging programs set up by uniform bureaucratic standards can often create barriers preventing the ethnic elderly from obtaining resources to which they are entitled (see especially Cuellar and Weeks, 1980).

Many data support the proposition of the disenfranchised minority elder. For example, although income levels for elderly blacks have changed for the better over the last 30 years—the percentage of those in poverty dropping from 62.5 percent in 1959 to 36.3 percent in 1977—this latest figure is still over *three times* the proportion of elderly whites in poverty (Jackson, 1980:167).

However, some researchers have suggested that aging exerts a leveling influence on ethnic differences. This *age-as-leveler* hypothesis suggests that growing old is a sufficiently potent process to cut across ethnic lines and mediate or level differences in the patterns of aging reflective of membership in distinct ethnic groups (Kent and Hirsch, 1969).

Research is just beginning in earnest to examine the overall viability of these two models of ethnic aging—multiple jeopardy versus age as leveler. In the first article of this section, Bengtson and Morgan rigorously test these hypotheses. They use large-scale survey techniques to examine various quality-of-life indicators and perceptions of aging among three ethnic segments of the American population.

ETHNICITY AS A RESOURCE

A second major theme in researching the cultural diversity of America's aged has portrayed ethnicity not as a handicap but as a resource (Cool, forthcoming). This emphasis emerges in this section's articles by Schweitzer and by Myerhoff. By comparing these works with the section's first selection, students can see quite clearly the different types of data produced by typical survey versus ethnographic research. The latter technique focuses on the qualitative aspects of ethnically based roles, attitudes and identity that emerge as a coping mechanism in accommodating to old age. We have already seen in Johnson's analysis of the Italian-American family (see Section II) how interaction mediated by values shapes the way that family roles acquire importance for the aged. Similarly Schweitzer, in her selection on American Indian aged, finds that traditional roles in family interaction and in linking the family to community ritual remain sources of significant prestige.

While much of the literature on the ethnic elderly has stressed the function of family organization, there is also recognition that:

. . . ethnicity offers the old a continuing identity and source of control which may be compartmentalized during different stages of the life cycle but which

remains available for use when needed or wanted. While ethnicity does not guarantee valued friendships for an older person it does provide a backdrop for shared understandings and values, which are often the foundations of friendship. (Cool, 1980:168).

In Myerhoff's article on a group of East European Jews this component of ethnicity is shown to facilitate not only the creation of meaningful attachments to nonkin age peers but also the establishment of a broader sense of community.

Vern L. Bengtson and Leslie A. Morgan

ETHNICITY AND AGING:
A COMPARISON OF THREE ETHNIC GROUPS

The "Social and Cultural Contexts of Aging" study conducted through the University of Southern California was one of the most far-reaching research projects yet to explore cultural diversity in the elderly population. This work not only collected the large-scale survey data, discussed in this first selection, but also sponsored in-depth anthropological field work represented in this section by the writing of Barbara Myerhoff (see Myerhoff and Simić, 1978; Myerhoff, 1978). In the following article sociologists Bengtson and Morgan analyze questionnaire data comparing middle-aged and elderly whites to black and Hispanic populations, the two groups containing the largest number of minority aged. The first part of their paper examines the double jeopardy versus age as leveler debate, using four quality-of-life indicators: income, perception of health, life satisfaction, and social interaction. Analyzing both the differences among groups as well as the change within age cohorts of the three populations, Bengtson and Morgan find dramatic confirmation of the double jeopardy hypothesis in terms of income deprivation and poorer perceptions of health by black and Hispanic elderly. Results for the other two variables are not so clear, with both advantages and disadvantages accruing to ethnic membership.

The authors also discuss variations among the three ethnic groups in terms of the perceptions of aging itself and problems people face in growing old. Some important differences were found, especially in the subjective assessments of when people consider themselves "old," the estimates of the years one has yet to live, and the judgments about the positive features of old age. Interestingly, despite large economic and health perception differences among the groups, each ranks finances and health as the two greatest problems faced in old age.

ETHNICITY IS INCREASINGLY RECOGNIZED as an important dimension of social differentiation in modern, pluralistic societies. By "ethnicity" we mean groups distinguishable from the majority population in terms of racial or national background and by virtue of shared history and cultural values. Aging is also increasingly considered a principal dimension of social organization, in that populations are comprised of groups who differ in behavior and orientation by virtue of their age. This article explores the interplay of two dimensions of social differentiation, ethnicity and age, utilizing explicitly comparative analysis from a sociological study of aging in three ethnic groups (blacks, Mexican Americans, and whites) recently completed in southern California.

It may seem obvious that groups that differ by ethnicity would have different orientations toward aging and old age. Certainly cross-cultural research has demonstrated that definitions of old age, its rights and obligations, problems and opportunities vary across cultures (Cowgill and Holmes, 1972; Myerhoff and Simić, 1978; Simmons, 1945). But it might also be argued that aging is a universal human challenge, bringing with it similar problems and perceptions, regardless of variations in cultural context (Bengtson, Dowd, Smith and Inkeles, 1975).

This essay was specially prepared for this book by the authors. Permission to reprint must be obtained from the authors and publisher.

Can ethnic differentiation be seen with greater clarity as one examines problems of growing old within various cultural contexts? Or are problems of aging generally common across groups to the point that social policy, programs, and theory may adopt a more universal strategy in dealing with problems of aging? The question addressed in this article, then, is to what extent there are observable ethnic or subcultural variations in the patterns of aging.

Two central issues emerge in explorations of the interplay of ethnicity and aging. The first has to do with the quality of life, which has long been considered problematic for the elderly who commonly experience decrements in status, health, and income (Streib, 1976; U. S. Senate Special Committee on Aging, 1971). Quality of life is also an issue for ethnic minorities as a consequence of discrimination and limited "life chances" (Mills, 1963). What, then, is the combined effect of aging and minority status on indicators of quality of life?

The second issue relates to social definitions of age and the aging process. The experience of aging depends, to a large extent, on socially defined patterns derived from shared and learned "definitions of the situation" which influence action and behavior (Berger and Luckmann, 1966). Thus, analysis of *perceptions* of aging and the way such perceptions contrast among identifiable subgroups is of considerable importance in understanding the phenomenon of aging. To what extent do perceptions of aging vary across ethnic subcultures?

Both of these issues are significant in establishing the social location and well-being of ethnic elderly in contemporary American society.

ETHNICITY, AGING, AND THE QUALITY OF LIFE

Ethnic and subcultural variations within the population of aged Americans, which have been increasingly discussed within the past decade, particularly as advocates for minorities (e.g., Asociacion Nacional Pro Persones Mayores and National Indian Council on Aging), point to the plight of elderly members of their communities (National Urban League, 1964; U. S. Senate Special Committee on Aging, 1971). Researchers have only begun to accumulate knowledge concerning ethnicity as a factor in the problems of the aged (see Blau et al., 1979).

At this point in scholarly analysis, there are two conflicting hypotheses of what happens to the quality of life when minority persons grow old in American society. These may be termed "double jeopardy" and "age as a leveler." Both hypotheses argue that there is a relationship between the changes arising from increased age and ethnic identification, but the proposed effects on quality of life are in opposite directions.

Double Jeopardy

The situation of minority or ethnic elderly persons has been characterized as one of "double jeopardy" or "multiple hazards" (Dowd and Bengtson, 1978; Jackson, 1970, 1971; National Urban League, 1964). This refers to the fact that being old constitutes a disadvantage in American society and that being a member of a minority or ethnic group may represent a distinct disadvantage. Persons who are both old and in a minority group experience the added effects of these two burdens and are expected to experience more severe problems and lower quality of life.

Like other older people in industrial societies, ethnic aged experience the devaluation of old age found in most modern societies (Arnoff et al., 1964; Cowgill and Holmes, 1972). Unlike other older people, however, these aged must bear the additional economic, social, and psychological burdens of living in a society in which racial equality remains more myth than fact. It has been noted that, compared to the white aged, most of the minority aged "are less well educated, have less income, suffer more illnesses and earlier death, have poorer quality housing and less choice as to where to live and where they work, and in general have a less satisfying quality of life" (U. S. Senate Special Committee on Aging, 1971). Evidence such as this, emphasizing the greater disadvantages of being both old and in a minority group, supports the double jeopardy hypothesis (Blau et al., 1979).

Age as a Leveler

The second hypothesis also suggests that there is a connection between patterns of aging and ethnicity. It argues, however, that aging leads to diminishing of the differences found at younger ages between the quality of life of majority and minority groups. According to the "age-as-a-leveler" hypothesis, problems of ethnic elderly may not be all that unique. While differences among ethnic groups are often observed, it must also be acknowledged that the aging individual, regardless of ethnic background, is subject to a variety of influences which cut across racial lines and may mediate or level differences which existed between groups in midlife (Kent and Hirsch, 1969).

As Dowd and Bengtson (1978) note, this hypothesis implies that differences between ethnic or subcultural groups are actually *reduced* as their members experience the common impacts associated with advancing age. The relative numbers of ethnic *minority* aged having good health and adequate income may be less than those of aged whites. If, however, the percentage differences between middle-aged blacks or Mexican Americans and their white counterparts are greater than in old age, it would be erroneous to simply rely totally on the double jeopardy argument. The social, economic, and physical consequences of aging may deal a relatively more severe blow to the *majority* aged, thereby reducing or leveling differences that existed among subcultural groups in youth and middle age.

There are, then, two explicit hypotheses on the dynamics of aging and ethnicity which both predict a decline in quality of life associated with aging. How do we test these two views with data? Ideally their proof would be based on longitudinal studies following groups of individuals from various subcultures over time to see how they age. More often, however, researchers must rely on cross-sectional studies that compare age and ethnic groups at one point in time. If cross-ethnic differences among older individuals are not as great as those found among middle-aged persons and all groups experienced a decline in the quality of life, there would be an indication that age exerts a leveling influence. If, on the other hand, the following conditions exist simultaneously,

evidence points to the double jeopardy explanation:

1. Differences between white and minority elderly which favor the white majority.
2. A significant decline in the quality of life within the minority(ies) as age increases.
3. a. Significant differences do *not* exist between subcultural groups in middle age, *or*

   b. Differences do exist between the middle-aged which favor the white respondents, but these are smaller than differences among the aged, *or*

   c. A significant difference exists in middle age which favors the minority(ies).

According to Dowd and Bengtson (1978) all three conditions must be met for double jeopardy to pertain.

ISSUES IN RESEARCH ON ETHNICITY AND AGING

In order to explore these two hypotheses on the quality of life and to establish information on the diversity of ethnic experience of aging in American society, it is necessary to carry out research specifically exploring minorities within the elderly population. Moreover, it is desirable, perhaps necessary, to achieve an explicitly comparative research design, enabling direct comparisons between comparable groups. Variables such as socioeconomic status are so highly associated with ethnicity in our society that they are most often glossed over in aging research.

The Social and Cultural Contexts of Aging study reported here involved a carefully designed sample allowing explicit comparison of ethnic and socioeconomic groups, and separation of the effects of ethnicity on the situation of older Americans. The sample of 1,269 individuals was drawn in Los Angeles county to represent three age groups (45–54, 55–64, 65–74), three ethnic groups (black, Mexican-American, and white), and two levels of socioeconomic status. This sampling design permits some rather unique, systematic comparisons among groups and examination of some relatively rare categories, such as older blacks in upper socioeconomic ranges.

One important limitation, however, was the lack of further ethnic differentiation among the white subsample. Undoubtedly many of these persons grew up in distinctive white ethnic climates, but it was not possible in this study to attempt to represent these various white ethnic groups. Moreover, the qualitative analyses carried out by anthropologists on this project (Myerhoff and Simić, 1978; Myerhoff, 1979) were expected to provide a more focused and informative portrait of at least two white ethnic groups.

Quality of Life

One set of analyses (Dowd and Bengtson, 1978) utilized the USC data to examine four dimensions reflecting quality of life: income, health, life satisfaction, and social interaction. These four factors can be used to evaluate the merits of the two hypotheses of ethnicity and aging.

Results from the USC survey suggest that in terms of *relative income* the minority elderly may indeed be characterized as experiencing "double jeopardy." While income of both white and minority respondents declined by age stratum, the mean income reported by older Mexican American and black respondents is considerably lower than any other age-ethnic subgroup in the sample ($3,360 and $3,490, respectively, compared to

$6,890 for whites age 65–74 and $14,700 among whites 45–54).[1] Further, the relative difference in income within the 30-year-age span represented in the sample studied here is much greater for minority respondents than it is for whites. The mean income reported by blacks changed 55 percent across the three age strata. Mexican Americans showed an even larger drop in the mean income (62 percent) from the youngest to the oldest age group. The income of older white respondents differed by only 36 percent. Thus, the rather large income "gap" that exists between middle-aged minority and white respondents is an even larger one among the respondents aged 65 or older, supporting the "double jeopardy" hypothesis. These differences in income cannot be explained by the socioeconomic status (SES), sex, or health differences that exist between whites and either Mexican Americans or blacks. Even with these variables held constant, the net incomes of the respondents over 65 are significantly different.

Similar results can be seen with respect to *self-rated health*. Health was measured by asking respondents, "In general, would you say your health is very good, good, fair, poor, or very poor?" Older minority respondents were significantly more likely to report poorer health than same-age white respondents, even with the effects of SES, sex, and income held constant (see Table 1). The distinctions in perceived health among

TABLE 1
Tri-Ethnic Comparisons of Quality of Life: Income, Health, and Life Satisfaction

	Blacks	Mexican Americans	Whites
Income			
Mean $ for 65–74-year-olds (1973)	$3,490	$3,360	$6,890
% change from youngest to oldest age group	–55%	–62%	–36%
Health			
% of 65–74-year-olds who label health "poor" or "very poor"	27.0%	23.2%	4.0%
% change from youngest to oldest age group	–13.2%	–6.3%	–2.3%
Life Satisfaction			
Tranquility			
Mean score for 65–74-year-olds	2.17	1.93	2.17
Change from youngest to oldest age group	–.02	–.15	+.22
Optimism			
Mean score for 65–74-year-olds	1.31	.98	1.43
Change from youngest to oldest age group	–.29	–.31	–.04

the three ethnic groups were less apparent among middle-aged respondents. As was the case with income, the self-assessed health of whites is better than that of minority respondents at each age stratum with the greatest disparity occurring among those aged 65 and older. While 27 percent of blacks and 23 percent of Mexican Americans between 65 and 74 years of age reported their health as "poor" or "very poor," only 4 percent of older whites gave this response. Consequently the label "double jeopardy" appears appropriate when describing the health self-categorizations of older blacks or Mexican Americans; the same may be true for other older minority ethnics.

A third dimension explored in Dowd and Bengtson's (1978) analysis concerned *subjective dimensions of life satisfaction*. Questions used to determine life satisfaction are listed in Appendix A. Two dimensions of satisfaction, tranquility and optimism, were analyzed separately in each ethnic group, with mixed results. Here there is less support for the double jeopardy hypothesis (see Table 1). On the first factor dimension, labeled "tranquility," there was little indication of age-group differences within or across ethnic strata. Although the tranquility scores for 65- to 74-year-old Mexican Americans are somewhat lower than for the 45–54-year-olds, the contrast is not statistically significant, and the scores of blacks are virtually the same, regardless of age. Interestingly, there is a slight increase in tranquility scores by age within the white sample.

On the second dimension, called "optimism," the responses of the Mexican American minority group do appear supportive of the "double jeopardy" hypothesis. Among the 449 respondents in this group there was a lower average score for each older age stratum, with optimism scores among aged respondents (age 65–74 years) significantly lower than scores for whites of the same age; and the contrast is greater in the older, as compared with the middle-aged group. However, no such indication of double jeopardy characterizes the black respondents—where on both tranquility and optimism, differences in comparison to the white sample of respondents in each age group become smaller with increasing age. On the tranquility dimension there is substantively no difference between 65- to 74-year-old black and white respondents, though in the 45- to 54-year-old age stratum blacks score

slightly *higher* than whites. In this black and white contrast controlling for income, SES, health, and sex, the hypothesis of age as a leveler receives some support while the double jeopardy hypothesis is not suggested by the data. While the black-white contrast suggests "aging as a leveler" to be the correct approach in analyzing life satisfaction, similar analysis with Mexican Americans supports double jeopardy. This is the first evidence supporting the age-as-a-leveler hypothesis, and indicates, in passing, the complexity of assessing ethnic contrasts in varying aspects of aging.

Indicators of social interaction were used to explore a fourth dimension of quality of life as varying by ethnicity, indicative of either the double jeopardy or age-as-leveler hypothesis. Primary group interaction indicates a source of reward to individuals in the course of daily living: directly in terms of potential assistance in times of need, indirectly as insulation against the breakdown in self-esteem and coping skills often associated with aging and described elsewhere as the "social breakdown syndrome" (Kuypers and Bengtson, 1971).

Four measures of social interaction are utilized to evaluate quality of life: frequency of contact with children, grandchildren, other kin (siblings and others), and friends, neighbors, and acquaintances. On the first two indicators Mexican Americans reported the most frequent interaction with younger generations. White and black respondents are very similar on the proportions seeing grandchildren, but older whites are more likely to have seen their children in the past week. Both white and Mexican-American subgroups showed increases in seeing children moving from the youngest age group to the oldest, while rates for the black subsample remained essentially the same.

Whites also evidenced no change across age levels in the proportion seeing grandchildren, while blacks reported a slight drop and Mexican Americans reported a significant increase when we move from youngest to the oldest age stratum. Mexican Americans seemingly increase their contact with younger generations of their families with increased age, while blacks evidence decline. The most striking difference is the marked increase in rates of contact for older whites with their adult children in comparison to their middle-aged majority peers. Since the two ethnic

TABLE 2
Tri-Ethnic Comparisons on Social Interaction

	Blacks	Mexican Americans	Whites
Social Interaction			
Children			
% who saw children within the last week (65–74-year-olds)	68.8%	85.2%	79.9%
% change from youngest to oldest age group	-0.4%	+14.0%	+24.3%
Grandchildren			
% who saw grandchildren within the last week (65–74-year-olds)	75.6%	82.9%	73.1%
% change from youngest to oldest age group	-3.2%	+7.3%	+0.6%
Other relatives			
% who saw other relatives within the last week (65–74-year-olds)	42.7%	40.2%	40.5%
% change from youngest to oldest age group	-8.5%	-22.7%	+2.1%
Friends, neighbors, etc.			
% who saw friends, neighbors, etc. within the last week (65–74-year-olds)	50.0%	31.6%	75.0%
% change from youngest to oldest age group	+5.4%	-7.2%	+7.1%

groups demonstrate different patterns of change over time, and since the Mexican Americans report such an objectively high rate of contact, these two indicators clearly do not support double jeopardy. Since the increase in contacts with children for whites bring them more into line in old age with minority rates, we seem to have a peculiar case of "age as a leveler."

In terms of contact with other kin, the cross-ethnic differences become smaller in increasing age strata. Weekly contacts among minorities, which are higher than those of whites in middle age, are diminished (especially among Mexican Americans) as age increases and becomes similar to that of whites in the oldest age category. White respondents report fairly stable levels of contact in all age groups, resulting in a *leveling* of ethnic differences with advancing age.

On the fourth dimension, frequency of contact with friends, neighbors, and acquaintances, whites reported higher levels of interaction at all age levels. Contact is higher for whites in each successive age stratum, and the cross-ethnic differentials in 65- to 74-year-olds are greater than in any other age category. Mexican Americans have the lowest contact of any ethnic group and that contact decreases slightly for the oldest (see Table 2). Both white and black subsamples reported that their weekly nonkin contacts

increased in older groups. While "double jeopardy" is suggested for Mexican Americans, the data for blacks do not comply with the second criterion of double jeopardy, a decline in the quality of life indicator as age increases.

The greater frequency of familial interaction among the ethnic minority respondents, particularly Mexican Americans, suggests that primary group needs of minority aged are more likely to be met within the extended family. But the fact that Mexican Americans also report the *lowest* amount of interaction with nonrelated individuals suggests a certain amount of social isolation beyond the family.

Other analyses have found that while levels of interaction with kin and rates of coresidence are higher among Mexican-American elderly, especially women, their expectations for contact with kin are also very high (Morgan, 1976; Ragan and Simonin, 1977). A study of widowed women drawn from this sample found that for Mexican-American widows the adequacy of contact with kin was an important factor in their satisfaction with life (Morgan, 1976). Even in light of objectively high levels of contact with family, Mexican-American elderly are more likely to be unsatisfied with how often they see children and grandchildren. These culturally defined expectations for contact differ for this group, and when they are unmet, result in lower life satisfaction (Morgan, 1976). The relative isolation of this group from contacts outside the family would seem to place them in an especially vulnerable position if their children adopt the standards of the majority culture for visiting with parents and grandparents.

In summary, analysis of the southern California community survey data on the quality of life suggests that differences among the ethnic groups do exist, but there is also support for the hypothesis that age exerts a leveling influence on some aspects of ethnic variation with advancing age. This selective support for each of the hypotheses reinforces the necessity of longitudinal studies to definitively explore age as a leveler versus double jeopardy. The data reviewed offer some support for Kent's suggestion that the problems older people face are substantially similar regardless of their ethnic background: "This is not to say that the same proportion of each group faces these problems; obviously they do not. The point, however, is that if we concentrate on the group rather than the problem, we shall be treating symptoms rather than causes" (1971:33).

Put differently, to presume that ethnic differences are alone sufficient to understand the personal and social situation of the aged ignores tremendous variation both across ethnic boundaries and within ethnic categories (as has been underscored, for example, by Jackson, 1970, 1971). The existence of double jeopardy, therefore, is an empirical, not a logical question. To assume otherwise would be to ignore the warning of Kent that "age may be a great leveler with regard to both racial and social influences . . ." (1971:49).

PERCEPTIONS OF AGING

Aging represents one of many aspects of reality that are socially defined and old age is a social category whose properties and problems are constructed within the context of shared expectations particular to specific groups. It is useful to examine evidence concerning perceptions of aging among contrasting groups to explore patterns of reality construction. To what extent are there marked ethnic differences in perception of aging? To what extent are there commonalities, despite ethnic or subcultural variations?

In the Social and Cultural Contexts of Aging project several indicators were used to examine ethnic contrasts in perceptions of aging. The first concerned *subjective assessments of age,* self-categorizations by respondents of whether they define themselves as "young," "middle-aged," or "elderly." Self-categorizations varied considerably by ethnic group membership.

Regardless of ethnic identification relatively few of the 45–54-year-olds considered themselves "old." Beyond the youngest respondents, however, the pattern of age identification began to diverge by ethnic category. Mexican-American respondents showed the most marked differences in terms of the percent considering themselves old, with black respondents following not far behind. Among Mexican-Americans, over 30 percent defined themselves as "old" by age 60, while the same proportions were not reached among the blacks until age 65 and among whites until almost age 70 (Bengtson, Kasschau and Ragan, 1977). It is also important to note that in none of these age-ethnic groups did more than about 60 percent of respondents define themselves old, even though their chronological ages reached to 75 years. And among white respondents the largest proportion of any age group defining themselves as old was found among those 69–71-year-olds, only 40 percent of whom selected this subjective age. These results correspond with the discussion of black and white elderly by Jackson (1970), who suggests that in the United States minority group members perceive themselves as "old" at a considerable earlier chronological age than whites because of the repeated hardships they have faced through a lifetime of economic and social disadvantage.

A different method of assessing subjective age is to ask respondents to *estimate the amount of time left to them to live.* This has been termed "awareness of finitude" by Munnichs (1968). These estimates may be expected to vary by social factors, since mortality rates indicate significant contrasts between males and females, between racial groups, and among economic status levels.

Results from the southern California survey again indicate significant ethnic differences in this perception of aging (Bengtson, Cuellar and Ragan, 1977). The black subsample as a group expressed the greatest longevity expectancy, with a mean of 26 years, and the Mexican Americans the least with a mean of 19 years (it will be recalled that these respondents range in age from 45 to 74 years old). The ethnic contrasts were maintained after controlling for potentially confounding effects of differences in socioeconomic status.

These results are somewhat surprising. The patterns of black responses are in marked contrast to age-specific mortality data showing differences between minorities and whites. According to current United States Census figures, life expectancy at age 50 for nonwhites is about 74 years, while for whites it is 76 years. At age 70 it is slightly under 12 more years for nonwhites, slightly over 12 for whites (Vital Statistics, USDHEW, 1972). Comparable census life expectancy data are not available for Mexican Americans, but it is estimated that these will be even lower than for blacks (Moore, 1971).

Thus, the blacks in this particular sample subjectively considered themselves to have more years to live than than the other two ethnic groups. Perhaps this is an indication of the "pride of survivorship" described by Jackson (1970) in the face of lifetime adversity as a minority group member. Ironically, while black respondents face some negative objective circumstances in old age their *subjective* responses appear somewhat more optimistic in terms of future survival than that of their white counterparts. This view of the future is also suggested in the fairly high scores on life satisfaction listed in Table 1.

A third aspect concerns major problems encountered in old age. In the USC survey we asked members of each ethnic group what were the *three greatest problems* they currently faced (Ragan and Simonin, 1977). Again there were cross-ethnic similarities as well as differences. All three ethnic groups reported finances as the number one problem (mentioned by 76 percent of the blacks and Mexican Americans, 67 percent of the whites). Health was the second greatest problem volunteered (48 percent of the Mexican Americans, 35 percent of the whites, 31 percent of the blacks). Although the two most frequently mentioned problems were the same across ethnic groups, additional concerns demonstrated ethnic

diversity. The third most common problems for the black, Mexican-American and white samples were crime (27 percent), transportation (10 percent), and morale (13 percent), respectively.

TABLE 3
"What Are the Three Greatest Problems You Are Facing These Days?"

Blacks	Mexican Americans	Whites
Finances 76%	Finances 76%	Finances 67%
Health 31%	Health 48%	Health 35%
Crime 27%	Transportation 10%	Morale 13%

Listing of greatest problems does not present a test for the two hypotheses discussed for quality of life, because the information is based on open-ended responses, which are not directly comparable. It is interesting, however, to note some suggestive evidence pertaining to the quality of life. First, the strongly dominant issues of health and finances were common across subcultural groups, suggesting a common experience and problems of aging. Beyond these two problems, however, there appears to be ethnic diversity, with minority respondents more often reporting concrete problems (i.e., crime and transportation) than their majority peers. While we cannot easily evaluate the relative seriousness of these problems (as opposed to low morale among whites), the more concrete, survival nature of crime and transportation endorse the probable validity of double jeopardy for ethnic elderly in this country.

A fourth and perhaps most general assessment of perceptions of age involved analysis of responses to opinion items regarding *characteristics* of old age, both positive and negative. The USC survey respondents were asked to agree or disagree to such statements as, "Most older people are set in their ways and unable to change," and "Older people can learn new things just as well as younger people can." A battery of items taken from previous studies was used to construct two scales (positive potential and negative attributes of aging) that measured the attitudes adequately among the diverse groups in the sample (Morgan and Bengtson, 1976).[2] These were then tested for significant differences, by ethnicity, age, and sex.

Results were somewhat surprising. First, there was substantial similarity among the various social categories represented in the survey on the scale measuring Negative Attributes of the Aged. Evaluations tended overall to be highly negative (indicating, for example, that many respondents agreed that "most older people spend too much time prying into the affairs of others"). Although overall differences by ethnicity did not attain significance, whites were less negative than were blacks or Mexican Americans. There were no statistically significant differences by age (though older respondents were slightly more negative than 45- to 54-year-olds) or by sex.

Second, there were group differences on the scale measuring Positive Potential of the Aged (questions such as "Older people can learn new things just as well as younger people can"). Ethnic differences were highly significant, with blacks the most positive, Mexican Americans the least positive. Age differences also emerged, with the oldest respondents the least positive. Again we see a positive view of aging among black respondents who seem to maintain positive expectations for themselves in spite of some negative concrete facts. It is important to reinforce, however, that in discussing perceptions of "the aged" most members of the sample do not define themselves as currently in this category, and are probably not referring to their own positive and negative traits.

In these data one sees perhaps the clearest example of the complex interplay between broadly shared cultural perceptions regarding old age and subgroups or ethnic variations. There is general agreement that old age has pervasive negative attributes; there are no significant ethnic variations on this theme. This may also be tied to the two most common problems of respondents which were the same for all ethnic groups. But there are wide group contrasts on assessments of positive aspects of aging. These data argue that there are cultural or subcultural differences in the definitions of age and the meaning of being old, and that these views color the experiences of persons as they age. These differences are likely to have a major impact on the ways in which members of ethnic and cultural groups experience aging and assimilate the changes common to later life.

CONCLUSIONS AND IMPLICATIONS

We are still far from having any clear answers about the interrelationships of ethnicity and aging in contemporary American society. The complexity of cross-ethnic research on aging is a continuing challenge to social scientists and policy makers in aging.

In terms of the two hypotheses on the quality of life, the data presented here seem to do little to settle the debate between supporters of the double jeopardy and aging-as-leveler perspectives. On some items, such as income and self-rated health, the disadvantage for minority elderly is striking. On other issues, such as levels of contact with kin, we see a more complex pattern where we must evaluate the varying expectations of groups to compare quality of life.

The Social and Cultural Contexts of Aging project provides selective support for each hypothesis, promoting the recognition that either hypothesis may be an oversimplification in attempting to explain *all* dimensions of the quality of life. It also points out the strong possibility of ignoring or underestimating variation among ethnic and subcultural minorities in American society. Each ethnic group brings unique characteristics and resources to the situation faced with aging, so that attempting to find one explanation applicable to all ethnic groups is subject to failure.

Perceptions of aging also vary by ethnicity, but do not do so consistently. In some cases, such as the social interaction of Mexican Americans with family, differing cultural "definitions of the situation" caution against imposing one standard of comparison of varying ethnic strata. What appeared in this case to be a positive factor in the quality of life of elderly Mexican Americans (i.e., higher family contact) was, in reality, a common source of lowered morale for members of the group. Utilizing a standard for comparison across all groups in this case ignores a major difference in the *salience* and *meaning* of life events across cultural milieus.

These results also point up important concerns of those responsible for formulating national and regional policies affecting the elderly. We must first acknowledge that until quite recently scientific and policy-relevant knowledge about ethnicity and aging has been lacking. Most of the research in social gerontology until 1972 involved respondents who are middle-class, white, predominantly native-born Americans. The resulting base of information underemphasized the wide diversity among the over 65 population and has had some unfortunate consequences.

Social policy for the elderly in the United States has been oriented to the needs of the white, English-speaking, and relatively well-educated individuals represented in earlier studies. The assumption being made was that these programs would also serve any diverse groups in the population. In the last several years, however, advocacy groups have attempted to focus attention on the diversity and unique problems of the minority elderly. Their efforts have been hampered by a critical lack of comparative information with which to assess the situation and needs of various minority groups of elderly. In short, information needed to understand ethnic or minority elderly and to develop programs for their particular needs is still quite limited.

Analysis of perceptions of age also has several important implications for researchers and policy makers in aging (Bengtson, Kasschau, and Ragan, 1977). First, the social categorization of individuals by age (as young, middle-aged, elderly, and frail or "dependent") may vary among subgroups, reflecting differential placement in terms of social stratification. For example, a person of a certain age could be defined as "middle-aged" in one cultural context and as "old" in another, changing her/his social status, resources, expectations for behavior, etc., simply by moving from one cultural milieu to another. Therefore the basic constructs of interest to gerontologists (time and aging) may have quite different meaning for one group of humans in contrast to another.

A second implication concerns the definition of "social problems." What is or is not seen as a difficulty associated with aging reflects what is collectively defined as normal or deviant, and these definitions may vary across societies, across locations within a given society, and across historical periods. However, this study found basis to assert the similarity among ethnic groups in at least two major problems of aging in contemporary American culture: finances and health.

Does ethnicity make a difference in aging? From the evidence reviewed in this chapter we can conclude that it does. On some objective issues, such as income, the difference and the "double jeopardy" are quite clear. But our conclusions must remain most tentative, pending further studies. Only by explicit, comparative research designs can we adequately explore the interplay between aging and ethnicity.

Ethnic group membership does appear to reflect an important dimension of social differentiation among the aged. In pluralistic populations, gerontologists would do well to acknowledge the importance of ethnic group membership as important characteristics that are manifest in patterns of behavior in old age. It is important to emphasize, however, that although minority status brings problems, membership in an ethnic group, with its shared culture, symbols, rituals, and meanings, is an important resource in dealing with the problems of aging. These potentials must be recognized, and indeed exploited by the elderly themselves and their advocates.

APPENDIX: LIFE SATISFACTION ITEMS

—Do you have a lot to be sad about?
—Do you feel that life isn't worth living?
—Do you worry so much that you can't sleep?
—Do you feel afraid?
—Do you feel bored?
—Do you feel lonely these days?
—Do you get upset easily?
—Do you feel that things keep getting worse as you get older?
—Do you feel that you have as much pep as you did last year?
—As you get older, do you feel less useful?
—Do you feel that life is hard for you?

NOTES

1. Figures are approximate, since responses were based on income categories which reflected thousand-dollar increments up to $10,000. Larger categories were used for upper income ranges (Dowd and Bengtson, 1978).

2. It should be mentioned that this analysis focused on a frequently overlooked problem of comparing attitudes of respondents from different social categories. It was found that the scales originally constructed contained serious problems of cross-group equivalency in terms of reliability and validity—the same questions appeared to have different meanings for black, Mexican-American, and white respondents. A second stage of analysis revealed two dimensions that could be justified as operating similarly across ethnic, sex, and age groups (see Morgan and Bengtson, 1976). These are the dimensions reported in the present discussion.

Marjorie M. Schweitzer

THE ELDERS: CULTURAL DIMENSIONS OF AGING IN TWO AMERICAN INDIAN COMMUNITIES

The history of contemporary American Indian groups is marked by extremes of physical and cultural genocide that resulted in drastic reduction of population, relocation to often sterile reservation lands, and forced "assimilation" of children in non-Indian schools. Today, Indian populations, especially on reservations, are often characterized by the highest levels of poor nutrition, housing, and health services to be found in America. Yet there is still very limited research detailing the meaning of old age for the American Indian in the contemporary context. Rather, many of the assumptions about the Indian aged stem from the anthropological "ethnographic present," prior to the inception of the reservation system, when traits such as communal sharing, mandated family and community care of the frail aged, and control by the aged of important ceremonial positions and esoteric knowledge were common. It is simply not known of many Indian groups to what extent such traits remain as a buffer to forms of multiple jeopardy.

However, we see in Schweitzer's research, conducted in two Oklahoma Indian communities, that ethnicity does indeed make a positive difference in linking elders to tribal functions and the extended family system. Although most political and curing roles have been lost, the aged have retained power in the public domain by remaining in demand as ritual specialists, information sources, and storytellers at tribal functions. The most enduring source of esteem is the family system, which not only facilitates intense intergenerational ties but also provides a context in which grandparents through ritual sponsorship can enhance the prestige of younger family members. However, Schweitzer also notes that the failure of federal programs to take account of ethnic distinctiveness has created impediments to the elderly Indians' making use of needed government services.

INTRODUCTION

Early ethnographic studies of American Indian cultures contributed much to anthropological theory and method. The research was based on the premise that the old people could provide details about traditional lifeways as they existed before the coming of white explorers and settlers had set up a chain of reactions which led to serious disruption of native cultures. Although much information about the elders themselves can be gleaned from these ethnographic reports, the roles and attitudes of aged women and men were not specifically the focus of the research. In recent years anthropologists have turned their attention to the study of the aged as a central concern (see, for example, Myerhoff, 1978; Keith, 1979; and Fry, 1980), but it can be noted that the amount of research on the aged in American Indian communities still remains small.

This article will assess the status of studies on Indian aged. Observations on the roles and attitudes of the elderly in two Oklahoma Indian communities will then be presented along with

This essay was specially prepared for this book by the author. Permission to reprint must be obtained from the author and publisher.

the implications of these data for agencies which plan and provide services for the old. Final comments will concern the importance of cultural factors in aging in American society.

STUDIES ON INDIAN AGING

Aging in Traditional Indian Cultures

In 1945 Simmons made the first attempt to correlate cultural and ecological factors with the position of the aged in preliterate societies. The analysis included data culled from the ethnographies of 16 North American tribes. A thorough commentary on the status of the aged in traditional Indian cultures still remains to be done but it is possible to make a few observations.

An active old age was of utmost importance as can be seen by the many useful tasks that old people performed. "Old Crow grandmothers were considered essential elements in the household, engaged in domestic chores . . . " while helping young mothers who were burdened with heavy work (Simmons, 1945:84). The grandmothers also sliced and dried the strips of meat after a bison hunt. These essential tasks provided a certain measure of old-age security but an even greater guarantee was achieved by the possession of property rights, skills, and special knowledge that was not dependent upon the strength of youth. Specialized roles acquired through the accumulation of experience and familiarity with skills associated with the rites of passage were frequently the domain of the elderly. Old women were midwives and old men played important roles associated with the newborn child. In the Omaha tribe old women attended the birth of a baby who was then frequently named by the grandfather. When that child began to walk, an old man provided him with his first pair of moccasins (Simmons, 1945:91).

Experience and knowledge were also important as old people led games, songs, and dances. They told stories which were a combination of "entertainment, instruction and moral admonition" (Simmons, 1945:98). A Polar Eskimo stated, ". . . to the words of the newly born none give much credence, but the experience of the older generation contains truth. When I narrate

legends, it is not I who speak, it is the wisdom of our forefathers . . ." (as quoted in Simmons, 1945:99). The myths and legends that were told often included stories which portrayed old women and old men in an especially favorable light. The terms *grandfather* and *old man* were used when addressing the gods, and the elderly often held the role of religious specialist. They were curing shamans and keepers of the songs, emblems, and medicine bags important in religious rituals.

The political domain as well as the family provided arenas where the aged had important status. Within the framework of the extended family a special relationship existed between grandparents and grandchildren which began at birth and lasted a lifetime. Children were cared for by grandparents and in turn the family cared for the old when they were feeble. The term *elder* traditionally referred to a leader or councilman and the political role that the aged often occupied. It was also used to convey respect.

The statuses held by the old merited respect, honor, and prestige and attitudes toward them were generally positive. Many tribes taught their children to venerate the old people, but it is safe to say that positive attitudes were produced in part by the individual qualifications brought to each role by the old person.

Although old-age status among Indian societies was marked by veneration, aged Indians at times became very vulnerable. When the infirmities of old age no longer allowed individuals to remain active, the old were sometimes neglected, abandoned, or helped to end their lives. The Eskimo provide the classic example (Guemple, 1969). The old Eskimo who was still capable of doing camp chores, taking care of children, marrying a younger spouse, or telling legends and stories had strategies which maintained a positive status. It was when a person was too frail and feeble to maintain these strategies that abandonment took place (Guemple, 1969:68–69).

Other hunter-gatherer groups and some sedentary agricultural people followed a similar pattern. The Plains Ioway recognized that there came a time in life when it was proper to accept an inevitable fate. As one man related:

In Ioway custom in the old days when a couple got real old they used to build themselves a little shelter down by the creek so they would not be a bother to their children. Their children would bring them only a little food and water. Finally they would die. The old people only did that if they thought they were being a burden to their children. (Schweitzer, field notes, 1976).

Even among the Hopi who revered their old people, the old were sometimes neglected when they reached the helpless and useless stage (Simmons, 1945:225).

Although the most often quoted explanation of abandonment is necessity, people in Western society often express shock at such practices. To account for the apparently casual acceptance of death under these circumstances in Eskimo culture, Guemple explores the Eskimo belief that old people do not really die (see Section I). The essence of an Eskimo resides in the name which, after death, waits in the underworld until it again enters the body of a newborn. Guemple suggests that because Eskimo know their *persona* lives on, they are indifferent to death.

Contemporary Studies on American Indian Aging

The recent research focusing on American Indian aging falls into three broad categories: (1) culture change studies concerned with the effects of historical, economic, and social changes on the roles of elderly Indians, (2) psychological studies of personality, and (3) statistical-demographic studies which focus on the needs and problems of aging Indians with recommendations for planning policy and providing services.

Culture Change Studies. The historical events accompanying European settlement of North America resulted in drastic and rapid culture change in Indian societies. In an attempt to identify the kinds of changes which have occurred and the effects of these changes on the position of the elderly, research has focused on the economy, the family, and ceremonials and rituals. Such data have allowed the authors to draw conclusions regarding the status of the elderly in the communities studied.

Low status for the aged occurs when the vital roles associated with traditional economic production are curtailed or destroyed and the emphasis is no longer on the extended family in

the traditional sense. Some reservation Navajo elderly have suffered loss of property because of a stock reduction program and the resulting pressure to relinquish their grazing pursuits to their heirs. With these changes came a loss of power and prestige. Prestige appears to be maintained, however, by older traditional Navajos in isolated areas of the reservation where pastoral pursuits by the elderly continue and the matrilineal extended family still exists (Levy, 1967:231–36). In the sphere of ritual many older Navajos are practicing medicine men. With the support of a medicine man school (Bergman, 1973:663–66), the honored position of medicine men may continue to be a position of prestige in the future.

Loss of power and prestige for the elderly in a Pima Maricopa community in Arizona is also tied in closely with changes in the economy as wage labor and land leasing have replaced the traditional subsistence agriculture (Munsell, 1972:127–32). Those elderly who remain in an extended family milieu are more likely to maintain a higher status as are the aged who perform useful tasks (tasks most likely to be done by women). A few families have become residentially mobile. These families are usually matricentric or grandparental groups in which women occupy an unusually high status, thus refuting the hypothesis that status of the aged will be low where residence is unstable (Cowgill and Holmes, 1972:9).

Evidence shows that in spite of the lack of economic or political power today, some Indian aged are able to occupy positions of power and prestige because of the cultural contributions they can make. This is especially true when the revival of moribund ceremonies and rituals depends directly on the knowledge that the elders have. The Coast Salish elders today occupy a high prestige status because of their contributions to the revival of ceremonies and tribal education programs. Not only do they contribute knowledge but they actively engage in the ceremonies and when needed develop new rituals within the limits of the traditional ideology (Amoss, 1981a:47–63; Amoss, 1981b:1–3, 14–17).

Central Oklahoma communities offer further evidence that although traditional economic and political roles no longer provide positions of importance for elderly nonreservation Indians, kinship ties remain strong. The elders are looked to for knowledge about traditional ways as younger Indians turn increasingly toward an Indian identity (Schweitzer and Williams, 1974:5–7, 9–10; Williams, 1980:101–11).

However, a study of the Wind River Shoshone living in Wyoming emphasizes the increasing orientation by the younger people to white values. The older generation holds values which focus on collateral kin (emphasis on the group), an orientation to the past, a feeling of subjugation to nature, and a sense of being rather than doing. The younger generation, on the other hand, identifies with the individual rather than the group, future orientation, mastery over nature, and on doing rather than being. The younger generation readily acknowledges whites as their reference group (Tefft, 1968:330–33).

Psychological Studies. TAT measures of age-graded changes (Goldstine and Gutmann, 1972) and projective tests (Gutmann, 1971) as well as a study of dreams (Krohn and Gutmann, 1971) of Navajo men are cited as support for a developmental psychology theory of aging. These analyses show a change from active orientation in younger men to a passive and magical orientation in older men. The authors suggest that these shifts of Navajo responses parallel universal shifts in other cultures that are both urban and literate. Objections to their theory are raised by Press's criticisms of Gutmann's work on the Maya (Goldstine and Gutmann, 1972:372). Press feels that culture change is a more plausible explanation and suggests that the active mastery ego status among the younger Navajo may be a new phenomenon, an interpretation which would not support a developmental theory of aging. Tefft's study of the Wind River Shoshone (1968) suggests that other Indian cultures also provide a valued sacred domain for aged Indians regardless of whether it is explained by a developmental psychology theory of aging or by culture change.[1]

Statistical-Demographic Studies. The social profile which has emerged from the compilation of statistical-demographic data available in 1970 on elderly American Indians has been bleak (Benedict, 1972; Block, 1979; Nixon, 1970; B. Williams, 1977, 1978). Data used by Benedict indicate a short life expectancy (only one out of three reached the age of 65), lack of education,

high rates of unemployment and inadequate income, chronic illnesses and disabilities, and a high rate of disease-related deaths (1972: 51-58). B. Williams's summary of the statistics available in 1970 for American Indian elderly showed that in 1969 89 percent of Indians 65 years of age and over received an income. Of those receiving income 71 percent received less than $2,000 and 84 percent received less than $3,000 compared with 54 percent and 69 percent respectively for all older persons. Half of the Indian elderly reported incomes below poverty level in 1969 (1978: 7–8). The proportion of poor older Indians below poverty level was about the same as for black elderly but about twice as high as for all older persons (p. 9). In 1970 14 percent of Indians 65 and older had obtained a high school diploma compared to 25 percent for all older people (p. 12). The average life expectancy for Indians in 1970 was equal to nonwhites in general but was about seven years less than for whites. As Williams notes ". . . there are many factors which cause the average age at death to be lower. These factors include infant mortality, lack of decent housing, inadequate nutrition, poor transportation systems, insufficient medical services, and poor communication systems" (as quoted in B. Williams, 1978:14, from Special Committee on Aging, United States Senate, *Advisory Council on the Elderly American Indian*, Working Paper, November 1971, p. 3).

The needs of today's American Indian elderly are being addressed by the National Indian Council on Aging. The needs fall into several categories: income, environmental conditions, legal problems, physical well-being, and legislation (Lyon, 1978; National Indian Council on Aging, 1979).[2] Many are the same problems addressed at the 1971 White House Conference on Aging and most of them remain unsolved.[3] Needs assessments have been made as well in specific Indian communities on reservations and in urban areas (Dukepoo, 1980; Rogers and Gallion, 1978; Murdock and Schwartz, 1978; Kaplan and Taylor, 1972; and Lustig, 1979).

Two observations can be made about the data in the above-cited literature. The first is the recognition that variations in Indian aging are determined in part by the dichotomies which exist: reservation versus nonreservation status, urban versus rural environment, federally recognized versus nonfederally recognized groups. Variations in cultural background found in different parts of the country add a further dimension.

The second important observation to be made is that cultural factors make a difference in how contemporary Indians perceive aging and in the strategies used to cope with it. There is a clear indication that aging is more than a biological process with the resultant physical problems that come with growing older. While no one can deny the damaging effect that low income and poor health can have, aging goes beyond these factors. The reports summarized here show strong indications that cultural factors affect the aging process.

AGING IN TWO OKLAHOMA INDIAN COMMUNITIES[4]

My interest in the cross-cultural aspects of aging as well as in American Indian cultures led me to study the roles and attitudes of contemporary elderly Indians, in short to determine what it was like to be old and Indian today.

The data presented here are derived from participant observation and informal interviews with people from two rural nonreservation central Oklahoma Indian tribes: the Oto-Missouri[5] and the Ioway. Both groups are located on lands that once were reservations occupied by the tribes when they were removed to Indian Territory in the late 1800s. Approximately 980 Oto-Missouri live in the Red Rock area in north central Oklahoma (Trimble, 1972:468) and about 70 Ioway live in the vicinity of Perkins near the Cimarron River (Trimble, 1972:269). The number of people 65 years of age and older in these groups was approximately 9 percent at the time of the 1970 census (Census of Population, 1970:12–13).[6]

The Oto and Ioway tribes are closely related linguistically, culturally, and historically. The languages are mutually intelligible and their early connections are believed to date to a time when they were originally bands (along with the Winnebago) of one tribe. The tribes were agricultural, bison-hunting Plains Indians who

lived in large earth lodges. Contact between the two tribes continues today because of intermarriages but more importantly because of a sense of shared culture and common heritage.

Who Are the Elderly? It has been asserted that the definition of old age (the elderly, the aged, the old, and more euphemistically the Senior Citizen) in middle-class white America is a formal one (Anderson, 1972:212). There has been widespread acceptance of the notion that "old" means being 65, an age at which people have been arbitrarily retired. Though retirement ages are changing (today it is 70 for some jobs) and one must only be 55 to use the local Senior Citizens Center, the definition of who is old remains a formal one, and one that carries with it a certain amount of negative connotation.

By contrast, the prevailing definition of "old" as revealed by my research in Oklahoma Indian communities is a functional definition (Schweitzer and Williams, 1974:3–4). People are defined as old according to the functions they perform, the roles they play, and the community and family positions they hold, rather than by the arbitrary and formal marker of chronological age. There are two basic dimensions of this functional definition. The positive dimension recognizes a person as an elder if he or she possesses knowledge about tribal ways and customs or occupies the respected role of grandparent or is the head of a family line. These positions carry with them an attitude of honor and respect and offer occasions for interaction between old people and other tribal members.

The second dimension of the functional definition has what might be considered a negative connotation. Thus, a person is old when one can no longer take care of oneself. If one has failing health, one is considered to be old even if the chronological age is, for example, around 45 to 50 years. Implicit in this perspective is the idea that if a person is active, that person is not old even if the age is 85.

The Positive Dimensions of Aging. Although the contemporary roles of the elderly are different in many ways from the traditional ones that were available in precontact times, the elderly Oto and Ioway today occupy a variety of positions. These carry with them prestige and power, although the degree is determined in part by an individual's personal qualifications. As in other societies (Simmons, 1945:63) one does not have power and prestige merely because one is old.

The positions exist in two main segments of the social structure: the roles within the extended family network and the roles which are a function of public tribal and intertribal activities. Because of the interconnectedness of the social relations between these segments, however, it is not always possible to separate family from the larger tribal dimensions.

Roles indicated by the demands of tribal interaction which are available to the elderly include ritual specialists at naming ceremonies and funerals, religious specialists in the Native American church, and as masters of ceremonies of the tribal dances and the yearly encampment. Another very important function of the elderly today is to share knowledge of traditional tribal ways, to teach the language to those willing to learn, and to pass down the songs and legends to the younger generation. A woman in her late seventies speaks of her husband:

People come to him and ask him things—how to do things in the old way. (In tribal government) there is a lot of paper work and we give that to the educated ones . . . . But for lots of other things people come to the old people to find out how to do things.

This function is especially important today as younger tribal members come to the realization that what remains of tribal lore and the understanding of tribal ways is contained in the memories of their grandparents and other older members of the tribe. This follows the current trend in many Indian tribes which finds middle-aged and younger individuals, who for one reason or another had earlier rejected Indian ways, now turning to their elderly to learn as much as possible of the old ways.

The elders of the tribes possess in addition to the specific roles a more diffuse role, a measure of prestige which exists regardless of the specific duties attached to the role. This can be observed on public occasions when references are made to following the wishes of the ancestors or when public recognition and acquiescence to the elders are made.

The most important social structure which operates within the Indian community remains that of the family. It is the family which provides the framework in which the elderly Indian occupies roles which constitute the most important area of power and prestige for old people. Part of that power is economic, attained through land holdings and lease monies. If prestige accrues in any context just for the sake of being old it is in the family context that it may occur. Indian grandparents have the potential of achieving prestige in part because of the long tradition of respect and honor for old people that is a part of the enculturation process whereby values are learned.

As in traditional times, the grandparent-grandchild relationship is a strong one. Adults, especially women, welcome becoming a grandparent and are proud to claim that status. It is customary for grandparents to raise grandchildren who have been left without a father or mother or both. A young man in his early twenties is one example. The grandfather, to whom the young man is very close, stated that "the young man's father died when he was a baby. We raised him." It is also customary for grandparents to raise grandchildren when parents work, a parent is sick, away on a job relocation, or when it eases the burden of too many children. Grandparents may choose to raise a handicapped child to ease the burden a young family faces. Grandchildren in turn are the ones who often provide special services for their aging grandparents. Implicit in this relationship is a special feeling of love and respect. As one grandmother put it:

Old people are useful in many ways. For one thing they could look after the kids. People never did let anyone else take care of their kids. Grandparents are very useful to patch clothes, sew on buttons, be there to look after the children when the mother and father had to go somewhere.

The interaction which occurs between members of the larger family is mirrored in the kinship classification system which reflects close relations between various members. Because of the continued existence of the patrilineal kinship system and the recognition of that system in nomenclature, an individual has an extended network within which to function. A great-uncle is called "grandfather" and a great-aunt is called "grandmother." These are terms of special respect. A great-aunt or great-uncle will also take on the obligations (such as giving advice or help) of the grandfather or grandmother role if one's own grandparent dies. The grandparent relationship may even be assumed by members of nonrelated extended families or by people in other tribes. This may be done out of respect for the deceased or because an individual particularly likes a younger person. The older person makes a statement at a public event in which he indicates that he wishes to assume the grandparent role. He may say, "I want Robert to call me grandfather. I want to take Edward's place and do for Robert like his own grandfather would."

The family network in the Oto and Ioway communities is extensive; many people are related in either close or more remote ways. The tribal groups provide the background against which the family relationships are enacted and provide an extension of those relationships through the community roles mentioned above. A traditional feature of social relationships in the Oto and Ioway tribes and important in the lives of the old revolves around a kind of fictive kinship in which an individual acquires a "special" friend. Special friends are chosen by mutual agreement between two people who declare their friendship publicly. One young woman said:

We used to play together when we were little girls. She gave me a gift at a public gathering declaring her desire for a lasting friendship before the people. I accepted her gift, acknowledging her as my friend.

A person may have several special friends but there is usually one who is considered to be the most special. It is customary to help a special friend who is preparing for a giveaway by giving gifts of goods or money, although the increased mobility of tribal members makes it more and more difficult to maintain frequent contact.[7]

The special friend role carries with it obligations which last into old age and even into death for it is the "special" friend who "puts the deceased away." The family makes all of the arrangements and provides the dishes, new cooking utensils, and food. The special friend and his or her family do the cooking and feed the people who come to pay their respects. The person who "puts the deceased away" humbles himself and does the bidding of the family. It is the special friend who sits with the deceased during the traditional four-day funeral celebra-

tion. If the special friend is no longer living, a relative of the special friend, perhaps a daughter, will sometimes perform the obligations at the funeral. In some instances the special friend will "talk" for the family, relating the circumstances of the person's death to the people gathered for the funeral feast and speaking for them during the giveaway, although the family often chooses a close member of the family to "talk" for them.

Even though family relationships remain important, increased mobility and migration have resulted in a weakening of kinship and friendship ties in these Indian communities. Moving away from the local community for economic reasons understandably results in branches of the family and community network becoming relatively inactive. There are, however, members of the network who return on special occasions (for example, for the four-day summer encampment and powwow) to reestablish ties with their families in particular and the community in general. A number of people who live in other towns in Oklahoma return frequently, some every weekend, to be with their friends and relatives.

In spite of the adverse influences of migration on kinship ties as younger members move away from the area and remain for years, there are those who eventually return to the community to stay. Some return after middle age to live the remaining years of their lives in the Indian community. Some return for the purpose of taking care of older relatives or at least to live near them. It is more usual to find a younger family member living with or near the older ones than it is to find the older ones moving in with the younger people. In one example three generations live near each other creating in effect a four-household, three-generational extended family. The old couple live in one house; living in the same block are two daughters and their children as well as a nephew and his family. Two sons take turns living in the house with the old folks or living on the allotment farm.[8] This pattern is reminiscent of the prereservation practice where a man's married children lived in nearby tipis during the bison hunt. Old people are not reluctant to be dependent on others when it becomes necessary but at the same time their right to make their own decisions is recognized and respected by others. This seems to be the reverse of white middle-class elderly who fight becoming dependent on their adult children but who often are forced to relinquish not only their right to decision making but their own homes as well.

Family and community or tribal roles sometimes merge as family activities are enacted within the framework of tribal activities. A noteworthy example is the ceremony which is performed at a dance in which a boy's grandfather or other honored elder places a roach headdress on the boy's head symbolically giving him the right to dance at other public dances.[9] After placing the roach the elder walks with the boy in a circle around the drum and the singers, symbolizing the "going-around-together" of the old and the young. After this special ceremony the family, including the grandparents, have a giveaway in which they give gifts of money, shawls, blankets, and food to friends and relatives. Important in both ceremonies—placing the roach and the giveaway—is the cementing of the bond between grandparent and grandchild, a symbol of the continuity from generation to generation. The symbolism represents not only close family ties but embraces the larger structure represented by tribal membership and tribal heritage.

Especially important in understanding the position of the elderly are two dimensions in the lives of Indians in general. First, activities in which elderly people partake are events which tend to be non-age-segregated. For example, at the annual encampments held by many Oklahoma tribes each year people of all ages participate in camp activities, eating and dancing together. Old people interact with the young as grandparents look after small children or carry the very young in their arms as they dance around the drum. At individual camp sites grandparents, adult sons and daughters, and grandchildren share camping chores and help each other prepare to dance. Other activities which include people of all ages are hand games, birthday dinners, and tribal meetings.

The second dimension which has a special implication for the elderly is the sharing which permeates the family, tribal, and intertribal networks. The intricacies of the sharing can perhaps be illustrated most easily by citing the example in which a grandmother honors her young granddaughter who has been chosen to be the head lady dancer at a powwow. To honor the young woman the grandmother requests a special dance after which she holds a giveaway. The cooperation of the family members who have contributed shawls, blankets, and money has enabled the grandmother to acquire enough material goods and cash to distribute. Giveaways are also held on other occasions in which sharing is carried out in a web of relationships in which older people have important roles.

The Elders. In general, attitudes among the Oto-Missouri and the Ioway toward elderly people today reflect an expression of respect, honor, and prestige—a concept which portrays old age and old people as positively valued. These attitudes are implicitly expressed in the ways in which old people are expected to fulfill important family and community roles and explicitly in verbal expressions of honor made about the old people on public and private occasions. While attitudes toward the elderly are not 100 percent positive, they do reflect the positive roles discussed above.

THE PROBLEMS OF OLD AGE

It is suggested here that the cultural features which define old age in these Indian communities and provide the positive dimensions just discussed also act in a negative way when brought face to face with values and attitudes inherent in the planning of policy and the providing of services by state and federal agencies. Indian perceptions of aging differ from those of the dominant society and cultural patterns result in different roles and preferences. In addition to these factors, historical events have added a further negative dimension.

Indian concepts of old age do not correlate with the formal definition of the dominant society. The policies concerning the elderly and the services provided by state and federal agencies have been guided for the most part by the formal definition of aging and thus have ignored some of the specific problems inherent in American Indian aging. The statistical reality of a shorter life span for American Indians works to their disadvantage because fewer live to reap old-age benefits. The demographic data for American Indians which agencies use as a basis for their planning are out of date and inaccurate.[10]

Grandmothers and grandfathers who fill the surrogate mother and father roles for grandchildren or other young people are not able to take advantage of Senior Citizens Centers which operate in the daytime. It is also difficult for them to take advantage of other services such as meal programs which assume they have no such responsibilities. It is especially difficult for citywide services to meet the needs of the urban elderly Indian because of food preferences, activity and visiting patterns, and family ties which are culturally different from the non-Indian patterns (Lustig, 1979:19–60; Kaplan and Taylor, 1972).

Social Security plans ignore the historical and cultural background of the elderly American Indian who often lacked the opportunities to work at jobs which lead to social security benefits (Johnson, 1975:7). The economic roles which some elderly fill with their homestead allotments and lease monies or welfare payments do not make them eligible for pension plans or Social Security which regular employment would provide.

The values of sharing and non-age-segregated activities which are implicit in Indian culture can be negative factors when placed in juxtaposition with the values of the white community. The Senior Citizens Center's regulation admitting only people who are 55 years of age and older is clearly antithetical to the life style and values of elderly Indian people who would find it exceedingly hard to conceive of being segregated from their family and friends in such a way. The emphasis in white society seems to be for more and more segregation while in the Indian community it is clearly on non-age-segregation.

The family is the unit in which the social relations of the elderly are embedded and in which the people receive care when they need it. Very few Oto and Ioway, for example, actually go to nursing homes. Rogers and Gallion's study shows that among Pueblo Indian elderly of New Mexico approximately two-thirds live in an extended family situation and only 9 percent live alone, whereas in the general population 27 percent live alone and 51 percent live only with a spouse (1978:484–85). These data indicate that family networks exist in Indian groups to which home care services might well be adapted.

It is also recognized that some Indian people have only limited contact with whites and feel uncomfortable with non-Indians, some of whom are either completely uninformed about their Indian neighbors or who exhibit outright hostility and discrimination. Senior Citizens Centers and congregate meal programs served at a public location are frequented by few Oklahoma Indians for some of these reasons.

The implications for policy and planning strongly indicate that cultural factors should be taken into consideration if people other than the white population are to be served (see Trela and Sokolovsky, 1979, for a discussion of ethnicity and policy for the aged). The testimony and tribal reports from both National Indian Conferences on Aging as well as the data gathered by the multi-ethnic research program carried out by the Center on Aging in San Diego (see, for example, Valle and Mendoza, 1978) corroborate the Oklahoma data presented here.

INDIAN AGING AND MINORITY STATUS

In discussing the relationship of minority status to aging, minority aging is characterized as one of double jeopardy (Dowd and Bengtson, 1978; Bengtson and Morgan, this volume): (1) the minority elderly experience devaluation similar to that found in the majority society and (2) they also bear economic, social, and psycholgical inequities because of poor education, low incomes, higher percentage of illness and earlier death, poorer quality housing, and less choice as to where they live and work as well as a less satisfying quality of life.

The data presented here, however, indicate that social structures and attitudes exist that provide support for the Indian elderly even though certain inequities exist which stem from a unique historical relationship to the majority society. But suggesting that these social structures do exist in the Indian community should not be interpreted to mean that there are no needs or that these needs are fully taken care of by the family and community. The way these needs are met, however, must take into consideration the values, behavior, and social networks which operate in the lives of elderly Indians.

Dowd and Bengtson (1978) also test the hypothesis that age acts as a leveler: As majority and minority individuals grow old, the extent of variation declines. The problems that all aged people face are in many ways similar, but it is my contention that cultural factors tend to negate the leveling influences in regions where traditional behavior, values, and attitudes remain. That the aged face similar problems inherent in growing old is not as important as the fact that there are different and varied perceptions and solutions used to meet these problems (see the conclusions in Bengtson and Morgan, this volume).

CONCLUSIONS

Historical events have eroded much of the traditional life style of American Indian cultures but it is clear that Indian people retain a strong sense of Indian identity. They are neither vanishing nor being completely assimilated. Nowhere is it more evident than in the attitudes and roles which are associated with Indian aged today. It is my hope that the needs of these individuals can be realistically met without the necessity of abandoning the positive aspects that Indian communities offer their aged people.

NOTES

1. See Gutmann (1976) for a general discussion of cross-cultural psychological studies of aging.

2. I have not attempted to summarize here the vast amount of data included in these two excellent reports by the National Indian Council on Aging. Both reports help to bring up to date the profile of Indian aged. The reports substantiate in many ways my own data on the definition of the elderly, the roles available, and the reasons for supporting the premise that cultural factors are important in determining solutions for the needs of Indian elderly.

3. The needs are clearly stated—the solutions seem harder to achieve. See Cooley et al. (1979) and Duncan (1977) for initial attempts to meet some of the needs.

4. I would like to thank the National Science Foundation for support of part of the research on which this paper is based. Support was by a Student Originated Studies Grant #GY-11477 during the summer of 1974 and a dissertation grant #BNS76-81127 for 1977–1978. I would especially like to express my appreciation to those people of the Oto-Missouri and Ioway tribes who offered me their friendship and who shared with me their perceptions of aging. Thanks go also to G. Edward Arquitt, Richard Miller, John Schweitzer and Ethel Murray Staley for reading a draft of this paper and making helpful comments. Unless otherwise indicated, the data cited here on Oklahoma Indian aging are from field work which took place from 1974 through 1980. This presentation makes no attempt to include data on Indians who, for one reason or another, are excluded from the networks described here.

5. Often referred to as Oto.

6. The 9.36 percent of the Indian population in Oklahoma that was 65 or older in 1970 contrasts rather sharply with the 1970 census figures for reservation tribes which show 5.74 percent in the 65 or older category (Census of Population, 1970:188).

7. The giveaway is just that: the giving of goods and money in the person's honor to friends, honored guests, to the singers and drummers and other persons who have special meaning to the family.

8. The Oto-Missouri and Ioway reservations in Oklahoma were allotted to individual tribal members as a result of the Dawes Act of 1887. The allotment farm referred to was inherited by the descendant of the original allottee.

9. The roach headdress is part of the costume used by Plains Indian male dancers.

10. Different criteria used for the identification of Indians result in inconsistent statistics on the number of Indians. Bureau of Indian Affairs figures usually include only those Indians who are eligible for different federal programs and do not include all Indians. Identifying urban Indians (45

percent of the Indian population in 1970) is especially difficult. All of these problems are compounded when trying to assess the needs and numbers of the elderly (Lyon, 1978:185–87; Block, 1979:185). It is hoped that the 1980 census will provide more complete and more accurate information on American Indians and Alaskan Natives than has been available to date (National Indian Council on Aging News, Spring 1980:6–7). See Poppy (1979:79–88) for discussion of the research project on Indian elderly needs assessment begun in January 1978 by the National Indian Council on Aging.

NUMBER OUR DAYS

The so-called "ethnic revival," as it is currently being manifested by third-generation Euro-Americans, centers on subjective identity markers (food, clothes, "roots," and so on) and a sense of belonging to a historically known past. What does this mean for the elderly? Perhaps most important is that a positive valuation of ethnicity can serve as a nondenigrating component of identity that is not readily destroyed by retirement or the "empty nest syndrome." The development of a common identity with age peers can be especially crucial for urban elderly who are isolated from their upwardly mobile children. This is dramatically seen in the anthropological research of Barbara Myerhoff.

In the following article Myerhoff powerfully combines life histories with general ethnographic methods to penetrate intimately the lives of quite aged East European Jews living in rooming houses and hotels in Venice, California. Culturally dispossessed from the village environment of early socialization and from their far-flung children, these elderly live in a social world that revolves around a local senior citizens center. The center is where they search for continuity in their lives, by means of their common Jewish heritage. It is important to note that most have never been strongly religious Jews but rather share a passionate *Yiddishkeit* (Jewishness) that links them through the retention of the Yiddish language and the occasional performance of ritual venerating a cultural past that survived even the Holocaust. In the center we see the elders as complex, real persons and ethnicity not as a preexisting given but as a cultural milieu created and manipulated by these people.

"Every morning I wake up in pain. I wiggle my toes. Good. They still obey. I open my eyes. Good. I can see. Everything hurts but I get dressed. I walk down to the ocean. Good. It's still there. Now my day can start. About tomorrow I never know. After all, I'm eighty-nine. I can't live forever."

DEATH AND THE OCEAN are protagonists in Basha's life. They provide points of orientation, comforting in their certitude. One visible; the other invisible: Neither hostile nor friendly, they accompany her as she walks down the boardwalk to the Aliyah Senior Citizens' Center.

Above all, Basha wants to remain independent. Her life at the beach depends on her ability to perform a minimum number of basic tasks. She must shop and cook, dress herself, care for her body and her one-room apartment, walk, take the bus to the market and the doctor, be able to make a telephone call in case of emergency. Her arthritic fingers have a difficult time with the buttons on her dress. Some days her fingers ache and swell so that she cannot fit them into the holes of the telephone dial. Her hands shake as she puts in her eyedrops for glaucoma.

Basha's daughter calls her once a week. She worries about her mother living alone and in a deteriorated neighborhood. "Don't worry about me, darling. This morning I put the garbage in the oven and the bagels in the trash. But I'm feeling fine." Basha enjoys teasing her daughter whose distant concern she finds somewhat embarrassing. "She says to me, 'Mammaleh, you're sweet but you're so *stupid*.' What else could a greenhorn mother expect from a daughter who is a lawyer?"

From *Number Our Days* by Barbara Myerhoff. Copyright © 1978 by Barbara Myerhoff. Reproduced by permission of the publisher, E. P. Dutton.

The statement conveys Basha's simultaneous pride and grief at having produced an educated, successful child whose very accomplishments drastically separate her from her mother. The daughter has often invited Basha to live with her, but Basha refuses.

Like most of the three hundred or so elderly members (late eighties and beyond) of the Aliyah Center, Basha was born, and spent much of her childhood, in one of the small, predominately Jewish, Yiddish-speaking villages known as *shtetls*, located within the Pale of Settlement of Czarist Russia, an area to which almost half the world's Jewish population was confined in the nineteenth century. Desperately poor, regularly terrorized by outbreaks of anti-Semitism initiated by government officials and surrounding peasants, *shtetl* life was precarious. Yet, in these provincial, self-sufficient, semirural settlements, a rich, highly developed culture flourished, based on a shared, sacred religious history, common customs and beliefs, and two languages—Hebrew for prayer and Yiddish for daily life. The folk culture, Yiddishkeit, reached its florescence there, and although it continues in various places in the world today, by comparison these expressions are dim and fading. When times worsened, Eastern Europe *shtetl* life often seemed to intensify proportionately. Internal ties deepened, and people drew sustenance and courage from each other, their religion, and their community. For many, life became unbearable under the reactionary regime of Czar Alexander II. The pogroms of 1881–82, accompanied by severe economic and legal restrictions, drove out the more desperate and daring of the Jews. Soon they were leaving the *shtetls* and the cities in droves. The exodus of Jews from Eastern Europe swelled rapidly; by the turn of the century, hundreds of thousands were emigrating, the majority to seek freedom and opportunity in the New World.

Even though she is now living in southern California, Basha dresses for the cold, wearing a babushka under a red sun hat, a sweater under her heavy coat. She moves steadily down the boardwalk, paying attention to the placement of her feet. A fall is common and dangerous for the elderly. A fractured hip can mean permanent disability, loss of autonomy, and removal from the community to a convalescent or old age home. Basha seats herself on a bench in front of the Center and waits for friends. Her feet are spread apart, well planted, as if growing up from the cement. Even sitting quite still, she has an air of determination about her. She will withstand attacks by anti-Semites, Cossacks, Nazis, historical enemies whom she conquers by outliving. She defies time and weather (although it is not cold here). So she might have sat a century ago, before a small pyramid of potatoes or herring in the marketplace of the Polish town where she was born. Patient, resolute, she is a survivor.

As the morning wears on, the benches fill. Benches are attached back to back: one side facing the ocean; one side the boardwalk. The people on the ocean side swivel around to face their friends, the boardwalk, and the Center.

Bench behavior is highly stylized. The half-dozen or so benches immediately to the north and south of the Center are the territory of the members, segregated by sex and conversation topic. The men's benches are devoted to abstract, ideological concerns—philosophical debates, politics, religion, and economics. The women's benches are given more to talk about immediate, personal matters—children, food, health, neighbors, love affairs, scandals, and "managing." Men and women talk about Israel and its welfare, about being a Jew, and about Center politics. On the benches, reputations are made and broken, controversies explored, leaders selected, factions formed and dissolved. Here is the outdoor dimension of center life; like a village plaza, it is a focus of protracted, intense sociability. All the elderly Jews in the neighborhood are Eastern European in origin. All are multilingual. Hebrew is brought out—usually by the men—for punctuating debates with definitive, learned points. Russian or Polish may be used for songs, stories, poems, and reminiscences. But Yiddish, the beloved *mama-loshen*, "mother tongue," of their childhood, binds these diverse people together. It is Yiddish that is used for the most emotional discussions. Despite their ideological differences, most of these people know each other well, having lived here at the beach for two and three decades.

About thirty years ago, Jews from all over the country began to immigrate to the beach community, particularly those with health problems or newly retired. Seeking a benign climate, fellow Jews, and moderately priced housing, they brought their savings and small pensions and came to live near the ocean. Collective life was and still is especially intense in this community because there is no automobile traffic on the boardwalk. Here is a place where people may meet, gather, talk, and stroll—simple but basic and precious activities that the elderly in particular can enjoy here all year round.

In the late 1950s, an urban development program resulted in the displacement of between four and six thousand of these senior citizens in a very short period. It was a devastating blow to the culture. "A second Holocaust," Basha called it. "It destroyed our *shtetl* life all over again." Soon after the urban development project began, a marina was constructed at the southern end of the boardwalk. Property values soared. Older people could not pay the taxes and many lost their homes. Rents quadrupled. As old hotels and apartments were torn down, housing became the most serious problem for the elderly who desperately wanted to remain in the area. While several thousand have managed to hang on, no new Center members are moving into the area because of the housing problem. Their Yiddish world, built up over a thirty-year period, is dying and extinction is imminent. Perhaps it will last another five or, at most, ten years. Whenever a Center member leaves, everyone is acutely aware that there will be no replacements. The sense of cultural doom coincides with awareness of approaching individual death. "When I go out of here, it will be in a box or to the old folks' home. I couldn't say which is worse," Basha said. "We've only got a few more years here, all of us. It would be good if we could stay till the end. We had a protest march the other day, when they took down the old Miramar Hotel. I made up a sign. It said, 'Let my people stay.'"

Yet the community is not a dreary place, and the Center members are not a depressed group. The sense of doom, by some miraculous process, functions to heighten and animate their life. Every moment matters. There is no time for deception, trivia, or decorum. Life at the Center is passionate, almost melodramatic. Inside, ordinary concerns and mundane interchanges are strangely intense, quickly heating to outburst. The emotional urgency often seems to have little to do with content. This caldronlike quality is perhaps due to the elders' proximity to death and the

realization that their remaining days are few. They want to be seen and heard from, before it is too late.

Center culture is in some respects thin and fragile, but its very existence must be seen as a major accomplishment, emerging spontaneously as a result of two conditions that characterize the members: social isolation and continuities between past and present circumstance. Several marked similarities exist between the circumstances of members' childhoods and old age. They had grown up in small, intimate Jewish communities—isolated, ethnocentric, surrounded by indifferent and often hostile outsiders. Previously, in Eastern Europe, they had been marginal people, even pariahs. They had strong early training in resourcefulness and opportunities to develop strong survival strategies. Then, as now, they had been poor, politically impotent, and physically insecure. Then, as now, they turned to each other and their shared Yiddishkeit for sustenance, constituting what Irving Howe has called a "ragged kingdom of the spirit." It was not a great shock for these people to find themselves once more in difficult circumstances, for they had never given up their conviction that life was a struggle, that gains entailed losses, that joy and sorrow were inseparable. They knew how to pinch pennies, how to make do, how to pay attention to those worse off than they and thereby feel useful and needed. They had come to America seeking another life and found that it, too, provided some fulfillments, some disappointments. And thus, they were now not demoralized or helpless.

Their culture was able to emerge as fully as it did because of their isolation from family and community, ironically, the very condition that causes them much grief. Yet, their isolation freed them to find their own way. Now they could indulge their passion for things of the past, enjoy Yiddishkeit without fear of being stigmatized as "not American." With little concern for public opinion, with only each other for company, they revitalized selected features of their common history to meet their present needs, adding and amending it without concern for consistency, priority, or "authenticity." It had taken three decades for this culture to develop to its present state of complexity, now a truly organic, if occasionally disorderly and illogical, amalgam of forms and sentiments, memories and wishes, rotating around a few stable, strong symbols and premises. Claude Lévi-Strauss has used the term *bricolage* to describe the process through which myths are constructed in preliterate societies. Odds and ends, fragments offered up by chance or the environment—almost anything will do— are taken up by a group and incorporated into a tale, used by a people to explain themselves and their world. No intrinsic order or system has dictated the materials employed. In such an inelegant fashion does the *bricoleur*, or "handyman," meet his needs.

Center culture was such a work of *bricolage*. Robust and impudently eclectic, it shifted and stretched to meet immediate needs—private, collective, secular, and sacred. Thus, when a Center Yiddish History class graduated, a unique ceremony was designed that pasted together the local event with an analogous, historical counterpart, thereby enlarging and authenticating the improvised, contemporary affair. And the traditional Sabbath ceremony was rearranged to allow as many people as possible to participate—making speeches, singing songs, reading poems—taking into account the members' acute need for visibility and attention. Two or even three women, instead of one, were required to light the Sabbath candles—one singing the blessing in Hebrew, one in Yiddish, one putting the match to the wick. Similarly, Center folk redefined the secular New Year's Eve, holding their dance a full day and a half before the conventional date, since this made it possible for them to get home before dark and to hire their favorite musicians at lower rates. These improvisations were entirely authentic. Somehow, midday December 30 became the real New Year's Eve and the later public celebration seemed unconvincing by comparison. In all this, no explicit plan or internal integration could be detected. Cultures are, after all, collective, untidy assemblages, authenticated by belief and agreement, focused only in crisis, systematized after the fact. Like a quilt, Center life was made up of many small pieces sewn together by necessity, intended to be serviceable and to last. It was sufficient for the people's remaining years.

I had made no conscious decision to explore my roots or clarify the meaning of my origins. I was one of several anthropologists at the Universi-

ty of Southern California engaged in an examination of ethnicity and aging. At first I planned to study elderly Chicanos, since I had previously done field work in Mexico. But in the early 1970s in urban America, ethnic groups were not welcoming curious outsiders, and people I approached kept asking me, "Why work with us? Why don't you study your own kind?" This was a new idea to me. I had not been trained for such a project. Anthropologists conventionally investigate exotic, remote, preliterate societies. But such groups are increasingly unavailable and often inhospitable. As a result, more and more anthropologists find themselves working at home these days. Inevitably, this creates problems with objectivity and identification, and I anticipated that I, too, would have my share if I studied the Center folk. But perhaps there would be advantages. There was no way that I could have anticipated the duration of the study or its great impact on my life. I intended to spend a year at the Center. In fact, I was there continually for two years (1973–74, 1975–76) and periodically for two more. In the beginning, I spent a great deal of time agonizing about how to label what I was doing—was it anthropology or a personal quest? I never fully resolved the question. I used many conventional anthropological methods and asked many typical questions, but when I had finished, I found my descriptions did not resemble most anthropological writings. Still, the results of the study would certainly have been different had I not been an anthropologist.

Sitting in the sun and contemplating the passsing parade on the boardwalk that first morning in 1973, I wondered how to begin. At eleven-thirty the benches began to empty as old people entered the Center for a "Hot Kosher Meal—Nutritious—65¢," then a new program provided by state and private funds. I followed the crowd inside and sat at the back of the warm, noisy room redolent with odors of fish and chicken soup, wondering how to introduce myself. It was decided for me when a woman, who I soon learned was Basha, sat down next to me. In a leisurely fashion, she appraised me. Uncomfortable, I smiled and said hello.

"You are not hungry?" she asked.

"No, thank you, I'm not," I answered.

"So, what brings you here?"

"I'm from the University of Southern California. I'm looking for a place to study how older Jews live in the city."

At the word *university*, she moved closer and nodded approvingly. "Are you Jewish?" she asked.

"Yes, I am."

"Are you married?" she persisted.

"Yes."

"You got children?"

"Yes, two boys, four and eight," I answered.

"Are you teaching them to be Jews?"

"I'm trying."

"So what do you want with us here?" asked Basha.

"Well, I want to understand your life, find out what it's like to be older and Jewish, what if anything makes Jews different from other older people. I'm an anthropologist and we usually study people's cultures and societies. I think I would like to learn about this culture."

"And what will you do for us?" she asked me.

"I could teach a class in something people here are interested in—how older people live in other places, perhaps."

"Are you qualified to do this?" Basha shot me a suspicious glance.

"I have a Ph.D. and have taught in the university for a number of years, so I suppose I am qualified."

"You are a professor then? A little bit of a thing like you?" To my relief, she chuckled amiably. Perhaps I had passed my first rite of entrance into the group.

For the next four years I was to be involved with these people, as an anthropologist doing field work, as a friend, and sometimes, as a family member. The anthropologist engages in peculiar work. He or she tries to understand a different culture to the point of finding it to be intelligible, regardless of how strange it seems in comparison with one's own background. This is accomplished by attempting to experience the new culture from within, living in it for a time as a member, all the while maintaining sufficient detachment to observe and analyze it with some objectivity. This peculiar posture—being inside and outside at the same time—is called participant-observation. It is a fruitful paradox, one that has allowed anthropologists to find sense and purpose within a society's seemingly illogical and arbitrary customs and beliefs. This assumption of the natives'

viewpoint, so to speak, is a means of knowing others through oneself, a professional technique that can be mastered fairly easily in the study of very different peoples. Working with one's own society, and more specifically, those of one's own ethnic and familial heritage, is perilous and much more difficult. Yet it has a certain validity and value not available in other circumstances. Identifying with the "other"—Indians and Chicanos if one is Anglo, blacks if one is white, males if one is female—is an act of imagination, a means for discovering what one is not and will never be. Identifying with what one is now and will be someday is quite a different process. And one day I will be a little old Jewish lady, and it is important for me to have some concrete expectations about that.

In working among the elderly—also, I suspect, among the very young—an exceptionally important part of one's information is derived from nonverbal communication and identification, this because the bodily state is such a large determinant of well-being for the growing and declining organism. At various times, I consciously tried to heighten my awareness of the physical state of the elderly by wearing stiff garden gloves to perform ordinary tasks, taking off my glasses and plugging my ears, slowing down my movements and, sometimes, by wearing the heaviest shoes I could find to the Center. Walking a few blocks in this condition became an unimaginably exhilarating achievement. Once by accident I stumbled slightly. The flash of terror I experienced was shocking. From close watching of the elderly, it seems I had acquired their need to avoid falling, although to one of my age and in good health, such a minor accident presents no real danger. This recognition occurred after I had been watching two very old women walk down the alley with great concentration, arms tightly linked, navigating impediments in slow-motion movements that were perfectly coordinated and mutually supportive. So great was their concern with balance, they might have been walking a high wire.

But I learned more than what old age would or could be in my work with the Center elderly. They provided a model of an alternative life style, built on values in many ways antithetical to those commonly esteemed by contemporary Americans. The usual markers of success were anathema to them. Wealth, power, physical beauty, youth, mobility, security, social status—all were out of the question. Without a future, lacking hope for change or improvement, they had devised a counter-world, inventing their own version of what made "the good life." It was built on their veneration for their religious and cultural membership and was full of meaning, intensity, and consciousness. This they had managed on their own, creating a nearly invisible, run-down world, containing a major lesson for any who would attend it. It was not the first time that an anthropologist had found in obscure, unworldly folk a message of wide applicability for the larger outside society.

The character of Center social life was distinctively tumultuous and dramatic. In part this was due to the tensions arising from contradictions within the members' ideology, most conspicuously, between their Zionism and internationalism, their agnosticism and Judaism, their identification with modern American society and their Eastern European past. All cultures are riddled with internal inconsistencies, but they do not generally produce the kind of social disorganization so evident at the Center. More troublesome than the inconsistencies in their beliefs were certain paradoxes or structural conflicts that disrupted solidarity and prevented their society from developing the stability it otherwise might have. Three paradoxes were particularly evident. First was people's need for passionate experiences, as opposed to their desire for dignity and harmony. Second, people had extreme need for each other socially and psychologically, with no corresponding material, economic need; this resulted in a peculiar imbalance that generated much strain and confusion. Finally, Center elders required witnesses to their past and present life and turned to each other for this, although it is a role properly filled by the succeeding generation. Lacking suitable heirs to their traditions and stories, they were forced to use peers who, they realized, would perish along with them, and thus could not assure the preservation of what they had witnessed.

Center people, like so many of the elderly, were very fond of reminiscing and storytelling, eager to be heard from, eager to relate parts of their life history. More afraid of oblivion than of pain or death, they always sought opportunities

to become visible. Narrative activity among them was intense and relentless. Age and proximity to death augmented the Jewish predilection for verbal expression. In their stories, as in their cultural dramas, they witnessed themselves, and thus knew who they were, serving as subject and object at once. They perpetually narrated themselves; they kept notes and journals, wrote poems and spontaneous reflections, and told their stories to all who would listen. Their histories were not devoted to marking their successes or unusual merits. Rather they were efforts at ordering, sorting, explaining—rendering coherent their long lives, finding integrating ideas and characteristics that helped them know themselves as the same persons over time, despite great ruptures and shifts. No doubt their emigrant experience and the loss of their original culture made them even more prone to seek continuity and coherence. Survivors, it is often noted, are strongly impelled to serve as witnesses to what has been lost. Often these materials are idealized and sentimentalized. Despite its poverty and oppression, *shtetl* life was often described as a golden age in comparison with much of the present, which was found lacking. In recounting the past, they kept that early life alive, weaving it into their present.

Here are excerpts from a statement dictated by Shmuel, one of the Center members and my principal informant. He died three days after he completed recording his life history.

Oh, how often in our dreams, like a bird, we fly back to the place of our birth, to that little Polish town on the Vistula, which would be to you a small speck on the map, maybe even too insignificant for a map. A few thousand people huddled together, hidden in the hills, but with a view in sight of the beautiful river. In this place, the population was nearly equal Poles and Jews. All were poor. There were the poor and the poorer still.

If you walked through the Jewish quarter, you would see small houses, higgledy-piggledy, leaning all over each other. Some had straw roofs, if shingles, some broken. No cobbles on the streets, and you might not even want to call them streets, so narrow and deep rutted from wagons. Everywhere, children, cats, geese, chickens, sometimes a goat, all together making very strong smells and noises. Always, the children were dirty and barefoot, always the dogs were skinny and mean, not Jewish dogs. They came over from Gentile quarters looking for garbage and cats. You would go along this way until you crossed the wooden bridge into the main platz. Here were the women on market day, sitting in the open, or in little wooden stalls if they were well-off.

The pogroms were all around us. Then the soldiers on horseback would tear through the town and leave dead Jews behind. One time, we heard the big bell ring out and there was no reason for it. We were so scared we hid in the synagogue. That was probably the worst place to go, but we were small boys. All night we stayed huddling together there and heard terrible noises outside—horses, screams, shouts. We were afraid to light the lamps or stove. In the morning some men came to get us. Someone, it must have been a Pole, had warned the Jews with the bells that the soldiers were coming through. Everyone got away very quickly, hiding in the forest and in neighbors' homes. Who knows what would have happened without the warning? As it is, the soldiers tore up the Jewish streets, broke windows, threw the furniture out. We came out into the sparkling sunshine and the streets were white like in winter. Everywhere were feathers from where those Cossacks cut up our featherbeds. Dead animals also on our streets.

The day comes to go. A summer day, beautiful. My father goes down to the cemetery and I with him. I couldn't stand to go too close to him. I loved him, but the pain that was coming out from him kept me away. Like flames, going out in waves. First he walked up and down. Finally, he gave the rabbi there some money to say prayers and keep up the graves. Then he walked over to the grave of his father. He cried, tears coming down his face. His hair was black and gray. Old as he was, there was a youthfulness about him, very remarkable. At this time, I saw that youthfulness go out from him forever, like the departure of a spirit. I could not take this sight in, and I hid my eyes. Still,

when I looked up, he stood there like a small boy crying. He walked over to the other graves, his mother's, his sisters' and brothers', then back to his father's. He started a conversation there, telling his father why he was leaving, asking him for forgiveness and a blessing. All the while his tears are running through his beard until his shirt front is drenched.

In that little town there were no walls. But we were curled up together inside it, like small cubs, keeping each other warm, growing from within, never showing the outside what is happening, until our backs made up a strong wall. It is not the worst thing that can happen for a man to grow old and die. But here is the hard part. When my mind goes back there now, there are no roads going in or out. No way back remains because nothing is there, no continuation. Then life itself, what is its worth to us? Why have we bothered to live? All this is at an end. For myself, growing old would be altogether a different thing if that little town was there still. All is ended. So in my life I carry with me everything—all those people, all those places, I carry them around until my shoulders bend. I can see the old rabbi, the workers pulling their wagons, the man carrying his baby tied to his back, walking up from the Vistula, no money, no house, nothing to feed his child. His greatest dream is to have a horse of his own, and in this he will never succeed. So I carry him. If he didn't have a horse, he should have at least the chance to be remaining in the place he lived. Even with all that poverty and suffering, it would be enough if the place remained, even old men like me, ending their days, would find it enough. But when I come back from these stories and remember that the way they lived is gone forever, wiped out like you would erase a line of writing, then it means another thing altogether for me to accept leaving this life. If my life goes now, it means nothing. But if my life goes, with my memories, and all that is lost, that is something else to bear.

NETWORKS, COMMUNITY CREATION, AND INSTITUTIONALIZATION: ENVIRONMENTS FOR AGING

"Our current institutions do not offer a choice between marginality and integration of the aged but simply between alternative forms of alienation."

—*Irving Rosow (1974)*

"The alienation of the aged from American life is not wholly barred from any creative solutions."

—*Margaret Clark and Barbara Anderson (1967)*

To some, growing old in America is akin to entering a state of oblivion. This pessimistic outlook is certainly reflected in the first quotation by Rosow. Such a view of aging is linked to conspicuous alienation from deep family and community ties, loss of work roles, devaluation of traditional knowledge, and aging itself in the context of a youth cult and an economic system based on "planned obsolescence." Regarding the United States, J. Scott Francher (1973) proposes that the themes represented in the glorification of the youthful, competitive, action-oriented "Pepsi generation" present a set of symbols both contradictory and psychologically harmful to the self-esteem of the old. What might be the consequences for the elderly of trying to adhere to the values represented by the Pepsi generation? Anthropologists Margaret Clark and Barbara Anderson (1967) found an indication of the answer to this question in their study of 1,200 San Francisco residents over the age of 60. Those

elderly who espoused values of self-reliance, productivity, and competitive interaction were the *most* likely to be institutionalized for mental illness. Yet the optimism of the second quotation opening this section stems from Clark and Anderson's analysis of those highly "adapted" aged in their sample. These were individuals who had fulfilled five "adaptive tasks":

1. Accept aging.
2. Reorganize life space.
3. Substitute sources of need satisfaction.
4. Reexamine the criteria for self-evaluation.
5. Reintegrate values and life goals.

Completion of these tasks was found to be associated with positive mental health and high levels of life satisfaction in later adulthood among the sample studied (see also Anderson, 1979).

However, understanding the viability of such models of successful aging in a rapidly changing urban, industrial society requires examining the actual interpersonal linkages through which survival is accomplished and the broader social arenas in which growing old and dying take place.

SOCIAL NETWORKS

As noted in the discussion of family interaction (see Section II), the elderly in industrial societies are not as isolated as previously suspected, at least in terms of frequency of contact and the exchange of some practical resources. Despite the proliferation of formal care-giving organizations and attendant personnel oriented toward senior citizens, growing attention has focused on the existence of "natural" support systems, *generated by the elderly themselves*. In seeking to understand the importance of informal social ties in meeting the needs of the elderly, one level of analysis has concentrated on the study of "social networks"— ego-centered sets of personal links and their interconnections generated among friends, kin, and neighbors (Cantor, 1979; Sokolovsky, 1980; Kahn and Antonucci, 1981; Wentowski, 1982). In anthropology and sociology network analysis has been particularly useful for studying urban settings where social action is not readily understood within the context of formal institutional structures such as the *matai* system of Samoa or the East African age sets.

The salience of a network approach to aging populations is clearly indicated by studies that show "the buffering effect of social support to moderate the relationship between acute stress . . . and criteria for well-being" (Kahn, 1979:85). In this section's first selection we see how network analysis is used to understand the adaptation of the inner-city elderly, a population often considered the most isolated, at risk, noninstitutionalized category of older Americans (Stephens, 1975; Lopata, 1978; Eckert, 1979, 1980; Cohen and Sokolovsky, 1980; Sokolovsky and Cohen, 1981b; Baxter and Hopper, 1981).

COMMUNITY CREATION

Overlapping the study of social networks, another level of analysis has investigated the conditions under which alternate roles and norms for the elderly are likely to be generated. Concern for this issue has been stimulated by the works of such gerontologists as Rosow, who has forcefully argued that "unlike earlier status changes in American life, people are not effectively socialized to old age" (1974:xii). Stimulated by growing age consciousness and segregation of the elderly from younger people, Arnold Rose (1962) in the 1960s predicted the emergence of an elderly subculture. According to Rose's theory, new

status systems would develop based on health and activity levels relevant to the aged themselves. While a general subculture of older citizens has not yet materialized, studies of various age-segregated residences of the old in France, Great Britian, and the United States have indicated that in fact such environments can enhance social integration. It is in such age-graded public housing (Hochschild, 1973; Ross, 1977; Goist, 1981), mobile home parks (Johnson, 1971; Angrosino, 1976), and private retirement communities (S. W. Byrne, 1974; J. Jacobs, 1974; Fry, 1977; Perkinson, 1980) that an ethnographic approach to aging has been most frequently used. The arguments favoring such new environments seem most clear in terms of social interaction, since "elders living in such communities appear to have more friends, see them more often, and show a higher level of social activity" (Rosow, 1970:63). This is especially clear in those instances where a strong sense of community crystalizes around the new social networks formed (Keith, 1980a). One of the few social scientists to analyze the common factors facilitating this process is Jennie Keith. Her article in this section shows that in diverse settings strong social bonds among the aged will be stimulated by: (1) norms of equality; (2) a transitional status for old age; (3) a high level of perceived threat from the outside world; and (4) a lack of strong cross-cutting social ties.

The research suggesting the benefits of age-segregated housing has far-reaching policy implications for urban planning that have not gone unchallenged. Foster and Anderson, while admitting that such communities can provide the basis for a healthier self-image and insulate against disquieting societal change, argue that such communities also represent an "escape the system" model of adaptation that operates by ignoring old age and emphasizing a cult of pseudoactivity (1978:294). They contrast this with what they feel is a more positive "confront the system" model that emphasizes accomplishing the five adaptive tasks delineated by Clark and Anderson (1967). However, accommodating to growing old is not merely a matter of personal adjustment; it is strongly influenced by the organization of the broader society in which people are embedded. Barbara Hornum, in the third article of this section, recognizes this point.

In her study of a wide variety of age-integrated, planned communities in Great Britain, Hornum shows that age-homogeneous environments are *not* the only ones that can provide a satisfying old age.

INSTITUTIONALIZATION: THE ULTIMATE SEGREGATION

The intense emotionalism surrounding the issue of residential segregation of the aged in our society is undoubtably due to the pervasive association of old age with institutionalization and nursing home placement. However, in thinking about environments that the elderly occupy, we must distinguish among age segments of this population. Indeed, fewer than 2 percent of the "young-old" (age 65 to 74) reside in institutions, as compared to 7 percent of the 75- to 85-year-olds and 16 percent of those over 85 (Tobin and Lieberman, 1976:211). Nursing homes are thus currently inhabited by the very old (the average age is 82). Nevertheless, although only one in 20 of those over 65 now live in such places, it is estimated that *one in four* will require at least some institutional care during the balance of their lives (Butler, 1975).

Various studies of nursing homes in the United States have documented the shocking conditions of this ultimate segregation—from which only 20 percent ever leave alive (Henry, 1963; C. Townsend, 1971; Mendelson, 1974; Moss and Halamandaris, 1977; Henderson, 1981). Yet, research on nursing homes in other societies has indicated that the atrocities attributed to our own nursing homes are not completely a function of institutionalization itself (Kayser-Jones, 1981a, 1981b; Rhoads and Holmes, 1981). In the final selection Maria Vesperi shows that the true horror of nursing home placement is not in the physical surroundings but in the means by which institutionalization symbolically redefines the person as a nonhuman, a nonentity—that is symbolically dead.

Jay Sokolovsky and Carl Cohen

NETWORKS AS ADAPTATION:
THE CULTURAL MEANING OF BEING A "LONER" AMONG THE INNER-CITY ELDERLY

Ironically, while measures of informal social interaction have been viewed as crucial in gerontological theory and research, most studies have failed to examine the qualitative features and cultural meaning that social networks hold for the elderly. Anthropologist Jay Sokolovsky and community psychiatrist Carl Cohen argue that failure to consider such data can foster severe misunderstandings about the inner-city aged population. Using an ethnographically guided network analysis to study elderly residents of Manhattan single room occupancy (SRO) hotels, they find this population to be far from total isolates. Rather, three network characteristics—(1) structural dispersion, (2) highly selective intimacy, and (3) variable activation of ties—link these self-identified "loners" to their urban environment in a culturally meaningful way.

WHILE NETWORK ANALYSIS HAS come to be a regularly used methodological tool, especially in urban anthropology, the data produced are often of heuristic rather than empirical value. Most studies avoid measuring the total size of egocentric networks, neglect to distinguish between levels of multiplexity, and do not consider temporal fluctuation. Failure to derive such data can lead to misinterpretation of simple participant observation and to making inappropriate linkages of network variables to other indices of behavior.

In such a way the literature on the inner-city elderly, especially those residing in Single Room Occupancy hotels (SRO's), has portrayed this population as totally "isolated" and with personal networks of little significance. Our research indicates that for many SRO residents this perception is largely incorrect and distorted by a tendency to study social linkages within the context of formal institutional structures rather than viewing the informally developed social matrix as *culturally significant in itself*. The goal of this paper will be to suggest how an anthropologically oriented network analysis can clarify the cultural meaning of social interaction for the SRO elderly.

THE INNER CITY AND THE "URBAN UNATTACHED"

Since the early formulations by Wirth (1938) of the effect of urbanism on social organization, the cultural condition of "unattached" city dwellers has presented a theoretical and methodological dilemma for researchers: how indeed to study people who appear to shun or retire from normal occupations, refuse to join voluntary associations, are not embedded in an ethnic enclave, and avoid the joys of married life and frequent family reunion. The urban focus of such a question has been the inner city, those "transient residential

Revised version of an article in *Urban Anthropology*, 7 (4), 1978, pp. 323–342. Reprinted by permission
The authors wish to thank Alan Laskow, Lynne Stein, John Stern, Ann Avitobile, David Burns, Mary Beckor, Mike Braverman, and the Murray Hill SRO Project for their assistance. Special thanks to the residents of the SRO hotels we studied who really made this research possible. The research was supported by grants from the Ittleson Foundation, New York Foundation, van Ameringin Foundation, the Commonwealth Foundation, and computer time provided by the University of Maryland Baltimore County.

areas, the Gold Coasts, and the slums that generally surround the central business district, although in some communities they may continue for miles beyond that district" (Gans, 1975).

Investigations of the impact of inner-city residence on social relations, especially for those residing in urban SRO hotels have depicted atomism and isolation at their zenith. The pioneer studies of hotel life all stressed the great anonymity, dissociation, and virtual absence of cultural meaning. The archetype of such a supposedly deculturized population is perhaps summed up best by Harvey Zorbaugh in analyzing "The World of the Furnished Rooms" in Chicago.

One knows no one, and is known by no one. One comes and goes as one wishes, does very much as one pleases, and as long as one disturbs no one no questions are asked . . . . The peculiar social relationships of the world of furnished rooms are reflected in the behavior of the people who live in this world . . . . They seem to reveal the same isolation, loneliness and tendency to personal disorganization . . . . The rooming house world is in no sense a social world, a set of group relationships through which the person's wishes are realized . . . . It is a world of atomized individuals. (1929:74–86)

Some recent studies have come to similar conclusions. Hertz and Hutheesing (1975) using a "loose" interview procedure and a sample of 19 individuals in a small (40-room) Manhattan rooming hotel describe tenants as "isolates" possessing a "nominal culture." This "nominal culture" life style is characterized by virtual lack of kin ties, contact with no more than one outside "friend," and an extreme bareness of communication inside and outside the hotel (p. 325).

The most emphatic denials of social interaction have stemmed from studies of the elderly components of such populations. Stephens in her study of a Detroit SRO categorizes these elderly as alienated lifelong "loners" who "have broken *all* ties to family, friends and for the most part do not attempt to replenish an impoverished repertoire of social relations." This aged population (90 percent male) is described as living in a "society of the alone" dominated by norms of freedom,

privacy, and utilitarianism. It is also maintained that those few aged women who live in the hotel have a particularly hard time in generating even the few utilitarian ties which the men maintain. Another recent study echos Stephen's analysis particularly with regard to female SRO residents. Lally et al. (1979), studying a number of Seattle hotels, focused on a small sample (16) of older women who had higher than average education for their age cohort and a majority of whom had worked in traditionally male occupations. Basing their writing on interviews, the authors depict these women as having only limited functional ties with hotel staff and nearby business proprietors as the respondents "consistently claimed to neither be friends with or even know other women in their hotels" (p. 70).[1] (1976:91).

Yet a small number of studies of inner-city areas have contradicted assumptions that life for the elderly there is totally disorganized and atomistic. Marjorie Cantor's work, crosscutting residential and ethnic segments of New York's inner-city aged, empirically demonstrates the extent of neighbor- and kin-based networks: "Over 80 percent sit and talk together with neighbors either in front of the building or in parks or in open spaces. Almost two-thirds have a visiting relationship with neighbors" (1975:26). Many eat together. More than half of the respondents reported having "intimate" friends within the neighborhood. Cantor further found that contrary to previous investigations, the inner-city elderly maintained important kin ties: Two-thirds reported seeing their children monthly.

Other studies of center-city aged by Tissue in Sacramento (1971), by Bild and Havighurst (1976) in Chicago, and Ehrlich's (1976) St. Louis hotel research, while not indicating the high interaction rates found by Cantor, show that many elderly maintain at least a few close personal ties. Anthropologically oriented studies of hotels in San Diego (Eckert, 1980), New York's Upper West side (Siegel, 1977) and the Mid-town area (Cohen and Sokolovsky, 1980; Sokolovsky and Cohen, 1981b) provide cultural and empirical data disputing the claims of total isolation for the SRO aged. It is the contention here that many of the inconsistencies in the literature stem from failure to measure the totality of social interaction and a limited perspective on the cultural adaptation of the inner-city elderly.

NETWORKS AND METHODOLOGY

In anthropology over the last two decades beginning with studies by Barnes (1954) and Bott (1957) the concept of "social network" has been used to distinguish the concrete informal ties of friendship, kinship, and neighborliness from those subsumed by the formal frameworks of bounded institutionalized groups or categories. In particular the analytic study of egocentric social matrixes, referred to here as personal networks, has accompanied a shift in anthropological concern away from "formal structure" and ideal individuals to concern with active persons generating patterns by their own decisions in all contexts of interaction (Barnes, 1972; Blau, 1964; Boissevain, 1968, 1974; A. Mayer, 1966; E. Wolf, 1966).

The study of social networks has stimulated a new look at the connection between action, sentiment, and structure which flows from the premise of Boissevain (1974) and Whitten and Wolfe (1973) that informal interaction not be rendered an insignificant residue of structured groups. Rather it is the *starting* point from which anthropologists can elucidate patterned aspects of culture. In this sense social networks are "a model in which links are seen as relating persons in social situations" (Wolfe, 1970:229). From such a broad model we are in a better position to appreciate what Boissevain labels the "place of non-groups in the social sciences" (1968). Such a model harnesses attention to actual interaction and not just categories, norms, or representations and fosters, as Whitten and Wolfe suggest, the avoidance of a "disorganization model" of social systems where bounded, corporate groups are not apparent (1973:738). Thus, dyadic-contracts (Foster, 1961), cliques, quasi-groups (Boissevain, 1968), action-sets (A. Mayer, 1966), and other types of coalitions become crucial interactive components of social systems which must be given as much sociological credence as clans,

labor unions, or agrarian states.

Diagrammatically, a network is similar to a circuit of potential communication and transactional channels. But if, as some suggest (Mitchell, 1969), the interest in networks for anthropology is the morphological characteristics of network channels and their implications for social behavior, then the nature of transactions that flow in these channels must be established empirically. In doing this we can understand the practical aspect of a personal network as a cultural "support system" involving "the giving and receiving of objects, services, social, and emotional supports defined by the receiver and the giver as necessary or at least helpful in maintaining a style of life" (Lopata, 1975:35).

In comparing personal networks it is seen that the linkages between the central ego and those in his social world are structurally diverse. That is, they may be recruited from different institutional activity fields or role relationships. Thus, networks may be drived from kinship relations (real or fictive), work or recreational activities, residential location, and so on. Other factors such as age, sex, socioeconomic class, ethnicity, or residential location may be crucial variables regulating recruitment in any activity field. Additionally the link to a given network member may be single stranded (uniplex) involving a single transactional context (e.g., casual conversation) or multistranded (multiplex) involving more than one content (e.g., talking, visiting, personal assistance, emotional support, etc.) and perhaps multiple role involvement—cousin, employee, friend. Variation is also found in the interconnectedness of an ego's social relations, typically represented by a network density, the ratio of actual links to potential ones.[2] In this way networks are also qualitatively diverse and therefore varying in intensity, intimacy, and structural design. There is also an important but seldom made distinction between minimally multiplex links with just two types of content and those of greater intensity involving 3–4 types of transactions. The strategic variation of these qualitative types of links in a person's network within different activity spheres may be an important aspect of human adaptation.

However, elucidating the culturally important aspects of networks presents a most difficult research task for anthropologists and sociologists: how to methodologically delimit the behavioral and cognitive organization of networks. In this respect Craven and Wellman (1973) have noted two broad strategies of network research. The first of these is the "whole-network" strategy which depicts all linkages among all the units who are members of a particular interacting population. Such a strategy is most feasible in extremely small, clearly bounded populations for which a limited number of variables are investigated (see especially Killworth and Bernard, 1974).

The second approach more commonly applied to urban studies is the "personal-network" strategy. This method involves choosing a starting unit—an individual chosen from the population—and obtaining a list of all other units to which he is linked. The major strength of this technique is that it permits sampling from a large population and the potential analysis of many variables where it would prove unmanageable to study a whole network. Yet this approach when used by sociologists and anthropologists can yield quite different types of data.

Sociologists in this context may generate data via sociograms and with typically restrictive questionnaires (e.g., "name your four best friends") which measure only partial personal networks and/or fail to consider qualitative aspects of interaction. While able to generate large samples, such methods seriously compromise the distinction between real and ideal behavior (Killworth and Bernard, 1974, 1976).

Anthropological studies of networks can correct for these problems with an emphasis on holistic analysis, ethnographic description, and a concern for the derived cultural meaning of behavior.[3] However, traditional anthropological techniques often have posed problems especially in investigating the behavioral quality of networks for more than just a handful of individuals. In one study, Boissevain (1974) tried to assess the impact of entire networks on personality in rural versus urban Malta. By asking respondents to name and describe all persons they knew, he wound up with potential networks so large (1,751 and 638) that from this burdensome level of analysis he derived a sample of only two individuals. As Boissevain concedes, this does not provide a good basis for comparative research.

NETWORK ANALYSIS PROFILE

It seems that the real challenge for an anthropologist in such studies is to produce both empirically comparative data and qualitative behavioral information on total personal networks of meaningful samples. It should also strive to add a temporal dimension. In an effort to approach this goal in a study of elderly SRO residents we combined participant observeation, a biographically oriented interview schedule, and the "Network Analysis Profile." The "Network Analysis Profile" comprises six sectors of interaction: hotel, outside nonkin, kin, management, public agency or health care professional, and social institution. (The "hotel" segment of the Network Analysis Profile is shown in Figure 1 on page 193.)

It is important to note that the Network Analysis Profile was only developed after about four months field work during which we casually observed behavior and talked to people about the extent and meaning of their social interaction. We found that open-ended questions—i.e., "how many friends do you have" or "how often do you see relatives"—evoked responses which were more attuned to the interview situation or the respondent's personality than actual interaction. While many would habitually proclaim themselves "loners" and strongly deny knowing anyone, observation of behavior indicated that this was often not the case. There were also a smaller number who claimed to be "good friends" with virtually everyone in the immediate area even though contact with these "friends" scarcely scratched the surface of human contact. Such observations lead us to be skeptical about network data obtained by requesting simple enumeration of network characteristics (as in the study by Hertz and Hutheesing, 1975).

Additionally we observed that some important personal contacts especially outside of the hotel were activated sporadically, in many cases timed to the monthly cycle of checks from the government. In this context studiously logging a person's activities continually for even a week might still fall short of recording salient parts of the personal network. It soon became apparent that one must ethnographically establish informed knowledge of typical behavior to ask culturally

NAME Ms. A.

CODE NUMBER

FORM A: HOTEL CONTACTS

DIRECTIONAL
CODE: 1. EGO TO OTHER
       2. OTHER TO EGO
       3. RECIPROCAL
N.A.: NOT ASCERTAINED

INTER-CONNECTIONS Write: form letter/ person number	NAME 1.Male 2.Female Age ___	ROOM NO. or address	RACE 1.Wt. 2.Blk. 3.Hisp. 4.Other 9.N.A.	OCCUP STATUS 1.Work 2.S.S. 3.SSI 4.Welf. 5.Pension 9.N.A.	LENGTH OF LINK (years)	CONTEXT OF LINK 1.Work 2.Friend 3.Kin 4.Hotel 5.Senior center 6.Other 9.N.A.	LAST SAW 1.Yester./ Today 2.Past Wk. 3.Past Mo. 4.Past 6 Mo. 5.Past Yr. 6.Past 5 Yr. 7.Plus 5 Yr. 9.N.A.	VISUAL CONTACT FREQUENCY 1.Daily 2.Few/wk. 3.1x/wk. 4.1x/mo. 5.2x/yr. 6.1x/yr. 7.1x/5 yr. 8.Less	TELEP. FREQ. same code as prior box	TIME OF DAY OF CONTACT 1.Day 2.Night 3.Day or Night 9.N.A.	CHANGE: MONTHLY SEASONAL 0.None 1.Monthly 2.Seasonal 3.Yearly
A_1	Eva, 2 68	Rm. 705	2	3	6	4	1	1	0	3	2-gone 2 weeks in summer

continued Form A

CONTENT OF RELATIONSHIP

	VISITS ROOM Direction 1,2,3	MEET IN LOUNGE	INFORMAL CONVERS'N	ADVICE Direc. 1,2,3	MONEY/ LOANS 1,2,3	DRINKING/ DRUGS Direc. 1,2,3	FOOD AID Direc. 1,2,3	MEDICAL AID Direc. 1,2,3	OTHER AID Direc. 1,2,3	EAT OUT TOGETHER	OTHER SOCIAL OUTINGS (parks, movies)	GLOBAL IMPORTANCE 1.Not import. 2.Important 3.Very import. 4.Most import. 9.N.A.	FRIENDSHIP 1.Not a friend 2.A friend 3.A good friend 4.Best friend 9.N.A.	SHARE INTIMATE THOUGHTS WITH 1.Yes 2.No 9.N.A.
			Freq. 0.None 1.1x/Mo. 2.Less 9.N.A.	Freq. 0.None 1.1x/Mo. 2.Less 3.N.A.	Freq. 0.None 1.1x/Mo. 2.Less 9.N.A.	Freq. 0.None 1.1x/Mo. 2.Less 9.N.A.	Freq. 0.None 1.1x/Mo. 2.Less 9.N.A.	Freq. 0.None 1.1x/Mo. 2.Less 9.N.A.	Freq. 0.None 1.1x/Mo. 2.Less 9.N.A.	Freq. 0.None 1.1x/Mo. 2.Less 9.N.A.	Freq. 0.None 1.1x/Mo. 2.Less 9.N.A.	4-depend on when I "feel crazy"	4	1-"Don't hold anything back from each other"
Direc.	3	1		3	3	3	3	3	3					
Freq.	1	1	1	1	$2-5	drink beer	cook for each other	care for when sick	care for emotional aid	2	0			

Frequency
0.None
1.1x/Mo.
2.Less
9.N.A.

Figure I: Network Analysis Profile Completed for Hotel Sector

meaningful questions about personal networks. This was accomplished in certain cases by accompanying tenants for several days as they interacted with their particualr version of the urban environment. In this way one became aware of the places and contexts in which social behavior is likely to take place (see Sanjek, 1978:260 for a similar discussion).

In seeking to maximize the correspondence between respondent statements and observed behavior it was found that the most efficient way to elicit accurate responses about networks, which were also comparable between respondents, was first to structure questions around each sector of interaction (e.g., hotel resident). Then within this cognitive context questions focused concretely on: characteristics of each network member (age, sex), expected sites of contact (e.g., hotel room, local bar), specific modes of transaction (casual conversation, medical aid), and finally emotional characteristics (perception of friendship, intimacy). In charting a tenant's association with each contact, the content of the link is delineated as is the frequency, duration, intensity, and directional flow of the relationship. We are primarily concerned here with links active within the prior year, with a minimum frequency of once every month for hotel residents, once every three months for nonresidents, and at least once a year for kin. In a given ego's network the interaction with other network members was determined by questioning ego and available network members, and by field observations. To develop data on network flux an attempt was made to ascertain network contacts prior to entering the hotel environment and also to inquire about fluctuation on a daily, monthly, and seasonal basis.

The data do not yield the entirety of human interaction at the lowest possible level of abstraction (Harris, 1964); rather, in striving to begin at a level of behavior which is of cultural significance for an aging population this method delineates the total egocentric personal network. Like all usable methodology the Network Analysis Profile is a compromise which seeks to obtain an adequate sample size without reducing the derived data to empirical triviality. While it does not totally eliminate the disparity between ideal and actual behavior, the Profile, by concretely structuring questions to recurrent patterns of behavior, attempts to minimize this difference. Individuals can be compared in terms of the entire quantitative and qualitative range of relations, and the actual proportional significance of different parts of an aged person's social world can be established. Moreover one can also establish a basis for comparing the number and intensity of multiplex ties in a person's network.

THE ENVIRONMENTAL SETTING: MIDTOWN SRO HOTELS

The environmental context of our study is 10 of the 27 SRO hotels in a one-half mile square area in Midtown Manhattan. In the 27 hotels, there are some 4,000 persons with about 15–20 percent over 65 years of age. These elderly SRO dwellers come from a variety of socioeconomic and geographical backgrounds, yet 90 percent are white (Bellevue Geriatrics Unit, 1976). They are nearly all single, widowed, or divorced and depend on government subsidies for their economic survival.

The hotel populations include increasing percentages of the mentally disturbed, the physically deteriorated with chronic illness, and especially the alcoholic. One neighborhood center serving this elderly population reports that 31 percent of its clientele have a history of chronic alcoholism or mental illness, 15 percent are homebound, and half are in need of outreach services (Murray Hill SRO Project, 1976). In our own sample, 15 percent admitted to a previous psychiatric hospitalization although the real figure is probably somewhat higher.

Ranging in size from 6–12 stories, the SRO's house between 90-400 persons. They are generally found in commercial areas on narrow side streets, squeezed in between office buildings, coffee shops, bars, small grocery and retail stores. A few vest-pocket parks dot the neighborhood, providing the only free convenient public areas for relaxation outside the hotel. There is rarely any public area inside a building where people can congregate and socialize. Only two of the 10 hotels had a tiny lounge area where informal gatherings could take place.

Some of the buildings retain elaborate carved granite facades left over from when the hotels housed a wealthier clientele. Yet the interior amenities habitually create an institutionally drab, depressing environ with narrow corridors on each floor leading to 12 or 14 nervously guarded rooms. The majority of these rooms are little more than roach infested cubicles barely accommodating a bed, clothes chest, and perhaps an illegal hot plate.

As highlighted in the mass media, these edifices are frequently the scene of muggings, prostitution, robberies, murders, and suicides. This was dramatized on the first day of field work in the summer of 1977. While talking to a desk clerk in a small hotel, a loud thud was heard outside. It turned out that a 38-year-old man who had recently been released from the Bellevue psychiatric wards took the elevator to his 12th floor room in a hotel across the street and jumped. The jumper crashed through the side window of a car killing the driver but miraculously avoiding death himself. It had been the second suicide attempt of the year, from that hotel, the previous one having been successful. It is such an environment which creates one of the largest high-risk elderly populations in our nation's older cities. Nevertheless, as Siegel (1977) suggests, culturally, the SRO presents the SRO dwellers with alternatives to urban slums, skid row, working and middle-class life styles. It appears that, as an ecological niche, these hotels represent "halfway" environments mediating between open society and the total institution. Most aged realize that if they are not able to maintain themselves in the SRO, a nursing home or perhaps skid row are the only alternatives, a thought which strikes terror in their hearts. There are in fact few viable alternatives for the poor urban elderly, a fact which planners are just beginning to realize (U.S. Senate Special Committee on Aging, 1978).

THE SAMPLE

For this investigation, data were collected (see Table 1) on the total personal networks of 96 elderly SRO tenants (49 females, 47 males) ranging in age from 60–93; 90 percent were white, 9 percent black and 1 percent Hispanic. These people have been living in their hotels for an average of 10.7 years with a minimum of 10 months and a maximum of 40 years. The average figure belies the fact that many have been living alone in apartments, boarding houses, or other hotels for a good part of their adult life. Only four persons in the sample were currently married or living with someone and it is important to note that these conjugal arrangements all began with the onset of old age.

Life histories reveal a variety of reasons for coming to the SRO: For some it was a way of continuing a life style marked by extreme

TABLE 1
Selected Demographic Characteristics of a SRO Hotel Elderly Population (N = 96)

Demographic Characteristics		
Age	Mean	71.9
	Mode	60.0
	Range	60–93
Years living alone	Mean	24.9
	Mode	15.0
	Range	0–68
Sex	Male	49%
	Female	51%
Race	White	90%
	Black	9%
	Hispanic	1%
Education	Elementary or less	33%
	Some high school/ High school graduate	36%
	Some college/ College graduate	31%
Occupation	White Collar	23%
	Blue Collar	77%
Ever married	No	39%
	Yes	61%
Time in hotels	Mean	16.9
	Mode	15.0
	Range	0–50
Time in Current hotel	Mean	10.7
	Mode	4.0
	Range	0–40

attempts to maintain American values of independence and personal autonomy; others found it conveniently situated near the sites of their former occupations; and some were placed there by public agencies. A good indication of the independent nature of this population is the fact that almost 40 percent have never been married. In comparison only 4.7–6.5 percent of the equivalent aged American population (U. S. Bureau of the Census, 1977) have never been married. This low rate of marriage is similar to that reported for other SRO populations (Ehrlich, 1976) and a cross-section of inner-city elderly (Tissue, 1971). It is perhaps indicative of a selective process which determines the type of people who spend their elderly years in a SRO.

NETWORK CHARACTERISTICS

What do the data tell us about the interaction of the SRO elderly with their interpersonal environment? As seen in Table 2 few of the individuals fit the common expectation of total isolation, with only two persons lacking any discernable personal network. The majority of tenants maintained a social matrix with total networks varying from 0–26 network members, having a mean of 7.5, and with three-quarters of the respondents having four or more persons in their personal support system. Males averaged only one person more than females in the size of their total personal networks, although this difference was statistically insignificant. Yet, these figures appear small in contrast to the very limited data showing a mean network size of 20–30 persons for a "normal" urban population (Pattison et al., 1975). The closest comparable study (Erickson and Eckert, 1977) indicates an average of 14 "acquaintances" for aged hotel dwellers. Unfortunately there is no mention of how this number was obtained.

While the average personal support system of our New York sample was rather small, significantly, 60 percent of these links involved multistrand relations and more than a third were complex links having three or more types of transactions. In terms of the cognitive and emotional importance of these ties only 23

TABLE 2
Total Network Characteristics of a SRO Hotel Elderly Population (N = 96)

All Spheres of Activity	Mean	Range	Percent None
Total contacts	7.5	0–26	2
Total multistran contacts	4.5	0–18	6
Total contacts involving three or more transactions	2.6	0–16	24
Total contacts rated "very important"	2.4	0–8	23
Total contacts considered "intimate"	.9	0–3	41.0

percent did not consider any of their contacts "very important" to them, but a considerably higher amount, 41 percent, possessed social matrixes devoid of persons described as intimate.

Perhaps the most surprising aspect of the data had to do with comparative interaction in the three personal activity fields we deciphered here: hotel resident, outside nonkin, kin. Contrary to the assertions of Shapiro (1971) and Stephens (1976), these hotels were not "closed urban villages." In fact, for a majority of the persons examined (see Table 3) at least one-half of their total network linked them to a social world outside the hotel walls, with 70 percent of all complex relations located there and one-fifth of the networks being exclusively focused outside of the hotel. While one-fourth of the SRO residents lacked any personal contact in their own hotels, only 6 percent shut themselves off from the outside world. An indication of the emotionally centrifugal nature of these networks was that while a relatively equivalent number of complex transactions occurred in the three interaction spheres, twice as many networks in both the outside nonkin and kin spheres contained at least one member deemed very important.

Despite an exaggerated lack of concern often expressed toward their kin network, family ties of these urban aged were not totally severed. For a

TABLE 3
Network Cqracteristics by Activity Sphere of a SRO Hotel Elderly Population (N = 96)

Sphere of Interaction	Network Characteristic	Mean	Range	Percent None
Hotel	Total contacts	2.7	0–15	26
	Total contacts three or more transactions	.8	0–6	57
	Total contacts rated "very important"	.4	0–5	76
Outside hotel: nonkin and kin combined	Total contacts	4.8	0–23	6
	Total contacts three or more transactions	1.8	0–16	—
	Total contacts jted "very important"	2.0	0–12	—
Outside nonkin	Total contacts	2.7	0–17	24
	Total contacts three or more transactions	1.1	0–16	61
	Total contacts rated "very important"	.8	0–4	51
Outside kin	Total contacts	2.1	0–12	29
	Total contacts three or more transactions	.7	0–10	66
	Total contacts rated "very important"	1.2	0–10	48

majority 10–20 percent of their total networks were composed of relatives. Almost 72 percent had interacted in some form with a kinsperson in the past year, yet it must be realized that for many this may amount to a single Christmas card, a few phone calls, or a half-hour visit. Indeed, the lowest frequency of contact and levels of material support are with kin. Only 17 percent of our sample had communicated with relatives on a weekly basis. This figure is in sharp contrast to data from a national survey on the elderly reporting that 82 percent claimed to have contact once a week with kin (Shanas et al., 1968). Nonetheless a majority of kin networks include

one relative rated as "very important" with the mean number of these important ties exceeding the figure for other spheres of interaction.

THE CULTURAL MEANING OF SRO NETWORKS

These data can give us just a glimpse of the cultural meaning of personal networks for this segment of the urban elderly. In this respect the more important question to ask is how do the total network configurations link these SRO dwellers to their urban environment? They have accomplished this by the generation of several interrelated network characteristics which I will refer to as (1) structural dispersion, (2) highly selective intimacy, and (3) variable activation of ties.

STRUCTURAL DISPERSION

I mean by structural dispersion that network contacts tend to be dispersed as widely as possible within the social world of the SRO tenant. This means that persons, especially males, will attempt to avoid getting deeply involved in a single close-knit clustering of friends. Such networks, which we have referred to elsewhere as "diffuse-cluster" configurations (Sokolovsky and Cohen, 1981b), show low levels of interconnect-edness, with density figures rarely exceeding 15 percent. These matrixes typically contain widely dispersed dyadic ties and occasionally small interconnected clusters (usually 2–4 persons) that are highly segregated from each other. Conforming to the often stated effects of urbanism on network morphology, when relations exist in all fields of interaction those in each sphere are handled separately. Thus a person's hotel contacts seldom know much about one's relatives and/or outside acquaintances.

The ideal effect of such a structure is to establish a flexible system of support which diminishes dependence on formal city institutions at the same time that it avoids enmeshing a person in a tight-knit set of personal ties. An example is the total active network of 64-year-old John P., an ex-truck driver who retired ten years ago when his leg was amputated after an accident. With the use of an artificial limb, he walks around the hotel neighborhood each day within a two-block radius. Within the hotel he has three personal contacts whom he sees almost every morning sharing conversation in front of the hotel. With one of these persons he reciprocally exchanges cigarettes while the other grocery-shops for him in exchange for "loans" of 50 to 95 cents. John does not feel close to any of these

people. Outside the hotel his nonkin ties involve two men he meets several times a week at a local bar. They spend a good part of the afternoon talking and drinking together, nursing a small number of beers but seldom delving into the intimate parts of each other's lives. Especially toward the end of the month when his funds are low, John will borrow one or two dollars from one of these men whom he has know for five years.

However, John's closest ties are with his four sisters who live in various parts of Queens, a 30–40-minute subway ride away. He manages to talk to at least one of the sisters every month most typically communicating over the telephone. Despite John's low income ($270 per month) which leaves him with about $5 per day after rent is paid, he has avoided plying his siblings for loans. He is able to visit in his elder sister's apartment occasionally (once every few months) where they talk, play cards, and eat. He rates all these persons as "very important" although he only confides in the oldest who was the only one to consistently visit him when he was in the hospital. A majority of networks generated by both males and females had this type of "diffuse-cluster" configuration. Yet, especially among women in poor health, another pattern appeared. This involved a small (3 to 5 persons), very interconnected, and multistranded set of personal relationships primarily linking hotel residents. These "cluster" networks may simply involve getting together at a regular time in a public place outside the hotel to eat, socialize, or play cards. However, especially for some elderly with chronic health problems and limited mobility, cluster configurations can provide the primary means of survival in the hotel.

Such was the case of Ms. A., a 66-year-old black woman, who due to a bad back retired from working as a housekeeper at the age of 60. Ms. A. finds it difficult to walk, spending most of the day in her small but neatly kept room. Once a day she goes to the hotel lobby for a short time but returns to her room where she waits for the daily visits from her three elderly friends or less frequently goes to visit in their rooms. The exchanges involved are quite varied and include visiting, food preparation and food borrowing, money loans, shopping, providing care during illness, and in the case of one of Ms. A's friends, the sharing of personal thoughts. Her three hotel friends do not stay long together in Ms. A.'s room but rather float in and out during the day, gossiping, sharing meals cooked on a hot plate, or drinking some beer. The section of Ms. A.'s Network Profile delineating the relationship to her best friend is shown in Figure 1.

HIGHLY SELECTIVE INTIMACY

The transactions involved in such networks run the gamut of human relations including casual conversation; emotional support; visiting; provision of food, drink, money, and medicine; watching television together or going out for meals or a walk in a park; or help in dealing with a city agency. Yet such exchanges do not automatically determine emotional relatedness or intimacy. Indeed a large number of dyadic ties are clearly utilitarian involving only one or two aspects of aid relations with hardly any intimate conversation or extension to nonessential realms of behavior. Such ties often develop among the roombound elderly with younger residents (25–45) who pick up food, medicine, or other essentials for a small set fee. In several of the hotels there are men in their fifties who, although they had been forced into retirement by medical problems, are relatively healthy and active and often helped or offered aid to the more frail elderly. These aid transactions are often more altruistic than those with much younger men, with such behavior indicating the care givers' cultural importance and generating a positive conception of self-worth from such helping behavior. Each hotel appears to have at least one willing aid giver who seems to be extremely competent in dealing with city institutions such as hospitals and the welfare or social security agencies. An elderly woman of 76, for the last 30 years, has been writing vehement and quite effective letters to virtually every city agency on behalf of tenants young and old whom she has befriended.

However, guiding the perception of the personal world SRO dwellers see around themselves is a good deal of fear and suspicion. They have little control over who will be residing on the other side of their drab wall and often lack a basis for mutuality in social relationships. The vast majority of the limited intimate ties found in their personal networks stem from a long-term association generated through occupational or kinship ties begun in earlier parts of the life cycle. In the SRO's a basis of common values and behavioral expectations is highly limited and leads to frequent misinterpretation of actions. As an example, in one hotel I had become friendly with two men, one 83 (Mike) and the other 56 (Al) who manifested a strong distrust of each other verging on hatred. The elder man prided himself on his independence while the other stressed his own willingness to help the more unfortunate in the hotel. The source of distrust stemmed from a recent incident where Mike, a diabetic, fainted while walking near the hotel. Al who was the only one around came over to help and began to take off Mike's coat. Mike woke up convinced he was a mugging victim and thinking Al was the perpetrator making off with the wallet in Mike's coat pocket. Despite Al's explanation of the event Mike has spread the word of Al's alleged thievery through the hotel causing the state of antagonism between the two men.

In essence, despite the close proximity of potential friends in the hotels, intimate social ties center on a few of the safest contacts which evoke a minimum of dependency. This is highlighted by an active denial of any important ties and an ethos of noninterference in other's lives. As one man put it, "I don't have any friends, don't have any time. I travelled all over the world and never cared for anyone else's business, just took care of my own. I go my way and you go yours, that's my thinkin'." It's important to note that despite this proclamation I often observed him spending a good part of his afternoon shopping for sick tenants and delivering food to their rooms, in most cases refusing compensation.

VARIBLE ACTIVATION OF TIES

One of the reasons the networks described may appear insignificant is that static quantitative measures of interaction would show these SRO elderly to be comparatively isolated. For example, employing a social contact score developed by Peter Townsend (1957) these New York elderly show an average of only 28 contacts per week. This is three times less than Townsend's English sample of elderly. In fact almost three-fourths of our sample would be considered "rather isolated" by their social contact score. Yet such a scale tells us little about the meaning and use of social relationships to people. As Jacobson (1973, 1975) argues, a low frequency of interaction need not prohibit the existence of enduring important relations but mandates that they be intermittently activated by residentially mobile urban dwellers. Although the SRO elderly are not themselves very residentially mobile, they are adapting to an urban area in which such mobility is extremely high especially among those social segments which mean the most to them: their older friends and kin. Thus, we see these people variably activating parts of their network in response to independence striving in an environment over which they have little control.

As one might expect social relationships are most frequently activated in the hotels. Over 70 percent of the sample had some weekly contacts, while the figures for outside acquaintances and kin are 44 percent and 20 percent respectively. If nonhotel ties are considered important, there will be an effort made to maintain contact at least once a year, even though face-to-face contact had not occurred in the previous ten years. This is a significant point as the outside nonkin personnel have remained part of an individual's network for an average of 19 years.

A number of respondents discussed persons with whom they had no contact in the last several years but whom they still considered a crucial part of their potential support network. However, when people focus their hopes on such potential, distantly maintained network ties they may be in grave difficulty in crisis situations. Such was the case with a poor 78-year-old woman. She bragged to me about her aloofness from her three hotel contacts and the help she expected to get from her two nearby cousins whom she had not seen in 15 years despite their sporadic attempts to involve her in family affairs. She had recently been mugged and needed several hundred dollars to buy food and pay the rent, and attempts to

borrow money from the cousins were sternly rejected.

Another important aspect of variable activation of ties is seen in a diurnal cycle. This day/night change in network functioning is related to living in a blighted urban niche. Cohen (1976), in studying the unattached elderly living in Midtown tenements, observed that while these persons had extensive personal networks during the day, there were virtually no contacts in the evening. Withdrawal of the personal support system appeared to be largely responsible for a marked exacerbation of neurotic symptoms in the nighttime. Cohen termed this phenomenon, "Nocturnal Neurosis of the Elderly." Similar to apartment dwellers, over three-fourths of our sample population had no linkages outside the hotel after dark. However, our data on the SRO aged point to a less severe diurnal pattern with two-thirds of all male and female residents having social contacts in the hotel both during the day and the evening.

CONCLUSIONS: LONERS VERSUS THE ALONE

The total impact of the above network characteristics is such that researchers and community workers often confuse the "single occupancy" situation of residing alone and the often repeated self-description of these elderly as "loners" with proof that they are socially isolated. In contrast we found that many self-proclaimed loners frequently had *larger* than average networks. They were also the most reluctant to acknowledge the significance of these ties. By proclaiming themselves loners the SRO aged do not so much define behavioral reality as they proclaim a world view which has been adaptive in their difficult urban environment. In effect their ideal self-image, which emphasizes self-sufficiency and independence, stimulates the organization of personal networks designed to limit the penetration of societal institutions into their lives. Specifically, network qualities of dispersion, selective intimacy, and variable activation enable these elderly to create support systems which

200

maintain a modicum of physical and emotional contact while making control of their lives by social forces difficult. Yet, this is done at a potentially great cost. Dependence on a relatively small network with only a few bonds providing significant support leaves an individual extremely vulnerable when a sudden crisis strikes.

From a certain perspective which measures cultural meaning by group-oriented activity the SRO elderly would indeed be isolated. However, empirically examining interaction shows: (1) Despite relatively low levels of social interaction, few are devoid of personal networks and many maintain some complex interpersonal relations. (2) Contrary to the common assumption of a complete cutoff with their cultural past, the greater part of most networks *outside* the hotel include persons known almost two decades but are only intermittently activated within a yearly cycle. (3) In contrast to the findings of other SRO studies, elderly women in our sample were found to be as capable as men in building systems of personal support.

Living in a small well-defined urban locality these hotel dwellers have dismissed open easy sociability with their closest neighbors. Yet as Suttles (1968:6) notes in his study of a Chicago slum: "On the basis of stochastic processes alone, one might expect that a distinct locality might become a common area within which people arrive at a fairly standard code for deciphering and evaluating one another's behavior." In the SRO the achievement of this common meaning is accomplished through the cultural stance of a loner in an environment perceived as threatening. As one man put it when asked if he anticipated getting involved with more than the four persons in his limited social world, "Don't want to know nobody else, so far no one's got anything against me."

NOTES

1. Lopata goes even further and suggests that the Chicago inner-city aged even "lack the ability to voluntarily engage in supportive relations" (1975:35).

2. Density can be calculated by the formula

$$\text{Density} = Na \Big/ \frac{N(N-1)}{2},$$

where Na is the actual number of relations linking people in ego's network (excluding ego) and N is the number of persons in that network.

3. For a full discussion of the problems with network analysis in the context of gerontological research, see Sokolovsky, 1980; Sokolovsky and Cohen, 1981a.

Jennie Keith

AGE AND INFORMAL INTERACTION

Contrasting popular images of retirement housing have included that of an "old fogey farm" and that of a "gilded ghetto" for the very rich. These notions are being shattered by the research of anthropologists and sociologists in such environments. Viewing "old people as people," Jennie Keith compares her work among retired French workers with the existing literature on age-homogeneous residences to uncover common factors that stimulate social interaction and the emergence of a feeling of community. As a consequence of the high density of age peers and the "liminal," ill-defined status of old age in industrial society, these environments are shown to provide a distinct arena in which new roles and social groupings can be created by the elderly themselves.

OLD PEOPLE'S SOCIAL CONTACTS with each other provide a *behavioral* map of age categorization. This behavioral and informal significance of age-mates may be quite distinct from formally organized groups, or from normative rules about what roles age-mates ought to or are desired to play. The clearest fact about the significance of age in the informal social lives of old people anywhere is that we know next to nothing about it. As in many other areas of inquiry, the formal and the normative have received more attention—they're easier to find—than the informal. What is known about informal ties is mainly quantitative, although we have little understanding of what we are counting. Yet creation and maintenance of roles for the elderly in industrial society must initially be rooted in the informal sphere (see Rosow, 1976:479), and much policy discussion concerns reinforcement of "natural support networks." The best information we have is about residents of special settings such as retirement communities—again, they're easier to find. The benefits to these people of peer ties . . . are so clear, however, and the trade-off costs so low, that what we do know about them is a strong stimulus to learning more about the role of age-mates in the lives of old people in more ordinary circumstances. In this article we will retrace the steps of the anthropologists who have investigated peer ties among old people, beginning with community studies of special settings, and then moving out into the wider world to hypothesize about the conditions and consequences of age ties for old people in general.

COMMUNITY STUDIES

The earliest firsthand research by anthropologists on old age was done in age-homogeneous communities (see Ross, 1977; Fry, 1979; Byrne, 1974; Hendel-Sebestyen, 1979). The broadest question behind these studies is whether age could provide a foundation for community; the consistent answer is yes. In mobile-home parks, highrise public housing, luxury condominiums, union and church sponsored residences, in the United States, France, and England, these ethnographers found both the emotional and the structural aspects of community. The old people studied feel they are part of a collectivity, that their destinies are woven together with those of other residents; and the routines of their daily lives trace the regular patterns of interaction that define social organization. Most of these patterns develop and exist outside of, or even in opposition to, more formal organization imposed by community managers or administrators (see

From *Old People as People: Social and Cultural Influences on Aging and Old Age* by Jennie Keith. Copyright © 1982 by Little, Brown and Company, Inc. Reprinted by permission.

Keith, 1980a, for a review of community creation in age-homogeneous settings).

The superficial characteristics of the various settings in which old people have formed communities are, at least to an anthropologist's eye, delightfully diverse. In the French residence, wine bottles appear on tables, food is a major focus of recreation, and factions line up along political cleavages. In Florida, old black men go fishing in a pond while Cuban women exchange gossip across balcony railings; in California, working class women quilt, crochet, and align themselves by Baptist church affiliations, while in a middle-class condominium, couples play bridge, golf, and gather in cocktail party cliques. However, the most important aspect of cultural diversity in these peer communities may be its superficiality.

Below the surface differences in style, and even language, are significant similarities. First of all, social organization exists, and [the] level of social activity is high. The fact that older people among themselves create full, patterned, active social lives deserves mention only because of the view taken by many younger people that complete lives for the old must be centered on *us*. These social lives are functional as well as fun. The extensive aid available from peers allows many older residents to be secure without giving up independence: Acceptance of help from a peer does not connote dependence in the way that support from a child or an institution might. The giver of help also acquires a precious superiority in what one observer has labelled the "hierarchy of poor dears" (Hochschild, 1973).

Second, the social organizations created in old-age communities are distinctive from the outside worlds in which they are embedded. . . . Responses to death and to sex are distilled into normative patterns markedly different in some ways from those outside. As morale is higher in age-homogeneous contexts even for members without high social participation, the existence of such shared norms seems to be the key feature linking age-homogeneity to morale. In addition, the emphasis on equality sharply differentiates the status ranking systems inside old people's communities from those outside them. As among the warriors of East African age-graded societies, ranking in terms of skills or activities exercised in the present, and particularly identified with the

group, is more acceptable than ranking based in the past, or on external scales: Being a good shot is an appropriate basis of status among warriors; being a good shuffleboard player, or an elected official inside the community is an appropriate basis of status in a retirement community. The significance of age itself is an excellent indicator of this distinctiveness in ranking. Age is typically irrelevant to rank inside an age-homogeneous community—although that perceived homogeneity may include a 30-year span of chronological age (Ross, 1977:66–84).

Other basic characteristics also take on different meaning inside old-age communities. Sex roles are often less distinct, and in some cases, although men and women participate in the communities differently, those differences are indicated in new ways. Ethnicity is a less imposing social border inside several multiracial United States age communities than in the society outside (Kandel and Heider, 1979; Wellin and Boyer, 1979). In the French residence where I lived (Les Floralies), politics was imported from the outside as the most significant social identity, but put to distinctive use inside, as Catholic holidays became Communist celebrations, and each leisure activity acquired a factional identity. Ethnically homogeneous communities display a similar "recycling" of cultural raw materials. Jewish old people in a Venice, California, Senior Citizens Center remain very Jewish, but in adaptation to the demands and restrictions of a new situation, rituals and symbols are created and modified out of the basic raw materials of Eastern European Jewish culture [see Section IV]. One old man celebrated his own birth-death day by finishing his speech, with the help of an oxygen mask, before the "angel of death" arrived. The man's will included a bequest to the Center to make possible a new ritual—celebration of his birthday for five more years, until he would have been 100. The Sabbath at the Center begins well before sundown, so that the old people can come and go safely in the dangerous neighborhood (Myerhoff, 1978). The expression and use of Jewishness at the Aliyah Center is as different from that outside it as the significance of Communism at Les Floralies is different from that in Paris at large.

Another reprise of the "old people are people" theme is the importance of conflict in these communities. Fighting is an activity we seldom associate with the old. Most people who worried about the boredom and depression I would surely face as a young member of an old-age community shared an image of old people as peaceable to the point of stagnation. As in any other community ever observed, communities of old people are scenes of battle as well as of cohesiveness. Whether factional allegiances are to Baptist churches or to political orientations, they are present, and can erupt into intense conflict. I was almost thrown out of Les Floralies for my alleged part in a complex election fight involving secret slates, clandestine meetings, accusations of corruption, attempts to influence senile voters, and ultimate insults impugning candidates' characters on the basis of their activities during the World War II Resistance. Difficult as such factional machination may make life for administrators, it is a sign of life from the old people who care enough for their community to fight about it.

Why so much conflict in old-age communities? Not because they are old people, but because they are new communities. In communities formed unintentionally, that is without a shared goal or ideology to define and launch them, conflict is likely to develop over what the definition of the emerging community should be. The likelihood of conflict increases with the lack of alternative options open to its members, and their consequent commitment to the one at hand. Like it or not, residents of many old-age communities perceive few alternatives, and assume that they will live out their lives there.

The essential finding about communities of old people is that they exist. This raises two questions: Why? and So what? To discover why, the first step is to compare cases and discover what they have in common. Here the answer is clear: They all have at least 50 percent old people. The variation in every other aspect of their settings, cultures, and formal organization puts great emphasis on their age-homogeneity as the key factor. What these communities seem to teach us is that when old people have access to their peers, they "take advantage of them" to create norms and behavior patterns that increase their well-being. That is, of course, the answer to "so what?" The people in old-age communities, compared to those in mixed-age settings, appear to have higher morale, greater opportunity for

social participation, and greater access to tangible support when they need it. Interpretation of the studies that show these results is, however, difficult (cf. Carp, 1976). They may compare people who moved into subsidized housing with those who did not, and better housing may have a lot to do with their good feelings about themselves and their lives. Those who move into resort areas may be divided into those who enter age-homogeneous communities and those who do not: Those in the retirement communities have higher morale, but the entire category of those who move across state lines is a statistical minority. Residents of HUD-subsidized housing may be compared in terms of whether they live in age-mixed or elderly projects; however, other differences among residents in age-mixed housing, such as class and/or ethnicity, may confound the results.

Where should the community studies lead us, then? Back out into the surrounding society. The levels of community, and their benefits, are striking enough to spur investigation to unravel the inconclusive evidence. To do this, the focus must be on age bonds themselves, viewed as distinctly as possible from type of housing, moving, and social attributes other than age. Will older people *outside* special settings use age-mates when they are available to create norms and social networks? If they do, will the material and emotional benefits observed in the old-age communities result?

AGE BONDS OUTSIDE OF COMMUNITIES

Direct evidence for the most straightforward source of age ties does exist outside of special communities. The availability of peers in the immediate residential area does stimulate actual contact with those peers. When "density" of age-mates in apartment buildings reaches 50 percent or more, for instance, the number of local friends increases (Rosow, 1967). The 50 percent "tipping point" is the same as in some of the formal communities, such as IdleHaven, where older people are only about half the population (S. K. Johnson, 1971). Even outside the residential concentration of apartment buildings, the proportion of older people in a neighborhood affects the likelihood that older people's friends will also be old (Rosenberg, 1970).

In case the availability-actuality relationship of old neighbors to old friends seems obvious, it must be remembered that proximity does *not* promote social closeness *across* age lines. Older people in more than one age-integrated setting have trekked across courtyards or upstairs to seek out other old people, rather than visiting the young neighbors placed next door by the social engineers (Rosenmayr and Köckeis, 1962; Alger, 1959). Old people, by choosing other old people as friends are, of course, acting just like young people.

In friendship choices, as in every other way, old people are diverse. Although general patterns of age homophily, facilitated by proximity, exist, there are individual attributes that increase "sensitivity" to age density. In Rosow's study of Cleveland apartment buildings, for instance, women, people over 75, and those who had experienced more extensive role losses, were more influenced in their friendship choices by availability of other old people; and age density had a stronger effect on members of the working class than on those in the middle class (Rosow, 1967).

The consequences of these age ties are apparently as beneficial outside as inside residential communities. Age density in the Cleveland apartments was positively related both to the use of neighbors as role models—increasing potential for definition of age norms—and to decreased anxiety about illness because neighbors became an important source of support. Similar findings appear in Philadelphia, where older people with active friendship networks have less need for support services, regardless of their actual physical health (Moss et al., 1976).

Knowing that age ties do exist when peers are available, that there is individual variation in response to that availability, and that peer ties have obvious benefits, the stage is set for a more thorough investigation of the conditions under which peers become important in older people's social networks, and the consequences of such informal age boundaries for the quality of their lives. Two sources of guidance are available for these explorations: general social theories about affiliation, which have not yet been thoroughly

applied to age; and cross-cultural data about age differentiation, which have not yet been "brought home" for integration into gerontological research.

CONDITIONS OF INFORMAL AGE BONDS

Homophily

The general principle of homophily [like attracts like] is intensified under two kinds of stress, one produced by lack of social definition, the other by what might be called overdefinition. Ambiguity is a painful aspect of new roles, which some individuals must define for themselves because their society has outlined a form but not yet filled in any content. Conflicting expectations of various role partners may also create ambiguities about priorities of response. Or the transition from one social role to another may strand individuals in a temporarily ambiguous status "betwixt and between." Older people are likely to experience all of these ambiguities, and with fewer of the social supports provided at earlier life stages. Since order and definition are a basic aspect of any human way of life, it is no exaggeration to call social ambiguity an inhuman stress. Others who have suffered in similar circumstances have found, logically enough, that the best assistance came from fellow sufferers. Since reduction of social ambiguity requires collective resolution, the most likely collectivity to turn to is composed of those with both the understanding and the motivation required.

New Roles

Divorced single parent is an example of a new role in American society, the lack of a positive definition for which has promoted bonds of friendship and mutual support distilled in some cases into formal organizations, such as Parents Without Partners. In the casual context of picnics or parties these role pioneers are also about the serious business of filling in norms of appropriate behavior for this newly numerous category. The school superintendent is a classic victim of role conflict, bombarded with irreconcilable expectations from various sets of role partners including teachers, parents, students, and fellow superintendents. Occupants of this strained role tend to socialize intensively among themselves (Gross et al., 1957). This peer contact offers blessed relief from conflicting demands, but in addition provides an opportunity for mutual development of strategies for managing the role's built-in ambiguities.

One of the first official social science labels applied to old age was "roleless role" (Burgess, 1950). Since it is new in the history of the human species to have an extended stage of life between work and death, the people Neugarten calls the "young-old" face a roleless role with a vengeance. Like school superintendents or divorcees, old people are people, but in this case, pioneering people in a profound sense. If new roles, with their ambiguity of norms and expectations, promote ties to peers, then older people should be even more likely to develop peer ties than others faced with undefined roles in a shallower sense. Given the stigma of old age in some modern societies, however, the comfort of peers may not be worth the price of public association with them. Old age is not really without definition, since it does have a negative valence. Ironically, what unhelpful social definition of age that does exist may be an impressive obstacle to peer creation of definitions positive and specific enough to provide guidance for a new life-stage.

The research required to discover the relationship between stigma and peer ties may be difficult to do because of the stigma itself. Even those peer ties that do exist may not be accurately reported. An older person who suspects the questioner of negative views toward the aged, or who shares many of those views, may minimize how many and how important are his or her ties to other old people. The tremendous emotional significance of family bonds leads to their being emphasized when people report about their social lives. That qualitative significance is, of course, crucial information, but it should not obscure the actual contact and support shared with peers. The only way to be sure of getting both kinds of data is to put in the hours of observation rather than relying only on reports (Keith, 1980c).

An excellent example of the rewards in accuracy and insight that may come from combining extended observation with interview report is anthropological research in single room occupancy hotels. The residents of these hotels are characterized by ferocious independence; their view of themselves as loners is probably their most precious possession. Asked direct questions about friendship ties or social support, they typically deny any. The only ties they do acknowledge are those with family. Anthropologists who have lived and worked in SROs, however, have learned that it is peer networks that make possible maintenance of the prized loner image [see the article by Sokolovsky and Cohen in this section]. Once they knew about the existence of these networks, the researchers could interview residents with specific questions about personnel, location, and function of specific network links. "You can't be a loner on your own" is an appropriate summary of these studies. Detailed "network profiles" reveal frequent and diverse social supports—hours of informal visiting, loans, shared food, help in emergencies, emotional unburdening, shared advice. This research has two kinds of significance: It adds more data to demonstrate the tendency toward peer grouping among the old; and it waves a warning flag against any attempt to study social networks without extensive observation of actual behavior (Cohen and Sokolovsky, 1980; Sokolovsky and Cohen, 1981b).

We have learned as much as we know about residents of old-age communities by moving in on them. To have the same extensive and qualitative understanding of the informal social lives of the majority of old people who do not live in these special settings, we need to come as close to moving in as possible. "Ethnographies of age" must also be done in the natural communities where most old people live, the footwork put in to follow out their social networks, and the listening hours accumulated to hear their perceptions and evaluations of life in old age.

Liminality
Liminality derives from the Latin word for threshold: It refers to a phase of transition from one social state to another. Couples on their honeymoon, recruits entering boot camp, pilgrims en route from profane to sacred space, initiates suspended between nonmembership and belonging are all in liminal states. Liminality is not only

between more structured states of existence, it is also an antithesis of normal structure. Most normal roles are "neutralized" in liminal periods. If hair styles represent social position, then initiands' heads are shaved. If speech usually indicates status relations, then verbal control is abolished and obscenity prevails. Special secret argots are often acquired and used during liminal experiences (see Legesse, 1973:115).

Individuals in liminal states are often perceived as temporarily not quite human—either more than human, i.e., sacred, or less than human, i.e., animalistic or not yet cultured enough to be fully human. As representative of the antithesis of what is fully ordered human social life in a particular setting, liminal individuals and experiences clarify by contrast the appropriate structures of ordinary life. This contrast is itself a structured opposition, and liminality is not without its own rules. If heads are to be shaved in antithesis to status marking hairstyles, then initiands do not have the choice of shaving or not shaving. If everyone at a personal growth seminar is supposed to strip in liberation from status-marking dress, then no one is free to keep clothes on.

Rituals of passage such as marriages or initiations provide roadmaps across the cultural no-man's land of liminality. The rite of passage itself is subdivided into a metaphor of the transition it both guides and represents. Each ritual is composed of three stages—separation, marginality, and reincorporation. The marginal, or liminal, stage is a fallow field for communality and creativity, as it offers temporary respite from status differentiation and normative structures (Turner, 1969). Learning with and from peers is a central aspect of many of these rituals. One particular characteristic of roles recruited by age is that they must be relearned repeatedly (Legesse, 1979). Unlike other social identities, age-roles by definition cannot be learned once and for all, as each age-linked stage requires resocialization.

Individuals who share experiences of the liminal often share feelings of *communitas*, unstructured, spontaneous, communal feeling. One of the poignant aspects of liminal experience is the difficulty of carrying these intense and diffuse feelings back out into the everyday world. The logical and empirical link between liminality and age peers is that the "social clocks" of many

cultures move age-mates through liminal stages together, so the egalitarian potentialities of age are accentuated in the combination of celebration and ordeal typical of most rites of passage. Liminality both evokes and is eased by solidarity with others in the same circumstances, and age-mates often experience liminal stages together.

Old people in industrial societies are, however, stranded in the liminal. Exit signs are clearly marked, but reincorporation is not on the map. Their choice is between cultural bushwhacking and clinging to the crumbling cliff of midlife roles. If liminality offers an opportunity for creativity, then older people in modern societies face opportunity on a fearful scale. As at other ages and in other cultures, creativity is most likely in the company of peers. Entire life-stages are defined as liminal in some other cultures; among the Boran of Kenya, the first and the last generation grades are liminal (Legesse, 1973:115). However, both the boundaries and the content of these temporarily marginal and sacred statuses are clearly specified and transient antistructure, rather than the permanent nonstructure surrounding the old in modern contexts.

Residents of old-age communities invent rites of passage and create the norms and roles that offer an end stage for the ritual to move toward. The move into an age-homogeneous community is itself a rite of passage; and, in addition, the specific patterns of socialization into many old-age communities follow the three-stage formula. At Les Floralies, for example, finding a permanent seat in the dining room was both the means and the metaphor for social incorporation (Ross, 1977, ch. 6). The broader question is whether liminality is a stimulus to peer bonding and mutual socialization outside separate residential settings. Strong hints in the yes direction come from the evidence that role loss makes individuals more "sensitive" to age density (Rosow, 1967). Widowhood in the United States is a poignant example of role exit into liminality without clear routes to reentry. The presence of other widows in the neighborhood does ease adjustment, through actual support as well as through reference groups which assist in the definition of new roles (see Z. S. Blau, 1961).

Asked in a symposium on *The Elderly of the Future* to make predictions from my perspective as an anthropologist, my first answer was that I foresaw a great deal of work for cross-cultural researchers. No topic is a better example than liminality of the amount of future work required to understand the social significance of age. If informal aspects of old-age sociability are little studied, then its liminal aspects—the antithesis of formal social organization—are, not surprisingly, understood least of all. Thorough understanding of liminality as a possible stimulus to informal peer ties will require several kinds of comparison. On a societal level, cultures in which older people categorically are and are not placed in liminal phases can be compared. Comparison must also focus—both within and among cultures—on variation in the collectivity of liminal experiences associated with age. In addition, individuals should be compared in terms of their perceived experiences of liminality to determine whether they define certain points in their lives as transitional, and whether they see those phases as associated with age, as idiosyncratic or shared with others, and whether those others are primarily identified as age-mates. All of the information about age-linked transitions must then be connected to fully charted networks of social interaction.

Stereotypes and Stigma

Social contact among people with some characteristics in common may also be stimulated by the opposite of ambiguity; certain kinds of external overdefinition may also push people together. Stereotyping and stigma by outsiders may make other victims of these negative overgeneralizations a blessed refuge. The double jeopardy here is that associating with other old people may reinforce some of the stereotypes, and perpetuate some of the stigma, from which peer ties offer temporary relief (Goffman, 1963; Ross, 1975). It seems most likely that older individuals who find negative responses the most shocking—that is, those who have enjoyed higher statuses throughout their lives—are the most reluctant to seek comfort whose price is visible association with similarly disvalued peers. Residential density of peers, for instance, has a stronger effect on the sociability of working class than middle-class old people (Rosow, 1967). Part of this difference is explained by the greater tendency of working class individuals to find their friends close to home, but the status discrepancy hypothesis may account for some difference too.

Threat

The extreme edge of overrecognition from outsiders is threat. Studies of community formation in many contexts—nation-states, utopias, squatters—show that a moderate level of threat from an identifiable source is a stimulus to communal feeling and organization. Comparison of the old-age communities rings in the "old people are people" theme again, as threat also appears as a source of community formation among them. Security is a major reason that old people choose to live in any age-homogeneous residential environment. This is partly provided by the closed areas and policing offered by organized communities, but it comes also from the absence of younger people who are seen as more dangerous than peers. In addition, inside age-homogeneous residences, old people such as the retired construction workers of Les Floralies, discover that they share fears of financial insecurity based on mistrust of the motives or judgment of younger directors or developers (see also Fry, 1979).

Whether perceived threat might promote peer networks outside of separate residential settings is not known, but plausible enough to be worth investigation. The old people who dance and pray together at the Aliyah Senior Center described by Myerhoff are, for example, painfully aware of the dangers in the streets and alleys surrounding it. The warmth and humanity inside the Center's walls bind its members even closer because of the contrasting cold world outside. Even the timing of Sabbath is redefined in the Aliyah world to preserve it as a haven from after-dark dangers. Certainly older people with peer supports—even outside of organized communities—do feel more secure (see also Moss et al., 1976; Rosow, 1967). The beneficial consequence argues for exploration of triggering conditions.

Cross-Cutting Ties

Age similarity, combined with other homogeneities, does promote informal ties. What happens when age is cross-cut, rather than paralleled by other social identities or allegiances? Raising this question is a reminder to restate the basic but productive principle that age bonds are most likely to develop when few cross-cutting ties are present. The explanatory productivity of this principle comes from its leading us to look for stages of the life course, cultural contexts, or social situations in which age has least "competition." Some anthropologists have even suggested that age has a residual quality, that it is *only* a significant principle in society when few others are available (Schurtz, 1902; Needham, 1974). A look across cultures, and down the life span, however, suggests that age often performs a more complicated balancing act of complementarity with other attributes.

In terms of times and places when age has little competition as a basis of social bonding, adolescence and old age are, in many cultures, the life-stages with fewest types of social linkage; age-mates and kin predominate. Intense peer ties among adolescents are stimulated by shared liminality, as well as by the classic ambiguities of a search for self-identity. It is also true that age-mates win partly by default, since in many social settings adolescents have not yet acquired the adult roles of work, parenthood, politics, religion, and so on, that would compete with age. One reason that the old gang fades into reminiscence is that its former members are too busy and divided by too many loyalties to maintain it (e.g., Whyte, 1955). However, we are less accustomed to thinking about the fact that a new gang may be formed or the old one revived *after* the roles of social maturity have receded.

In the culturally defined life careers of many societies, adolescence and old age are symmetrical transitions in and out of social maturity, with a parallel lack of competition for age ties at the same time that liminality and need for socialization make them attractive. In a rural Hungarian village, for instance, revival of the old gang is exactly what occurs. Adolescent peer group sociability fades during adult years, but is the basis for social contact and emotional support once again in old age (Fel and Hofer, 1969). Very little is known about such waxing and waning of peer ties in modern societies. There are enough tantalizing bits of evidence, however, to tempt researchers to a real feast. In the two classic studies of residential density and age bonds, the areas with greatest age density also had greatest residential stability, suggesting revival or mainte-

nance rather than creation of age friendships (Rosow, 1967; Rosenberg, 1970). The age community studies show the possibility of reviving a pattern of peer ties, but with new personnel. A San Francisco survey found that the scores for "friendship participation" (number plus contact) declined through middle-age, then rose in the sixties (Lowenthal et al., 1975:51). The *meaning* of friendship appeared similar for adolescents and older people in another United States study which found that for both age categories friends were valued as sources of status definition (Gibbs-Candy, 1976).

The task is to disentangle the individual experiences, community characteristics, and cultural expectations producing the various patterns. Are individuals with intense and satisfying peer group ties at adolescence, for example, most likely to revive them later, either with the same individuals or with others? One unexpected benefit to some deaf Americans is the lasting peer bonds created by attending special schools. These peer supports, intensified by a shared understanding of handicap and a shared communication system learned in a collective socialization experience, persist into old age (Becker, 1980). Are residentially stable neighborhoods likely to promote peer ties, regardless of age density? Might age density combined with residential instability also promote peer groups of "new" older people precisely because they do not have deep roots in the community (see Fennell, 1981)?

"Generation gap" has been a provocative tag for the relationships, or nonrelationships, of adolescents to their parents. The abrasive potential of relations between adjacent generations is another similarity between adolescents and older people: Both have problems of role shift and authority with the generation in the middle. In cross-cultural view, alternate generation bonds appear when authority is vested in the middle-age category, the most common circumstance (Sweetser, 1956). The conflictual rub of adjacent generations may also stimulate grouping among age peers. Among the Tiv of Northern Nigeria, for example, the adult men within a kin group control cattle which younger men need to obtain brides. Since in this polygynous society the older men would prefer to have additional wives themselves, there is a conflict of interest. Among the Tiv it is the young man's age-mates who bring a horizontal leverage through the age organization against the vertical pull of kinship. This pattern has been hypothesized to be general: When the kin group impedes the younger persons' access to social maturity, age grouping is likely to appear (Eisenstadt, 1956).

An even broader pattern may be that when the household is not *adequate* to prepare the young for participation in the wider society, age groups are likely to appear as an interstitial or interlinking sphere. Here the argument is abstract. If the principles guiding social relationships within the household are not those that predominate in the outside world, then a transition is necessary. Links among family members, who are usually the majority of residents in a household, are typically particularistic and ascribed—that is, guided by the sex, age, and kinship attributes of individuals, and focused on them as particular individuals rather than as members of a category. In some societies, where kinship is the type for social relation in every domain, norms of interaction acquired in the household may be extended appropriately beyond it, but societies in which universalistic and achieved principles predominate outside the household require a transition. Universalistic norms emphasize categorical rather than personal attributes. According to universalistic principles, people would be recruited to government jobs by scores on examinations, rather than by family connections. Achieved attributes are those acquired through life by individuals, in contrast to ascribed characteristics which are determined, usually permanently, at birth. Age groups, melding universalistic and ascriptive criteria, are, according to Eisenstadt, the perfect response. Extended schooling outside the home, for instance, is the setting for just the kind of transitional age grouping he predicts.

Stepping back to view the entire life course in many societies suggests again that there may be a structural parallel between adolescence and "young" old age. If one is the transition into and the other the transition out of social maturity, then perhaps Eisenstadt's argument about interlinking spheres could be extended to old age. The key question becomes, what is the transition into at the later stage? Is there the same asymmetry of structural principles to stimulate age grouping? A

shift toward more particularistic relationships would fulfill the conditions, and nothing is more particularistic than a family. Family ties do become more predominant, at least as sources of support for older members of many modern societies (Shanas et al., 1968; Shanas, 1979a). Although the concrete mapping of kinds and quality of social networks is not yet available to test Eisenstadt's abstract hypothesis, the hints we have make exploration look well worth the effort. . . .

CONCLUSION

Age symbolizes, evokes, and protects equality among peers. Peer ties should be most numerous and significant in informal social networks under conditions that promote an emphasis on equality. When the information available about peer ties is plotted in time and space, several patterns suggest when these conditions will be present. Peer ties develop as an egalitarian or horizontal balance to the vertical strain of hierarchy. Material as well as social needs may be met by peers in a spirit of reciprocity that does not require admission of dependence. A world of age-mates insulates from external ranking members of an age-grade temporarily or permanently excluded from power. The sometimes painful equality of shared status transitions also bonds peers together as colearners and coteachers. Shared experience of liminality is a powerful source of communal feeling in a context that goes beyond negation of ranking to a temporary irrelevance of all structure. Access to age peers under various conditions appears to promote social ties that provide both material and emotional benefits. In liminal circumstances, there may be, in addition, a spontaneous ferment of social creativity. Older people in many modern societies are exposed to all of these conditions. When peers are available, we should therefore expect that old people, like other people, will be linked to these age-mates in informal networks that provide both tangible and intangible support. Our surprise when we find these networks—and our slowness to look for them in the first place—are signs of the difficulty we have reminding ourselves that old people are indeed people. . . .

Barbara Hornum

THE ELDERLY IN BRITISH NEW TOWNS: NEW ROLES, NEW NETWORKS

Although the development of planned communities is not a recent phenomenon, its impact on the lives of the elderly is little known. Barbara Hornum in the following article uses the British experience with New Town development to explore how both macro and micro cultural variation shape the new roles and networks that the elderly develop in these new environments. Not only are the towns themselves quite varied but so are the resident groups of elderly: Some are long-term residents of the general area; others were New Town pioneers who have aged there; and yet others have migrated there after they were already old. Hornum shows that the planned towns have a wide variety of housing options purposely built for the aged, facilitating the integration of the aged as a vital part of the community. Although the United States has few towns identical to those studied in Britain, the author reveals how the British experience can have important implications in planning future environments for the aged in this country.

INTRODUCTION

THE BRITISH NEW TOWNS reflecting the dream of Ebenezer Howard have stood since 1948 as models for urban planners and developers. Since these are living communities, they can be studied as segments of larger cultural systems and, as such, they provide insights into how the different segments of the population can have their needs met.

There are two aspects of culture: the broad spectrum of norms and values that permeate the social system and provide it with its underlying value orientation, and the specific responses to these that are focused and directed towards a unique segment of the population. We can think of the first as macrocultural elements because of the extent of their influence. The second area can be deemed microcultural because it reflects and channels the values and themes of the wider culture. There is further a dual process with

interaction and response going in both directions. Because of this movement of values and the potential for applying them in different ways, we can expect to find variation in their manifestation.

There are a number of dilemmas typically faced by the aged in post industrial society. When circumstances promote physical and social mobility of children as an ideal, spatial and emotional gaps may appear between the generations. Frequent contacts as part of an interactive kinship network may diminish, and those ties that remain are apt to become attenuated. Different life styles for parents and children can also lead to communication difficulties even when the emotional bonds are strong.

In addition, the mores of an achievement-oriented world view are likely to foster desires for independence and "standing on one's own feet." Conflicting pressures may be manifest as a result of the relatively low fixed incomes of many elderly, especially as these are eroded further by high inflation. Thus, older individuals may want to be able to maintain their own households, but

This essay was specially prepared for this book by the author. Permission to reprint must be obtained from the author and publisher.

can find it hard to do so because of increasingly tight budgets. If mobility is at all impaired as health needs alter, the aged may feel increasingly vulnerable in terms of their holding on to their autonomy. The availability of alternative options for living arrangements enables older people to exercise their choices based on personal preferences, and does not lock them into any one residential-social model.

RELATIONSHIP OF MACRO AND MICROCULTURAL ELEMENTS

When we examine the position of the elderly in the British New Towns, we can see that it is influenced by the beliefs of the general population, as these have been translated into relevant social policy. All of the elderly in Britain are entitled to rent rebates, subsidized medical care, etc., if necessary. In old, established communities, the elderly are frequently invisible, and an understanding of the social aspects of aging related to role expectation and use of available resources may be difficult. Within the British New Towns, however, the elderly hold a unique position, because they represent a small, if highly perceptible, group. Further, the "newness" of the New Towns permits an assessment of how networks and roles emerge and are used. In addition, variations by region, initial purpose of the towns, social class, and population mix can be investigated, as these may influence perceptions of and responses to the conditions of aging.

DEVELOPMENT OF NEW TOWNS

In the 1940s, the British government promulgated a New Towns policy. The desire to control random suburban sprawl led to the establishment of a "green belt" around London in which no new development would be permitted. There was also a need to deal with the problem of continued growth and congestion within London, and other

industrial cities, such as Birmingham and Liverpool. The New Towns Act of 1946 gave power to the Minister of Housing and Local Government (now held by the Secretary of State for the Environment) to designate New Towns throughout Britain, and to appoint Development Corporations to plan, construct, and administer them.[1]

As of 1980, the New Towns are in varying stages of development, with more than 600,000 inhabitants. A New Towns Commission has been established by the Central Government, and Development Corporations are being phased out in several of the older, established New Towns. Recently, it has been decided that rental housing and related assets shall be transferred to local housing authorities in these "old" New Towns, and the social development responsibilities will then be completely carried by local government.

Since the earliest "overspill" New Towns,[2] others have been established to meet a wider variety of conditions. Some were designated to help support the development of a particular industry and to alleviate unemployment. Others aid in the coordination of the development/redevelopment of relatively large urban areas, which may encompass a number of existing towns and villages. Still other New Towns have been designated to help halt depopulation of an area.

CATEGORIES OF NEW TOWNS

The first group of New Towns was begun in the period of 1947–50. The majority of these were intended to relieve congestion in London, and to provide housing and employment for the people so dispersed (Osborn and Whittick, 1977:57; Diamond, 1972:57). Of this group, *Bracknell* is to be examined here. Other New Towns were designated to bring together scattered population, traditionally focused on one local industry, and to provide these people with opportunities for improved housing and subsidiary facilities along with augmenting regional economic growth. *Glenrothes* in Scotland falls into this category. The additional early New Towns also included those built to maintain existing industry by preventing depopulation of a region because of poor housing and/or community services. *Cwmbran*, in Wales, is an example of such a community. These initial New Towns had original target populations that ranged from 10,000 to 50,000. Since the focus of this paper is on the categories of elderly within the New Towns, the three cases selected for comparison come from this initial group.

The second wave of New Towns was designated in the 1960s. Some of these, such as Northampton, England, and Irvine, Scotland, were intended to be grafted on to already existing communities, augmenting and enlarging housing and services as well as fostering new economic growth. Still others, like Milton Keynes in England, were seen as serving to integrate a large number of towns and villages, forming regional complexes. With the exception of *Newtown*, all of the second wave have much larger target populations than the earlier towns. Indeed, the planned population of Milton Keynes is 250,000, far larger than a town (Osborn and Whittick, 1977:58; and Diamond, 1972:59). All of the towns differ then in purpose at inception, size, location, and objective. The differences are rooted in the values of the regions, and affect the perceptions of need for and delivery of services. The limitations of space, and the need to focus on the interface of the macro and microcultural elements, necessitate only a brief glimpse of some of these new communities.

POPULATION FACTORS

In the older and thus more established New Towns, even those that were not affiliated with preexisting villages or towns, second- and sometimes third-generation residents are heavily represented in the population. The people have grown older along with the New Town; many of them are now in their fifties and sixties. Large numbers of them have chosen to remain in the New Town upon retirement, shifting if necessary from their original residence to "purpose-built" housing. In fact, the rate of out-migration from New Towns is only about 5 percent per year. Many of these people still see themselves as pioneers, or founders of the communities in which they live.

In the more recent New Towns, the population is composed of incomers and the original

indigenous inhabitants of the area. Most newcomers are young married couples with small children who have assured jobs in the new environment. Their older relatives thus become a priority category for housing in the New Town. Government regulation additionally specifies that some housing provision be made in specially built accommodations for those over 65. The indigenous population is typically representative of a small rural community whose ancestors have lived in the area for a long time. This population may indeed contain a high proportion of people above 65. Therefore, even in the newest New Towns, there will be an older segment of the population for whom provision must be made. Population mix is yet another critical factor in producing variation.

The New Towns selected for analysis were chosen because they varied in when, where, and why they were built. Each one has a unique population mixture as well. Thus an understanding of them, first individually and then as a whole, can enable us to see how their regional and planning differences produce variations in structural arrangements (social forms) and cultural behavior (roles) for the elderly. These, out of 18 New Towns surveyed, will serve as case studies. A major aim is to give some qualitative understanding of the variation in New Town segregation and what this means for the life of the aged. The diversity of *Bracknell*, *Glenrothes*, and *Cwmbran* by type and region leads to their selection as the core case models. Space necessitates that *Northampton*, *Irvine*, and *Milton Keynes* shall only have brief mention useful in highlighting other dimensions of difference for older people. The ethnographic information primarily comes from interviews with residents (middle-aged and elderly), social service workers, health care personnel, directors of housing and recreational facilities, and volunteer groups collected from 1972 through 1979.

BRACKNELL: AN "OVERSPILL" TOWN

Bracknell, in the Royal County of Berkshire, is located 28 miles west of London. Railway service to London is frequent, with trains running at least every thirty minutes; the journey may take as little as forty minutes. Historically, Bracknell was a small settlement. At its 1949 date of designation, it had approximately 5,000 inhabitants, a cattle market, a high street with shops, and six small light industrial factories. The original designation covered an area of 1,870 acres, including and surrounding the old town. August 1951 marked the completion of the first buildings, and the occupation of the first house. The original population target of 25,000 was enlarged in 1963 to 60,000, and the designated area expanded to 3,285 acres. Elaborate networks of roads and sewers run through and connect the different estates of the town. There are more than 12,000 dwellings; over 40 factories and their extensions, many of them in electronics; schools, shops, and many recreational facilities. In addition, a major factor in the uniqueness of Bracknell is the fact that several large, and a number of small, companies have established their headquarters there. The presence of these headquarters and the demand for skilled workers in the electronics field has led to a middle-class ethos. The political orientation of the county, the district, and Bracknell itself is predominantly Conservative.

With the completion of the designated area, Bracknell will have a town center, three industrial areas, and nine residential neighborhoods. Each of these will provide amenity shopping, a church, a meeting hall, a pub, a primary school, and play areas. Some of the neighborhoods are now settled, while others are just now being completed. These neighborhoods reflect some of the changes in town planning from 1949 to 1978. Some are traditional in layout, others segregate traffic and pedestrians, while the newest have modified this strict segregation.

Demographically, the original population, pre-1949, reflected the homogeneity of a small rural community. Many of the people had ancestors who had lived in Bracknell for generations; others had moved in from small villages and farms because of the market. Beginning in 1951, the New Town influx was largely composed of young married couples with small children. The majority of these newcomers came from West London. Most of them live and work in Bracknell, attracted by the economic opportunities. As their

children grow up and marry, they too have applied for housing in the New Town. In addition, special housing arrangements exist to enable the elderly, retired parents of the incomers, to also live in Bracknell. This has resulted in the existence of a number of three-generation families. At the present time, the first generation of New Town residents includes an evergrowing proportion of over 50s.

The separation of the housing estates and the existence of inadequacies in the mass transit system appear to be a constraining element in the ability of the elderly, who may not drive, to move freely outside of the local shopping area or into the town center. Nonetheless, the increasing array of "purpose-built" housing continues to make Bracknell an attractive place to retire.[3]

The elderly themselves fall into three major groupings. There are those, now mostly above 70, who once formed the stable core of settled middle-aged farmers, small merchants, and professionals in the pre-New Town period, thirty years ago. There are the parents of the first New Town residents who have been slowly moving into Bracknell as they retired in order to be close to their children; they are also generally over 70. Finally, there are those of the frontier population who migrated from London in the early 1950s, and who constitute the "young elderly," being between 50 and 70. This latter group, while itself preretirement, is the largest segment of the older population, and the most likely to play an advocacy role in future programs for seniors.

It is this last group that tends to have the most positive set of perceptions of Bracknell. The New Town has been the locus within which they raised their children, made friends, established careers, and felt themselves to be in the vanguard of an exciting experiment. While the majority of this group are renters, they also make up the largest proportion of the roughly 30 percent homeowners within Bracknell. Technicians, white-collar workers, and professionals, they see themselves as solidly part of the middle class. Conservative in their politics, they are supporters of the status quo. Over the years, they have made a number of enduring friendships, both at work and within their particular residential estate. These associations, plus a fondness for the traditional architectural styles of these earliest estates, tend to work against their moving to purpose-built housing in the newer areas where it is available. Since they are still agile physically, many of them continue to occupy the larger homes in which they raised their now-grown families. Inadvertently, they thus block the free flow of younger families into these established residential areas. Although not yet in need of specialized facilities for the elderly, they seem to give most support to fostering those services that can help people stay as long as possible and as happily as possible in their own homes. Because of the length of residence in Bracknell, they participate in a number of informal, free associational networks. Thus, some of the housewives from this group pool the cab fare and taxi into and out of the town center on a weekly basis to do their marketing. The persistence of such patterns can incidentally facilitate the ease with which this group can maintain its current life style even past retirement.

Even though the members of this group may have younger kin living in the newer estates, representing those born and raised in Bracknell New Town, they tend to see them primarily on a once-a-week, Sunday dinner basis. The active lives of the first generation, many of whom are still employed, allow them to support the independence of the second generation. Exceptions to this occur when grown, married children are able to locate in the same estates on which they were raised, thereby placing them in closer proximity to their parents. In their dealings with their own parents, who have moved to Bracknell in order to be with children and grandchildren, there are elements of strain and some intergenerational conflict. The parents come to Bracknell expecting to return to the sorts of kinship patterns and social interaction patterns they had known in London. However, ten, twenty, or even thirty years have elapsed since these "children" moved to Bracknell, and they have established "new" ties. To these children, once-a-week contact over a meal is ample; to their recently uprooted parents, it is not.

The elderly newcomers to Bracknell seem to be experiencing some sense of culture shock. They have left behind siblings and lifetime friends in order to reestablish what they feel will be the tight, three-generational families they remember from their own pre-World War II youth. General social and cultural change, as well as alterations in the life styles of their children and grown

grandchildren, vitiates this sustained, close contact. Feeling uprooted, there may be an initial period of fear and loneliness. As long as both partners of a couple are alive and healthy, this is held in check. But when one spouse either dies or becomes ill, the need for external support intensifies. Many of the older people in this group seem to come at least once a week to day centers, like the Johnstone Court Day Center, where they can make new friends, have a reason to get dressed up, and find people with life experiences similar to their own. Had these parents moved shortly after their children, the old interaction patterns might have remained strong, and possibly even blocked the development of new kinds of dependencies. The temporal lag results in a kind of role reversal. The children are now the "old hands" who have knowledge of Bracknell as a community. It is they who must introduce their parents to the "proper" way of doing things. Yet they really do not have the time nor the mutuality of interest, despite bonds of affection, to truly want to see their parents on a daily basis. "Mum going to the day center means she doesn't expect to have me pop in every day. She is making new friends, and they can grouse about the way things ought to be."

If they have moved directly into a bungalow or "granny flat," they will seek to stay in it as long as health permits, and will freely use available services such as Meals on Wheels and Home Help. Others, feeling themselves less able, may have moved directly into a sheltered housing scheme.[4] These, along with those bungalows in rows, do offer structured networks within which the older person may find new patterns of friendship relatively rapidly, and set up appropriate conditions for exchanges of services. This is more difficult for the incomers living in a flat or bungalow in an integrated housing arrangement, unless they are within walking distance of relatives. In the absence of this, the day center becomes a vital connection to other people. A few of the more extroverted elderly in this group have established tentative reciprocal exchanges of child minding for lifts to the market with their younger neighbors.

Clearly, this group, however, has faced not only the normal role changes of advancing in the life cycle, but some unique role changes tied to their late life relocation as well. These reciprocal exchanges with youthful neighbors do not replace kinship ties at the emotional level. But they are satisfying in that they expand the physical horizon of the older person who may not have a car available. There is also the enhanced sense of usefulness that comes from being able to return favors with services that are valued by others. It should be noted that this is only one aspect of networking, and is generally not considered by the elderly to be as important as maintaining contacts with their own children and grandchildren. Nor is it as relevent to their ultimate satisfaction with Bracknell as frequent contacts with peers.

The last group to be discussed is composed of those elderly now living within the designated New Town area who were part of the indigenous pre-New Town population. Some of these people are still ambivalent about Bracknell, even after thirty years, and think nostalgically about the small town they have idealized over the years. Many of this group inhabit housing stock that predates the New Town and lacks central heating and indoor toilet facilities. Because of ancestral associations, they are reluctant to leave these homes for modern purpose-built housing. Increasing frailty is the only reason for such a move; and, even this will be offset as much as possible by the use of Home Help services, Meals on Wheels, and Visiting Nurses. The indigenous elderly are less apt to use the facilities of the day center, but will turn instead to various parish churches that may offer social activities. If their children have remained in the area, either in Bracknell proper or in one of the surrounding communities, kin networks are also maintained. And, because these people have lived their entire lives in the area, existing patterns of reciprocity and friendship tend to endure into old age. The presence of the New Town has introduced structural change, but personal role changes are not generally radical because of the geographic and network continuity.

GLENROTHES: BALANCING INDUSTRIAL GROWTH

Glenrothes, Scotland, was designated as a New Town in 1948. Its location, originally selected

because of the proximity to coal reserves, has placed it far enough away from Edinburgh to prevent it from becoming a "bedroom" suburb. Even though the town was to be based mainly on the needs of the Rothes Colliery (coal mine), there was recognition of some need to create balancing industry. This proved fortunate, because after years of difficulty, the mine was closed in 1961. With this, the original planning objective had to be altered, and Glenrothes was redesignated as a growth point for Central Scotland. The target population was increased to 55,000. Even though an overspill agreement exists with Glasgow, it has not operated to any extent. Glenrothes appears to grow only insofar as employment in and around the town grows.

Two factors make Glenrothes unique. First, its physical location is exceptionally attractive with wooded hills and the River Leven. Second, from its inception, the connection between the New Town and the Fife County Council has been extremely close. Unlike all other UK New Towns, Glenrothes does not have a Special Development Order creating the New Town Corporation as a Planning Authority. Instead, the Fife County Council administers planning as well as educational, health, and welfare services. Additionally, Glenrothes' location in the center of Fife makes it ideal as a location for the Fife Regional Council itself. Further, the projected population growth to 95,000 by the year 2000 will make it the largest town in Fife.

Over 16,000 people work in Glenrothes in companies as varied as fashion jewelers and mining manufacturers. The five industrial estates house over 160 companies, and employment is growing, with a number of international companies represented. Over 70 percent of the work force is either skilled or professionally qualified, which gives a middle-class base to the town. Housing is grouped in several precincts, each with shops, pubs, meeting rooms, and churches readily accessible. The Town Center is in the process of expansion, but since this is relatively new, contact between the residents of the different precincts has taken an unusual format. Wirz (1975) comments on the unusually strong club membership of those over 60 in Glenrothes. My feeling is that this operates for several reasons. First, association because of common interest countered the lack of a Town Center and drew people together from the various precincts. Second, with nearly all of the residents newcomers, the need for affiliation was high. Finally, the middle-class background of most of the residents and their relatively high education, reflecting the strong Scottish emphasis on this, foster an interest in organized activity. Innovation in programs has been basic to Glenrothes, the first New Town to have a permanent town artist.

Demographically, Glenrothes by design and location was populated by incomers. The slow period of growth prior to 1963 reflected the lack of stability of the colliery. Thus the majority of those living in Glenrothes today moved to the town after 1963. They were attracted to the employment opportunities in skilled, white-collar, service, and professional occupational areas. Many of these people came from other areas of Scotland, a few from other parts of the UK, and some from the U.S. and continental Europe. The varied backgrounds and range of experience provide an interest in the outside world and in travel unusual in the New Towns.

The formal arrangements for the elderly do not differ radically from those in other New Towns. However, many of these have been built recently because of the fact that most of the earlier housing was designed to meet the needs of families. Nonetheless, there is a growing awareness of developing needs for varied purpose-built accommodations, sheltered housing, and geriatric day and residential facilities. Many of these have been completed or are in process. Support in the form of opening up meeting rooms for clubs for the elderly, and the provision of an office for Age Concern are also part of the arrangements made in Glenrothes to aid the elderly. Constraining factors seem to be the typical ones of distance between housing precincts and poor mass transit.

A high percentage of the elderly in Glenrothes are the "young" old because of the age and patterns of development of the town itself. Statistics in 1977 indicated that 2.4 percent of the residents were between 65 and 69. At that time, there were 5.9 percent who were between 55 and 64 years of age, and some of this group have now passed their 65th birthdays. Seniors 70 and over constituted 3.0 percent of the 1977 population breakdown. Therefore, there is a

growing segment of the population in Glenrothes with a vital interest in matters pertaining to the life style of "pensioners." Certainly a core of "seniors" seems to interact with both the official and unofficial organization of the town. These people are concerned, visible, and know how to "work" the system.

The older population of Glenrothes does not break naturally into categories. True, there are a few people who have moved to Glenrothes after retirement elsewhere in order to be closer to children who work for one of the industries in the New Town. There are also a few of the above-75-year-olds who have always lived in Fife District, but not in Glenrothes. The local authorities are placing them in sheltered housing or old people's homes as their advancing age and increasing frailty necessitate some minimal supervision. But the majority of those between 55 and 70 seem to have lived in the town for fifteen-plus years, have been active in the employment and social scene of Glenrothes, and are continuing their energetic concern for the maintenance of what they feel is a "highly livable community." They hold very positive views of the New Town, and are action oriented when there are things they do not like.

Typical of the values held was the concept of "help for self-help." Older people are encouraged to be as independent as possible, to reach out and transmit skills and knowledge across the generations, and to maintain an interest in personal and intellectual growth. The elderly women and men have been asked to volunteer to work with adolescents after school, to teach them skills like baking and woodworking. In some cases, strong friendships have grown up across the generations as a result of these contacts. Staying in touch, keeping fit, and reaching out to others are all encouraged by organizations throughout the town. Whether it is working with youngsters, helping shop for or read to some of the less-well aged, learning a new skill, or answering the telephone in the Age Concern office, it is expected that senior citizens will do as much for others as they can, and in so doing will benefit personally. This seems to permeate the world view of the elderly in Glenrothes, and is openly articulated by them. Thus, as has been noted, a very high percentage of the elderly in Glenrothes are *active* club members. What is impressive is the outward focus and strong interest in a wide range of affairs expressed by the older people of Glenrothes.

Ties of common interest and friendships based on shared participation in activities have created a strong network of older people that operates beyond the level of regular meetings. Many of those active in one group are active in others. They are thus part of a larger interlocking networking pattern that touches volunteer groups like Age Concern, and also reaches into the Development Corporation and the County Council. Some of the involvement of older people may be the result of the efforts of the Age Concern paid organizer, the only one appointed to a voluntary association in Scotland. Certainly she has been able to reach out to a wide number of old people. She has also been able to act as an advocate for them with the health services, the churches, social services, and the local authorities. Nonetheless, the desire for involvement seems to spring genuinely from a very dynamic group of older people who appear to have by and large translated their energy from raising families and holding paid employment to other spheres of interest. It is true that many of the people involved came from what could be classified as white-collar or skilled craft positions whereby we could see them as middle class. Yet this would be too simplistic an explanation for their belief that they can control their own lives. Having had successes in other spheres of activity, they do not see passivity as an adjunct of growing older. While not everyone subscribes to this view, enough do and are able to motivate the rest.

Their roles have changed as their statuses have altered, but they have apparently accepted these changes without feeling it necessary to cut themselves off from participation in the ongoing affairs of Glenrothes. Networking and reciprocity seem strongly based on free association. Many of the older people have children living as far away as Australia. Since they, themselves, rarely come from the vicinity of Fife, their other kin are also likely to be geographically distant. Dependency on kinship-rooted ties and networks neither seems possible nor desirable to them. Given a life history of perceiving themselves to have been responsible for directing their own lives, they are strongly motivated to push the services of

Glenrothes to help them continue to maintain high levels of control.

CWMBRAN: PROVIDING BETTER SERVICES

Cwmbran, Wales, is the third of the New Towns discussed to be designated just after 1948. It is the first New Town to be built in Wales. This "Valley of the Crow" had an existing concentration of industry already located in or near to it. Thousands of people used to travel daily to work in the area. One of the main factors behind the New Town designation was to provide homes for those who worked in existing regional industries. Coal mining, tinplate works, chemical industries, brick, tile, and pipemaking were the original major industries. Their development was helped by the Monmouthshire Canal and later by the railroads. The depression of the 1930s, however, had a heavy impact on the region. For a long period, over half the working population was unemployed. Concerted government action at the end of the 30s and the advent of World War II brought an economic reversal to the area. The various manufacturing industries established employ a high percentage of the workingmen of Cwmbran. Many of the women, however, are employed by electronics industries. The class base was, and still is, primarily working class.

At the time of designation, the indigenous population was about 12,000, mostly living in a hamlet and in two small townships. This original population had to be integrated with the newcomers. Additionally, planners had to work around the problems of a site traversed by a river, two railways, and a canal. There are five main residential neighborhoods with various religious, social, educational, and shopping facilities. These neighborhoods are grouped around the Town Center. Despite the population growth from 12,000 to nearly 45,000, the vast majority of the incomers (70 percent) are from the surrounding county area. Another 10 percent come predominantly from South Wales. The remainder come from other parts of Britain. The strong county orientation of both the pre-New

Town and post-New Town population has important social and cultural consequences. Affiliation with Cwmbran may be recent, but ties to the wider area are of long duration.

The formal arrangements for the elderly are particularly good due to the unique situation of Cwmbran having two housing authorities: the Urban Council and the Development Corporation. Eventually, in 1968, two spheres of concern were worked out. The Development Corporation would assume responsibility for general housing; the Urban Council would concentrate on building accommodations for the elderly. Nine special schemes of sheltered housing have been completed, and plans exist for at least 300 purpose-built dwellings. In addition, the very large Central Recreation Area and the Oakfield Gardens with its benches and band platform provide free leisure resources which can be used by the elderly for recreational purposes. The primary constraining factor in terms of the mobility of those elderly who do not drive is the dearth of frequent public transportation.

The connection of the Urban District Council with the housing in Cwmbran meant that, for a New Town, there is a large group of older people who have been housed in the town from its initial designation. Since the vast majority of all residents come from within the county, the homogeneity of the incomers and the indigenous population is striking. Not having had to face either drastic uprooting themselves, nor having to deal with "foreigners," the general perception of Cwmbran is a positive one.

The values and concerns of the elderly in Cwmbran center about religion and family. Close kinship ties and strong family discipline related to duty mean that relatives form the primary networks of contact and exchange. Nonetheless, the degree of contact between elderly parents and their adult daughters, once a major source of affiliation, is altering. The increasing employment of women in the electronics industries of Cwmbran has led to a growing number of elderly who can no longer count on their daughters' daily visits. Where the older parent, chiefly the grandmother, is still physically agile and residential proximity is good, she may act as child minder for her working daughter. Even where the daily ties have been attenuated, long-standing

patterns of filial respect remain strong. This bears a striking similarity to the relationships of grown children to "Mum" as found by Young and Willmott in their 1957 study of family and kinship patterns in East London.

Free associational contacts largely center around the particular religious body to which the older person belongs. A few people have ties that reflect common interests, such as choral singing. Beyond this, lifetimes spent within Monmouthshire, if not in Cwmbran, ensure that old friendship patterns can also be sustained.

Earlier retirement for men and increasing employment for women are creating shifting authority patterns within the family—nuclear and extended. Roles are changing both within and across generations. We would anticipate that one area of change should be visible as the first generation of working women become grandmothers. These women, employed outside of the home, will not have the availability to back up and support their own daughters by an exchange of chores; at least not until their own retirement. Still another prospect is that grandfathers, having retired early while their wives are still working, will seek to spend increased time with their grandchildren.

NEWER ALTERNATIVE MODELS

Both Northampton and Irvine are unusual for New Towns in that they involve the deliberate and continued grafting together of old existing communities with extant traditions, and the designated New Towns. It is hoped that the alliance of old and new, past and future, will be ever-present factors of life. Further, it is expected that since the majority of the elderly will be from the predesignation period, there will be few responses to the New Towns as such except through an increase in services. The newcomers will have heightened opportunities to be introduced by the indigenous populations to the existing traditions. Role models for the elderly are thus likely to remain those of earlier local generations. There are many long-term kinship and friendship ties as well as stable associations that may go back to childhood experiences. People are traditional in preferring home, church, or pub as meeting places. They prefer to rely on those they know, either kin or friends, rather than strangers. How long informal patterns of mutual aid can be sustained will be a question for the future.

In contrast to the deliberate conjunction of old and new is the "showcase" new "city" of Milton Keynes. Milton Keynes was designated primarily to provide housing and employment for workers from London. Roughly 70 percent of those over 60 are part of the predesignation population. The remainder have come in as priority tenants for purpose-built housing. As yet, these two groups seem to maintain separation from one another. The indigenous elderly largely rely on existing extended kinship and friendship networks (Mather, 1978:46–48). A high proportion of incoming elderly must establish new local friends, and often do so by selecting some form of grouped housing. Milton Keynes should provide an opportunity for research into many facets of conscious networking.

IMPACT OF VARIATION

It should be abundantly clear that while the various British New Towns do have many similarities, they are also quite different from one another. The diverse factors of location, original and projected size of population and land area, degree of proximity to the town center, composition of the population in terms of ratio of indigenous residents to incomers, and the purpose behind the actual New Town designation as well as its date of inception, all lead to variation in the types of networking possibilities that exist. The roles all people enter into, and this includes the elderly, are tied not only to the social reality of the statuses they hold, but to their perceptions of these statuses. Assessments of alternatives are influenced by the elements of the macroculture as these either appear to limit or to extend the feasible boundaries of behavior.

When dealing with Britain, then, the development of the "welfare state" and its entitlements is a very strong factor in the overall macroculture of that society. Indeed, the creation of New Towns as consciously planned experiments to improve the well-being of one or more segments of the population should not be overlooked. They thus form an interpretive manifestation of the general culture even while containing shaping or macrocultural elements of their own.

Certainly none of the towns discussed is planned primarily for the elderly, yet in the overall concept of creating what could be a total design for living, there has been a latent awareness that any given population will eventually change and age. Emphasis was placed on creating a "natural" atmosphere, and this was seen as requiring a population mixed by social class as well as stage of life. Creating one central activity hub in the Town Center, balanced by localized amenity provisions within walking distance of the residents of the dispersed housing area, was one attempt to facilitate easy physical mobility. The use of community-based meeting centers, either especially designed, or based in a school or converted house but again placed in most of the decentralized housing locales, was also intended to make it convenient for people to join together should they wish to do so. The commitment in most of the towns to including at least some pedestrian walkways was also intended to aid both the very young and the old in being able to walk safely despite automobile traffic. (That these walkways are seldom used because they tend to elongate the time of moving from point A to B shows that structural variables can be ignored.) Most importantly, *while there may be some seclusion by age within each area, there is not total isolation.* Right next to a sheltered housing unit or a row of grouped Old People's Dwellings, there will be mixed housing to accommodate families of different sizes.

In the English New Towns located close to London, the existence of generally good rail connections and the proximity of major highways prevent feelings of being isolated or cut off. At the same time, the original legislative requirement that someone in each household be employed in the town or related to such an employee worked against the development of bedroom suburbs. Only in recent years has some housing been allocated and set aside for priority groupings, including the single parent and the senior citizen.

Therefore, for most of those living in these towns, pressures were strong to foster ties not simply to a house, but to a community.

Thus we can see that conscious planning of spatial arrangements, transportation facilities, and meeting places can augment existing networks or help to create new ones. The recognition on the part of architects, urban planners, and service deliverers of the links between the special needs of any population and the general cultural world view seems almost mandatory. Exposition of these connections can certainly be one of the important contributions of anthropology.

CONCLUSION

In all of the New Towns, certain changes will occur. Gradually they will all move from the supervision of the various development corporations to autonomy as towns within the standard political authorities of their regions. The growth will be tied to total regional planning. Because of the history of the New Towns as units of planned change, where discussion by residents has generally been encouraged about the direction of that change, continued self-advocacy is likely. And this includes expressions of self-interest by the elderly.

Individually and collectively, the British New Towns meet the vision set forth by Margaret Mead (1973) when she wrote about the need for three generations to live side by side in communities that are self-contained because they have adequate facilities and varied housing for people with different needs. She called for places for sharing formal and informal contacts. She suggested communities where people could stay throughout their lives, shifting types of accommodations, but not having to leave familiar streets or known people. In particular, she addressed the needs of the elderly when she wrote:

There must be provision for older people to walk to shopping centers, to visit each other, and to visit the playground or the nursery; there must be housing which they can afford and manage without undue strain, and where they will be safe. The special needs of older people, both men and women, can be

determined only by careful observation combined with a chance for them to participate in the planning process (Mead, 1973:247)

The New Towns seem to hold three groups of elderly: those who have always lived in the area, if not in the New Town; those who have aged along with the New Town and are planning their retirement; and those who have moved as elderly people into the New Towns. Each group is free to select from the various living options available in the New Towns. But some distinct patterns do emerge. The incoming elderly seem to prefer either sheltered accommodations or grouped Old People's Bungalows which provide them with structured peer contacts. The indigenous aged seem to seek residences that will have proximity to friends and kin. Thus they may choose "granny flats" or bungalows, but tend to see sheltered housing as something for their later stages of aging, perhaps when widowed. The New Town "pioneers" whose maturation has paralleled the community's seem to prefer purpose-built housing on the estates in which they have always lived. In instances where this is lacking because of planning oversights, they will move based on established contacts, e.g., club associates. This is the most active group of elderly in any of the New Towns, and seems prepared to lobby with Development Corporation staff and Council politicians for the services they deem necessary.

Cross-cultural translation of the New Town concept has not been notably successful in the United States. There are a number of major differences in the general culture that have resulted in the U.S. New Towns like Columbia, Maryland, and Reston, Virginia, becoming quasi-suburban enclaves of the affluent. Unlike the British New Towns, there was no prolonged preliminary discussion and analysis resulting in planned and full-ranging legislative acts. Nor is there any governmental control over the development corporation activities. Rather, the American New Towns have emerged like apotheoses from the minds of private developers. Further, the determined population class mixture of the British developers has proved difficult to implement here. While Columbia does have some industry, both it and Reston primarily employ office workers, service workers, and merchants.[5]

The upper income base of the American New

Towns also still prevents many retired people from considering Columbia or Reston as communities.[6] The rate and rental rebate schemes that are uniformly available to all residents of Britain are not available here except as conditions associated with welfare. This means that supplementary subsidies that the older person in Britain can take as a right of citizenship and can use to increase housing alternatives and options are simply not part of American cultural prerogatives. In addition, services such as Home Helps, administered through local authorities on sliding scales, are only possible in the U.S. via private agencies, and are thus quite costly, placing them beyond the reach of most senior citizens. American notions of independence for the elderly seem of the "sink or swim" variety, rather than being the "help for self-help" apparent throughout Britain. In contrast, as part of the mandate for the British New Towns, some housing must be provided for designated priority groups, including the elderly. This housing is purpose-built, and is to provide a range of choices from the "granny flat," to the "Old Person's Dwelling," to sheltered housing. By deliberate design, older people are encouraged to see the British New Towns as possible communities. Such designated inclusion is not commercially profitable, and does not exist in the New Towns of the United States.

The older residents of the British New Towns are encouraged to stay within these communities by the attention given to their special needs. Existing networks of relatives and friends are augmented by the readily extended social services available within the agency networking of the New Town structure. Aging in any society brings correlated role changes. People who were employed become retired; parents see their children grow and in turn become parents themselves; physiological changes occur and are realities; most of the social positions change as individuals advance through the life cycle. These changes can be seen as bringing advantages such as greater leisure to garden or visit with friends; to learn German or serve as a volunteer; to do any or all of these activities or others. This positive view seems to be part of the perceptions of the elderly in the different New Towns of Britain, even though some see the changes as outside their control and others feel they can shape them. Yet in the

United States, many senior citizens appear to believe that isolation, loneliness, and diminishing income are inevitable for them. Whether these perceptions are accurate or are derived from changes in status and network arrangements, they nonetheless have impact on the self-images of those who subscribe to them. Even the affluent elderly who can select and pay for residences in comfortable retirement communities are steered into what are essentially gilded age ghettos (Kuhn, speech at Drexel University, March 3, 1976). Studies like Keith (1980a; and Keith, in this volume) have pointed out the benefits for network formation within age-homogeneous communities. Yet given adequate support services, other housing options might also provide these (Riesenfeld et al., 1972). Carp (1976) has pointed out the need to be careful about drawing conclusions from the existing data. Since the elderly are a heterogeneous group, different segments of it can be expected to have different needs. The opportunity to remain vital elements in a multigenerational community does not appear to be a realistic option for many senior citizens in the United States.

Do prospects for the elderly in America seem amenable to improvement? Is there adaptive potential growing out of the British New Town experience from which we can benefit? Both these questions will be explored in this concluding section.

One certainly hopes that the prospects for the elderly in this country will improve, at the very least, through the provision of a wider range of alternatives from which the elderly, as a diverse population, can meet a broad spectrum of needs and interests. At the general cultural level, the fostering of a view of old age as a dynamic stage of life involving people who are still contributing to society and not simply waiting for death could influence both role expectation and implementation. Perceptions that senior citizens have a great deal to offer to other people, young and old, could lead to the creation of positions for them on civic planning commissions, boards of community centers, as advisors to educational institutions, and as consumer advocates. Their increasing visibility as shapers and mediators of the system would help personal self-esteem as well as give them continued social value. Equally important would be the opportunities such structured involvement would provide for being able to have impact on formulating programs touching their own lives.

In looking at the British New Towns as models for innovative ideas about living that can be adopted even without using the actual New Town formula, it is noteworthy that planning for the housing, transportation, and social needs of older people can be done based on future population projections. Thus, anticipation of demographic changes can indicate a declining primary school population simultaneous with increased longevity after retirement. Hence schools and community centers could be designed for flexible, multipurpose use across the age spectrum.

Further, an awareness that one segment of the community may have increasing leisure could encourage provision for this group to be able to offer this leisure as an exchange commodity. Thus in Glenrothes, one found retired men and women working with teen-agers to help them learn certain skills. The teen-agers in turn reciprocated by running errands for the senior citizens. A change in the social positioning of the elderly may be liberating in providing them with more time to advance hobbies and what were formerly secondary interests, and to transform these into primary activities. Balanced reciprocity can be additionally beneficial in the establishment of new networks that can help to replace older ties attenuated by life cycle alterations. When the elderly are instrumental in attaining positive new roles for themselves, it is projected that what they do will be seen as valuable to society as a whole, and that this will lead to greater willingness of the social planners to incorporate the elderly into social-structural arrangements.

The different New Towns discussed display tremendous variety. This should prove useful in assessing what can be applied in the United States according to the needs of special groups and/or divergent localities. Thus the use of congregate housing for the elderly within the center of a town in an area of low population density makes dependence on either the private automobile or mass transit less important. There are, of course, limits to adaptation based on the improbability of American government aid close to the British scale. Yet federally subsidized construction loans could be tied to the inclusion of some purpose-built, subsidized housing in many private developments. Design awards could be made for housing/living plans produced by senior citizens and tied to the above. Yet another lesson from the British New Towns is that "help for self-help" involving both the younger elderly and the older elderly tends to lead to the development of programs that are realistic and effective.

No modern society seems able to continue to afford the social and economic costs of trial-and-error learning. Both short- and long-term planning programs should come off the drawing boards simultaneously, and should include some built-in receptivity for modification.

In British New Towns, the elderly are seen as a vital and valued resource contributing to the population mix that is in turn perceived as necessary to the existence of any successful community. This view of older people as contributing to the welfare of the total population means that the macro and microculture show interaction and correspondence of values. Senior citizens in the United States, in order to maximize the systemic possibilities for increased life style options, have the potential of working with their new status as retired people to lobby for changes in the macroculture. In order to be able to do this, they may be able to use models from places like Glenrothes to assess the pressure points that need to be manipulated. The emergent role adjustments and networking affiliations that have been seen in the British New Towns provide insights into how this can be done.

NOTES

1. The Development Corporation is not a Town Council; it exists alongside and cooperates with local authorities. It is these county, regional, and district councils that are responsible for education, police, fire, water, public transport, social work, public health, libraries, and many other social and civic needs.

2. Essentially, an "overspill" New Town is one officially designated to alleviate congestion in a major city such as London. These towns are to provide both housing *and* employment within the New Town boundaries.

3. Purpose-built housing is housing designed to meet the needs, real and potential, of a special group of people. Thus, light sockets will be placed at waist level to avoid difficulties in mobility, or the space beneath a sink will be designed to accommodate a wheel chair.

4. Sheltered housing offers those elderly who feel themselves to be vulnerable, or are so perceived by others, a chance to maintain independent status with some external supervision. Typically, sheltered housing will consist of apartment-type accommodations, usually with intercoms, that are compacted together within a single building. There will be an administrator who lives in the building, and who has access to a general communications board with lights and buzzers.

5. This may be changing, at least in Columbia, where out of 26,473 jobs, 10,109 are in the industrial sector with 4,100 more in construction.

6. As of March, 1979, there were three apartment complexes at Columbia, Maryland, subsidized by the state of Maryland using Section 8 funds. In a personal communication from Dr. Jay Sokolovsky, he indicated these three apartment complexes have varied facilities and do mix the elderly with other special need population segments. Rent is based on 25 percent of income, and a few tenants may also qualify for utility subsidies. According to his conversation with the manager of one complex, Dr. Sokolovsky was told that many of the older people have moved to Columbia to be near relatives. "The place I visited is especially attractive and right off a main business area-village center. As in England, a problem exists in transport beyond the area, but it seems the residents are forming voluntary associations to deal with this" (personal correspondence from Dr. Jay Sokolovsky, August 29, 1980).

Maria Vesperi

THE RELUCTANT CONSUMER: NURSING HOME RESIDENTS IN THE POST-BERGMAN ERA

Horror stories of physical abuse, starvation, and improper medical care typify our image of American nursing homes. Why? we ask. Anthropologist Maria Vesperi goes to the root of this question. Using her work role as a nurse's aid in a nursing home she presents the insider's view from the perspectives of both the "victimized" elderly and the underpaid, disillusioned staff. In a series of case studies Vesperi illustrates the pervasive system of infantilization, depersonalization, and dehumanization that residents encounter. Here we see in action the type of double bind Teski described in the first article of this book. Society segregates these people due to the "symptoms" of old age, yet once they are in the isolated environment, any attempt to call attention to these symptoms leads to ridicule, abuse, or forced isolation. The only means of protest left to the residents are purposeful incontinence and self-starvation, conditions that serve only to increase the hostility of nursing home personnel.

A misguided welfare system, greedy proprietors, and the breakdown of the extended family are usually suggested as the true impediments to humane care. But Vesperi questions whether nursing home atrocities are simply a matter of failing to get what we pay for. Rather, she maintains that it is our cultural concept of old age and its paradoxical link to a notion of cure that shapes the quality of institutionalized care.

"I feel guilty about lying to the patients, but what can you do? For example, that Mrs. D put up quite a fuss the first night. Said she wanted to go home, wouldn't stay another minute. So we told her: 'Look here, you've already engaged the room for the night. You might as well stay and then we'll call a cab for you in the morning.'

"'You mean I've already paid for it? Then I'll stay right here.'

"Of course [with a chuckle], she was determined to get her money's worth. That kind of reasoning usually calms them right down. And the next morning, well . . . that's Margo's [the head nurse] problem!"

— *Nurse's aide, night shift, Martindale Nursing Home[1]*

IN RECENT YEARS, MUCH attention has been focused upon fraudulent business practices and their effect on the delivery of services in private institutions for the elderly. Repeatedly, the news media have been filled with the works of those anxious to contribute to our most recent ongoing documentation of atrocity. Unfortunately, what satisfies the need of a newly awakened public for comprehension and analysis must appear to the nursing home resident as merely so much flagellation of the conscience. Thus far, most arguments pro and con have been directed toward the middle generation as taxpayers ("Just see what has happened to Medicaid!"), or as child-parents responsible for the care of their parent-children ("Could this be your mother, father, or great-uncle Herman?!").

Yet the most compelling atrocity remains that which is told from the perspective of the victim;

Revised slightly from an article in *Practicing Anthropology*, 3:1:23–24, 70–78, 1980. Reprinted by permission.

without this perspective, injustice cannot be held in context. Abstract horror, in any genre, exists only to titillate an audience. In our fascination with primal cause and effect, we smugly identify the source of the problem—an unfeeling welfare system, the breakdown of the extended family unit, the money-mongering proprietors of old folks' homes. Thus the nursing home "scandal" becomes just another aspect of consumer advocacy. The services have been defined, and we are determined to see them faithfully executed on the bodies and minds of our elderly population. One rarely encounters an attempt to reappraise these services themselves. Our pronouncements about what the aging individual needs and wants are predicated upon an unquestioned conceptualization of what old age *is*.

BACKGROUND

In an attempt to uncover this conceptualization and its effect upon nursing home residents, I obtained employment as a nurse's aide in two institutions for the elderly. The following material is drawn from the Martindale Nursing Home, where I worked 32 hours weekly for a period of eight weeks. Martindale is a conventional private nursing facility, designed to accommodate 50 patients and employing over 30 staff members. Located in a small rural Massachusetts community, Martindale is not associated with a nursing home chain or other business conglomerate. Here violations are of the most shop-worn, petty type—occasional skimpy suppers, night shift aides "ghosting" for the required LPN, and (I suspect) a tendency to look the other way while local doctors collect pocket money from Medicaid. Bathroom facilities are inadequate, but otherwise the living areas are clean, well lighted, and not particularly overcrowded. Planned recreational activities for the ambulatory are vapid but numerous. The casual investigator will find little of the physical neglect or flagrant health code violations so evident in many similar institutions.

Yet a comparative survey would find Martindale residents no more satisfied than those unfortunate inhabitants of Bernard Bergman's now spectral Manhattan "Towers."[2] While the public may rest content with surface legislation or the prosecution of a few profiteers, the subtle, complex problems faced by institutionalized elderly have remained essentially untouched. The brief case studies presented below may provide an introduction to the underlying issues involved.

THE RESIDENTS

Mrs. O'Rourke: Age 89

Mrs. O'Rourke provided a dramatic example of the rapid estrangement from self which often occurs upon admission to a nursing home. As one veteran staff member commented, "They either go under in the first week or they hang on the same forever." Mrs. O'Rourke was one of those who "went under," both physically and emotionally, within the first few days of her stay at Martindale. Her admission was characterized by the usual degree of ambivalence on the part of her family. They felt guilty about placing her in an institution, and yet they could no longer provide the constant supervision necessary to prevent her from wandering into the street and falling down stairs. On arrival, Mrs. O'Rourke was responsive and alert, ate well, and was fully continent. Her only "difficulty" was a tendency to wander outside or from room to room, which she managed with some speed despite her severely deformed feet and advanced curvature of the spine. The family placed her at Martindale with the expectation that her promenades would be supervised, and that she would be living in a safe environment where accidental injury would be less likely to occur.

Unfortunately, Mrs. O'Rourke's seemingly innocuous behavior proved to be the least tolerated of all patient activities at Martindale. When the nurses discovered that she could not be relied upon to "stay put" in her allotted chair hour after hour, day after day (as most of the first-floor residents were expected to do), she was placed on a strong dose of sedatives. This was done without her knowledge or consent. The woman was given no official indication, then or ever, of this change in her regimen. The first time I saw her after the medication had been ordered, she muttered dazedly: "I don't know what happened . . . . I've never felt like this before . . . ."

Sedation did not curb Mrs. O'Rourke's desire to explore, but it did make her even less steady on her feet and more inclined to injury. Since patient accidents and the accompanying implication of negligence are among the greatest fears of nursing home administrators, a Posey Belt was ordered for Mrs. O'Rourke. (For those unfamiliar with the term, "Posey Belt" is the euphemistic brand name for a peculiar type of physical restraint. It looks something like a thin cotton vest worn backwards, with long end-straps that can be wrapped around a chair and secured behind to restrain the patient in an upright, sitting position.) These devices were used daily on seven of the 50 patients at Martindale.

Within a week of her arrival at the home, Mrs. O'Rourke was under 24-hour sedation and daily physical restraint. She was soon to be confined in bed also, when it was discovered that she enjoyed rummaging through bureau drawers at night. The drastic personality changes and "real" behavioral disturbances which followed can be directly attributed to the staff-imposed conditions described above. Formerly in full control of her bowel and bladder functions, Mrs. O'Rourke immediately became incontinent. The symbolic implications of incontinence are discussed below; it is sufficient to remark here that this behavior had a direct physical motivation as well. Restrained and/or bedridden residents were dependent upon the aides to provide bedpans or escort them to the toilet. In Mrs. O'Rourke's case, she was untied from bed at 7:00 A.M. and immediately restrained in a chair. To remain continent, she would have been obliged to wait through breakfast and the employees' first coffee break— until at least 9:30 or 10:00—before it would be "her turn" to get dressed and use the bathroom.

During this time, Mrs. O'Rourke's relations with her two roommates became increasingly strained. She had been placed in a room with two fully mobile younger women, not unreasonable considering her original state of mental and physical well-being. These women seemed threatened and somewhat frightened by her rapid and unexpected decline, and they soon began to express resentment at sharing a room with an incontinent patient. Realizing that they could

exercise no control over room assignments and that a deaf ear would be turned to any request for a change, they began to vent their anger and resentment upon Mrs. O'Rourke herself. They first tried to ignore her attempts at communication—one woman would turn off her hearing aid and close her eyes while the other sat staring out the window with her back to the room. When this proved ineffective, they turned to ridicule and threats of abuse. One of them was eventually apprehended in the act of slapping the unfortunate Mrs. O'Rourke. Their comments reinforced the staff's belief in sedation and restraint as effective, legitimate means of patient management: "I think she needs another pill." "Sue (an LPN) *really* knows how to tie her down!" "Can't you give her something to shut her up?"

Mrs. O'Rourke responded to this treatment in a number of ways. A small person with exceptionally strong and nimble fingers, she often managed to wriggle out of her bonds and then her clothes as well. She would prance around the room naked, infuriating her roommates and causing embarrassment for the nurses whenever visitors were present. If she could not get loose, she would spread her legs and pose in attitudes regarded as obscene by the others. She also began to swear vociferously, to point threateningly at people, and to make faces. When she managed to slip out of bed at night she would go through the other women's bureau drawers, scattering clothes and shrieking at the top of her lungs.

To an outsider coming in at this point and attempting to evaluate the course of Mrs. O'Rourke's treatment, sedation and physical restraint might not seem unreasonable in light of her actual behavior. However, such an observer could not know that these disturbances appeared *after the fact*, as the *result* and not as the cause of treatment. To one who had known Mrs. O'Rourke from the date of admission, her behavior seemed a tragic but completely logical choice drawn from a highly circumscribed range of expression. The nurses could not prevent her from cursing and shrieking, nor could they stop her from urinating in her chair or on the floor. On the other hand, they could not really force her to eat, and she ultimately proceeded to the hunger strike as the last possibility for active protest available to individuals in her situation (see below). Thus Mrs. O'Rourke was caught in an inexorable web of action and counteraction. While her "treatment" had provided the initial stimulus for deviant behavior, this behavior only served to justify continued restraint and sedation in the eyes of the doctor, the Martindale staff, and her equally unfortunate roommates.

Jennie Farlo: Age 87

Until the accident which brought her to Martindale, Jennie Farlo had lived the dream of many less fortunate elderly people—a fully independent life. She had maintained her own seven-room home, kept her personal affairs in order, and enjoyed the company of numerous friends and neighbors. "I even mowed my lawn," she told me with pride. In January, 1974, Jennie lost her footing on the cellar stairs; she sustained a broken shoulder and a severe blow to her self-confidence. She went directly to Martindale upon release from the hospital, and had been in residence there for about six months when I arrived.

Jennie's dilemma was a common one among older people who live alone. Although she enjoyed good health and was eager to resume normal activities, the slow-mending injury to her right arm hampered her mobility with regard to basic self-care tasks. She could no longer get dressed, comb her hair, climb safely in and out of the tub, or prepare a hot meal. Like many independent people with temporary physical impairments, Jennie preferred a short period of "convalescence" in a nursing home to the real or imagined prospect of "putting a burden on anybody." She displayed an innocent faith in the belief that the goal of convalescence was recovery, and that the nurses would relate with professional pride to indications of permanent improvement.

My initial contacts with Jennie were highly encouraging: She was the *only* resident at Martindale who voluntarily articulated a plan for the future that seemed within the range of her personal and financial limitations. She assured me that her stay at the home was temporary—"Until this damn arm is better." She then proceeded to outline a full course of action: the selling of her old house, distribution of excess furniture, searching for a suitable apartment, and a gradual resumption of the exchange of services with friends and neighbors that had enabled her to

remain independent in the past. "I do for them, they do for me." The maintenance of reciprocal relations was a core concept in Jennie's attempt to repudiate the institutional structuring of experience among the elderly.

Sharing fully in Jennie's enthusiasm, I was led to remark upon her progress during a conversation with other staff members. My comments were met with mild derision, followed by an outpouring of resentment about Jennie's independent attitude, her "meddling" with the other patients, and her frequent absences from the premises. I was told that "a lot of these old people" had "ideas" about going home. They would leave all right, the staff assured me, but only in a box.

While Jennie expressed complete confidence in the intentions and ability of the nurses, their underlying assumptions about her limited potential as an old person were communicated in several ways. The doctor had prescribed physical therapy for her shoulder. Whatever he had intended, the net result was an occasional halfhearted attempt on the part of an LPN to manipulate her arm. This was augmented by frequent, patronizing admonitions to "Do your exercises, Jennie." The impact of this paradoxical message left Jennie in a peculiar position. On the one hand, the staff was clearly communicating that her therapy was not to be taken seriously, that positive results were unlikely, and that such an old woman should learn to accept her limitations rather than wasting the time and energy of staff members in pursuit of a futile endeavor. On the other hand, since she was admonished arbitrarily whether she completed the exercises or not, the assumption projected was that she was "lazy," that she "didn't really *want* to go home," and that she secretly enjoyed her position of dependence. Neither message was an accurate response to Jennie's attitude or to problems that might interfere with her treatment. Yet these assumptions were in congruence with the institutional conceptualization of old age, within which elderly people command no potential for future development.

The evident discrepancy between Jennie's stated intentions and her actual behavior with regard to therapy must be viewed as a parallel response to the situation outlined above. Her primary concern was with the implications of passive dependency associated with old age. She seized any opportunity to leave the premises with friends. These excursions symbolized her ability to maintain independent contact with the outside world, while the enthusiasm of her many companions reaffirmed her self-worth in the face of the assumption that she was simply "too old" to merit serious therapy. Within the nursing home she displayed a rare interest and concern for other residents—visiting them in their rooms, sympathizing with their misfortunes, and serving as general confidante. This strategy enabled her to maintain herself as a temporary visitor, distinct from the other "patients." She could make symbolic statements about her own "health" by demonstrating that she was not threatened by her association with the others, for whom she had energy and concern to spare.

In short, Jennie pursued every available activity energetically—except the exercises that were necessary for the full rehabilitation of her arm. One might expect her to respond to the nurses' perfunctory admonishments with indignation and an increased demonstration of diligence, but instead she just smiled sheepishly and attempted to change the subject. All around her, "old" men and women younger than herself were languishing on their beds, and she knew that for them "medical attention" meant no more than custodial care. She accepted this with equanimity; after all, what more could be done for a person who had given up hope and clearly expressed a will to die? Thus she did not deny the institutional conceptualization as a working hypothesis for the staff; she felt that it was based on experience. In her own case, she believed the nurses "kept after her for her own good"; they "knew" old people and were merely trying to prevent her from following in the footsteps of countless others.

Thus Jennie was confronted with a need to renounce the nursing home image and to embrace it at the same time—demonstrating to others that she was still a whole, autonomous person while admitting with a sheepish grin that she was in danger of lapsing into dependency and defeat. Jennie's freedom from debilitating disease and her strong outside friendships enabled her to maintain the first aspect of this double identification, although not without its own set of internal contradictions. The second aspect, however, was much more problematical. Not only did Jennie

confirm staff expectations with vacant smiles and evasive answers, she also began to replicate unknowingly the conditions that had led to hopelessness for so many before her. She knew the nurses' verdict for those "complainers" who worried about their bodies all day; they were guilty of old age and could expect a life sentence at Martindale. It was easier for Jennie to "forget about" doing her exercises in the excitement of preparing for an outing with friends. Thus she began to close the door on her only avenue of escape—without continuous therapy she would never regain sufficient strength in her arm and shoulder.

When I said goodbye to Jennie at the end of my stay, she invited me to visit her "at home." I returned a full year later, to find that she still occupied a room at Martindale.

Daren Gilroy: Age 79

In recent years, state governments have been concerned with the phasing out of "custodial care" facilities, particularly in the areas of juvenile correction and mental health. Conscious of rehabilitation statistics and the actual or threatened dismantling of several such institutions, administrators must continue to proclaim that their goal is to return inmates and patients to the community. By a quick twist of logic, the blame for institutional inadequacy is often shifted onto residents themselves. If only we could make "other arrangements" for past failures, the chronic offenders and the "hopeless" mental patients who do not respond to treatment, we could then proceed to the "real" work—curing the ready and willing of their social afflictions. The individual designated "custodial" becomes a young psychiatric patient grown old. As a result, private nursing homes have contracted with the state to provide care for an increasing number of psychiatric hospital residents.[3]

Of the 50 people living at Martindale during the period of my employment, five were former residents of state mental hospitals, five were classified as retarded, and a number of others had been placed there by the Veterans' Administration. (The majority of the latter were diagnosed as suffering from Korsakoff's Syndrome.)[4] While these classifications may appear fortuitous, they are often rigidly maintained within nursing homes. Labels such as mental patient, brain-damaged alcoholic, and retarded are prominent in determining the quality of interaction between residents and staff, and also among the residents themselves.

The former psychiatric patients at Martindale were not characterized by an unusual degree of evident motor disturbances. All resided on the second floor, an area reserved for self-care patients who were believed to require a minimum of supervision. Two of the five were extremely withdrawn, appeared to be absorbed in internal monologue, and rarely initiated conversation with others. The third, Daren Gilroy, provided a tragic illustration of the consequences of "benign neglect" as it was practiced within the nursing home situation. Daren seemed desperately aware of his condition, and made frequent attempts to overcome the barrier between himself and those around him. These efforts were often frustrated by his extremely rapid and garbled speech pattern, which combined with an unusually thick Irish brogue to render his conversation quite difficult to grasp. Needless to say, the staff made no effort to decipher his speech. They referred often to his "diagnosis" (schizophrenic reaction), accused him of "always hallucinating," and generally left him to his own devices.

Like many other residents at Martindale, Daren found his frustration turning gradually to self-hatred and self-destructiveness. A proud man who was constantly humiliated by his own limitations, he began to experience a difficulty in urination control not uncommon among men of his age group. He was obviously embarrassed by the evidence of his spotted pants, and tried to conceal this as much as possible. Still unsatisfied, he tied a string tightly around his penis in a last desperate attempt to prevent further accidents. It is not known how long he continued this painful practice, but by the time it was discovered he was suffering intensely and had caused himself irreparable physical damage.

Marcella Darlon: Age 96

For this I must return to my first two days at Martindale, which were spent familiarizing myself with institutional organization and the tasks I would be expected to perform. I followed other employees around, asking questions and providing assistance when required. On the third day I was given my first independent assignment: to

wash, dress, and otherwise care for the institution's oldest resident. I approached her bed with trepidation. What should I say? How should I proceed? How could I make these tasks less depersonalizing, less coercive than what I had observed? I introduced myself hesitantly, explaining that I was new and unfamiliar with the established routine. Marcella remained in the same position, her eyes averted and her body rigid. A small-boned, emaciated woman, she could not have weighed more than 75–80 pounds. Every tendon was visible in the slightest movement of arm or head. Once full breasts lay flat against the clear outline of her ribcage. The fingers of both hands, severely crippled by arthritis, were frozen in odd attitudes. As I continued, consulting her about procedure and asking her preferences, she gradually began to respond. I concluded sadly that she was surprised by my attitude—it had been a long time since she was consulted about what nightgown she wanted to wear or whether she preferred to sit up or to remain in bed.

As my contacts with Marcella became more frequent, I realized that she suffered from the effects of a common staff misinterpretation. She seemed preoccupied with the past, and often returned to a time when her own mother was ill and dependent upon her for care. "When can I go home? I have to go! I have a sick mother at home . . . she must be worried. She doesn't even know where I am! Will you call her for me and tell her that I'm here?" This train of thought, combined with the fact that Marcella's soft voice demanded strict attention to every word, led the staff to conclude that she was "senile" and hopelessly confused. Thus it was taken for granted that she was unaware of her surroundings and consequently insensitive to slights and open ridicule (of which she received her full share). Verbal abuse was not considered cruel—after all, "she didn't even know the difference."

Unfortunately, nothing could be further from the truth. Marcella *was* trapped between two conflicting interpretations of reality, but to choose one over the other simply generated a new set of contradictions. The juxtaposition of past and present called forth unbearable guilt and anxiety; she had abandoned "a sick mother" to become a patient herself. Yet to wrench free of the past and confront the present alone was even more disorienting, for within the reality of institutional routine she was no longer considered a person. Our discussion of unpleasant incidents (which she remembered all too well) often ended with a question: "What have I done? I've been good, I know I have. Why don't they like me?" Unable to make sense of the institutional conceptualization of old age and its relation to her established sense of self, she would return again to the safety of past identity. However, such retreats invariably served to reinforce the diagnosis of "senility" and render the emotional deprivation of the present even more untenable. Unable to walk or to use her hands, too weak and discouraged to lash out or even hold her own in a verbal battle, Marcella could command few outlets for her anger and frustration. She referred to herself unhappily as "a very old woman," but did not articulate a desire for death. It was some time before I realized that this issue had already been resolved.

Marcella had eaten almost nothing during the three months prior to my arrival. Staff members found this behavior uncharacteristic, as she had apparently maintained a good appetite before. Since Marcella could not take her meals without assistance, I had ample opportunity to observe her at mealtime. I tried to determine her favorite foods, with the intention of bringing a few things from home. My efforts were met with an evasive smile. It eventually became clear that Marcella's behavior was unrelated to the quality of food itself, for she had determined to die by starvation.

As the weeks passed, Marcella became increasingly weak and debilitated. After meals, her tray would be returned to the kitchen almost untouched. The first round of disinterested speculation began—how long would she last? While aides dutifully continued to record her food intake on their charts, starvation was never mentioned as a possible factor contributing to her decline. She was "just too old." "It's better this way." Never was she credited with the conscious decision to hasten her own death.

One day, I arrived at Martindale to find Marcella's bed empty. Her meager belongings were packed neatly in plastic bags, awaiting removal by the relatives who "never seemed to visit anymore." Staff members breathed a sigh of relief, hoping that her successor would be a little more self-sufficient. The plastic bags remained for some time—sterile, impersonal symbols of a sterile, impersonal death.

Mr. Newberry: Age 84

Mr. Newberry fell down in his room during the staff's extended morning coffee break. The aides assigned to his section rushed to see what had happened; the rest remained peacefully munching their toast. Mr. Newberry was helped into bed and examined by a practical nurse, but his demands for immediate medical attention were ignored. The coffee break continued, now enlivened by sarcastic imitations of the patient and his complaints. A quiet and unassuming man, he was immediately classified as a "complainer," a "baby," a "hypochondriac." When Mr. Newberry still refused to quiet down after an hour and a half had elapsed, the doctor was grudgingly contacted. The physician ordered an amulbance immediately; it was soon discovered that Mr. Newberry had suffered a broken hip and would require extended hospitalization.

SELF-ORIENTATION WITHIN THE NURSING HOME CONTEXT

In each case outlined above, specific aspects of policy and procedure at Martindale can be linked directly to the physical and emotional decline of its residents. Yet these accounts contain no concrete evidence upon which legal action against the home could be based. For instance, nursing home personnel would be puzzled by a request that they discuss with patients the effects of depressants and other awareness-altering drugs. They would no sooner seek informed consent from a "senile" old woman than from a two-year-old child. (As is the case with children, family members and attending physicians are entrusted with such decisions.) Distressing as it may seem, the administrative staff at Martindale expressed confidence in the belief that it had provided a reasonably viable environmental and social setting for its resident population. Policy is directly informed by the definition of what an old person is, wants, and needs as constructed within the framework of an institutional setting. Yet staff members do not rely upon a formally articulated definition of aging to provide guidelines for appropriate action. The institutional image of the resident does not emerge whole but remains in its refracted state—each part linked to the proper custodial or supervisory task. Thus residents often find that aspects of their self-image have lost significance for others, or that they have become enmeshed in the contradictions generated by the superimposition of new needs and motivations.

For example, Mr. Newberry's experience provides a dramatic illustration of a demoralizing dilemma which confronts all nursing home residents—the drastic curtailment of physical self-determination. In many cases, the aging men or women who voluntarily enter a home have recently attempted to come to grips with the discrepancy between their established sense of well-being and the effects of a debilitating injury or illness. They may feel "just a little too tired" to get out of bed; others conclude that they are old, sick, and incapable of continuing full independent activity. Once the possibility of "old age" has been introduced, the individual may act upon its implications in an attempt to demonstrate a capacity for continued adult decision making. Thus the resolution to enter a nursing home becomes the "sensible" thing to do. Recognizing a need for regular medical care, such individuals feel that they have further secured the privilege of access already granted to them as adults capable of self-diagnosis.

Once inside the institution, however, such concepts take on a new meaning. The "sicknesses" associated with "age" are not regarded as curable or worthy of intensive treatment by nursing home personnel. Outside, the individual was advised to seek treatment for the symptoms of old age. Inside, he or she is ridiculed for calling attention to these same symptoms. Instead of an adult capable of knowing when treatment is needed, the person becomes a "complainer" or "hypochondriac" who would probably medicate himself to death if the nurses paid any attention. Thus the nursing home situation often provides no greater access to the physician or to hospital care. In fact, as Mr. Newberry discovered, this access may actually be delayed. Unlike the average person, who is free to decide when

specialized medical attention is needed, the nursing home resident must battle an intermediary staff member for the privilege. She alone is authorized to distinguish between "real" sickness and "complaining." She may frequently be inclined to ignore the resident's request altogether or to substitute a placebo, "ordered" by a physician who has never actually been contacted.

At Martindale, the living room is always crowded and one can never be assured of a seat on the front porch. But what appears to be congregation is, in actuality, only concentration. Ten people sit motionless before the television for hours without exchanging a word, except perhaps to bicker over station selection. Lasting friendships are few. Residents rarely address each other by name—many are unable to identify their own roommates when asked. Sharing and exchange of personal services are very rare. Accidental clothing mixups are simultaneously interpreted as "theft" by both parties. Unequal distribution of small favors by an administrator or recreation director occasions jealousy and fighting.

Many nursing home residents see themselves as unfortunate but still autonomous individuals accidentally juxtaposed. Each sees justification for ill treatment in the behavior of others ("Can't you give her something to shut her up?"), but few realize that they are subjected to the same a priori attitudes and assumptions, the same institutional conceptualization of old age, which governs the relations among their neighbors. By the same token, only those who arrive at Martindale equipped with the knowledge gleaned from former institutional experience can perceive the staff as "employees," subject to the unique dictates of their own work situation. Thus every manifestation of oppression becomes particularized, internalized, or both: Nurse A is "just a bitch," nurse B "doesn't like me," nurse C "picks on me for my own good." The frequent occurrence of unpleasant incidents keep most Martindale residents in a state of protective isolation. Any possibility for collective response to institutional injustice is precluded.

Yet from within their carefully guarded stronghold of autonomy, residents sense that they have somehow been "misunderstood." Drawing upon a long lifetime of experience, the individual has grown confident in the ability to predict the range of response which his or her presence will evoke in others. In a nursing home situation, however, the basis for such prediction is radically removed. Staff members respond to an impersonal, stereotyped image of old age which need not articulate with individual demeanor at all. Martindale residents vary greatly in their comprehension of this situation. Some, like Mrs. O'Rourke, are hopelessly sedated before they can achieve full awareness of their surroundings. Others, demoralized by the abrupt separation from home, conclude that they really *have* changed for the worse—how else could they lose their grip on family and friends and be reduced to institutional living?

However he or she has come to assess the hows and whys of staff-patient "misunderstandings," each resident is confronted with the desire to *act* upon felt injustices. Slights, ridicule, false assumptions (shouting in the ear of a "deaf" man who is in perfect command of his hearing)—every incident leaves the resident burning with indignation. According to the institutional conceptualization of old age at Martindale, the elderly man or woman is presumed to be suffering from a severe perceptual handicap: deaf to insults, dumb with regard to the accurate communication of needs and emotions, and blind to cracks in the thin veneer of concern which covers the daily routine. Withdrawal from adult activity is considered a normal adjustment. Thus any active response to conditions, such as running away, physical violence, or verbal retaliation, is judged inappropriate or deviant and "treated" accordingly with drugs and/or physical restraint. Accepted as problems but not as protests, such actions are ineffective for residents' purposes. What remains is the possibility to attack the institution and its employees at their most vulnerable point—their collective identity as a medical facility administered and staffed by professionals.

CONTRADICTIONS INHERENT IN THE NOTION OF CURE

When employed outside of the usual hospital context, the term *patient* often indicates a relationship of dependency and helplessness. For the ambulatory person who is motivated to enter Martindale because of loneliness, temporary physical impairment, or a desire to avoid "burdening" relatives, the term evokes resentment and a gradual erosion of self-confidence. Thinking of themselves as patients removes the locus of decision making and places it beyond their control, for the implication becomes inevitability rather than choice. This is particularly tragic with regard to the older person who has arrived for purposes of "convalescence" after an operation or injury. Such people find identification as patients hard to reconcile with their former life styles, particularly when the patient role is not substantiated by anything which resembles *treatment*. Every employee wears white, but few do more for the resident than change beds or deliver admonishments. Only the most debilitated receive actual "medical" care; the bulk of the nursing is done by untrained aides who are no more qualified to clothe, bathe, or supervise the residents than their own families. An ambulatory person such as Jennie Farlo, who strives to appear as "healthy" and as "busy" as possible, poses a serious threat to the professional identity of staff members. By demonstrating that there is nothing the staff can do for them, these "patients" bring forth an uncomfortable reminder of the custodial duties performed by nursing home employees.

SYMBOLIC PROTEST

For the person who *does* suffer from a severely debilitating disease, the concept of passive helplessness and dependency provides a framework for depersonalization and withdrawal. Here the most frequent response is to become incontinent—a problem which is often misinterpreted when it occurs among older people. The immediate assumption in such a case is that the person has simply lost control over basic functions. This has not been borne out by my observations; in fact, even those individuals who appear to be least in contact with their surroundings manifest frequent awareness of incontinence.

For the debilitated, restrained, and/or sedated person, incontinence provides one of the few remaining possibilities for protest. Its most immediate effect is a significant workload increase for unpopular employees. Yet staff anger does not stem entirely from the work increase, or from the knowledge that they are being manipulated by residents. More significantly, incontinence provides a powerful symbolic negation of the aide's professional self-image. Making beds and dressing or feeding patients remain within the domain of "nurselike" responsibility; this is further fortified by strict refinement of procedure and adherence to routine. With regard to the institutional hierarchy, however, incontinence emerges as the dividing line between nurse and custodian. Passing through a room, a supervisor admonishes the appropriate aide: "He's wet!" The patient stares innocently into space, the administrator continues her tour—the only one obliged to further identify with the spreading puddle of urine is the aide herself. Such incidents often lead to expression of bitter resentment over the nature of the work required. Incontinence serves as the most frequent catalyst for job reassessment, after which staff members are left severely demoralized and convinced that they are engaged in a futile, thankless enterprise.

While incontinent behavior affords one of the few effective means by which the institutional conceptualization of old age can be turned back upon its perpetuators, the incontinent resident is ultimately caught in what Gregory Bateson (1972) has referred to as the double bind. For the person who has completely incorporated the notions of passivity, physical worthlessness, and denial of intellectual capability set forward by the nursing home, incontinence becomes a logically justifiable activity. Yet while incontinence "makes sense" when one perceives him/herself as passive-dependent, the individual must also struggle with the usual self-consciousness and shame experienced by any adult who has failed to reach the bathroom in time. This conflict is replicated also in the attitudes of staff members, who expect incontinence from "old people" and yet continue to express disgust when confronted with an "adult" who consistently wets the bed.

Failure to eat constitutes the other form of symbolic protest that must be mentioned in this context. Although few residents carry this to the conclusion achieved by Marcella Darlon—actually starving themselves to death—many engage in some form of food-related protest. While the food at Martindale is both nutritionally sound and prepared under sanitary conditions (no small consideration in relation to the flagrant health code violations practiced elsewhere), evidence of institutional presupposition emerges in the planning of the daily menu. Meals are monotonous; the same dishes are served frequently and with little attention to variation. For most residents, dinner is a disheartening affair. There is no communal dining room; the self-contained meal, served at bedside, symbolizes the profound isolation of institutional living and evokes sharp contrast to the past—when meals were shared with friends, relatives, and co-workers. This is particularly true for the women, most of whom continue to speak of their own cooking with great pride. "We always ate so well at home." "This would never find its way to my table." "If only I could get my own meals. . . ." Each meal brings residents fresh reminders that they are no longer considered capable of providing for themselves.

On the most rudimentary level, any functional self-definition of a nursing home must include the provision of basic life support for those unable to live alone. Thus many residents feel that they cannot accept even the most essential services without both admitting their own dependency and offering passive approval to the institutional status quo. To accept food would imply acquiescence to institutional authority and acceptance of the nursing home's assessment of individual needs. To seek the companionship of others at mealtime would indicate a recognition of collective status and shared ontology. As I have suggested, such recognition is very difficult for residents to achieve. The only alternative is to reject food altogether, thus negating both one's own dependency and the institution's ability to adequately perceive and fulfill one's needs.

The symbolic effectiveness of food refusal is parallel to that observed in cases of incontinence. The untrained employee arrives at Martindale with "medical" expectations about the nature of the work to be performed. Until the recent intensification of media coverage, the *nursing* home (as distinct from the "rest" or "retirement" home) was perceived by the community as a legitimate medical facility. This expectation is immediately contradicted by the institutional conceptualization of "old age diseases." As illustrated in the case of Jennie Farlo, recovery does not emerge as a reasonable or viable goal. Thus staff members do not perceive patient disabilities as professionally challenging; they consider rehabilitative efforts to be unrewarding and pointless. While the practical nurse may garner some professional satisfaction from administering injections, dispensing medicine, and other technical responsibilities, the aide finds it least problematic to concentrate upon her "nurturant" function. This articulates well with the conceptualization of the old person as childlike, dependent, and intellectually deficient or "senile." If the patient cannot be expected to "recover" from old age, he/she can at least be provided with the basic necessities of life—thus substituting a "humanitarian" motive for a frustrated curative one. By refusing to accept food, the resident undermines this last stronghold of paramedical identity. When the validity of the aide's most basic task is no longer acknowledged, she is forced to confront the full implications of her situation.

THE STAFF

The aide in an average nursing home is notoriously underpaid, enjoys few fringe benefits, and commands virtually no possibilities for advancement. Those who regard Medicaid fraud as the primary factor in the nursing home issue may attribute poor staff-patient relations to economic dissatisfaction. It might be assumed that simply forcing avaricious proprietors to provide more work incentives will cause the vicious circle of humiliation and counter-humiliation to magically disappear. Yet most permanent employees at Martindale frame job expectation and demand within an economic framework of traditional marriage. Older staff members regard their husbands as the primary wage earners; they seek money for a child's college expenses or to provide "a few extras" at home. Young employees see their work situation as temporary; they are saving for a house, or to start a family. Most look forward impatiently to the day when they will be fully supported by their husbands.

Thus while most employees agree, when

questioned, that wages at Martindale are "pretty low," this issue is not openly cited in their discussions of working conditions. Group insurance plans have been proposed, not once but many times, and these have been consistently rejected by employees. "I might as well stay on my husband's insurance." "I'm already covered." "As long as he's working. . . ." The sample attitude extends to the absence of other benefits, such as advancement and seniority. Any provision for the future, any attempt to achieve job security, is perceived as infringement upon a male domain. Among Martindale employees, a woman's economic activity is restricted to the specific. The worker who values her job for its long-term, generalized subsistence value can only undermine her husband's position as locus of financial responsibility.

Caught between their emergent identity as workers and their adherence to traditional female roles, staff members seek to transform the exchange value of their labor into a potential for economically desituated, "humanitarian" social action. Most employment opportunities open to the unskilled female worker disclose the unadorned exchange of time for money. Yet there remains a residual category of "service" jobs (including nurse's aide, teacher's aide, and companion) which afford an approximation of the volunteer ethic. The nursing home employee ministers to the sick, thus asserting the self while remaining within an established nurturant role. Of course she gets paid, but not much. The community must regard her work as socially useful; she becomes virtuous in the wake of another's inadequacy. As one Martindale aide remarked:

I can't stand people like Mrs. D's daughter. Always so suspicious and critical. "Why don't you do this for Mother and when can you see about that?" I'd like to see her in here changing the incontinent patients . . . . Families can just leave the old people and then go about their business, but somebody has to take care of them.

The newly recruited nurse's aide arrives at her post equipped with an untenable set of expectations. It is not surprising that her fragile optimism soon hardens into vindictive resentment or callous resignation. At Martindale, deterioration of morale takes place within the first few weeks. Unable to achieve an overview of their own exploitation within an employer-employee relationship, staff members trace their disappointment to the residents themselves. If they are bored, it is because they regard old people as inherently uninteresting. If they feel alienated, unfulfilled, and infinitely replaceable, it is because they see residents as "too senile" to appreciate the uniqueness of their individual contributions.

Just as residents particularize the conditions of their oppression by focusing upon one-to-one interactions with employees, so workers predicate the existence of unpleasant job requirements upon the bodies of residents themselves. Since work assignments rotate regularly and changes in the patient population are frequent, staff members are not inclined to make long-term assessments of working conditions. Each section of the home is evaluated according to the particular patient configuration of which it is comprised. Some days are judged "good," others "bad," depending upon the physical requirements of individuals. If Mr. B defecates three times in his chair and then proceeds to smear it all over himself and anyone who comes near, it is a "bad" day for the person assigned to his section. If Mrs. M is judged too sick to leave her bed, thus obviating the need to get her dressed, combed, and up in her chair, it is a "good" day for the aide responsible. Staff members wish wholeheartedly for the death of incontinent or otherwise troublesome residents. My fear that a woman left sleeping with her face buried in a pillow might suffocate was met with the straightforward reply: "What difference does it make? That much less for us to do."

CONCLUSION

In her well-documented analysis of fraudulent nursing home management, Mary Mendelson notes: "The nursing home as a money making enterprise is quite new in America. As recently as the 1930's there were only a handful of nursing homes in this country, and those were mostly of the mom-and-pop type that is now disappearing" (Mendelson, 1974). Previously, poorhouses,

prisons, and assorted denominational organizations had provided the last residence for elderly men and women who were both destitute and alone. Those with families could almost always rely on a place to sleep and a degree of material support, even when provided grudgingly. The rapid proliferation of nursing homes in recent years has often been associated with a perceived change in attitude toward the elderly. It has been said that we have lost respect, that our sense of filial responsibility has been diminished, and that we have substituted a frenzied youth worship for our traditional veneration of hoary wisdom and experience. Others indicate that modifications in the structure of the extended family have led to the severing of contacts between the elderly and their immediate relatives. Jules Henry's (1963) discussion of "dynamic obsolescence" suggests that our treatment of the elderly is symptomatic of a more widespread cultural malaise.

While the primacy of the nuclear family cannot be ignored, studies of inter-generational relations have indicated that the majority of older people can continue to rely on moral and/or material support from children, grandchildren, and siblings (Shanas, 1968, 1979a). Yet existing nursing homes are full to overflowing, and the "industry" has entered a period of rapid expansion. What about the growing number who cannot be explained away as homeless or without resources—those who enter private institutions voluntarily or are placed there by their families? Why have we become so willing to abandon our aging relatives to the care of others, when a few years ago such treatment was reserved for the disenfranchised?

Commitment to any institution places a particular set of demands upon the family as well as upon the individual directly involved. We provide a number of rationalizations for these situations—justifications which the family is induced to believe even if the treatment overshadows the cure. But the nursing home resident is not "sick enough" to be placed in a hospital, and not "disturbed enough" to require inpatient psychiatric care. But he or she is, in most cases, "old enough" to be retired from the work force, and to require a degree of personal assistance from other family members. American society has a solution for the dependent and unemployable. If they cannot produce they can at least consume, unknowingly in the case of a young child who does not discriminate between television advertising and the desire for yet another toy, and unwillingly in the case of the old person who is confined to an expensive private nursing home "for his own good."

While it might appear that this exploitative manipulation of the elderly would be recognized and resisted, *it is this very economic aspect* which serves to mediate the transfer of responsibility and allows the family to substitute others for its own presence. The town poorhouse and the exclusive home may be indistinguishable from the perspective of the patient—both constitute a complete separation from family, a drastic curtailment of freedom, and a deliverance into the hands of strangers whose attitude can be described as impersonal at best. What separates the "responsible" decision to place a relative in a nursing home from the admission of failure implicit in other forms of institutionalization is the distinction between public and private. The private nursing home demands an extended financial commitment: Thus the family feels that it has bought the right to an exclusive, personal-

ized service. The greater the cost, the more powerful is the symbolic expression of responsibility and concern. As mentioned above, this reasoning may extend to the man or woman who decides independently to enter a home. Successfully meeting the demands for payment can (initially) transform an admission of failure into a reaffirmation of the independent ability to secure services. In recent years, the families of those dependent upon Medicaid have also come to approach the nursing home with confidence; they somehow feel that the tone has been set and that the aura of "private" care will be extended equally to all residents.

Each time a new nursing home "scandal" is exposed, we stare at our emptying pockets in disbelief. All those tax and private dollars—perhaps we've left something else out? We love a Bernard Bergman; he brings us back to the comfortable equation of money and responsibility. Of course we've done right by our elderly. Just dispose of those cheaters who mismanage our funds, restore the services that have been contracted for, and everything will be just fine for Great-Uncle Herman. Or will it?

NOTES

1. All personal and place names have been altered to protect the anonymity of residents.

2. Bernard Bergman was a New York nursing home magnate who received much negative publicity during 1974–75 in connection with an establishment known as the "Manhattan Towers." Extensive media coverage of poor conditions and neglect led to a temporary upsurge of public concern with the quality of nursing homes. Unfortunately, opinion focused more on the tangible quality of physical facilities than on the quality of care and the underlying issue of institutionalization itself.

3. See also Eisdorfer and Stotsky (1977:735–40) for a discussion of institutionalization and the elderly psychiatric patient.

4. Korsakoff's Syndrome, also known as Korsakoff's psychosis, is a chronic organic brain syndrome linked to prolonged alcohol abuse. Symptoms include confusion, hallucination, and memory loss.

BIBLIOGRAPHY

Abarbanel, J. S. 1974. Prestige of the Aged and Their Control over Resources: A Cross-cultural Analysis. Paper presented at the annual meeting of the Gerontological Society, Portland.

Abrahams, R. G. 1978. "Aspects of Labwor age and generation grouping and related systems." Pp. 37–67 in P. T. W. Baxter and U. Almagor (eds.), Age, Generation and Time: Some Features of East African Age Organization. London: Hurst.

Abrams, P. 1970. "Rites de passage: The conflict of generations in industrial society." Journal of Contemporary History 5:175–90.

Acra Ne Feirme. 1973. Farm Inheritance and Succession. Dublin: Irish Farm Center.

Acsadi, G. and J. Nemeskeri. 1975. History of Human Life and Mortality. Budapest: Akademiai Kiado.

Adams, B. N. 1971. "Isolation, function and beyond: American kinship in the 1960's." Pp. 163–85 in C. B. Broderick (ed.), A Decade of Family Research and Action. Minneapolis, Minn.: National Council on Family Relations.

———. 1980. The Family: A Sociological Interpretation. Chicago, Ill.: Rand McNally.

Adams, D. L. 1971. "Correlates of satisfaction among the elderly." Gerontologist 11:64–68.

Adams, F. M. 1972. "The rule of old people in Santo Tomas, Mazaltepec." Pp. 103–27 in D. O. Cowgill and L. D. Holmes (eds.), Aging and Modernization. New York: Appleton-Century-Crofts.

Alba, R. 1976. "Social assimilation among American Catholic national origin groups." American Sociological Review 41: 1030–46.

Alberoni, F. 1971. "Classes and generations." Social Science Information 10: 41–67.

Alger, J. F. 1959. Activity Patterns and Attitudes toward Housing of Families in Specially Designed Apartments for Aged in Ten New York City Projects. Ithaca, N.Y.: Cornell University Housing Research Center.

Alston, J. P. and C. J. Dudley. 1973. "Age, occupation, and life satisfaction." Gerontologist 13:58–61.

American Samoa Health Coordinating Council. 1979. American Samoa Plan for Health, 1978–1983. Pago Pago, American Samoa: Government of American Samoa.

Amoss, P. 1981a. "Cultural centrality and prestige for the elderly: The Coast Salish case." Pp. 47–64 in C. Fry (ed.), Dimensions: Aging, Culture and Health. Brooklyn, N.Y.: J. F. Bergin.

———. 1981b. "Coast Salish elders." In P. Amoss and S. Harrell (eds.), Other Ways of Growing Old. Stanford, Calif.: Stanford University Press.

Amoss, P. and S. Harrell. 1981. Other Ways of Growing Old: Anthropological Perspectives. Stanford, Calif.: Stanford University Press.

Anderson, B. 1972. "The process of deculturation—its dynamics among United States aged." Anthropological Quarterly 45(4):209–16.

———. 1979. The Aging Game: Success, Sanity, and Sex after 60. New York: McGraw-Hill.

Angrosino, M. 1976. "Anthropology and the aged." Gerontologist 162:174–80.

Arensberg, C. (1937) 1968. The Irish Countryman. Garden City, N.Y.: Natural History Press.

Arensberg, C. and S. T. Kimball. (1940) 1968. Family and Community in Ireland. Cambridge, Mass.: Harvard University Press.

Arnhoff, F., H. Leon and I. Lorge. 1964. "Cross-cultural acceptance of stereotypes toward aging." Journal of Social Psychology 63:41–58.

Arth, M. 1968. "Ideals and behavior: A comment on Ibo respect patterns." Gerontologist 8:42–44.

———. 1972. "Aging: A cross-cultural perspective." Pp. 352–64 in D. Kent, R. Kastenbaum and S. Sherwood (eds.), Research Planning and Action for the Elderly. New York: Behavioral.

Asmarom, L. 1979. "Age sets and retirement communities." Pp. 61–69 in J. Keith (ed.), The Ethnography of Old Age. Special issue of Anthropological Quarterly 52 (1).

Atchley, R. C. 1971. "Disengagement among professors." Journal of Gerontology 26:476–80.

———. 1980. Social Forces in Later Life. Belmont, Calif.: Wadsworth.

Balikci, A. 1970. The Netsilik Eskimo. Garden City, N.Y.: Natural History Press.

Banfield, E. 1958. The Moral Basis of a Backward Society. Glencoe, Ill.: Free Press.

Barfield, R. E. and J. N. Morgan. 1970. Early Retirement: The

Decision and the Experience and a Second Look. Ann Arbor, Mich.: Institute for Social Research.

Barnes, J. A. 1954. "Class and committees in a Norwegian island parish." Human Relations 7:39–58.

———. 1972. "Social networks," Addison-Wesley Module in Anthropology, No. 26. Reading, Mass.: Addison-Wesley.

Bart, P. 1969. "Why women's status changes in middle age: The turn of the social ferris wheel." Sociological Symposium 3:1–18.

———. 1972. "Depression in middle aged women." In J. Bardwich (ed.), Readings on the Psychology of Women. New York: Harper & Row.

Barth, F. 1966. Models of Social Organization. London: Occasional Papers of the Royal Anthropological Institute of Great Britain and Ireland, No. 23.

——— (ed.). 1969. Ethnic Groups and Boundaries. Boston: Little, Brown.

Bateson, G. 1950. "Cultural ideas about aging." In E. P. Jones (ed.), Research on Aging. Berkeley: University of California Press.

———. 1956. "Toward a theory of schizophrenia." Behavioral Sciences 1:251–64.

———. 1958. "Language and psychotherapy—Frieda Fromm-Reichman's last project." Psychiatry 21:96–100.

———. 1972. Steps to an Ecology of Mind. New York: Ballantine Books.

Baxter, E. and K. Hopper. 1981. Private Lives/Public Space: Homeless Adults on the Streets of New York City. New York: Community Service Society.

Baxter, P. T. and U. Almagor (eds.). 1978. Age, Generation and Time. London: Hurst.

Beall, C. (ed.). 1982. Biocultural Perspectives on Aging. Special issue of Social Science and Medicine 16(2).

Beardsley, R. K., J. W. Hall and R. E. Ward. 1959. Village Japan. Chicago, Ill.: University of Chicago Press.

Beaubier, J. 1976. High Life Expectancy on the Island of Paros, Greece. New York: Philosophical Library.

———. 1980. "Biological factors in aging." Pp. 23–41 in C. Fry (ed.), Aging in Culture and Society. Brooklyn, N.Y.: J. F. Bergin.

Becker, G. 1980. Growing Old in Silence. Berkeley: University of California Press.

Bell, I. P. 1970. "The double standard: Age." TransAction (November–December): 75–80.

Bellevue Geriatrics Unit. 1976. Personal communication. Bellevue Hospital, New York.

Benedict, Robert. 1972. "A profile of Indian aged." Pp. 51–58 in Minority Aged in America, Papers from a Symposium Triple Jeopardy: The Plight of Aged Minorities, April 17, 1971, Detroit, Michigan. Ann Arbor: Institute of Gerontology of Michigan.

Benedict, Ruth. 1934. Patterns of Culture. Boston: Houghton Mifflin.

———. 1938. "Continuities and discontinuities in cultural conditioning." Psychiatry 1 (May): 161–67.

———. 1946. The Chrysanthemum and the Sword. Boston: Houghton Mifflin.

Benet, S. 1974. Abkhasians: The Long-living People of the Caucasus. New York: Holt, Rinehart & Winston.

———. 1976. How to Live to Be 100. New York: Dial Press.

Bengtson, V. L. 1970. "The generation gap: A review and typology of social-psychological perspectives."

Youth and Society 3:7–32.

———. 1973. The Social Psychology of Aging. New York: Bobbs-Merrill.

Bengtson, V. L., J. B. Cuellar and P. K. Ragan. 1977. "Stratum contrasts and similarities in attitudes toward death." Journal of Gerontology 32(1):76–88.

Bengtson, V. L., J. J. Dowd, D. H. Smith and A. Inkeles. 1975. "Modernization, modernity, and perceptions of aging: A cross-cultural study." Journal of Gerontology 30:688–95.

Bengtson, V. L., E. Grigsby, E. M. Corry and M. Hruby. 1977. "Relating academic research to community concerns: A case study in collaborative effort." Journal of Social Issues 33(4):75–92.

Bengtson, V. L., P. O. Kasschau and P. K. Ragan. 1977. "The impact of social structure on the aging individual." In J. Birren and K. W. Schaie (eds.), Handbook of the Psychology of Aging. New York: Van Nostrand Reinhold.

Berger, P. L. and T. Luckmann. 1966. The Social Construction of Reality. New York: Doubleday.

Bergman, R. L. 1973. "A school for medicine men." American Journal of Psychiatry 130(6):663–66.

Bernardi, B. 1955. "The age system of the Masai." Annali Lateranesi 18:257–318.

Bierstedt, R. 1950. "An analysis of social power." American Sociological Review 15:730–38.

———. 1965. Review of Blau's Exchange and Power in Social Life. American Sociological Review 30:789–90.

Biesele, M. and N. Howell. 1981. "The old people give you life: Aging among !Kung hunter-gatherers." Pp. 77–98 in P. Amoss and S. Harrell (eds.), Other Ways of Growing Old. Stanford, Calif.: Stanford University Press.

Bild, B. R. and R. J. Havighurst. 1976. "Senior citizens in great cities: The case of Chicago." Gerontologist 16:63–69.

Bischofberger, O. 1972. The Generation Classes of the Zanaki (Tanzania). Studia Ethnographica Friburgensia, Volume 1. Fribourg: University Press.

Bixby, L. E. 1976. "Retirement patterns in the United States: Research and policy interaction." Social Security Bulletin 39(August):3–19.

Blau, P. M. 1964. Exchange and Power in Social Life. New York: John Wiley.

———. 1973. Old Age in a Changing Society. New York: New Viewpoints.

Blau, Z. S. 1961. "Structural constraints on friendship in old age." American Sociological Review 36:429–39.

Blau, Z. S., G. T. Oser and R. C. Stephens. 1979. "Aging, social class and ethnicity." Pacific Sociological Review 22(4):501–25.

Blenkner, M. 1965. "Social work and family relationships in later life." In E. Shanas and G. Streib (eds.), Social Structure and the Family: Generational Relations. Englewood Cliffs, N.J.: Prentice-Hall.

Block, M. R. 1979. "Exiled Americans: The plight of Indian aged in the United States." Pp. 184–92 in D. Gelfand and A. Kutzik (eds.), Ethnicity and Aging—Theory, Research, and Policy. New York: Springer.

Bohannan, P. 1981. "Food of old people in center-city hotels." Pp. 185–200 in C. Fry (ed.), Dimensions: Aging, Culture and Health. Brooklyn, N.Y.: J. F. Bergin.

Boissevain, J. 1968. "The place of non-groups in the social sciences." Man 3(4):542–56.

———. 1974. Friends of Friends. New York: St. Martin Press.

Bond, K. 1976. "Retirement history study's first four years: Work, health, and living arrangements." Social Security Bulletin 39 (December):1–14.

Borgese, E. 1964. The Ascent of Women. New York: George Braziller.

Borthwick, M. 1979. Cultural Factors affecting the Truk District Aging Program. Paper presented at Conference on U. S. Federal Programs in Micronesia, Kolonia, Ponape.

Bott, E. 1957. Family and Social Networks. London: Tavistock.

Bottomore, T. B. 1968. Classes in Modern Society. New York: Vintage.

Brody, H. 1973. Inishkillaine: Change and Decline in the West of Ireland. Harmondworth: Penguin.

Bronfenbrenner, U. 1974. "The origins of alienation." Scientific American 231:53–61.

Bultena, G. L. 1969. "Relationship of occupational status to friendship ties in three planned retirement communities." Journal of Gerontology 24(4):461–64.

Bultena, G. L. and V. Wood. 1969. "The American retirement community: Bane or blessing." Journal of Gerontology 24(2):209–17.

Burch, E. 1975. Eskimo Kinsmen: Changing Family Relationships in Northwest Alaska. American Ethnological Society Monograph No. 59. New York: West.

Burgess, E. 1950. "Personal and social adjustment in old age." In M. Derber (ed.), The Aged in Society. Urbana: University of Illinois Press.

Burić, O. 1976. "The zadruga and the contemporary family in Yugoslavia." Pp. 117–38 in R. F. Byrnes (ed.), Communal Families in the Balkans: The Zadruga. Notre Dame, Ind.: University of Notre Dame Press.

Butler, R. 1975. Why Survive? Being Old in America. New York: Harper & Row.

Byrne, J. J. 1971. "Systematic analysis and exchange theory: A synthesis." Pacific Sociological Review 14:137–46.

Byrne, S. W. 1974. "Arden, an adult community." Pp. 123–52 in G. Foster and R. Kemper (eds.), Anthropologists in Cities. Boston: Little, Brown.

Cameron, P. 1967. "Ego strength and happiness of the aged." Journal of Gerontology 22:199–202.

———. 1968. "Masculinity-femininity in the aged." Journal of Gerontology 25:63–65.

Cameron, S. W. 1974. "The politics of the elderly." The Midwest Quarterly 15:141–53.

Cantor, M. 1975. "Life space and the social support system of the inner city elderly of New York." Gerontologist 15:23–27.

———. 1979. "Neighbors and friends: An overlooked resource in the informal support system." Research on Aging 1: 434–63.

Cantril, H. 1965. The Pattern of Human Concerns. New Brunswick, N.J.: Rutgers University Press.

Carleton, W. 1973. Wildgoose Lodge and Other Stories. Cork: Mercier.

Caro Baroja, J. 1963. "The city and country: Reflections on some ancient common-places." Pp. 27–40 in J. Pitt-Rivers (ed.), Mediterranean Countrymen. Paris: Mouton and Co.

Carp, F. M. 1968. "Some components of disengagement." Journal of Gerontology 23: 382–86.

———. 1976. "Housing and living environments of older people." Pp. 244–77 in R. Binstock and E. Shanas (eds.), Handbook of Aging and the Social Sciences. New York: Van Nostrand Reinhold.

Caudill, W. 1958. The Psychiatric Hospital as a Small Society. Cambridge, Mass.: Harvard University Press.

Cheng, E. 1978. The Elder Chinese. San Diego, Calif.: Campanile Press.

Clark, M. 1967. "The anthropology of aging: A new area for studies of culture and personality." Gerontologist 7:55–64.

———. 1972. "Cultural values and dependency in later life." Pp. 263–74 in D. Cowgill and L. Holmes (eds.), Aging and Modernization. New York: Appleton-Century-Crofts.

———. 1973. "Contributions of cultural anthropology to the study of the aged." Pp. 78–88 in L. Nader and T. Maretzki (eds.), Cultural Illness and Health. Washington, D.C.: The American Anthropological Association.

Clark, M. and B. Anderson. 1967. Culture and Aging: An Anthropological Study of Older Americans. Springfield, Ill.: Charles Thomas.

Clark, M. and M. Mendelson. 1969. "Mexican American aged in San Francisco: A case description." Gerontologist 9:90–95.

Cohen, C. 1976. "Nocturnal neurosis of the elderly." Journal of the American Geriatric Society 24:86–88.

Cohen, C. and J. Sokolovsky. 1980. "Social engagement versus isolation: The case of the aged in SRO hotels." Gerontologist 20:36–44.

Cohler, B. and M. Lieberman. 1979. "Personality changes across the second half of life: Findings from a study of Irish, Italian and Polish American men and women." Pp. 227–45 in D. E. Gelfand and A. Kutzik (eds.), Ethnicity and Aging. New York: Springer.

Coleman, J. S. 1973. "Loss of power." American Sociological Review 38:1–17.

Collier, J. 1974. "Women in politics." Pp. 89–96 in M. Rosaldo and L. Lamphere (eds.), Woman, Culture, and Society. Stanford, Calif.: Stanford University Press.

Collins, R. 1975. Conflict Sociology: Toward an Explanatory Science. New York: Academic Press.

Comfort, A. 1979. The Biology of Aging. New York: Elsevier.

Cool, L. E. 1976. Outsiders in Their Own Land: Ethnicity and the Dilemma of Aging Corsicans. Unpublished doctoral dissertation submitted to Duke University.

———. 1980. "Ethnicity and aging: Continuity through change for elderly Corsicans." Pp. 149–69 in C. Fry (ed.), Aging in Culture and Society. Brooklyn, N.Y.: J. F. Bergin.

———. Forthcoming. "Ethnic identity: A source of community esteem for the elderly." Anthropological Quarterly.

Cooley, R. C., D. Ostendorf and D. Bickerton. 1979. "Outreach services for elderly native Americans." Social Work (March): 151–55.

Cottrell, F. 1960. "The technological and societal basis of aging." Pp. 92–119 in C. Tibbetts (ed.), Handbook of Social Gerontology: Societal Aspects of Aging. Chicago and London: University of Chicago Press.

Cottrell, L. 1942. "The adjustment of the individual to his age and sex roles." American Sociological Review 7:617–20.

County Kerry Committee of Agriculture. 1972. County Kerry Agricultural Resource Survey. Tralee: Kerryman.

Covello, L. 1972. The Social Background of the Italian American School Child. Totowa, N.J.: Rowman Littlefield.

Cowgill, D. 1971. A Theoretical Framework for Considerations of Data on Aging. Paper delivered to the Society for Applied Anthropology, April, Miami.

———. 1972a. "Aging in American society." Pp. 243–61 in D. Cowgill and L. Holmes (eds.), Aging and Modernization. New York: Appleton-Century-Crofts.

———. 1972b. "A theory of aging in cross-cultural perspective." Pp. 1–13 in D. Cowgill and L. Holmes (eds.), Aging and Modernization. New York: Appleton-Century-Crofts.

———. 1974a. "The aging of populations and society." The Annals of the American Academy of Political and Social Sciences 415:1–18.

———. 1974b. "Aging and modernization: A revision of the theory." Pp. 123–46 in J. F. Gubrium (ed.), Late Life: Communities and Environmental Policy. Springfield, Ill.: Charles Thomas.

Cowgill, D. O. and L. D. Holmes (eds.). 1972. Aging and Modernization. New York: Appleton-Century-Crofts.

Craven, P. and B. Wellman. 1973. "The network city." Sociological Inquiry 34:57–88.

Creighton, M. 1978. A Case for Mandatory Retirement. Paper presented at the annual meeting of the Pacific Sociological Association, Spokane, Washington.

Cresswell, R. 1969. Une Communaute Rurale de L'Irlande. Paris: Institute de Ethnographie.

Cronin, C. 1964. "New thoughts on the theory of disengagement." Pp. 3–18 in R. Kastenbaum (ed.), New Thoughts on Old Age. New York: Springer.

———. 1970. Sting of Change: Sicilians in Sicily and Australia. Chicago, Ill.: University of Chicago Press.

Cuellar, J. 1978. "El senior citizens club: The older Mexican-American in the voluntary association." Pp. 207–30 in B. Myerhoff and A. Simić (eds.), Life's Career—Aging. Beverly Hills, Calif.: Sage.

Cuellar, J. and J. Weeks. 1980. Minority Elderly Americans: A Prototype for Area Agencies on Aging. Executive Summary. San Diego, Calif.: Allied Home Health Association.

Cumming, E. 1964. "New thoughts on the theory of disengagement." In Robert Kastenbaum (ed.), New Thoughts on Old Age. New York: Springer.

Cumming, E. and W. Henry. 1961. Growing Old: The Process of Disengagement. New York: Basic Books.

Cumming, E., L. R. Dean, D. S. Newell and I. McCaffrey. 1960. "Disengagement: A tentative theory of aging." Sociometry 23:23–25.

Cutler, N. E. 1974. "Aging and generations in politics: The conflict of explanations and inference." In A. R. Wilcox (ed.), Public Opinion and Political Attitudes. New York: John Wiley.

Cutler, S. J. 1973. "Voluntary association participation and life satisfaction: A cautionary note." Journal of Gerontology 28:95–100.

Dahrendorf, R. 1959. Class and Class Conflict in Industrial Society. Stanford, Calif.: Stanford University Press.

Datan, N. et al. 1970. "Climacterium in three culture contexts." Tropical and Geographical Medicine 22:77–86.

Davies, D. 1975. The Centenarians of the Andes. Garden City, N. Y.: Anchor Press.

Davis, D. L. 1979. Women's Status and Experience of Menopause in a Newfoundland Fishing Village. Paper

presented at the annual meeting of the American Anthropological Association, November, Cincinnati, Ohio.

deBeauvoir, S. 1972. The Coming of Age. Tr. P. O'Brian. New York: Putnam's.

Decker, D. 1978. "Sociological theory and the social position of the aged." International Journal of Contemporary Sociology 15:303–17.

———. 1980. Social Gerontology. Boston: Little, Brown.

Diamond, D. 1972. "New towns in their regional context." Pp. 54–65 in H. Evans (ed.), New Towns: The British Experience. New York: John Wiley.

Djilas, M. 1958. Land without Justice. New York: Harcourt, Brace.

Dougherty, M. 1978. "An anthropological perspective on aging and women in the middle years." In E. Bauwens (ed.), The Anthropology of Health. St. Louis: C. V. Mosby.

Douglas, M. 1966. Purity and Danger. London: Routledge and Kegan Paul.

Dowd, J. J. 1975. "Aging as exchange: A preface to theory." Journal of Gerontology 15:303–17.

———. 1978. "Aging as exchange: A test of the distributive justice proposition." Pacific Sociological Review 21:351–75.

———. 1980. Stratification among the Aged. Monterey, Calif.: Brooks/Cole.

Dowd, J. J. and V. L. Bengtson. 1978. "Aging in minority population, an examination of the double jeopardy hypothesis." Journal of Gerontology 33(3):427–36.

Dowty, N. 1971. Women's Attitudes towards the Climacterium in Five Israeli Sub-cultures. Doctoral dissertation submitted to the University of Chicago.

Duberman, L. 1976. Social Inequality: Class and Caste in America. Philadelphia: J. B. Lippincott.

Dukepoo, F. C. 1980. The Elder American Indian. San Diego: Campanile Press.

Duncan, G. 1977. "The Inter-Tribal Council in California, Inc." Pp. 147–50 in S. E. Percil (ed.), Comprehensive Service Delivery Systems for the Minority Aged. San Diego: Campanile Press.

Dunne, D. 1970. "Lose the heart—destroy the head." The Corridor Echo: Journal of St. Mary's Hospital, Castlebar (February):22–35.

Durkheim, E. 1964. The Division of Labor. New York: Free Press.

Dyson-Hudson, N. 1963. "The Karimojong age system." Ethnology 2 (3):353–401.

———. 1966. Karimojong Politics. London: Oxford University Press.

Eckert, K. 1979. "Urban development and renewal: High risk factors for the elderly." Gerontologist 19:496–502.

———. 1980. The Unseen Elderly: A Study of Marginally Subsistant Hotel Dwellers. San Diego: Campanile Press.

———. Forthcoming. "Dislocation and relocation of the urban elderly: Social networks as mediators of relocation stress." Human Organization.

Edwards, J. N. and D. L. Klemmack. 1973. "Correlates of the satisfaction: A reexamination." Journal of Gerontology 28:497–502.

Ehrlich, P. 1976. "Invisible" Elderly Needs and Characteristics of Aged "Single Room Occupancy" Downtown Hotel Residents. St. Louis:

Institute of Applied Gerontology.

Eisdorfer, C. and B. A. Stotsky. 1977. "Intervention, treatment, and rehabilitation of psychiatric disorders." In J. E. Birren and K. Schaie (eds.), Handbook of The Psychology of Aging. New York: Van Nostrand Reinhold.

Eisenstadt, S. N. 1956. From Generation to Generation. New York: Free Press.

———. 1965. Essays on Comparative Institutions. New York: John Wiley.

———. 1971. "Continuities and changes in systems of stratification." Pp. 61–81 in B. Barber and A. Inkeles (eds.), Stability and Social Change. Boston: Little, Brown.

Elliott, H. W. 1886. Our Arctic Provinces: Alaska and the Seal Islands. New York: Scribner's.

Emerson, R. M. 1962. "Power-dependence relations." American Sociological Review 27:31–41.

———. 1972. "Exchange theory, parts 1 and 2." In M. Zelditch and B. Anderson (eds.), Sociological Theories in Progress. Volume 11. Boston: Houghton Mifflin.

Epstein, A. L. 1969. "The network and urban social organization." Pp. 77–116 in J. C. Mitchell (ed.), Social Networks in Urban Situations. Manchester: Manchester University Press.

Erickson, R. and K. Eckert. 1977. "The elderly poor in downtown San Diego hotels." Gerontologist 17:440–46.

Erlich. V. St. 1972. "Americki zivotni stil (The American life style)." Zagreb: Sociologija 14:43–59.

Evans, E. 1957. Irish Folk Ways. London: Routledge and Kegan Paul.

Evans-Pritchard, E. E. 1936. "The Nuer: Age sets." Sudan Notes and Records 29 (2):233–69.

———. 1937. Witchcraft, Oracles, and Magic among the Azande. Oxford: Oxford University Press.

———. 1940. The Nuer. Oxford: Oxford University Press.

Fallers, L. 1965. Bantu Bureaucracy. Chicago, Ill.: University of Chicago Press.

Fallers, M. 1960. The Eastern Lacustrine Bantu. London: International African Institute.

Fandetti, D. V. and D. E. Gelfand. 1976. "Care of the aged: Attitudes of white ethnic families." Gerontologist 16:544–49.

Federal Council on the Aging. 1981. The Need for Long Term Care. Washington, D.C.: U. S. Department of Health and Human Services.

Fel, E. and T. Hofer. 1969. Proper Peasants: Traditional Life in a Hungarian Village. Chicago, Ill.: Aldine.

Fennell, V. 1981. "Older women in voluntary organizations." In C. Fry (ed.), Dimensions: Aging, Culture, and Health. New York: Praeger.

Finley, G. Forthcoming. "Modernization and aging." In T. Field et al. (eds.), Review of Human Dzvelopment. New York: Wiley-Interscience.

Fischer, D. H. 1978. Growing Old in America. Oxford: Oxford University Press.

Flint, M. 1975. "The menopause: Reward or punishment?" Psychosomatics 16:161–63.

———. 1976. "Transcultural influences in peri-menopause." Pp. 41–56 in A. A. Haspels and H. Musaph (eds.), Psychosomatics in Peri-Menopause. Lancaster: MTP Press Limited.

Flower, R. 1947. The Irish Tradition. Oxford: Clarendon.

Foner, A. 1975. "Age in society: Structure and change."

American Behavioral Scientist 19:144–68.

Foner, A. and D. I. Kertzer. 1978. "Transitions over the life course: Lessons from age-set societies." American Journal of Sociology 83:1081–104.

Fortes, M. 1962. The Web of Kinship among the Tallensi. London: Oxford University Press.

Fosbrooke, H. A. 1948. "An administrative survey of the Masai social system." Tanganyika Notes and Records 26:1–50.

Foster, G. 1961. "The dyadic contract: A model for the social structure of a Mexican peasant village." American Anthropologist 63(6):1173–92.

Foster, G. and B. Anderson. 1978. Medical Anthropology. New York: John Wiley.

Francher, J. S. 1973. "'It's the Pepsi generation': Accelerated aging and the television commercial." International Journal of Aging and Human Development 4(3):245–55.

Freilich, M. (ed.). 1970. Marginal Natives: Anthropologists at Work. New York: Harper & Row.

Freuchen, P. 1961. Peter Freuchen's Book of the Eskimos. Cleveland: World Publishing.

Friedl, E. 1967. "The position of women: Appearance and reality." Anthropological Quarterly 40:97–108.

———. 1975. Women and Men: An Anthropologist's View. New York: Holt, Rinehart & Winston.

Friedman, E. 1960. "The impact of aging on social structure." In C. Tibbetts (ed.), The Handbook of Social Gerontology: Societal Aspects of Aging. Chicago and London: University of Chicago Press.

———. 1967. "Age, length of institutionalization and social status in a home for the aged." Journal of Gerontology 22:474–77.

Fry, C. 1977. "Community as community: The aged graded case." Human Organization 36:115–23.

———. 1979. "Structural conditions affecting community formation among the aged." In J. Keith (ed.), The Ethnography of Old Age. Special issue of Anthropological Quarterly 52(1):7–18.

———. 1980. Aging in Culture and Society, Comparative Viewpoints and Strategies. Brooklyn, N. Y.: J. F. Bergin.

———. 1981. Dimensions: Aging, Culture and Health. Brooklyn, N.Y.: J. F. Bergin.

Fry, C. and J. Keith. 1980. New Methods for Old Age Research. Chicago, Ill.: Center for Urban Policy (Loyola).

———. 1982. "The life course as a cultural unit." In M. Riley (ed.), Aging from Birth to Death. Volume 2. Boulder: Westview Press.

Fuller, A. H. 1961. Buraji: Portrait of a Lebanese Moslem Village. Cambridge, Mass.: Harvard University Press.

Fuller, C. E. 1972. "Aging among South African Bantu." Pp. 51–72 in D. O. Cowgill and L. D. Holmes (eds.), Aging and Modernization. New York: Appleton-Century-Crofts.

Gans, H. 1975. "Urbanism and suburbanism as ways of life: A re-evaluation of definitions." Pp. 189–206 in J. Friedl and N. Chisman (eds.), City Ways: A Selective Reader in Urban Anthropology. New York: Thomas Y. Crowell.

Geertz, C. 1973. The Interpretation of Cultures. New York: Basic Books.

Gelfand, D. 1982. Aging: The Ethnic Factor. Boston: Little, Brown.

Gelfand, D. E. and A. J. Kutzik (eds.). 1979. Ethnicity and Aging. New York: Springer.

Giallombardo, R. 1966. Society of Women. New York: John Wiley.

Gibbs, J. L., Jr. 1965. Peoples of Africa. New York: Holt.

Gibbs-Candy, S. E. 1976. A Developmental Exploration of the Functions of Friendship in Women. Paper presented to the 29th annual meeting of the Gerontological Society, October, New York.

Giddens, A. 1973. The Class Structure of the Advanced Societies. London: Hutchinson & Co.

Gilford, R. and D. Black. 1972. The Grandchild-Grandparent Dyad: Ritual or Relationship? Paper presented at Gerontological Society meetings, San Juan, Puerto Rico.

Glascock, A. and R. Braden. 1981. Transitions of Being: Death and Dying in Cross-Cultural Perspective. Paper presented at the annual meeting of the American Anthropological Association.

Glascock, A. and S. L. Feinman. 1980. "Holocultural analysis of old age." Comparative Social Research 3:311–32.

———. 1981. "Social asset or social burden: Treatment of the aged in non-industrial societies." Pp. 13–31 in C. Fry (ed.), Dimensions: Aging, Culture and Health. Brooklyn, N.Y.: J. F. Bergin.

Glazer, N. and D. P. Moynihan. 1963. Beyond the Melting Pot. Cambridge, Mass.: M.I.T. Press.

———. 1975. Ethnicity: Theory and Experience. Cambridge, Mass.: Harvard University Press.

Glenn, N. D. and R. Zody. 1970. "Cohort analysis with national survey data." Gerontologist 10:233–40.

Gluckman, M. 1950. "Kinship and marriage among the Lozi of northern Rhodesia and the Zulu of Natal." Pp. 140–206 in A. R. Radcliffe-Brown and C. D. Forde (eds.), African Systems of Kinship and Marriage. London: Oxford University Press.

Goffman, E. 1961. Asylums. Garden City, N.Y.: Doubleday.

———. 1963. Stigma: Notes on the Management of Spoiled Identity. Englewood Cliffs, N.J.: Prentice-Hall.

Goist, D. 1981. "Adaptive strategies of the elderly in New England and Ohio." Pp. 85–107 in C. Fry (ed.), Dimensions: Aging, Culture and Health. Brooklyn, N.Y.: J. F. Bergin.

Gold, S. S. 1960. "A cross-cultural comparison of changes with aging in husband-wife roles." Student Journal of Human Development (University of Chicago) 1:11–15.

Goldstein, M. and C. Beall. 1981. "Modernization and aging in the third and fourth world: Views from the rural hinterland in Nepal." Human Organization 40(1):48–55.

Goldstine, T. and D. Gutmann. 1972. "A TAT study of Navajo aging." Psychiatry 35:373–84.

Goode, W. 1963. World Revolution and Family Patterns. New York: Free Press.

———. 1978. The Celebration of Heroes: Prestige as a Control System. Berkeley: University of California Press.

Goody, J. 1976. "Aging in nonindustrial societies." In R. Binstock and E. Shanas (eds.), Handbook of Aging and the Social Sciences. New York: Van Nostrand Reinhold.

Grattan, F. J. H. 1948. An Introduction to Samoan Custom. Apia, Western Samoa: Samoa Printing and Publishing Company, Ltd.

Greeley, A. 1974. Ethnicity in the United States. New York: John Wiley.

Gregory, A. (Lady). 1903. Poets and Dreamers. Dublin: Hodges, Figgis.

Gross, N., W. Mason and A. McEachern. 1957. Explorations in Role Analysis: Studies of the School Superintendency Role. New York: John Wiley.

Gubrium, J. F. 1973. The Myth of the Golden Years: A Socioenvironmental Theory of Aging. Springfield, Ill.: Charles C. Thomas.

Gubser, N. J. 1965. The Nunamiut Eskimo: Hunters of Caribou. New Haven, Conn.: Yale University Press.

Guemple, L. 1969. "Human resource management: The dilemma of the aging Eskimo." Sociological Symposium 2:59–74.

———. 1980. "Growing old in Inuit society." In V. Marshall (ed.), Aging in Canada: Social Perspectives. Toronto: Fitzhenry and Whiteside.

Guillemard, A. M. and R. Lenoir. 1974. Retraite et Échange Social. Paris: Centre d'Etude des Mouvements Sociaux.

Gulliver, P. H. 1953. "The age set organization of the Jie tribe." Journal of the Royal Anthropological Institute 83:147–68.

———. 1958. "The Turkana age organization." American Anthropologist 60:900–922.

———. 1963. Social Control in an African Society. London: Routledge and Kegan Paul.

Gutmann, D. 1968. "Aging among the Highland Maya: A comparative study." Pp. 444–52 in B. Neugarten (ed.), Middle Age and Aging. Chicago, Ill.: University of Chicago Press.

———. 1969. "The country of old men." Occasional Papers in Gerontology, No. 5. Ann Arbor: University of Michigan—Wayne State University.

———. 1971. "The hunger of old men." TransAction 72:55–66.

———. 1974. "Alternatives to disengagement: The old men of Highland Druze." Pp. 232–45 in R. Levine (ed.), Culture and Personality: Contemporary Readings. Chicago, Ill.: Aldine.

———. 1976. "The cross-cultural perspective: Notes toward a comparative psychology of aging." Pp. 302–26 in J. E. Birren and K. W. Schaie (eds.), Handbook of the Psychology of Aging. New York: Van Nostrand Reinhold.

———. 1980. "Observations on culture and mental health in later life." Pp. 429–44 in J. Birren and W. Sloan (eds.), Handbook of Mental Health. New York: Van Nostrand Reinhold.

Hall, C. 1961. "Samoa: America's shame in the South Seas." Reader's Digest (July): 111–16.

Hall, E. T. 1977. Beyond Culture. New York: Doubleday.

Hallpike, C. R. 1972. The Konso of Ethiopia: A Study of the Values of a Cushitic People. Oxford: Clarendon.

Halper, T. 1978. "Paternalism and the elderly." In S. Spicker, K. Woodward and D. van Tassel (eds.), Aging and the Elderly. Atlantic Highlands, N.J.: Humanities Press.

Halpern, J. M. and D. Anderson. 1970. "The zadruga: A century of change." Anthropologica 12:83–97.

Halsell, G. 1976. Los Viejos—Secrets of Long Life from the Sacred Valley. Emmaus: Rodale Press.

Hamer, J. H. 1970. "Sidamo generational class cycles: A political gerontocracy." Africa 40 (1): 50–70.

———. 1972. "Aging in a gerontocratic society: The Sidamo of southwest Ethopia." Pp. 15–30 in D. O. Cowgill and L. D. Holmes (eds.), Aging and Modernization. New York: Appleton-Century-Crofts.

Hammel, E. A. 1967. "The Jewish mother in Serbia or les structures alimentaires de la parenté." Pp. 55–62 in W. G. Lockwood (ed.), Essays in Balkan Ethnology. Berkeley, Calif.: Kroeber Anthropological Society Special Publications, No. 1.

———. 1968. Alternate Social Structures and Ritual Relations in the Balkans. Englewood Cliffs, N.J.: Prentice-Hall.

———. 1969. "Economic change, social mobility and kinship in Serbia." Southwestern Journal of Anthropology 25:188–97.

Hammel, E. A. and C. Yarbrough. 1973. "Social mobility and durability of family ties." Journal of Anthropological Research 29(3):145–63.

Hammond, D. and A. Jablow. 1976. Women in Cultures of the World. Menlo Park, Calif.: Benjamin/Cummings.

Harlan, W. H. 1968. "Social status of the aged in three Indian villages." Pp. 469–75 in B. Neugarten (ed.), Middle Age and Aging. Chicago, Ill.: University of Chicago Press.

Harner, M. 1972. The Jivaro: People of the Sacred Waterfalls. New York: Doubleday, Natural History Press.

Harper, E. B. 1969. "Fear and the status of women." Southwestern Journal of Anthropology 25:81–95.

Harris, L. and Associates. 1975. The Myth and Reality of Aging in America. Washington, D.C.: National Council on the Aging.

Harris, M. 1964. The Nature of Cultural Things. New York: Random House.

Hart, C. W. and A. R. Pilling. 1961. The Tiwi of North Australia. New York: Holt, Rinehart & Winston.

Hauser, P. 1976. "Aging and world-wide population change." Pp. 58–116 in R. Binstock and E. Shanas (eds.), Aging and the Social Sciences. New York: Van Nostrand Reinhold.

Havighurst, R. J. 1968. "Personality and patterns of aging." Gerontologist 8:20–33.

Havighurst, R. J., B. L. Neugarten and S. S. Tobin. 1964. "Disengagement, personality, and life satisfaction in the later years." Pp. 319–24 in P. F. Hanson (ed.), Aged with a Future. Copenhagen: Munksgaard.

———. 1968. "Disengagement and patterns of aging." Pp. 161–72 in B. Neugarten (ed.), Middle Age and Aging. Chicago, Ill.: University of Chicago Press.

Hawkes, E. W. 1916. The Labrador Eskimo. Canada Department of Mines, Geological Survey Memoir 91. Anthropological Series No. 14. Ottawa: Government Printing Bureau.

Haynes, M. S. 1962. "The supposedly golden age for the aged in ancient Greece (a study of literary concepts of old age)." Gerontologist 2:93–98.

———. 1963. "The supposedly golden age for the aged in ancient Rome." Gerontologist 3:26–35.

Hendel-Sebestyn, G. 1979. "Role diversity: Toward the development of community in a total institutional setting." In J. Keith (ed.), The Ethnography of Old Age. Special issue of Anthropological Quarterly 52(1):19–28.

Henderson, J. N. 1981. "Nursing home housekeepers: Indigenous agents of psychosocial support." Human Organization 40:300–305.

Henry, J. 1963. Culture Against Man. New York: Vintage Books.

———. 1977. "Forty-year-old jitters in urban married women." Pp. 262–68 in Annual Editions, Readings in Anthropology 77/78. Guilford, Conn.: Dushkin.

Hertz, E. and O. Hutheesing. 1975. "At the edge of society: The nominal culture of urban hotel isolates." Urban Anthropology 4(4):317–32.

Hinnant, J. 1980. "Age grade organization: An explicit model for the aging process." Pp. 146–54 in C. Fry and J. Keith (eds.), New Methods for Old Age Research. Chicago, Ill.: Center for Urban Policy.

Hochschild, A. R. 1973. The Unexpected Community. Englewood Cliffs, N.J.: Prentice-Hall.

———. 1975. "Disengagement theory: A critique and proposal." American Sociological Review 40:553–69.

Hoestetler, J. A. and G. E. Huntington. 1967. The Hutterites in North America. New York: Holt, Rinehart & Winston.

Holding, E. M. 1942. "Some preliminary notes on Meru age-grades." Man 42 (31):58–65.

Holmberg, A. 1969. Nomads of the Long Bow. Garden City, N.Y.: Natural History Press.

Holmes, L. 1972. "The role and status of the aged in a changing Samoa." Pp. 73–89 in D. Cowgill and L. Holmes (eds.), Aging and Modernization. New York: Appleton-Century-Crofts.

Homans, G. C. 1961. Social Behavior: Its Elementary Forms. New York: Harcourt, Brace and World.

Horowitz, I. 1975. "Race, class and the new ethnicity." Worldview 18(1):46–53.

Huntingford, G. W. B. 1953. The Nandi of Kenya. London: Routledge and Kegan Paul.

Hurault, J. 1971. "Les classes d'âge dans le systeme social des Bamiléké (Cameroun)." Pp. 308–19 in D. Paulme (ed.), Classes et Associations d'Âge en Afrique d l'Ouest. Paris: Plon.

Hyde, D. n.d. The Religious Songs of Connacht. Dublin: Gill.

Ianni, F. A. J. and E. R. Ianni. 1975. "The godfather is going out of business." Psychology Today (December): 87–92.

Inkeles, A. and D. H. Smith. 1970. "The fate of personal adjustment in the process of modernization." International Journal of Comparative Sociology 11:81–114.

Ishikawa, W. 1978a. The Elder Guamanian. San Diego, Calif.: Campanile Press.

———. 1978b. The Elder Samoan. San Diego, Calif.: Campanile Press.

Ishizuka, K. 1978. The Elder Japanese. San Diego, Calif.: Campanile Press.

Jackson, J. J. 1970. "Aged Negroes: Their cultural departures from statistical stereotypes and rural-urban differences." Gerontologist 10:140–45.

———. 1971. "Compensatory care for the black aged." In Minority Aged in America. Occasional paper No. 10. Ann Arbor: University of Michigan Press.

———. 1980. Minorities and Aging. Belmont, Calif.: Wadsworth.

Jacobs, A. H. 1958. Masai Age-Groups and Some Functional Tasks. Paper read at conference held at the East African Institute of Social Research, Makerere College, Kampala, Uganda.

Jacobs, J. 1974a. Fun City: An Ethnographic Study of a Retirement Community. New York: Holt, Rinehart & Winston.

———. 1974b. "An ethnographic study of a retirement setting." Gerontologist 14(6):483–87.

Jacobson, D. 1973. Friendship and Social Order in Urban Uganda. Menlo Park, Calif.: Benjamin/Cummings.

———. 1975. "Mobility, continuity, and urban social organization." Pp. 358–75 in J. Friedl and N. Chrisman (eds.), City Ways: A Selective Reader in Urban Anthropology. New York: Thomas Y. Crowell.

Jay, E. 1964. "The concepts of 'field' and 'networks' in anthropological research." Man 64:127–39.

Jenness, D. 1922. The Life of the Copper Eskimos. Report of the Canadian Arctic Islands. Ottawa: Government Printing Bureau.

Johnson, C. L. 1976. "The principle of generation among the Japanese in Honolulu." Ethnic Groups: An International Periodical of Ethnic Studies 1:13–35.

———. 1977. "Interdependence, reciprocity and indebtedness: An analysis of Japanese American kinship relations." Journal of Marriage and the Family 39(5):351–62.

———. 1978. "The maternal role in the contemporary Italian family." Pp. 234–45 in B. B. Caroli, R. Horner and L. Tomasi (eds.), The Italian Immigrant Woman in North America. Toronto: The Multicultural Historical Society.

———. 1979. "Family support systems to elderly Italian Americans." Journal of Minority Aging 3(1):34–41.

Johnson, H. 1975. American Indians in Transition. Economic Development Division, Economic Research Service, U. S. Department of Agriculture, Agricultural Economic Report No. 283. Washington, D. C.: U. S. Government Printing Office.

Johnson, S. K. 1971. Idle Haven: Community Building among the Working Class Retired. Berkeley: University of California Press.

Jolly, C. and F. Plog. 1979. Physical Anthropology and Archeology. 2d edition. New York: Alfred A. Knopf.

Juliano, R. 1973. "Origin and development of the Italian community in Philadelphia." Pp. 233–62 in J. E. Bodnar (ed.), The Ethnic Experience in Pennsylvania. Louisburg: Bucknell.

Kaberry, P. 1939. Aboriginal Women. New York: Gordon Press.

Kahana, E. and B. Kahana. 1971. "Theoretical and research perspectives on grandparenthood." Aging and Human Development 2:261–68.

Kahn, R. 1979. "Aging and social support." Pp. 77–91 in M. Riley (ed.), Aging from Birth to Death. AAAS Selected Symposia Series. Boulder: Westview Press.

Kahn, R. and T. Antonucci. 1981. "Convoys of social support: A life-course approach." Pp. 383–405 in S. Kiesler, J. Morgan and V. K. Oppenheimer (eds.), Aging: Social Change. New York: Academic Press.

Kandel, R. and M. Heider. 1979. "Friendship and factionalism in a tri-ethnic housing complex in North Miami." In J. Keith (ed.), The Ethnography of Old Age. Special issue of Anthropological Quarterly 52(1):29–38.

Kaplan, H. and B. Taylor. 1972. Economic and Social Problems of the Elderly Urban Indian in Phoenix, Arizona. Phoenix: LEAP, City of Phoenix.

Kardiner, A. et al. 1945. The Psychological Frontiers of Society. New York: Columbia University Press.

Katz, S. 1978. "Anthropological perspectives on aging." Annals of the American Academy of Political and Social Sciences 438:1–27.

Kayser-Jones, J. 1981a. Old, Alone and Neglected: Care of the Aged in Scotland and the United States. Berkeley: University of California Press.

———. 1981b. "Quality of care for the institutionalized aged: A Scottish-American comparison." Pp. 233–55 in C. Fry (ed.), Dimensions: Age, Culture and Health. Brooklyn, N. Y.: J. F. Bergin.

Keesing, F. and M. Keesing. 1956. Elite Communication in Samoa. Stanford, Calif.: Stanford University Press.

Keith, J. 1980a. "Old age and community creation." Pp. 170–97 in C. Fry (ed.), Aging in Culture and Society. New York: Praeger.

———. 1980b. "'The best is yet to be': Toward an anthropology of age." Annual Review of Anthroplogy 9:333–64.

———. 1980c. "Participant observation." Pp. 8–26 in C. Fry and J. Keith (eds.), New Methods for Old Age Research. Chicago, Ill.: Center for Urban Research (Loyola).

———. 1981. "Old age and age differentiation: Anthropological speculations on age as a social border." Pp. 453–88 in S. Kiesler, J. Morgan and V. K. Oppenheimer (eds.), Aging: Social Change. New York: Academic Press.

———. 1982. Old People as People: Social and Cultural Influences on Aging and Old Age. Boston: Little, Brown.

Keith, J. (ed.). 1979. The Ethnography of Old Age. Special issue of Anthropological Quarterly 52(1).

Kennedy, R. J. 1973. The Irish: Emigration, Marriage and Fertility. Berkeley: University of California Press.

Kent, D. P. 1971. "The Negro aged." Gerontologist 11: 48–50.

Kent, D. P. and C. Hirsch. 1969. Differentials in Need and Problem Solving Techniques among Low Income Negro and White Elderly. Paper presented at the 8th International Congress of Gerontology, Washington.

Kenyatta, J. 1938. Facing Mount Kenya: The Tribal Life of the Kikuyu. London: Secker & Warburg.

Kerckhoff, A. 1966. "Family patterns and morale in retirement." Pp. 173–92 in I. Simpson and J. McKinney (eds.), Social Aspects of Aging. Durham, N. C.: Duke University Press.

Kertzer, D. 1982. "Generation and age in cross-cultural perspective." In M. Riley (ed.), Aging from Birth to Death. Volume 2. Boulder: Westview Press.

Kertzer, D. and J. Keith (eds.). Forthcoming. Age and Anthropological Theory. Ithaca, N. Y.: Cornell University Press.

Kertzer, D. I. and O. B. B. Madison. 1981. "Women's age-set systems in Africa: The Latuka of Southern Sudan." Pp. 109–30 in C. Fry (ed.), Dimensions: Aging, Culture and Health. Brooklyn, N. Y.: J. F. Bergin.

Kiefer, C. 1971. "Notes on anthropology and the minority elderly." Gerontologist 11:94–98.

———. 1974. "Lessons from the Issei." Pp. 167–97 in J. Gubrium (ed.), Late Life: Communities and Environmental Policy. Springfield, Ill.: Charles Thomas.

Killworth, P. and H. Russell Bernard. 1974. "Catij: A new sociometric and its application to a prison living unit." Human Organization 33(4):335–50.

———. 1976. "Informant accuracy in social network data." Human Organization 35:269–86.

Kleemeier, R. W. 1954. "Moosehaven: Congregate living in a community of the retired." American Journal of Sociology 59:347–51.

Kline, C. 1975. "The socialization process of women." Gerontologist 15:486–92.

Kluckhohn, C. 1967. Navaho Witchcraft. Boston: Beacon Press.

Knipe, E. E. 1971. Attraction and Exchange: Some Temporal Considerations. Paper presented at annual meeting of the Southern Sociological Society, Atlanta.

Komorita, S. S. 1977. "Negotiating from strength and the concept of bargaining strength." Journal for the Theory of Social Behavior 7:65–79.

Koty, J. 1933. Die Behandlung der Alten und Kranken bei den Naturvoelken. Stuttgart: W. Kohlhammer.

Krohn, A. and D. Gutmann. 1971. "Changes in mastery style with age: A study of Navajo dreams." Psychiatry 34:289–300.

Kuypers, J. and V. L. Bengtson. 1971. "Generational difference and the 'developmental' stake." Aging and Human Development 2(1): 249–60.

Lally, M. et al. 1979. "Older women in single room occupant (SRO) hotels: A Seattle profile." Gerontologist 19:67–73.

Lambert, H. E. 1947. "The use of indigenous authorities in tribal administration: Studies of the Meru of Kenya Colony." Communication No. 16, School of African Studies, University of Capetown.

———. 1956. Kikuyu Social and Political Institutions. London: Oxford University Press.

Lamphere, L. 1974. "Strategies, cooperation, and conflict among women in domestic groups." Pp. 97–112 in M. Rosaldo and L. Lamphere (eds.), Woman, Culture, and Society. Stanford, Calif.: Stanford University Press.

Landtman, G. 1938. The Origin of the Inequality of the Social Classes. Chicago, Ill.: University of Chicago Press.

Lansing, S. 1980. "Being old in Bali." Parabola 5(1):34–37.

Laughlin, C. D., Jr. and E. R. Laughlin. 1974. "Age generations and political process in So. Africa." Africa 44(3):266–79.

Leaf, A. 1975. Youth in Old Age. New York: McGraw-Hill.

Lee, R. B. and I. Devore. 1976. Kalahari Hunter-Gatherers. Studies of the !Kung San and Their Neighbors. Cambridge, Mass.: Harvard University Press.

Legesse, A. 1973. Gada. New York: Free Press.

———. 1979. "Age-sets and retirement communities." In J. Keith (ed.), The Ethnography of Old Age. Special issue of Anthropological Quarterly 52(1):61–69.

Leggett, J. C. 1972. Race, Class, and Political Consciousness. Cambridge: Schenkman.

Lehman, E. W. 1977. Political Society: A Macrosociology of Politics. New York: Columbia University Press.

Lemon, B. W., V. L. Bengtson and J. A. Peterson. 1972. "An exploration of the activity theory of aging: Activity types and life satisfaction among in-movers to a retirement community." Journal of Gerontology 27:511–23.

Lenneberg, E. H. 1967. Biological Foundations of Language. New York: John Wiley.

Lenski, G. 1966. Power and Privilege: A Theory of Social Stratification. New York: McGraw-Hill.

Lenski, G. and J. Lenski. 1978. Human Societies: An Introduction to Macrosociology. New York: McGraw-Hill.

Leonard, O. E. 1967. "The older rural Spanish-speaking people of the Southwest." Pp. 239–61 in E. G. Youmans (ed.), Older Rural Americans. Lexington: University of Kentucky Press.

Levine, R. 1963. "Witchcraft and sorcery in a Gusii community." Pp. 221–55 in J. Middleton and E. Winter (eds.), Witchcraft and Sorcery in East Africa. New York: Praeger.

———. 1965. "Intergenerational tensions and extended family structures in Africa." Pp. 188–204 in Ethel Shanas and Gordon Strieb (eds.), Social Structure and the Family. Englewood Cliffs, N. J.: Prentice-Hall.

Levison, A. 1975. The Working-Class Majority. New York: Penguin.

Levy, J. 1967. "The older American Indian." Pp. 221–38 in E. G. Youmans (ed.), Older Rural Americans. Lexington: University of Kentucky Press.

Lewis, M. and R. Butler. 1972. "Why is women's lib ignoring the older women?" International Journal of Aging and Human Development 3(3):223–31.

Lindbergh, A. M. 1963. Dearly Beloved: A Theme and Variations. New York: Popular Library.

Lipman, A. 1961. "Role conceptions and morale of couples in retirement." Journal of Gerontology 16:267–71.

———. 1970. "Prestige of the aged in Portugal: Realistic appraisal and ritual deference." Aging and Human Development 1:127–36.

Lipman, A. and K. J. Smith. 1969. "Functionality of disengagement in old age." Journal of Gerontology 23:517–21.

Lopata, H. 1966. "The life cycle of the role of housewife." Sociology and Social Research 51:5–22.

———. 1971. "The living arrangements of American urban widows." Department of H.E.W., Administration on Aging, Mimeo No. 34. Washington, D. C.: U. S. Government Printing Office.

———. 1972. "Role changes in widowhood: A world perspective." Pp. 275–303 in D. Cowgill and L. Holmes (eds.), Aging and Modernization. New York: Appleton-Century-Crofts.

———. 1973. Widowhood in an American City. Cambridge: Schenkman.

———. 1975. "Support systems of elderly: Chicago of the 1970's." Gerontologist 15:35–41.

———. 1978. "The absence of community resources in support systems of urban widows." Family Coordinator 27(4):383–88.

Lopreato, J. 1970. Italian Americans. New York: Random House.

Low, A. P. 1906. Report on the Dominion Government Expedition to Hudson Bay and the Arctic Islands. Ottawa: Government Printing Bureau.

Lowenthal, M. F. and D. Boler. 1965. "Voluntary versus involuntary social withdrawal." Journal of Gerontology 20:363–71.

Lowenthal, M. F. and D. A. Chiriboga. 1972. "Transition to the empty nest: Crisis, challenge, or relief?" Archives of General Psychiatry 26:8–14.

Lowenthal, M. F. and B. Robinson. 1976. "Social networks and isolation." In R. Binstock and E. Shanas (eds.), Handbook of Aging and the Social Sciences. New York: Van Nostrand Reinhold.

Lowenthal, M. F., M. Thurner and D. Chiriboga. 1975. Four Stages of Life. San Francisco: Jossey-Bass.

Lowenthal. R. A. 1974. Tharaka Age-Organization and the Theory of Age-Set Systems. Ann Arbor:

University of Michigan Microfilms.

Lozier, J. and R. Althouse. 1974. "Social enforcement of behavior toward elders in an Appalachian mountain settlement." Gerontologist 14:69–80.

———. 1975. "Retirement to the porch in rural Appalachia." International Journal of Aging and Human Development 6:7–15.

Lukes, S. 1973. Individualism. New York: Harper & Row.

Lustig, J. 1979. The Needs of Elderly Indians in Phoenix, Arizona: Recommendations for Services. Phoenix: Affiliation of Arizona Indian Centers, Inc.

Lyon, J. P. 1978. The Indian Elder: A Forgotten American. Final Report on the First National Indian Conference on Aging, June 15–17, Phoenix, Arizona. Albuquerque, N.M.: Adobe Press.

Maddox, G. L. 1969a. "Activity and morale: A longitudinal study of selected elderly subjects." Social Forces 42:195–204.

———. 1969b. "Growing old: Getting beyond the stereotypes." Pp. 5–16 in R. Boyd and C. Oakes (eds.), Foundations of Practical Gerontology. Columbia: University of South Carolina Press.

Maddox, G. and E. B. Douglas. 1974. "Aging and individual differences: A longitudinal study of social, psychological, and physiological indicators." Journal of Gerontology 29:555–63.

Maeda, D. 1978. "Aging in Eastern society." Pp. 45–72 in D. Hobman (ed.), The Social Challenge of Aging. London: Croon Helm.

Mair, L. 1934. An African People in the 20th Century. London: Routledge.

———. 1969. African Marriage and Social Change. London: Cass.

Manuel, R. Forthcoming. Minority Aging: Sociological and Psychological Issues. Westport, Conn.: Greenwood Press.

Marcus, E. E., E. Gebauer, M. Levin and P. N. D. Pirie. 1974. Report on the 1974 Census of American Samoa. Honolulu: East-West Center.

Marcuse, H. 1964. One Dimensional Man: Studies in the Ideology of Advanced Industrial Society. Boston: Beacon Press.

Markson, E. 1979. "Ethnicity as a factor in the institutionalization of the ethnic elderly." Pp. 341–56 in D. Gelfand and A. Kutzik (eds.), Ethnicity and Aging. New York: Springer.

Marshall, L. 1976. "Sharing, talking and giving." In R. B. Lee and I. Devore (eds.), Kalahari Hunter-Gatherers: Studies of !Kung San and their Neighbors. Cambridge, Mass.: Harvard University Press.

Martin, R. 1971. "The concept of power: A critical defence." British Journal of Sociology 22:240–57.

Martin, W. C. 1973. "Activity and disengagement: Life satisfaction of in-movers into a retirement community." Gerontologist 13:224–27.

Mather, B. 1978. New City Life for the Elderly. Milton Keynes, England: Social Development Directorate.

Matthews, S. H. 1975. "Old women and identity maintenance: Outwitting the grim reaper." Urban Life 4: 105–15.

———. 1977. Negotiation by Default: The Social Definition of Old Widows. Paper presented at the meeting of the Society for the Study of Social Problems, Chicago.

Maxwell, E. K. and R. J. Maxwell. 1980. "Contempt for the elderly: A cross-cultural analysis." Current Anthropology 24:569–70.

Maxwell, R. 1970. "The changing status of the elders in Polynesia." International Journal of Aging and Human Development 1:137–46.

Maxwell, R. and P. Silverman. 1970. "Information and esteem." International Journal of Aging and Human Development 1:361–92.

———. 1981. Gerontocide. Paper presented at the annual meeting of the American Anthropological Association.

Maxwell, R. J., E. Krassen-Maxwell and P. Silverman. 1978. The Cross-Cultural Study of Aging: A Manual for Coders. New Haven, Conn.: HRAF Press.

Mayer, A. 1966. "The significance of quasi-groups in the study of complex societies." Pp. 97–122 in M. Banton (ed.), The Social Anthropology of Complex Societies. ASA Monograph, No. 4. New York: Praeger.

Mazess, R. and S. Forman. 1979. "Longevity and age exaggeration in Vilcabamba, Ecuador." Journal of Gerontology 34(1):94–98.

McArdle, J. and C. Yeracaris. 1979. Respect for the Elderly in Pre-industrial Societies as Related to Their Activity. Paper presented at the annual meeting of the Gerontological Society of America.

McCabe, J. 1979. The Status of Aging Women in the Middle East: The Process of Change in the Life Cycle of Rural Lebanese Women. Unpublished doctoral dissertation submitted to Duke University.

McKain, W. C. 1972. "The aged in the USSR." Pp. 151–65 in D. O. Cowgill and L. D. Holmes (eds.), Aging and Modernization. New York: Appleton-Century-Crofts.

McLaughlin, V. 1971. "Patterns of work and family organization: Buffalo's Italians." Journal of Interdisciplinary History 2(2):299–314.

Mead, M. 1928a "The role for the individual in Samoan culture." Journal of the Royal Anthropological Institute 58:481–95.

———. (1928b) 1964. Coming of Age in Samoa. New York: William Morrow.

———. 1951. "Cultural contexts of aging." Pp. 49–51 in No Time to Grow Old. New York State Legislative Committee on Problems of Aging, Legislative Document No. 12.

———. 1967. "Ethnological aspects of aging." Psychosomatics 8(4):33–37.

———. 1973. "New towns to set new life styles." Pp. 241–54 in I. L. Allen (ed.), New Towns and the Suburban Dream. New York: Kennihat Press.

Mead, M. and N. Calas (eds.). 1953. Primitive Heritage. New York: Random House.

Mendelson, M. 1974. Tender Loving Greed. New York: Alfred A. Knopf.

Messenger, J. 1969. Inis Beag. New York: Holt, Rinehart & Winston.

Middleton, J. 1953. The Kikuyu and Kamba of Kenya. London: Routledge & Sons.

Mills, C. W. 1963. Power, Politics, and People. New York: Ballantine Books.

Mindel, C. and R. Habenstein. 1976. Ethnic Families in America. New York: Elsevier.

Mitchell, J. C. 1969. Social Networks in Urban Situations. Manchester: University of Manchester Press.

Mizruchi, E. 1977. Abeyance Process and Time: An Exploratory Approach to Age and Social Structure. Paper presented at the Working Conference on Time and Aging, Maxwell Policy Center on Aging, Casenovia, New York.

Moen, E. 1978. "The reluctance of the elderly to accept help." Social Problems 25: 293–303.

Moore, J. 1971. "Mexican Americans." Gerontologist 11:30–35.

Moore, M. J. 1981. "Physical aging: A cross-cultural perspective." Pp. 27–40 in F. Berghorn and D. Schafer (eds.), The Dynamics of Aging. Boulder: Westview Press.

Morgan, L. A. 1976. "A re-examination of widowhood and morale." Journal of Gerontology 31:687–95.

Morgan, L. A. and V. L. Bengtson. 1976. Measuring Perceptions of Aging across Strata. Paper presented at the annual meeting of the Gerontological Society, October 15, New York.

Morioka, K. 1966. Life Cycle Patterns in Japan, China, and the United States. Paper presented at Sixth World Congress of Sociology, Tokyo.

Moss, F. and V. Halamandaris. 1977. Too Old Too Sick Too Bad: Nursing Homes in America. Germantown: Aspen Systems Corporation.

Moss, L. and W. Thompson. 1959. "The Southern Italian family: Literature and observation." Human Organization 18:35–41.

Moss, M., L. Gottesman and M. Kleban. 1976. Informal Social Relationships among Community Aged. Paper presented to the 29th annual meeting of the Gerontological Society, October, New York.

Mulkay, M. J. 1971. Functionalism, Exchange, and Theoretical Strategy. New York: Schocken.

Munnichs, J. M. 1968. Old Age and Finitude: A Contribution to Psycho-gerontology. New York: S. Karger.

Munsell, M. R. 1972. "Functions of the aged among Salt River Pima." Pp. 127–32 in D. Cowgill and L. Holmes (eds.), Aging and Modernization. New York: Appleton-Century-Crofts.

Murdock, G. P. and D. R. White. 1969. "Standard cross-cultural sample." Ethnology 8:321–69.

Murdock, S. H. and D. F. Schwartz. 1978. "Family structure and the use of agency services: An examination of patterns among elderly native Americans." Gerontologist 18:475-81.

Murphy, J. M. and C. C. Hughes. 1965. "The use of psychophysiological symptoms as indicators of disorder among Eskimos." Pp. 108–60 in J. M. Murphy and A. H. Leighton (eds.), Approaches to Cross-Cultural Psychiatry. Ithaca, N.Y.: Cornell University Press.

Murphy, Y. and R. F. Murphy. 1974. Women of the Forest. New York: Columbia University Press.

Murray Hill SRO Project. 1976. Personal communication. New York.

Myerhoff, B. 1978. Number Our Days. New York: E. P. Dutton.

Myerhoff, B. G. and A. Simić (eds.). 1978. Life's Career—Aging: Cultural Variations in Growing Old. Beverly Hills, Calif.: Sage.

Nadel, S. F. 1952. "Witchcraft in four African societies." American Anthropologist 54:18–29.

Nahemow, N. 1979. "Residence, kinship and social isolation among the aged Baganda." Journal of Marriage and the Family 41(1):171–83.

Nahemow, N. and B. N. Adams. 1974. "Old age among the Baganda: Continuity and change." Pp. 147–66 in J. F. Gubrium (ed.), Late Life: Communities and Environmental Policy. Springfield, Ill.: Charles Thomas.

National Indian Council on Aging. 1979. The Continuum of Life: Health Concerns of the Indian Elderly. Final Report on the Second National Indian Conference on Aging, August 15–18, Billings, Montana. Albuquerque, N.M.: Adobe Press.

National Urban League. 1964. Double Jeopardy: The Older Negro in America Today. New York: National Urban League.

Needham, R. 1974. "Age, category and descent." In R. Needham (ed.), Remarks and Inventions. London: Tavistock.

Neugarten, B. 1968. "Adult personality: Toward a psychology of the life cycle." Pp. 137–47 in B. Neugarten (ed.), Middle Age and Aging. Chicago, Ill.: University of Chicago Press.

Neugarten, B. and N. Datan. 1973. "Sociological perspectives on the life cycle." Pp. 53–69 in P. Baltes and K. Schaie (eds.), Life-Span Developmental Psychology. New York: Academic Press.

Neugarten, B. and D. Gutmann. 1968. "Age-sex roles and personality in middle age." Pp. 58–71 in B. Neugarten (ed.), Middle Age and Aging. Chicago, Ill.: University of Chicago Press.

Neugarten, B. and R. Kraines. 1965. "Menopausal symptoms in women of various ages." Psychosomatics 16:161–63.

Neugarten, B. L. and K. K. Weinstein. 1964. "The changing American grandparent." Journal of Marriage and the Family 26:199–204.

Neugarten, B., R. Havighurst and S. Tobin. 1961. "The measurement of life satisfaction." Journal of Gerontology 16:134–43.

Neugarten, B. et al. 1963. "Women's attitudes towards the menopause." Vita Humanica 6:140–51.

Nixon, R. M. 1970. "Text of Indian message." Congressional Quarterly Almanac, pp. 101–15A.

Norbeck, E. 1953. "Age grading in Japan." American Anthropologist 55:373–83.

Nord, W. R. 1969. "Social exchange theory: An integrated approach to social conformity." Psychological Bulletin 71:174–208.

Novak, M. 1972. The Rise of the Unmeltable Ethnic. New York: Macmillan.

O'Brien, J. and D. Lind. 1976. Book review of The Honorable Elders by Erdman Palmore. Gerontologist 19:560–61.

O'Crohan, T. 1951. The Islandman. Oxford: Clarendon.

O'Hare, A. and D. Walsh. 1974. Irish Psychiatric Hospital Census, 1971. Dublin: Medico-Social Research Board.

Oliver, D. 1951. The Pacific Islands. Cambridge, Mass.: Harvard University Press.

Ortner, S. 1974. "Is female to male as nature is to culture?" Pp. 67–87 in M. Rosaldo and L. Lamphere (eds.), Toward an Anthropology of Women. Stanford, Calif.: Stanford University Press.

Osako, M. 1979. "Aging and family among Japanese Americans: The role of ethnic tradition in the adjustment to old age." Gerontologist 19:448–55.

Osborn, F. J. and A. Whittick. (1963) 1977. New Towns:

Their Origins, Achievements, and Progress. Boston: Routledge and Kegan Paul.

O'Suilleabhain, S. 1967. Irish Wake Amusements. Cork: Mercier.

———. 1974. The Folklore of Ireland. London: Batsford.

O'Sullivan, M. 1957. Twenty Years A-Growing. London: Oxford Press.

Ottenberg, S. 1971. Leadership and Authority in an African Society: The Afikpo Village-Group. Seattle: University of Washington Press.

Palmore, E. 1968. "The effects of aging on activities and attitudes." Gerontologist 8:259–63.

———. 1971. "Attitudes towards aging as shown by humor." Gerontologist 11:181–86.

———. 1975a. The Honorable Elders. Durham, N.C.: Duke University Press.

———. 1975b. "What can the USA learn from Japan about aging?" Gerontologist 15:64–67.

———. 1975c. "The status and integration of the aged in Japanese society." Journal of Gerontology 30:199–208.

———. 1976. "The future status of the aged." Gerontologist 16:297–302.

Palmore, E. and K. Manton. 1974. "Modernization and the status of the aged: International correlations." Journal of Gerontology 29:205–10.

Palmore, E. and F. Whittington. 1971. "Trends in the relative status of the aged." Social Forces 50:84–91.

Parenti, M. 1978. Power and the Powerless. New York: St. Martin's Press.

Parsons, T. 1975. "Some theoretical considerations on the nature and trends of change of ethnicity." Pp. 53–83 in N. Glazer and D. Moynihan (eds.), Ethnicity: Theory and Experience. Cambridge, Mass.: Harvard University Press.

Patterson, G. J. 1979. "A critique of the new ethnicity." American Anthropologist 81(1):103–5.

Pattison, M. et al. 1975. "A psychosocial kinship model for family therapy." American Journal of Psychiatry 132(12):1246–51.

Peristiany, J. G. 1939. The Social Institutions of the Kipsigis. London: Routledge & Sons.

Perkinson, M. 1980. "Alternate roles for the elderly: An example from a Midwestern retirement community." Human Organization 39:219–26.

Peterson, R. 1978. The Elder Philipino. San Diego, Calif.: Campanile Press.

Pitskhelauari, G. 1981. The Long-Living of Soviet Georgia. Tr. and ed. G. Lesnoff-Caravaglio. New York: Human Sciences Press.

Pitt, D. 1970. Tradition and Economic Progress in Samoa. Oxford: Oxford University Press.

Pitt, D. and C. MacPherson. 1974. Emerging Pluralism: The Samoan Community in New Zealand. Auckland: Longman Paul.

Place, L. 1981. "The ethnic factor." Pp. 105–226 in F. Berghorn and D. Schafer (eds.), Dynamics of Aging. Boulder: Westview Press.

Plath, D. W. 1964a. "Where the family of God is the family: The role of the dead in Japanese households." American Anthropologist 66(2):300–317.

———. 1964b. The After Hours. Berkeley: University of California Press.

———. 1972. "Japan: The after years." Pp. 133–50 in D.

Cowgill and L. Holmes (eds.), Aging and Modernization. New York: Appleton-Century-Crofts.

———. 1973. "Ecstasy years—old age in Japan." Pacific Affairs 46:421–28.

———. 1980. Long Engagements: Maturity in Modern Japan. Stanford, Calif.: Stanford University Press.

Poppy, M. L. 1979. "Needs assessment in minority aging research." Pp. 79–88 in E. P. Stanford (ed.), Minority Aging Research, Old Issues—New Approaches. San Diego, Calif.: Campanile Press.

Pospisil, L. 1963. Kapauku Papuan Economy. New Haven, Conn.: Yale University Publications in Anthropology.

———. (1964) 1971. Kapauku Papuans and Their Law. New Haven, Conn.: Human Relations Area Files.

Powers, E. A. and G. L. Bultena. 1976. "Sex differences in intimate friendships of old age." Journal of Marriage and the Family (November):739–47.

Prasad, S. B. 1964. "The retirement postulate of disengagement theory." Gerontologist 4:20–23.

Press, I. 1967. "Maya aging: Cross-cultural projective techniques and the Dilemma of interpretation." Psychiatry 30:197–202.

Press, I. and M. McKool, Jr. 1971. Social Structure and Status of the Aged in Peasant Society. Paper delivered to the Society for Applied Anthropology, April, Miami.

———. 1972. "Social structure and status of the aged: Toward some valid cross cultural generalizations." Aging and Human Development 3:297–306.

Prins, A. H. J. 1970. East African Age-Class Systems: An Inquiry into the Social Order of Galla, Kipsigis, and Kikuyu. Westport, Conn.: Negro University Press.

Quinn, N. 1977. "Anthropological studies on women's status." Annual Review of Anthropology 6:181–225.

Radcliffe-Brown, A. R. 1967. African Systems of Kinship and Marriage. London: Oxford Press.

Ragan, P. K. and J. E. Grigsby. 1976. Responsibility for Meeting the Needs of the Elderly for Health Care, Housing, and Transportation. Opinions reported in a survey of blacks, Mexican Americans, and whites. Western Gerontological Society, San Diego.

Ragan, P. K. and M. Simonin. 1977. Community Survey Report. A brief report reproduced for dissemination, March.

Rasmussen, K. 1908. People of the Polar North. London: Kegan Paul, Trench, Trubner and Co.

Rhoads, E. and L. Holmes. 1981. "Mapuifagale, Western Samoa's home for the aged: A cultural enigma." International Journal of Aging and Human Development 13(2):121–35.

Riesenfeld, M. J., R. J. Newcomer, P. V. Berlant and W. A. Dempsey. 1972. "Perceptions of public service needs: The urban elderly and the public agency." Gerontologist 12:185–90.

Riesman, D. 1972. "Some questions about the study of American character in the twentieth century." Pp. 34–44 in S. D. Feldman and G. W. Thielbar (eds.), Life Styles: Diversity in American Society. Boston: Brown and Company.

Riley, M. W. 1973. "Aging and cohort succession: Interpretations and misinterpretations." Public Opinion Quarterly 37:35–49.

———. 1976. "Age strata in social systems." Pp. 189–217 in

R. H. Binstock, E. Shanas and Associates (eds.), Handbook of Aging and the Social Sciences. New York: Van Nostrand Reinhold.

Riley, M. W. and J. Waring. 1976. "Age and aging." Pp. 355–413 in R. K. Merton and R. Nisbet (eds.), Contemporary Social Problems. New York: Harcourt Brace Jovanovich.

Riley, M. W., M. Johnson and A. Foner. 1972. Aging and Society. Volume 3, A Sociology of Age Stratification. New York: Russell Sage.

Robertson, J. F. 1976. "Significance of grandparents—perceptions of young adult grandchildren." Gerontologist 16:137–40.

———. 1977. "Grandmotherhood: A study of role conception." Journal of Marriage and the Family 39(1):165–74.

Rockstein, M., J. A. Chesky and M. Sussman. 1977. "Comparative biology and evolution of aging." In C. E. Finch and L. Hayflick (eds.), The Biology of Aging. New York: Van Nostrand Reinhold.

Rogers, C. J. and T. E. Gallion. 1978. "Characteristics of elderly Pueblo Indians in New Mexico." Gerontologist 18:482–87.

Rohner, R. P. et al. 1978. "Guidelines for holocultural research." Current Anthropology 19:128–29.

Rosaldo, M. Z. 1974. "Woman, culture, and society: A theoretical overview." Pp. 17–42 in M. Rosaldo and L. Lamphere (eds.), Woman, Culture, and Society. Stanford, Calif.: Stanford University Press.

Rosaldo, M. and L. Lamphere (eds.), 1974. Woman, Culture, and Society. Stanford, Calif.: Stanford University Press.

Rose, A. 1962. "The subculture of aging: A topic for sociological research." Gerontologist 2:123–27.

———. 1964. "A current theoretical issue in social gerontology." Gerontologist 4:46–50.

———. 1965. "The subculture of the aging." In A. Rose and W. Peterson (eds.), Older People and Their Social World. Philadelphia: F. A. Davis.

Rosenberg, G. 1970. The Worker Grows Old. San Francisco: Jossey-Bass.

Rosenmayr, L. 1977. "The family—a source of hope for the elderly." In E. Shanas and M. B. Sussman (eds.), Family Bureaucracy and the Elderly. Durham, N.C.: Duke University Press.

Rosenmayr, L. and E. Kockeis. 1962. "Family relations and social contacts of the aged in Vienna." In C. Tibbitts and W. Donahue (eds.), Social and Psychological Aspects of Aging. Volume 1. New York: Columbia University Press.

Rosow, I. 1967. Social Integration of the Aged. New York: Free Press.

———. 1970. "Old people: Their friends and neighbors." American Behavioral Scientist 14:59–69.

———. 1974. Socialization to Old Age. New York: Free Press.

———. 1976. "Status and role change through the life span." In R. H. Binstock and E. Shanas (eds.), Handbook of Aging and the Social Sciences. New York: Van Nostrand Reinhold.

Ross, J. 1975. "Learning to be retired: Socialization into a retirement residence." Journal of Gerontology 29(2):211–23.

———. 1977. Old People, New Lives.

Chicago, Ill.: University of Chicago Press.

Rothman, R. A. 1978. Inequality and Stratification in the United States. Englewood Cliffs, N.J.: Prentice-Hall.

Ruel, J. J. 1958. Kuria Generation Sets. Paper read at conference held at the East African Institute of Social Research, Makerere College, Kampala, Uganda.

Ruse, F. 1968. "Land owning groups and initiations." In R. Lee and I. DeVore (eds.), Man the Hunter. Chicago, Ill.: Aldine.

Ryder, N. B. 1965. "The cohort as a concept in the study of social change." American Sociological Review 30:843–61.

Sanday, P. 1974. "Female status in the public domain." Pp. 189–206 in M. A. Rosaldo and L. Lamphere (eds.), Woman, Culture, and Society. Stanford, Calif.: Stanford University Press.

Sangree, W. H. 1965. "The Bantu Tiriki of western Kenya." Pp. 41–80 in J. L. Gibbs, Jr. (ed.), Peoples of Africa. New York: Holt, Rinehart & Winston.

———. 1966. Age, Prayer, and Politics in Tiriki, Kenya. New York: Oxford University Press.

Sanjek, R. 1978. "A network method and its use in urban Ethnography." Human Organization 37(3):257–69.

Sayers, P. 1962. An Old Woman's Reflections. London: Oxford University Press.

Schaie, K. W. 1973. "Methodological problems in descriptive developmental research on adulthood and aging." In J. F. Nesselroade and H. W. Reece (eds.), Life Span Developmental Psychology: Methodological Issues. New York: Academic Press.

Schapera, I. 1930. The Khoisan Peoples. London: Routledge and Kegan Paul.

Scheper-Hughes, N. 1979. Saints, Scholars and Schizophrenics: Mental Illness in Rural Ireland. Berkeley: University of California Press.

Schlegel, A. 1977. Sexual Stratification. New York: Columbia University Press.

Schurtz, H. 1902. Alters Klassen und Männerbunde. Berlin: Reimer.

Schwartz, T. 1978. "The size and shape of a culture." Pp. 215–52 in F. Barth (ed.), Scale and Social Organization. Oslo, Norway: Universitesforlaget.

Schweitzer, M. M. and G. C. Williams. 1974. The Elderly Indian. Paper presented at the National Science Foundation meetings, December 26, Washington, D.C.

Service, E. R. 1966. The Hunters. Englewood Cliffs, N.J.: Prentice-Hall.

Shanas, E. 1962. The Health of Older People. Cambridge, Mass.: Harvard University Press.

———. 1963. "Some observations on cross-national surveys of aging." Gerontologist 3:7–9.

———. 1968. "Family help patterns and social class in three countries." Pp. 296–305 in B. Neugarten (ed.), Middle Age and Aging. Chicago, Ill.: University of Chicago Press.

———. 1973. "Family-kin networks and aging in a cross-cultural perspective." Journal of Marriage and the Family 35(3):505–11.

———. 1979a. "The family as a social support system in old age." Gerontologist 192:169–74.

———. 1979b. "Social myth as hypothesis: The case of the family relations of old people." Gerontologist 19:3–9.

Shanas, E. and M. Sussman. 1981. "The family in later life: Social structure and social policy." Pp. 211–31 in S.

Kiesler, J. Morgan and V. K. Oppenheimer (eds.), Aging: Social Change. New York: Academic Press.

Shanas, E., P. Townsend, D. Weederburn, H. Friis, P. Milhojano and J. Stehouwer. 1968. Older People in Three Industrial Societies. New York: Atherton Press.

Shapiro, J. 1971. Communities of the Alone: Working with Single Room Occupants in the City. New York: Association Press.

Shaw, M. E. and P. R. Costanzo. 1970. Theories of Social Psychology. New York: McGraw-Hill.

Sheehan, N. 1976. "Planned obsolescence: Historical perspectives on aging women." Pp. 59–68 in K. Riegel and J. Meacham (eds.), The Developing Individual in a Changing World. Volume 1. Chicago, Ill.: Aldine.

Sheehan, T. 1976. "Senior esteem as a factor of societal economic complexity." Gerontologist 16:433–40.

Shelton, A. J. 1965. "Igbo aging and eldership: Notes for gerontologists and others." Gerontologist 5:20–23.

———. 1967. "Igbo child-rearing, eldership and dependence: Further notes for gerontologists and others." Gerontologist 7:236–41.

———. 1972. "The aged and eldership among the Igbo." Pp. 31–49 in D. O. Cowgill and L. D. Holmes (eds.), Aging and Modernization. New York: Appleton-Century-Crofts.

Sheppard, H. L. 1976. "Work and retirement." In R. Binstock and E. Shanas (eds.), Handbook of Aging and the Social Sciences. New York: Van Nostrand Reinhold.

Shils, E. 1975. Center and Periphery: Essays in Macrosociology. Chicago, Ill.: University of Chicago Press.

Siegel, H. 1977. Outposts of the Forgotten, New York City's Welfare Hotels and Single Room Occupany Tenements. Edison: Transaction Books.

Siemaszko, M. 1980. "Kin relations of the aged: Possible consequences of social services planning." Pp. 253–91 in C. Fry (ed.), Aging in Culture and Society. Brooklyn, N.Y.: J. F. Bergin.

Silverman, P. and R. J. Maxwell. 1972. An Anthropological Approach to the Study of the Aged. Paper at the meetings of the Gerontological Society, December, San Juan, Puerto Rico.

———. 1978. "How do I respect thee? Let me count the ways: Deference towards elderly men and women." Behavior Science Research 13:91–108.

———. 1982. "Cultural variation in the status of old people." In P. Sterns (ed.), Old Age in Preindustrial Society. New York: Holmes and Meier.

Silverman, S. 1967. "The life crisis as a clue to social function." Anthropological Quarterly 40:127–38.

Simić, A. 1967. "The blood feud in Montenegro." Pp. 83–94 in W. G. Lockwood (ed.), Essays in Balkan Ethnology. Berkeley, Calif.: Kroeber Anthropological Society Special Publications, No. 1.

———. 1973a. The Peasant Urbanites: A Study of Rural-Urban Mobility in Serbia. New York: Seminar Press.

———. 1973b. "Kinship reciprocity and rural-urban mobility in Serbia." Urban Anthropology 2: 206–13.

———. 1974. "Urbanization and cultural process in Yugoslavia." Anthropological Quarterly 47:211–27.

Simić, A. and B. Myerhoff. 1978. Life's Career—Aging. Beverley Hills, Calif.: Sage.

Simmons, L. W. 1945. The Role of the Aged in Primitive Society. New Haven, Conn.: Yale University Press.

———. 1946. "Attitudes toward aging and the aged: Primitive societies." Journal of Gerontology 1:72–95.

———. 1952. "Social participation of the aged in different cultures." Annals of the American Academy of Political and Social Science 279:43–51.

———. 1959. "Aging in modern society." In Toward a Better Understanding of Aging. Seminar on Aging, September 8–13, 1958, Aspen, Colorado. New York: Council on Social Work Education.

———. 1960. "Aging in preindustrial society." Pp. 62–91 in C. Tibbetts (ed.), Handbook of Social Gerontology: Societal Aspects of Aging. Chicago, Ill.: University of Chicago Press.

———. 1962. "Aging in primitive societies: A comparative survey of family life and relationships." Law and Contemporary Problems 27:36–51.

Sinnott, J. D. 1977. "Sex-role inconsistency, biology, and successful aging." Gerontologist 17:459–63.

Smelser, N. J. 1963. A Theory of Collective Behavior. New York: Free Press.

Smith, R. 1961a. "Cultural differences in the life cycle and the concept of time." Pp. 83–112 in R. Kleemeier (ed.), Aging and Leisure. New York: Oxford University Press.

———. 1961b. "Japan: The later years of life and the concept of time." Pp. 95–100 in R. Kleemeier (ed.), Aging and Leisure. New York: Oxford University Press.

Sokolovsky, J. 1980. "Interactional dimensions of the aged: Social network mapping." Pp. 75–100 in C. Fry and J. Keith (eds.), New Methods for Old Age Research. Chicago, Ill.: Center for Urban Policy.

———. 1982. Teaching the Anthropology of Aging and the Aged: A Curriculum Guide and Topical Bibliography. Chicago, Ill.: Association for Anthropology and Gerontology.

Sokolovksy, J. and C. Cohen. 1981a. "Measuring social interaction of the urban elderly: A methodological synthesis." International Journal of Aging and Human Development 13:233–44.

———. 1981b. "Being old in the inner city: Support systems of the SRO aged." Pp. 163–81 in C. Fry (ed.), Dimensions: Aging, Culture and Health. Brooklyn, N.Y.: J. F. Bergin.

Solamon, S. and V. Lockhart. 1980. "Land ownership and the position of the elderly in farm families." Human Organization 39:324–31.

Sommers, T. 1974. "The compounding impact of age on sex, another dimension of double standard." Civil Rights Digest 7(1):3–9.

Sontag, S. 1972. "The double standard of aging." Saturday Review of the Society 95 (September 23):29–38.

Southall, A. and P. C. W. Gutkind. 1957. Townsmen in the Making. Kampala: East African Institute of Social Research.

Sparks, D. 1975. "The still rebirth: Retirement and role discontinuity." Journal of Asian and African Studies 10:64–74.

Spencer, P. 1965. The Samburu: A Study of Gerontocracy in a Nomadic Tribe. Berkeley: University of California Press.

———. 1973. Nomads in Alliance: Symbiosis and Growth among the Rendille and Samburu of Kenya. London: Oxford University Press.

Spencer, R. 1959. The North Alaskan Eskimo. Bureau of

American Ethnology, Bulletin 171.

Stanford, E. P. 1978. The Elder Black. San Diego, Calif.: Campanile Press.

Stefánsson, W. 1914. The Stefánsson-Anderson Arctic Expedition of the American Museum. Anthropological Paper of the American Museum of Natural History, Volume 14, Part 1.

Stein, H. and R. Hill. 1977. The Ethnic Imperative: Examining the New White Ethnic Movement. University Park: Pennsylvania State University Press.

Stephens, J. 1975. "Society of the alone: Freedom, privacy, and utilitarianism as dominant norms in the SRO." Journal of Gerontology 30(2): 230–35.

———. 1976. Loners, Losers and Lovers: A Sociological Study of the Aged Tenants of a Slum Hotel. Seattle: University of Washington Press.

Stewart, F. 1977. Fundamentals of Age-Group Systems. New York: Academic Press.

Stone, E. 1978. "It's still hard to grow up Italian." New York Times Magazine (December 17): 42–106.

Streib, G. F. 1968. "Disengagement theory in sociocultural perspective." International Journal of Psychiatry 6:69–76.

———. 1972. "Old age in Ireland: Demographic and sociological aspects." Pp. 167–81 in D. Cowgill and L. Holmes (eds.), Aging and Modernization. New York: Appleton-Century-Crofts.

———. 1976. "Social stratification and aging." Pp. 160–85 in R. H. Binstock and E. Shanas (eds.), Handbook of Aging and the Social Sciences. New York: Van Nostrand Reinhold.

Streib, G. F. and R. B. Streib. 1978. Retired Persons and Their Contributions: Exchange Theory. Paper presented at the 11th International Congress of Gerontology, Tokyo.

Sussman, M. B. 1965a. "The isolated nuclear family: Fact or fiction?" Social Problems 6:333–40.

———. 1965b. "Relationships of adult children with their parents in the United States." Pp. 62–92 in E. Shanas and G. Streib (eds.), Social Structure and the Family: Generational Relations. Englewood Cliffs, N.J.: Prentice-Hall.

Suttles, G. 1968. The Social Order of the Slum. Chicago, Ill.: University of Chicago Press.

Suttles, G. D. and D. Street. 1970. "Aid to the poor and social exchange." In E. O. Laumann, P. M. Siegel and R. W. Hodge (eds.), The Logic of Social Hierarchies. Chicago, Ill.: Markham.

Sweetser, D. A. 1956. "The social structure of grandparenthood." American Anthropologist 58:656–63.

Synge, J. M. 1960. Complete Plays. New York: Vintage.

Tallmer, M. and B. Kutner. 1970. "Disengagement and morale." Gerontologist 10:317–20.

Tax, S. 1960. "The celebration: A personal view." In S. Tax and C. Callender (eds.), Issues in Evolution. University of Chicago Centennial Discussion. Chicago, Ill.: University of Chicago Press.

Taylor, G. B. 1972. "Social development." Pp. 124–33 in H. Evans (ed.), New Towns: The British Experience. New York: John Wiley.

Tefft, S. K. 1968. "Intergenerational value differentials and family structure among the Wind River Shoshone." American Anthropologist 70:330–33.

Tissue, T. L. 1968. "A Guttman scale of disengagement potential." Journal of Gerontology 23:513–16.

———. 1971. "Old age, poverty, and the central city." International Journal of Aging and Human Development 2:235–48.

Tobin, S. and M. Lieberman. 1976. Last Home for the Aged. San Francisco: Jossey-Bass.

Tobin, S. S. and B. L. Neugarten. 1961. "Life satisfaction and social interaction in aging." Journal of Gerontology 16:344–46.

Tooker, E. 1964. "An ethnography of the Huron Indians." Bulletin of the Bureau of American Ethnology 190: 1–183.

Torry, W. 1978. "Gabra age organization and ecology." Pp. 183–206 in P. T. W. Baxter and U. Almagor (eds.), Age, Generation and Time: Some Features of East African Age Organization. London: Hurst.

Townsend, C. 1971. Old Age: The Last Segregation. New York: Grossman.

Townsend, P. 1957. The Family Life of Old People. Glencoe, Ill.: Free Press.

Treas, J. 1977. "Family support systems for the aged." Gerontologist 17:486–91.

———. 1979. "Socialist organization and economic development in China: Latent consequences for the aged." Gerontologist 19:34–43.

Trela, J. and J. Sokolovsky. 1979. "Culture, ethnicity and policy for the aged." Pp. 117–36 in D. Gelfand and A. Kutzik (eds.), Ethnicity and Aging. New York: Springer.

Trimble, J. E. 1972. An Index of the Social Indicators of the American Indian in Oklahoma. Prepared for the Office of Community Affairs and Planning, State Planning Office, State of Oklahoma, Oklahoma City.

Troll, L., S. Miller and R. Atchley. 1979. Families in Later Life. Belmont, Calif.: Wadsworth.

Turnbull, C. 1965. Wayward Servants. Garden City, N.Y.: Natural History Press.

Turner, V. 1952. The Lozi Peoples of North-Western Rhodesia. London: International African Institute.

———. 1969. The Ritual Process. Chicago, Ill.: Aldine.

Uchendu, V. 1965. The Igbo of Southeast Nigeria. New York: Holt, Rinehart & Winston.

U.S. Bureau of the Census. 1963. U.S. Census of Population: 1960. Volume 1: Characteristics of the Population, Parts 54–57: Outlying Areas. Washington, D.C.: U.S. Government Printing Office.

———. 1970. Subject Report: American Indians. Washington, D.C.: U.S. Government Printing Office. PC9(2)-1F:12–13.

———. 1977. Current Population Reports. Washington, D.C.: U.S. Government Printing Office.

U.S. Senate Special Committee on Aging. 1971. The Multiple Hazards of Age and Race: The Situation of Aged Blacks in the U.S. Washington, D.C.: U.S. Government Printing Office.

———. 1978. Single Room Occupancy: A Need for National Concern. An Information Paper. Washington, D.C. U.S. Government Printing Office.

———. 1981. Developments in Aging: 1980. Part 1. Washington, D.C.: U.S. Government Printing Office.

Valle, R. and L. Mendoza. 1978. The Elder Latino. San Diego, Calif.: Campanile Press.

Vatuk, S. 1975. "The aging woman in India." Pp. 142–63 in A. de Souza (ed.), Women in Contemporary India. Delhi: Manohar.

Vicoli, R. 1979. "The Italian Americans." The Center Magazine 7:4.

Vital Statistics of the United States. 1972. Life Tables, 1972. Volume II, Section 5. U.S. Department of Health, Education, and Welfare. Washington, D.C.: U.S. Government Printing Office.

Wallace, A. 1970. Culture and Personality. New York: Random House.

Wallace, W. L. 1969. Sociological Theory. Chicago, Ill.: Aldine.

Waring, J. M. 1975. "Social replenishment and social change: The problem of disordered cohort flow." American Behavioral Scientist 19:237–56.

Warner, L. 1937. A Black Civilization. New York: Harper & Brothers.

Watson, W. and R. Maxwell (eds.). 1977. Human Aging and Dying. New York: St. Martin's Press.

Weber, M. 1958. The Protestant Ethic and the Spirit of Capitalism. New York: Charles Scribner's Sons.

Weeks, J. and J. Cuellar. 1981. "The role of family members in the helping networks of older people." Gerontologist 21:388–94.

Weiss, K. 1981. "Evolutionary perspectives on human aging." Pp. 25–58 in P. Amoss and S. Harrell (eds.), Other Ways of Growing Old. Stanford, Calif.: Stanford University Press.

Wellin, E. and E. Boyer. 1979. "Adjustments of black and white elderly to the same adaptive niche." In J. Keith (ed.), The Ethnography of Old Age. Special issue of Anthropological Quarterly 52(1): 39–48.

Weltfish, G. 1965. The Lost Universe. New York: Basic Books.

Wentowski, G. 1982. "Reciprocity and the coping strategies of older people: Cultural dimensions of network building." Gerontologist 21:600–609.

Werner, D. 1981. "Gerontocracy among the Mekranoti of central Brazil." Anthropological Quarterly 54(1):15–27.

Whitten, N. and A. Wolfe. 1973. "Network analysis." Pp. 717–46 in J. Honigmann (ed.), Handbook of Social and Cultural Anthropology. Chicago, Ill.: Rand McNally.

Whyte, W. F. 1955. Street Corner Society: The Social Structure of an Italian Slum. Chicago, Ill.: University of Chicago Press.

Williams, B. 1977. American Indian Population 55 Years of Age and Older: Geographic Distribution, 1970. Part 1 of 2. Statistical Reports on Older Americans. U.S. Department of Health, Education, and Welfare Publication, Office of Human Development Services, Agency on Aging, National Clearinghouse on Aging.

———. 1978. Social, Economic and Health Characteristics of Older American Indians. Part 2 of 2. Statistical Reports on Older Americans. U.S. Department of Health, Education, and Welfare Publication, Office of Human Development Services, Agency on Aging, National Clearinghouse on Aging.

Williams, G. C. 1980. "Warriors no more: A study of the American Indian elderly." Pp. 101–11 in C. Fry (ed.), Aging in Culture and Society, Comparative Viewpoints and Strategies. Brooklyn, N.Y.: J. F. Bergin.

Wilson, M. 1949. "Nyakyusa age-villages." Journal of the Royal Anthropological Institute 79:21–25.

———. 1951. Good Company: A Study of Nyakyusa Age-Villages. London: Oxford University Press.

———. 1957. Rituals of Kinship among the Nyakyusa. London: Oxford University Press.

———. 1977. For Men and Elders: Change in the Relations of Men and Women among the Nyakyusa-Ngonde People. New York: Africand.

Wirth, L. 1938. "Urbanism as a way of life." American Journal of Sociology 44:1–24.

Wirz, N. H. 1975. Social Aspects of Planning in New Towns. Farnborough, England: Saxon House.

Woehrer, C. 1978. "Cultural pluralism in American families: The influence of ethnicity on special aspects of aging." Family Coordinator 27:329–40.

Wolf, E. 1966. "Kinship, friendship, and patron client relations in complex societies." Pp. 1–22 in M. Banfield (ed.), The Social Anthropology of Complex Societies. ASA Monograph, No. 4. New York: Praeger.

Wolf, M. 1972. Women and the Family in Rural Taiwan. Stanford, Calif.: Stanford University Press.

Wolfe, A. 1970. "On structural comparisons of networks." Canadian Review of Sociology and Anthropology 4(7):226–44.

Wood, V. and J. F. Robertson. 1976. "The significance of grandparenthood." Pp. 278–304 in J. Gubrium (ed.), Time, Roles and Self in Old Age. New York: Human Science Press.

Wrong, D. H. 1964. "Social inequality without social stratification." Canadian Review of Sociology and Anthropology 1:5–16.

Yancey et al. 1976. "Emergent ethnicity: A review and reformulation." American Sociological Review 41:391–402.

Yanigasako, S. 1978. "Variance in American kinship: Implicators for cultural analysis." American Ethnologist 5(1):15–29.

Yap, M. 1962. "Aging in underdeveloped Asian countries." In C. Tibbitts and W. Donahue (eds.), Sociological and Psychological Aspects of Aging. New York: Columbia University Press.

Yeats, W. B. 1933. Collected Poems. New York: Macmillan.

———. n.d. Irish Folk Stories and Fairy Tales. New York: Grossett and Dunlap.

Youmans, E. G. 1969. "Some Perspectives on Disengagement Theory." Gerontologist 9:254–58.

Young, F. W. and A. S. Bacdayan. 1965. "Menstrual taboos and social rigidity." Ethnology 4:225–40.

Young, M. and P. Willmott. (1957) 1967. Family and Kinship in East London. London: Penguin Books.

Zajonc, R. B. 1968. "Attitudinal effects of mere exposure." Journal of Personality and Social Psychology, Monograph Supplement 9:1–127.

Zorbaugh, H. 1929. The Gold Coast and the Slum: A Sociological Study of Chicago's Near North Side. Chicago, Ill.: University of Chicago Press.

NAME INDEX

SUBJECT INDEX